ORIGINAL NARRATIVES
OF EARLY AMERICAN HISTORY

REPRODUCED UNDER THE AUSPICES OF THE
AMERICAN HISTORICAL ASSOCIATION

GENERAL EDITOR, J. FRANKLIN JAMESON, PH.D., LL.D., LITT.D.

DIRECTOR OF THE DEPARTMENT OF HISTORICAL RESEARCH IN THE
CARNEGIE INSTITUTION OF WASHINGTON

NARRATIVES OF EARLY VIRGINIA

BRADFORD'S HISTORY OF PLYMOUTH PLANTATION

WINTHROP'S JOURNAL "HISTORY OF NEW ENGLAND"
(2 vols.)

NARRATIVES OF EARLY CAROLINA

NARRATIVES OF EARLY MARYLAND

NARRATIVES OF EARLY PENNSYLVANIA, WEST NEW JERSEY,
AND DELAWARE

NARRATIVES OF NEW NETHERLAND

EARLY ENGLISH AND FRENCH VOYAGES

VOYAGES OF SAMUEL DE CHAMPLAIN

SPANISH EXPLORERS IN THE SOUTHERN UNITED STATES

SPANISH EXPLORATION IN THE SOUTHWEST

NARRATIVES OF THE INSURRECTIONS

NARRATIVES OF THE INDIAN WARS

JOHNSON'S WONDER-WORKING PROVIDENCE

THE JOURNAL OF JASPAR DANCKAERTS

NARRATIVES OF THE NORTHWEST

NARRATIVES OF THE WITCHCRAFT CASES

THE NORTHMEN, COLUMBUS, AND CABOT

ORIGINAL NARRATIVES
OF EARLY AMERICAN HISTORY

NARRATIVES OF EARLY PENNSYLVANIA WEST NEW JERSEY AND DELAWARE

1630—1707

EDITED BY

ALBERT COOK MYERS

New York
BARNES & NOBLE, INC.

NOTE

THE first of the illustrations in this volume is a facsimile of a portion of an excellent map entitled "Novi Belgii Novæque Angliæ necnon Pennsylvaniæ et Partis Virginiæ Tabula," by N. J. Visscher, a prominent Dutch map-engraver of the middle of the seventeenth century. The whole map embraces, as the title implies, all those parts of New England, the Middle States, and Maryland which at that time had been settled by white men or had become known, more or less accurately, through their explorations. The whole map measures twenty-two by nineteen inches. The part which has been selected for reproduction in this volume covers the regions especially involved in the narratives printed therein. The map is chosen as representing the state of things at the time when Swedish occupation of the Delaware River region gave way to Dutch. Its date cannot be later than June 28, 1656, since a copy of it accompanied a report of that date from the directors of the Dutch West India Company to the States General of the United Netherlands. On the other hand it can hardly have been finished before February, 1655, since in that month the directors of the West India Company authorized the publication of the first edition of Adriaen van der Donck's *Beschrijvinge van Niew Nederlant,* which has no map, while the second edition, published in 1656, has a map copied partly from Visscher's. I am informed by Mr. Wilberforce Eames of the New York Public Library, to whom I am indebted for much information respecting the map, that, though the map was formerly reputed exceedingly rare, there are probably now in this country a dozen or twenty copies of it in this form. Twenty-eight years later Visscher's son published a reissue of the map from a plate retouched with the addition of Philadelphia and other places and names belonging to subsequent history.

The second illustration in the volume is a reproduction of Thomas Holme's "Portraiture of the City of Philadelphia." Thomas Holme

(1624–1695), a captain in Cromwell's army, and afterward a Quaker living in Ireland,[1] was in April, 1682, appointed by Penn surveyor-general of Pennsylvania, and sailed immediately for that province. As one of the three "Commissioners for Settling the Colony," he laid out the city of Philadelphia in the autumn of that year. He also drew up this map or plan of the city, which was printed in London in 1683 as part of the *Letter to the Committee of the Free Society of Traders*. It will be seen (page 224) that the title of the pamphlet refers to it, in the words, "with a Portraiture or Plat-form thereof [*i. e.*, of Philadelphia], wherein the Purchasers Lots are distinguished by certain numbers inserted, directing to a Catalogue of the said Purchasors Names." The catalogue is not reproduced in this volume, but the explanation of the city's plan will be found in its place, near the map. The original map measures $11\frac{1}{2}$ x $17\frac{1}{4}$ inches; our reproduction is reduced about two-fifths in each dimension.

The plan here presented did not in all details remain permanently in effect. From the Delaware River to Eleventh Street, indeed—counting the Delaware water-front, or Front Street, as the first—it is substantially the plan of the corresponding area of the present city. But as early as 1684, all the streets west of the eleventh were moved eastward, and the street marked Broad Street on the "Portraiture," and still so called, became the fourteenth instead of the twelfth; while the street next east of the Schuylkill water-front remained, and still remains, Twenty-Second Street.

J. F. J.

[1] A fuller account of his life may be seen on p. 242, note 1; a letter from him on p. 292.

CONTENTS

NARRATIVES OF EARLY PENNSYLVANIA, WEST NEW JERSEY, AND DELAWARE

EDITED BY ALBERT COOK MYERS

NARRATIVES OF EARLY PENNSYLVANIA WEST NEW JERSEY AND DELAWARE

FROM THE "KORTE HISTORIAEL ENDE JOUR-
NAELS AENTEYCKENINGE," BY DAVID
PIETERSZ. DE VRIES, 1630–1633, 1643 (1655)

INTRODUCTION

THE scene of action of the collection of narratives assembled in this volume is Delaware Bay and River, that broad waterway which lies central to what is not only the domain of three great commonwealths but in a deeply significant historical sense the keystone region of the American Nation. Of the twenty pieces selected, covering a period of three-quarters of a century, this first narrative, as well as the succeeding one by Captain Yong, brings clearly to view the low-lying forest shores of the great estuary in its primitive simplicity of the red man's day, untouched as yet, save for two abandoned sites, by the oncoming, all-transforming complexities of the white man's civilization. Explorers, traders, and adventurers, in the main under the auspices of the enterprising Dutch, had made more or less brief visits to the territory, and the Dutch laid claim to it as a part of New Netherland. An economic incentive, the lure of the enriching beaver trade with the Minquas Indians of the Susquehanna and Allegheny River valleys, a traffic which was readily tapped from the Delaware, was the prime cause, in general, for this earlier interest, and, later, for settlement prior to the Dutch conquest. Very soon the expanding Swedish and English nations were to seek locations on the river and at intervals to come into effective competition with the Dutch for this profitable trade.

The following extracts are translated from a quaint little Dutch book, a small black-letter quarto of [8+] 192 pages, published at Alkmaar, Holland, in 1655. It bears this somewhat lengthy title, so characteristic of books of that age:

*Korte Historiael, ende Journaels Aenteyckeninge van verscheyden
Voyagiens in de vier deelen des Wereldts-Ronde, als Europa,
Africa, Asia, ende Amerika gedaen, Door D. David Pietersz. de
Vries, Artillerij-Meester vande Ed: M: Heeren Gecommitteerde
Raden van Staten van West-Vrieslandt ende 't Noordenquartier.
Waer in verhaelt werd wat Batailjes hy te Water gedaen heeft:
Yder Landtschap zijn Gedierte, Gevogelt, wat soorte van Vissen,
ende wat wilde Menschen naer 't leven geconterfaeyt, ende van de
Bosschen ende Ravieren met haer Vruchten. t' Hoorn. Voor
David Pietersz. de Vries, Artillerij-Meester van 't Noorder-
quartier. Tot Alckmaer, by Symon Cornelisz. Brekegeest,
Anno 1655.*

This title, as turned into English by the general editor in
his sketch of the work and its author, in *Narratives of New
Netherland* (1909), pages 183–185, reads: "Short Historical
and Journal-Notes of various Voyages performed in the Four
Quarters of the Globe, viz., Europe, Africa, Asia, and America,
by David Pieterszoon de Vries, Artillery-Master to the Noble
and Mighty Lords the Council of West Friesland and the Northern Quarter [of the Province of Holland], wherein is set forth
what Battles he delivered on the Water, Each Country, its
Animals, its Birds, its Kinds of Fishes, and its Wild Men
counterfeited to the Life, and its Woods and Rivers with their
Products."

The illustrations, which seem to be etchings on copper,
comprise an interesting portrait of the author and eighteen
other plates, twelve of which depict American scenes but are
for the most part appropriated from the earlier work of
Champlain.

David Pieterszoon de Vries, the author, wrote these
reminiscences of a quarter of a century of world voyaging, in
the leisurely retirement of later years in his ancestral city of
Hoorn, in North Holland. He was born in 1593 in Rochelle
on the west coast of France, whither his father went from

Hoorn, after the murder of William of Orange in 1584. His mother was of Amsterdam origin. When he was four years old his parents returned to Holland, and there De Vries chiefly lived, apparently in Hoorn, although he states that he was experienced in merchandising from his youth both in Holland and in France. He refers to partners in Amsterdam and Rochelle as concerned with him in his mercantile voyages. A religious man of strong Calvinistic convictions, he writes in a plain but vivid style and his book both internally and externally has well stood the tests of trustworthiness. His part in the voyages, although sometimes as commander, was usually as a supercargo. He was a bold and skilful seaman, and a considerable portion of the work is given to navigating and sailing directions.

The six voyages which De Vries describes began in 1618 —when he was a young man of twenty-five—with a voyage for grain to the Mediterranean, in which he took part in a successful engagement with some Turkish galleys off the coast of Greece. In his second voyage, 1620–1623, he went to Newfoundland and carried a cargo of fish to the Mediterranean, where he won a notable fight against privateers off the Spanish coast and accepted a brief service under the Duke of Guise, admiral of France. From 1627 to 1630 he was occupied with his third voyage to the East Indies, of which he gives a long account.

The fourth, fifth, and sixth voyages were made to the New World. The first and last of these American voyages include accounts of two visits to the Delaware, both of which are here presented. The first of these extracts covers the first part of the fourth voyage, from the formation of the patroonship in 1630 to the departure of De Vries from the Delaware, March 6, 1633. The remainder of the voyage, the part omitted from our text, relates to Virginia and Manhattan and the return to Holland in midsummer of the same year. The fifth voyage, 1634–1636, was taken up with the planting of a colony in Guiana and with trading trips to Manhattan and Virginia. In the sixth voyage, 1638–1644, De Vries was chiefly employed in vain attempts to establish settlements on Staten Island and at Tappaan (Vriesendael).[1] Then he sailed again to the Delaware and from October 12 to 20, 1643, made a briefer visit to the river, as recounted in the second of the extracts of our text. After wintering in Virginia he arrived in Holland in June, 1644. Having now passed his fiftieth year, he withdrew from the adventurous life of the sea. Nothing seems to be known of him after the publication of his book.

All the parts of De Vries's book relating to Newfoundland, New Netherland, and Virginia, as translated and edited by Henry C. Murphy, were published in 1853 by James Lenox, and in 1857 by the New York Historical Society in its *Collections*, second series, III. 1–129. The extracts concerning the Delaware, as here given, are taken from the *Collections*, pp. 15–32, 121–123, and carefully revised from the original Dutch text, pp. 94–107, 183–185, by Mr. A. J. F. van Laer, archivist of the state of New York.

A. C. M.

[1] For this period and the preceding visit to Manhattan, see *Narratives of New Netherland*, in this series, pp. 186–234.

FROM THE "KORTE HISTORIAEL ENDE JOUR-NAELS AENTEYCKENINGE," BY DAVID PIETERSZ. DE VRIES, 1630-1633, 1643 (1655)

AFTER I had been at home from the Indies two months, I met, at Amsterdam, Samuel Godyn, a merchant, who bade me welcome, as an old acquaintance, and asked me where I came from? I said from the East Indies. In what capacity? I told him as supercargo. He inquired whether it was my intention to remain at home. I said, yes. But he asked me if I wished to go as a commander to New Netherland; they wanted to plant a colony there, and would employ me as sub-patroon, according to the privileges [approved] by the Lords States [General], and granted by the [Council of] Nineteen of the West India Company to all patroons. I gave him for answer that the business suited me well, but I must be a patroon, equal with the rest. He said that he was content that it should be so. So we five first took steps to establish this patroonship; namely, Samuel Godyn, Gilliame van Rensselaer, Bloemaert, Jan de Laet, and myself, David Pietersz. de Vries. But more were afterwards admitted into the company; namely, Mathys van Ceulen, Nicolas van Sittorigh,[1] Harinck Koeck,[2] and Heyndrick Hamel, and we made a contract with one another, whereby we were all placed on the same footing. We then equipped a ship[3] with a yacht for the

[1] Given as Nicolaes van Sitterich in list of Directors of the Amsterdam Chamber of the West India Company, in de Laet, *Historie ofte Iaerlijck Verhael.*

[2] Johan van Harinck-houck in the same list.

[3] The ship *De Walvis*, of about 150 lasts, commanded by Captain Peter Heyes, with a cargo of bricks, provisions, a large stock of cattle and twenty-eight colonists, arrived in the Delaware in the spring of 1631. They made a settlement on the bank of the Hoorn (or Hoere) Kill, calling it Swanendael. "They engaged in whaling and farming and made suitable fortifications, so that in July of the same year their cows calved and their lands were seeded and covered with a fine crop." Five additional colonists joined the colony, probably from New Amsterdam, making the total number thirty-three. They built a brick house inside the palisades. *Van Rensselaer Bowier Manuscripts*, p. 240; Amandus Johnson, *The Swedish Settlements on the Delaware*, pp., 170-171.

purpose of prosecuting the voyage, as well to carry on the whale fishery in that region, as to plant a colony for the cultivation of all sorts of grain, for which the country is very well adapted, and of tobacco. This ship with the yacht sailed from the Texel[1] the 12th of December, with a number of people and a considerable number of animals, to settle our colony upon the South River, which lies in the thirty-eighth and a half degree, and to conduct the whale fishery there. As Godyn had been informed that many whales kept before the bay, and the oil was worth sixty guilders a hogshead, they thought that they might realize a good profit thereon and at the same time cultivate that fine country.

The 20th of the same month, we understood that our yacht was taken by the Dunkirkers the day after it ran out of the Texel, through the carelessness of the large ship, which had lagged behind the yacht, in which there was a large cargo, intended for exploration of the coast of New France. The large ship proceeded on the voyage, having on board some people to land at the island of Tortugas in the West Indies, which island we had made a contract with sixty Frenchmen to hold for us as a colony under their High Mightinesses the Lords States [General] and the West India Company.

Anno 1631. In September our ship returned from New Netherland and the West Indies. It was said to have disembarked a number of people on Tortugas, but [to have] found that the French had been killed by the Spaniards, and further [to have conveyed] the rest to the South River[2] in New Netherland, and [it] brought a sample of oil from a dead whale found on the shore. [The captain] said that he arrived there too late in the year. This was a losing voyage to us; because this captain, Peter Heyes, of Edam, whom we had put in command, durst not sail by the way of the West Indies with only one ship of eighteen guns, where he must have made good the expense of this voyage. He was a person who was only accustomed to sail to Greenland, where they make the voyage in three or four months, and then come home.

---

[1] The Texel, the island at the mouth of the Zuyder Zee in Holland.

[2] This was the colony at Swanendael, present Lewes, Delaware, thus brought there in 1631 by the ship *De Walvis*, and shortly after destroyed by the Indians as hereafter recounted by De Vries.

Anno 1632. The 12th of February we again entered into
an agreement to equip a ship and yacht for the whale fishery,
to which many objections were raised because we had had
such a losing voyage, and no returns from the whale fishery,
and saw no prospect of any. But Samuel Godyn encouraged
us to make another attempt. He said the Greenland Company had two bad voyages with Willem van Muyen, and afterwards became a thrifty company. It was therefore again resolved to undertake a voyage for the whale fishery, and that I
myself should go as patroon, and as commander of the ship
and yacht, and should endeavor to be there in December, in
order to conduct the whale fishing during the winter, as the
whales come in the winter and remain till March.

Before sailing out of the Texel, we understood that our
little fort[1] had been destroyed by the Indians, the people
killed—two and thirty men—who were outside the fort
working the land.

The 24th May, sailed out of the Texel with the ship and
yacht, with a northeast wind.

The 26th of the same month, at night, we ran aground
through the carelessness of the mates, to whom I gave particular directions, before I went to bed, to throw the lead frequently, and keep the freighter, which was a large ship, and
drew full three feet more water than we did, upon our lee;
but they not following their orders, we grounded upon the
Bree-Banck[2] before Dunkirk. We fired a shot, so that our
companion came to anchor. My yacht came under my lee,
but could not stand it there on account of the surf. I then
made our crew lower the boat and also two Biscayan shallops[3]
and they fled the ship. But I would not leave, and kept both
of the mates by me, who dared not leave me for shame, seeing
that I remained aboard. Eight or nine plain sailors remained
also and I then learned to know the crew well. Those men
who had appeared fierce as lions, were the first to escape in
the boat. Bumping and tossing along, we got into four
fathoms water, where I let the anchor fall, and set to pump-

[1] At Swanendael.

[2] Bree-Banck, one of the largest shoals before Dunkirk, in France, about
four miles from the coast.

[3] Convenient rowboats used by Basque fishermen.

ing and got the ship dry. At the same time, the day broke, when we saw our boat and the two sloops tossing about; but when they saw the ship once more afloat they came on board again, and told us that had the night continued two hours longer, they would have headed for the lighthouse and rowed into Dunkirk. We weighed anchor again and sailed for the coast of England, and, on the 28th, ran into Portsmouth, and hauled the ship into the king's dock, where we repaired her.

The 10th of July, we sailed from Portsmouth to Cowes in the Isle of Wight.

The 12th of the same month, the ship *New Netherland*, of the West India Company, arrived here—a large ship, which was built in New Netherland, and which was bound for the West Indies, whither I had good company.

The 1st of August, with a good northeast wind, weighed anchor, and made sail with my ship and yacht, in company of the ship *New Netherland*.

The 2d, passed Land's End, and laid our course for the Canary Islands.

The 13th, we saw Madeira on our larboard, and a Turk came towards us, but as soon as he observed that we were stout ships, he hauled off from us, and we sailed for him. The evening growing dark, I fired a shot for my yacht to come by me. When night came on, we pursued our course, but the *New Netherland* followed the Turk by night, which seemed to us folly, because we had not got near him by day. We then separated from the *New Netherland*.

The 14th, towards evening, we saw the Isle of Palms on our lee, and set our course from thence to Barbados.

The 4th of September, we came in sight of Barbados, and the next day, the 5th, towards evening, arrived at the Island of St. Vincent. The Indians put out with their canoes and came on board of us. I observed the great astonishment of this people. Their canoes or boats getting full of water, they sprang overboard, and with great dexterity lifted up both ends with their shoulders in the water, emptied out the water, and then clambered in again; many of our people, in such circumstances, would have drowned, if their boat got full of water, and they had no other aid than their bodies and the sea. While here, we had fifteen good [supplies of] refreshments, bananas, pine-apples, and various Indian fruits. We anchored in the Great Channel in 23 fathoms.

On the 5th, arrived here also the ship *New Netherland,* which was separated from us at Madeira.

On the 8th, we weighed anchor, and passed by the islands of Martinique, Dominica, Guadeloupe, Montserrat, Redonde, and Nevis, arrived the 20th[1] before St. Christopher, where we found some English ships, and obtained a supply of water.

The 11th, weighed anchor, in order to sail to St. Martin. Half-way between St. Martin and St. Christopher, we met a French ship with a large sloop in company, which veered considerably towards us, as if he sought to commit some hostility towards us, but I kept my course and spoke him not. I let the prince's flag[2] fly aloft, and the red flag behind. When he saw this, he hauled off and passed at a good distance on my lee. Towards evening, we arrived at the roadstead of St. Martin and let our anchor fall. We found before the fort three flutes[3] under Dirck Femmesz. of Hoorn, two from Waterland,[4] and the third an Englishman.

The 11th of September, as I lay before the fort with my yacht, the above-named master of the flutes came on board, and inquired if I had not met a French ship. I said, "Yes, sir." And whether he had not attacked me? I said, "No." Had we been a small ship, he perhaps would have done so: for he [Femmesz.] said that he [the Frenchman] had sworn to pay off the first Hollander whom he should meet, because they had shot and killed two of his men from the flute, which was not creditable to them. He told me that this French ship had come into the harbor some days ago, and that the captain was a Knight of Malta, and the vessel a royal yacht of the King of France, in search of Spaniards. When he was taken ashore by the commander of the fort, he inquired whether there was any one who could speak French. The captain of the soldiers understanding French, he requested that the captain might

---

[1] Evidently a misprint for the 10th.

[2] The flag of Prince Frederick Henry of Orange-Nassau, stadtholder of the Dutch republic.

[3] A *fluit* (flute) is a three-master of about 600 to 700 tons burden.

[4] Waterland, a district in the province of North Holland, between Amsterdam and Monnickendam.

go with him to interpret what should be said. So the captain went from the fort with this knight in his skiff to the flutes. Having reached them, the Knight desired that they should sell him a barrel of tar, for money and kind words, as they had enough and he had long sailed in the West Indies; but they gave him a rude answer—that they did not wish to have him in their ships—if the captain of the fort wished to come on board their ships he might, but he must depart with the boat. The Knight stood perplexed at such an answer, when he had met them with every courtesy. At length he said to the captain, his interpreter, that they would return to the fort, [as] he wished to make his complaints to the commander-in-chief. Coming to the commander, he exhibited his royal commission, and inquired of the commander whether he had not as much right to go in the roadstead where these flutes were, as they?—that they were friends;—that all the ports and harbors in France were open to us. The commander said, "Yes." Then the Frenchman weighed anchor, and wished to come to anchor by them in order to careen his ship a little, as the water was shallow there. When they saw the Frenchman had weighed his anchor, they hauled one behind the other, and began to fire upon him, and shot two of his men; when the Frenchman again let his anchor fall, went to the fort and complained of the hostilities which these brutes had committed against him, and desired that the commander, with his officers, should take note thereof; and made his protest. But he was lost on his return voyage, with his ship, people and all, which has caused great comfort to these shipmasters, as he would otherwise have made sport enough for them; but the quarrel was thereby terminated. This we learned afterwards.

The 12th of September, I had room made in the ship [to take in salt], in case the whale fishery in New Netherland should fail, as salt brought a good price in the Fatherland. This day the ship *New Netherland* arrived here, which I had left lying at St. Vincent to refresh. With her arrived the ship *Gelderia*, which belonged also to the Company, and also two flutes from Hoorn; of one of these, Cornelis Jansz. Niels was master; the other flute was the *Falcon*, and the master was named Gerrit Jansz.

The 27th of this month, we had our cargo of salt, as much as we wanted, and made ourselves again ready to sail to Nevis, to take in wood and water, because they were both better there than at St. Christopher, and there is also a fine sandy bay for the boats to land. The captains of the flutes, who had committed the hostilities against the Frenchman, inquired of me whether they might sail with me to Nevis, in order to provide themselves with wood and water, so as to sail directly for Holland, as they were afraid of the Frenchman, who had called out to them that he wished to meet them when they went to take in water; and they did not mount more than six or eight guns. I gave them for answer, that I was willing that they should sail with me, because they were our citizens, but that I could not prevent any hostility of the Frenchman happening to them, since my ship was no more defensible than theirs. If they wished, however, to sail with me, they could.

The 29th, weighed anchor with my yacht to get under sail, but they remained. By evening I arrived before the island of Nevis. I went ashore to the governor, an Englishman, named Luttelton.[1] He requested me to take aboard some captive Portuguese, and to put them, on my way to St. Christopher, on board an English ship called Captain Stoon's;[2] which I could not refuse him, if I had them only three or four hours in the ship. Maerten Thysz.,[3] from Zeeland, had put these Portuguese ashore here.

The 1st of November, took my leave of the governor of Nevis, and weighed anchor. At noon, came to the great roadstead where the English are. There was a governor, named Sir Warnar.[4] Here I immediately got rid of the Portuguese

[1] Littleton.

[2] Captain John Stone (d. 1634), who figures also in the narratives of William Bradford, of Plymouth, and John Winthrop, of Boston, was an Englishman living for a time on the island of St. Christopher in the West Indies and later in Virginia, whence he engaged with his vessel in the intercolonial trade He was not over-scrupulous in his conduct and dealings; for instance, he made the Dutch Governor Van Twiller drunk in order to secure consent to seize a Plymouth bark laden with furs. His murder by the Indians on his own ship in the Connecticut River was one of the immediate causes of the Pequot war in New England.

[3] Probably Admiral Maarten Thijssen, who later became famous in Swedish naval service under the name of Martin Thijson Anckarhjelm.

[4] Sir Thomas Warner (d. 1649), the English governor of the island of St. Christopher, appointed to that office in 1627 and knighted in 1629.

prisoners, gave them over to the Englishman, who wished to sail in company with me to St. Martin.

The 2d, weighed anchor, with my yacht and the Englishman, of London, who had the Portuguese prisoners, whom he was to carry to Porto Rico. He left his barge behind, to follow him with some goods to St. Martin. We arrived in the evening at the anchorage before St. Martin, where we found the whole fleet there still which we had left there. I asked the captains of the flutes why they had not followed me when I weighed anchor. They answered that they thanked me for the offer which I had made them, but they had determined to remain by each other, and expected that they would be ready together, and the *Gelderland* would go with them.

The 4th, the Englishman, expecting his boat from St. Christopher, knew not what it meant that it staid so long, as it should have followed us at noon. This Englishman wished much to sail with me to the latitude of Porto Rico, which I must pass.

The 5th of this month, took my leave at the fort of our governor and the captains, and weighed anchor with my yacht also; having a fair sail set, I could not wait longer for the Englishman's boat. We understood afterwards that this boat was placed in great distress; that it was driven to the leeward by a strong wind, and being in want of provisions and water, the men cast lots whom they should first kill for the others to eat for food; having at length felled one, they fed themselves therewith, till they finally reached the island of Saba, where they subsisted on what they found there, and were afterwards recovered in great distress, but he who was eaten up for their subsistence was gone.

The 14th, in the thirty-second degree of latitude, the Bermudas to the east of us, encountered a severe storm from the northwest, and it was sheer luck that we managed to take in our sails; all around the waters swirled as if it were an hurricane; it blew so, that standing beside each other we could not understand each other. I feared when I saw the yacht, that it would finally capsize, so dreadful was it to see so small a yacht, of ten lasts, save itself from such a storm. This storm continued until the 18th, but towards the last the wind veered entirely west.

The 1st of December, threw the lead, in the thirty-ninth degree of latitude, in fifty-seven fathoms, sandy bottom; found out afterwards that we were then fourteen or fifteen leagues[1] from the shore. This is a flat coast. Wind westerly.

The 2d, threw the lead in fourteen fathoms, sandy bottom, and smelt the land, which gave a sweet perfume, as the wind came from the northwest, which blew off land, and caused these sweet odors. This comes from the Indians setting fire, at this time of year, to the woods and thickets, in order to hunt; and the land is full of sweet-smelling herbs, as sassafras, which has a sweet smell. When the wind blows out of the northwest, and the smoke is driven to sea, it happens that the land is smelt before it is seen. The land can be seen when in from thirteen to fourteen fathoms. Sand-hills are seen from the thirty-fourth to the fortieth degree, and the hills rise up full of pine-trees, which would serve as masts for ships.

The 3d of the same month, saw the mouth of the South[2] Bay, or South River, and anchored on sandy ground at ten fathoms; because it blew hard from the northwest, which is from the shore, and as we could not, in consequence of the hard wind, sail in the bay, we remained at anchor.

The 5th, the wind southwest, we weighed anchor, and sailed into the South Bay, and in the afternoon lay, with our yacht, in four fathoms water, and saw immediately a whale near the ship. Thought this would be royal work—the whales so numerous—and the land so fine for cultivation.

The 6th, we went with the boat into the river,[3] well armed, in order to see if we could speak with any Indians, but coming by our house,[4] which was destroyed, found it well beset with palisades in place of breastworks, but it was almost burnt up. Found lying here and there the skulls and bones of our people whom they had killed, and the heads of the horses and cows which they had brought with them, but perceived no Indians and, without having accomplished anything, returned on board,

---

[1] "Fourteen or fifteen [Dutch] miles," or English leagues; forty-two or forty-five English miles, the Dutch mile being equal to three English miles.

[2] Called Delaware Bay by the English.

[3] The Hoorn or Hoere Kill, the present Lewes Creek, in Delaware.

[4] At Swanendael, now Lewes, Delaware.

and let the gunner fire a shot in order to see if we could find any trace of them the next day.

The 7th, in the morning, we thought we saw some smoke near our destroyed house; we landed opposite the house, on the other side of the river, where there is a beach with some dunes. Coming to the beach, looked across the river towards the house where we had been the day before, and where we thought in the morning we had seen signs of smoke, but saw nothing. I had a cousin of mine with me from Rotterdam, named Heyndrick de Liefde, and as a flock of gulls was flying over our heads, I told him to shoot at it, as he had a fowling-piece with him, and he shot one on the wing, and brought it down. With it came a shout from two or three Indians, who were lying in the brush on the other side of the river by the destroyed house. We called to them to come over to us. They answered that we must come into the river with our boat. We promised to do so in the morning, as the water was then low, and that we would then talk with them, and we went back to the ship. Going aboard, we resolved to sail in the river with the yacht, as otherwise in an open boat we might be in danger of their arrows.

The 8th of December, we sailed into the river before our destroyed house, well on our guard. The Indians came to the edge of the shore, near the yacht, but dared not come in. At length, one ventured to come aboard the yacht, whom we presented with a cloth dress, and told him we desired to make peace. Then immediately more came running aboard, expecting to obtain a dress also, whom we presented with some trinkets, and told the one to whom we had given the cloth garment, that we had given it to him because he had most confidence in us—that he was the first one who came in the yacht, and should they come the next day with their chief called *Sakimas*, we would then make a firm peace, which they call *rancontyn marenit*. An Indian remained on board of the yacht at night, whom we asked why they had slain our people, and how it happened. He then showed us the place where our people had set up a column, to which was fastened a piece of tin, whereon the arms of Holland[1] were painted. One

---

[1] *Hollandtsche-Thuyn*, literally, Holland yard, or enclosure, referring to the emblem of the Seven United Provinces, which shows the Dutch lion defending

of their chiefs took this off for the purpose of making tobacco-pipes, not knowing that he was doing amiss. Those in command at the house made such an ado about it, that the Indians, not knowing how it was, went away and slew the chief who had done it, and brought a token of the dead to the house to those in command, who told them that they wished they had not done it, that they should have brought him to them, as they wished to have forbidden him to do the like again. They then went away, and the friends of the murdered chief incited their friends—as they are a people like the Italians, who are very revengeful—to set about the work of vengeance. Observing our people out of the house, each one at his work, that there was not more than one inside, who was lying sick, and a large mastiff, who was chained—had he been loose they would not have dared to approach the house—and the man who had command, standing near the house, three of the bravest Indians, who were to do the deed, bringing a lot of beaver-skins with them to exchange, asked to enter the house. The man in charge went in with them to make the barter; which being done, he went down from the loft where the stores lay, and in descending the stairs, one of the Indians seized an axe, and cleft the head of our agent who was in charge so that he fell down dead. They also relieved the sick man of life; and shot into the dog, who was chained fast, and whom they most feared, twenty-five arrows before they could despatch him. They then proceeded towards the rest of the men, who were at their work, and going among them with pretensions of friendship, struck them down.[1] Thus was our young colony destroyed, causing us serious loss.

The 9th, the Indians came to us with their chiefs, and sitting in a ring, made peace. Gave them some presents of duffels,[2] bullets, hatchets, and various Nuremberg trinkets. They promised to make a present to us, as they had been out a-hunting. They then departed again with great joy of us, that we had not remembered what they had done to us, which

Dutch territory, represented by a lion rampant inside a stockade, the lion holding in his right paw a sword and in his left paw a bundle of seven arrows, with the motto: *Eendracht maakt Macht* (In Unity is Strength).

[1] The colonists were all killed save one Theunis Willemsen.

[2] A kind of coarse cloth.

we suffered to pass, because we saw no chance of revenging it, as they dwelt in no fixed place. We began to make preparations to send our sloops to sea, and to set up a kettle for whale-oil, and to erect a lodging-hut of boards.

Anno 1633. The 1st of January, at about eight o'clock in the morning, I sailed with the yacht, the *Squirrel*, up the South River, to see whether I could obtain any beans from the Indians, as our stock-fish was consumed, and the porridge, now doubled, began to grow short. Towards evening we stopped, as it was calm, and the ice, which the tide brought down, opposed us, and we cast anchor in eight fathoms. Saw a whale at the mouth of the South River.

The 2d, in the morning, fine and pleasant, saw two large whales near the yacht. Wished much that we could have had the shallops, with the harpooners, which were lying at Swanendael. We weighed anchor with the tide, and by evening came a good mile before Reed Island,[1] where we cast anchor, and saw fires on the land. Supposed that they were made by Indians out a-hunting; but an hour afterwards a canoe came alongside. They said that they were a-hunting, but would not come aboard, from which we drew unfavorable conclusions; but they answered they would come aboard early in the morning.

The 4th, after we had chopped some wood, as it began to freeze, weighed anchor with the tide, made sail, and entered about a cannon-shot past Red Hook,[2] where we anchored before a kill, because it began to freeze; so that in case the ice should stop us, we could haul in there to secure the yacht.

The 5th, we weighed anchor in the morning, and sailed before the little fort named Fort Nassau,[3] where formerly some families of the West India Company had dwelt. Some Indians had begun to gather there and wished to barter furs,

[1] Evidently the present Reedy Island.

[2] Red Hook, near Mantes, now Mantua Creek, New Jersey. "Mantaes hoeck . . . about a long half league below the destroyed" Fort Nassau (Andreas Hudde, in 1662).

[3] Fort Nassau, built by the Dutch in 1623 and occupied by them at intervals until the building of Fort Casimir, 1651, was on the Delaware River near the south side of the mouth of the present Big Timber Creek, Gloucester County, New Jersey.

but I desired to trade for their Turkish beans,[1] because we had no goods to exchange for peltries, and our stores had been given away at Swanendael for the purpose of making the peace, so that there were not more than two pieces of cloth left of our goods, and two kettles, for which we wanted corn. As far as we could observe, the Indians were very scrupulous.[2] They told us that we ought to haul into the Timmer Kill.[3] There was a squaw of the Sankitans,[4] who cautioned us not to go entirely into the kill, as she knew that they intended to make an attack upon us. When we told her that if she would relate to us everything in regard to the attack, we would give her a cloth garment, as we did, she confessed to us that in Count Ernest's River[5] they had seized a shallop with Englishmen and killed the Englishmen.

The 6th, we weighed anchor, and came before the Timmer Kill, where we made everything ready, to see what the Indians would do. While lying there, a crowd of Indians came marching up, bringing beaver-skins with them, and boarding the yacht forty-two or forty-three strong. A portion of them began to play tunes with reeds, in order that they might not cause in us any suspicion, but we kept ourselves strictly upon our guard, as there were only seven of us in the yacht, and there were forty-two or forty-three of the Indians. When we found the traffic at its height, we ordered them to go ashore immediately, or we would shoot them all. Their *sachem* took an armful of beaver-skins which he wanted to present to us in order to tempt us, but we desired them not, and gave him for answer that they must make their way to the shore, as we knew that they had evil designs in their heads, that Manetoe (that is, the Devil, whom they call Manetoe) had told us so. They went ashore again, and their villainy was frustrated, God be praised and thanked! If one is a little on his guard against this people, there is, with God's help, no difficulty with the Indians. But, as far as I can observe, those that are in the Company's sloops give the Indians too much liberty, and so accidents occur which otherwise, with friendship, might

---

[1] Indian corn.   [2] Shy.
[3] The present Big Timber Creek, in Gloucester County, New Jersey.
[4] Or Sankikans. Delaware Indians, living at the falls at Trenton, and above.
[5] Not identified.

be prevented. These Indians were from Red Hook, otherwise called Mantes, and had a number of English jackets [1] on, which gave me more cause of suspicion, as those were not clothing for them, or trading goods. When they were all on land again, there soon came three or four others, who desired that we would trade for their goods; but we answered them that we did not want any beaver-skins, but wished corn for food.

The 7th, the chief, whom they call *sackima*, of the Armewanninge, another but neighboring nation, came to us. His name was Zee Pentor, and to him we interpreted our adventure. He said he had heard that they had been on board of our boat strong. He requested us to return soon to the Timmer Kill with the yacht, whereat I was suspicious. I told my interpreter to ask him why he was not willing to bring the corn here. He answered that where we were lying, it was too muddy and low to get on board, and it was too cold to go through the mud. So we said to him that we would go to the fort again, where it was hard and dry to come aboard, with which he was well content, and was again conveyed to the shore, saying that when we arrived at the fort, he would come aboard again.

The 8th, weighed anchor early in the morning, and came to again before the fort, which we saw was full of Indians, and more and more constantly coming. This gave us no favorable impression, because of the great numbers of the Indians. When they had all assembled in the fort, a canoe—which is a boat hollowed out of a tree—came at last from the fort to board us, in which were nine chiefs, sachems from nine different places. I saw among them the one who had intended to destroy us; he had thrown off the English clothes, and put on those made of skins, of which I immediately warned my interpreter. The nine seated themselves in a circle and called us to them, saying they saw that we were afraid of them, but that they came to make a lasting peace with us, whereupon they made us a present of ten beaver-skins, which one of them gave us, with a ceremony with each skin, saying in whose name he presented it; that it was for a perpetual peace with us, and that we must banish all evil thoughts from us, for they had

---

[1] *Kaesjacken*, probably intended for "cassocks."

now thrown away all evil. I wanted to make presents to them through the interpreter, to each one an axe, adze, and pair of knives, but they refused them, declaring that they had not made us presents in order to receive others in return, but for the purpose of a firm peace, which we took for truth.

The 8th of January, we wished to give them something for their wives, but they said we must give it to them on shore. As it was late, they went ashore again, and said they would come the next day with corn, and they sent aboard that evening seven or eight youth, which showed a good peace with them.

The 9th, they came aboard again in the morning, and brought Indian corn of different colors, for which we exchanged duffels, kettles, and axes. We also obtained some beaver-skins, all in good feeling. There came that day about fifty of them into the yacht, but we kept ourselves constantly on our guard.

The 10th, in the morning, traded for some beaver and corn; and in the afternoon drifted off with the ebb tide, and in the evening went aground on the shoal near Jaques Island,[1] where we remained one tide.

The 11th, weighed anchor in the morning, and by evening arrived about a league and a half above Minqua's Kill,[2] where we anchored, and saw a whale there that evening, which spouted six or seven times. We were surprised to see a whale seven or eight leagues up into fresh water.

The 12th, weighed anchor again, and arrived at the mouth of the river; in the evening we came to anchor where the thicket is.

The 13th, weighed anchor with the ebb, and at noon came to the ship at Swanendael, where our men were rejoiced to see us. We found that they had shot two whales, but they furnished little oil.

The 18th, the goods were placed in our yacht, and we sailed again up the South River. By evening arrived between Minqua's Kill and Reed Island, where we came to anchor. It

---

[1] Jaques or Jacob's (James's) Island, as given on Lindström's map of 1655, was probably Chester Island.

[2] Minquas Kill, now Christina Creek, which flows into Delaware River at Wilmington, Delaware.

began to freeze. We anchored here because the tide was
running down.

The 19th, weighed anchor with the tide, and came within
a league of Jaques Island. As it began to freeze, and it was
difficult to go on, it became necessary to haul into a kill
which was near us. Found it a fine creek, where the water
was two fathoms deep at high tide; but the current was
strong, and [the creek] not above thirty feet wide. The ice
began to trouble us some by the rubbing of the current. We
quickly cut a number of trees, and fastened them in the ground,
before and behind, in order to lie clear of the ice. This is a
fine country, in which many vines grow wild, so that we gave
it the name of Wyngært's Kill.[1] Went out daily, while here,
to shoot. Shot many wild turkeys, weighing from thirty to
thirty-six pounds. Their great size and very fine flavor are
surprising. We were frozen up in this kill from the 19th to
the 3rd of February. During this time, perceived no Indians,
though we saw here and there, at times, great fires on the land,
but we saw neither men nor canoes, because the river was
closed by the ice.

The 3d of February, we hauled out of the kill, as the river
was open again, and sailed to Fort Nassau, where we had left
the Indians before, but found no one there now, and saw no
Indians. It began to freeze again, and we hauled into a kill
over against the fort, as we were apprehensive, if we should
be frozen in there, we might be in danger. When we had
lain in this kill eight days to avoid the ice flow, there came a
canoe, in which sat an old Indian with a squaw, who brought
with them some maize and beans, of which we bought a quantity. We could not understand from the Indian how it was
that we saw no Indians. It seemed as if he were unwilling to
tell us; he always looked frightened as if he were fleeing, ran
frequently ashore, looked to and fro, so that we could perceive
there must be something. They hauled the next day out of
the kill, and passed between the cakes of ice and the shore,
which we could not do with our yacht.

The 11th, full fifty Indians came over the river from the

---

[1] Wyngaert's Kill, if Jaques Island is correctly identified as Chester Island,
was evidently Chester Creek, within one Dutch or three English miles of Jaques
Island.

fort upon the ice, with pieces of canoes, directly to our yacht, into which they could step from the shore, and spoke to us. They were Minquas,[1] who dwell north of the English of Virginia [colony]. They came on a warlike expedition, and six hundred more were to come. They are friendly to us, but it would not do to trust them too far, as they do anything for plunder. I determined, as the flood-tide began to make, that we must haul into the mouth of the kill, so that they could not come upon us on foot and master us, which would never do. Hauling out of the kill about five-and-twenty paces, we could not get any further, because there was not water enough. I told the master of the yacht that he must direct the crew to throw some ballast overboard, but he could not induce them to do it. I then went to them, and asked them whether they would rather trust to the mercy of these barbarians, or throw away the ballast. They answered that while we were in the river, our lives were at the mercy of the ice. I replied that God, who had so long aided us, would help us. Finally, I said that I had three flasks of brandy in my locker, and would give them one of them, if they would throw the ballast overboard, and we would all help to do it. When the yacht got afloat, we were driven by the current and with the ice and the ebb tide, which was almost spent, a thousand paces below the kill, between two high pieces of ice, which had fallen on the shore; this happened at nightfall. They all raised a great shout, when they saw that we were driven nearer to the river. In the morning, at daybreak, they saw that we were lying between the two pieces of ice, with the bowsprit over the shore, and came running to the yacht. We stood, eight of us, on our arms.

The 12th, we kept them off, as they sought to come into the yacht by the bowsprit, while we were lying, bow on land, between the two pieces of ice. At length the water rose, so that the yacht and the ice floated, and we were to be driven at God's mercy with the ice, which was our great enemy, while the land was our enemy on account of the Indians. We were finally driven up the river, where there was a dry sand-bar

[1] The regular habitat of these Indians was about the heads of Chesapeake Bay in Maryland, and in the lower part of the Susquehanna River Valley and beyond to Lake Erie. See *post*, pp. 70, 103.

running almost to the middle of the river. We were afraid we should be driven upon it by the ice, when God provided two canoes to float by us, which we immediately hauled before the bow, one on each side, and broke the ice with them. Then setting the foresail, as there was a good wind, in order to sail up the river with the tide, we passed, by the aid of God, the Vogel-Sant,[1] which was our great peril at this place, and arrived at the beautiful island when the tide began to run, and we managed to get to the shore, with the side to the shore lengthwise with the bow. At last, the water began to fall rapidly, and we found that there was a sand-bank along the shore. We immediately set about making the mast fast to [some] good stout trees on land, by means of a rope, and to protect ourselves against arrows. The next day, the 13th, three Indians of the Armewamen came before the yacht. They told us that they were fugitives—that the Minquas had killed some of their people, and they had escaped. They had been plundered of all their corn, their houses had been burnt, and they had escaped in great want, compelled to be content with what they could find in the woods, and came to spy out in what way the Minquas had gone away—the main body of their people lying about five or six hours' journey distant, with their wives and children. They told us also, that the Minquas had killed about ninety men of the Sankiekans; that they would come to us the next day, when the sun was in the southeast, as they were suffering great hunger, and that the Minquas had all left and gone from us, back to their country.

The 14th, at night, it began to rain hard, and the wind was from the southwest, which makes it warm there. In the morning we had high-water, which caused the yacht to float finely. We loosened the rope from the tree, to which it had been made fast, in order to prevent the yacht from falling over, because the shore was so shallow there, and let her drift into the river, as the ice was already very soft, like snow. We resolved not to wait for the Indians, as they had been driven away, and could not assist us in those things for which we had

---

[1] Probably Egg Island, or Reedy Island. It may be identified with the island referred to in the grant of the Dutch Governor Kieft, in 1646, to Planck and others for a tract of land on the west side of the Delaware River "almost over against the little island 'T Vogelssant."

come, so that it was a hopeless voyage for us. Going down the river, we arrived below the Minqua's Kill, where we took in some stone for ballast, which we could not obtain elsewhere in the morning. This is a very fine river, and the land all beautifully level, full of groves of oak, hickory, ash, and chestnut trees, and also vines which grow upon the trees. The river has a great plenty of fish, the same as those in our fatherland, perch, roach, pike, sturgeon, and similar fish. Along the sea-coast are codfish, the different kinds of fish which are in our fatherland, and others. After we had taken in some ballast, we went further down the river, and came to its mouth. We fished with our seines, and caught in one draught as many as thirty men could eat of perch, roach, and pike.

The 20th, we weighed our anchor, and with a northwest wind sailed out of the bay, which is ten leagues long, and so wide, that in the middle of it you can hardly see from one shore to the other. It is full of shoals between which are channels, from six to seven fathoms deep, but the deepest channel is on the west side. In order to run up by soundings, as you come from sea to Cape Hinloopen, which lies in thirty-eight degrees and twenty minutes, the shoal of the bank, which stretches from Cape Hinloopen over the bay, reaches Cape May, and when you have passed this a league and a half, and come into the river, so that Cape Hinloopen is south of you, run in then northwest along the west shore, and you will be out of danger of the banks, and keep the west side, where you should keep sounding, but do not get nearer to it than a depth of two fathoms, if the ship be a large one, and this will take you directly to the South River. When you come to the mouth of the river, where it is full two leagues wide, there is a shoal before it, on which, at low tide, there is not more than six or seven feet of water. This you must keep to starboard, and you will see a bushy point ahead on the west side, along which you must hold your course; that is the right channel, the water being three and a half fathoms at low tide, but inside, in the river, it is six or seven fathoms. The tide rises and falls here from five to six feet. By evening, we arrived again at the ship, in which there was great rejoicing to see us, as we had been gone over a month. They did not imagine that we had been frozen up in the river, as no pilot or astrologer could conceive, that in a latitude from the thirty-eighth and a half to the thirty-ninth, such rapid running rivers could freeze. Some maintain that it is because it lies so far west; others adduce other reasons; but I will tell how it can be, from experience and what I have seen, and that is thus: inland, stretching towards the north, there are high mountains, covered with snow, and the north and northwest winds blow over the land from these cold mountains, with a pure, clear air, which causes extreme cold and frost, such as is felt in Provence and Italy, which I have often experienced when I was at Genoa, when the wind blew over the land from the high mountains, making it as cold as it was in Holland. I have found by experience in all countries, during winter, that when the wind blows from the land, the hardest frost makes. It is so in New Netherland also, for as soon as the wind is southwest, it is so warm that one may stand naked in the woods, and put on a shirt.

The 5th of March, determined to make a voyage to the English in Virginia, as we had failed to obtain corn in the South River, in consequence of the war among the Indians, as before related, by which we were placed in such danger, and the grain of the Indians was destroyed; and as we thought that we should not be able to find a sufficient store of it at Fort Amsterdam, on the great [North] river, to serve us on our return voyage to Holland, we therefore deemed it advisable to sail to the English in Virginia. Although there had never been any one there from this quarter, I said, as I had escaped the danger in the South River, I would be the first one of our nation to venture to the English in Virginia, from these parts, as the distance is not more than thirty leagues from the South River or Cape Hinloopen.[1] . . . .

[*Anno* 1643, *October*.] The 12th, at daylight, the wind from the southeast straight on a leeshore, and it began to blow hard. We were in twelve fathoms water. When it was day, the skipper

---

[1] De Vries sailed out of Delaware Bay, March 6, 1633, for Virginia, as he proposed above, and was hospitably received by Sir John Harvey, Governor of Virginia. Returning to Swanendael March 29 he found that his people had caught seven whales, but had obtained only thirty-two cartels of oil. The expedition then departed for New Amsterdam and finally arrived in Holland by midsummer. The remaining paragraphs are from the narrative of 1643-1644.

asked me if I knew where I was. I told him we must run into
eight or nine fathoms, when we should be able to distinguish the
land; but he was afraid of the shore, as he had never been here.
Finally ran into shallower water, when he asked me if I knew the
country. I said, Yes; and I saw that we were by Cape May,
before the South River. He then inquired of me whether we
could not sail straight in. I said, No; that it was all over
full of shoals, that we must enter at the southwest side. He
then threw the lead, and had four fathoms, at which he was
startled. I told him he must lay down the lead; that we must
now depend on my knowledge to get in; that it was all a
shoal there. We then came by Cape Hinloopen in deep
water, when I told him he might throw the lead, and he would
find eight to nine fathoms, as he ran into the South Bay, close
by the shore. We sailed in by the shore, and he said: "I
was in this same place over seven weeks, and there were Indians here on land, and a-fishing, and I went ashore with my
skiff and spoke Spanish to them, but they could not understand me. It was so full of shoals, I ran again out to sea and
proceeded to New England." Then I said to the skipper:
"Had you known the Indian language as I know it, you would
not have sailed to New England. This land is called Swanendael, and these Indians destroyed a colony in the year 1630,
which I began. Had you been able to speak to them, they
would have taken you up the river to the Swedes, or to our
people, who would have informed you that you had passed by
the Virginias." I sailed up the bay west by north along the
west shore; at evening came before the river by the wild
thicket, where we anchored in four fathoms, hard bottom,
and in the morning weighed anchor.

The 13th, sailed by Reed Island, and came to the Verckens
Kill, where there was a fort[1] constructed by the Swedes, with
three angles, from which they fired for us to strike our flag.
The skipper asked me if he should strike it. I answered him,
"If I were in a ship belonging to myself, I would not strike it
because I am a patroon of New Netherland, and the Swedes
are a people who come into our river; but you come here by
contrary winds and for the purposes of trade, and it is there-

---

[1] Fort Nya Elfsborg, built by the Swedes in 1643, a short distance below
the mouth of Varkens Kill (now Salem Creek, New Jersey).

fore proper that you should strike." Then the skipper struck
his flag, and there came a small skiff from the Swedish fort,
some Swedes in it, who inquired of the skipper with what he
was laden. He told them with Madeira wine. We asked
them whether the governor was in the fort. They answered,
No; that he was at the third fort[1] up the river, to which we
sailed, and arrived at about four o'clock in the afternoon,
and went to the governor, who welcomed us. He was named
Captain Prins,[2] and a man of brave size, who weighed over
four hundred pounds. He asked the skipper if he had ever
been in this river before, who said he had not. How then had
he come in where it was so full of shoals? He pointed to me,
that I had brought him in. Then the governor's trader, who
knew me, and who had been at Fort Amsterdam, said that I
was a patroon of Swanendael at the entrance of the bay, destroyed by the Indians in the year 1630, when no Swedes were
known upon this river. He (the governor) then had a silver
mug brought, with which he treated the skipper with hop
beer, and a large glass of Rhenish wine, with which he drank
my health. The skipper traded some wines and sweetmeats
with him for peltries, beaver-skins, and staid here five days
from contrary winds. I went to Fort Nassau, which lies a
league higher up, in which the people of the West India Company were. I remained there half a day, and took my leave
of them, and returned at evening to the governor of the
Swedes.

The 19th, I went with the governor to the Minckquas
Kil, where their first fort[3] was, with some houses inside, where
they carried on their trade with the Minqua Indians; our ship
came down the river also. In this little fort there were some
iron guns. I staid here at night with the governor, who
treated me well. In the morning, the ship was lying before
the Minckquas Kil. I took my leave of the governor, who
accompanied me on board. We fired a salute for him, and
thus parted from him; weighed anchor and got under sail,
and came to the first fort. Let the anchor fall again, and
went on land to the fort, which was not entirely finished; it
was made after the English plan, with three angles close by

[1] Fort Nya Göteborg or New Gothenburg, on Tinicum Island.
[2] Governor Johan Printz.   [3] Fort Christina.

the river. There were lying there six or eight brass pieces, twelve-pounders. The skipper exchanged here some of his wines for beaver-skins.

The 20th of October, took our departure from the last fort, or first in sailing up the river, called Elsenburg. The second fort of the Swedes is named Fort Christian; the third, New Gottenburg. We weighed anchor and sailed from the river; arrived at noon at Cape Hinloopen, and put to sea. Set our course along the coast southwest, quite southerly at first.

RELATION OF CAPTAIN THOMAS YONG, 1634

INTRODUCTION

CAPTAIN THOMAS YONG, an Englishman, the author of tho narrative which follows, was one of the many early seekers for the northwest passage from Atlantic to Pacific waters. It was mainly in pursuit of this famous quest that he explored Delaware Bay and River. Before leaving the river he wrote these observations, and sent them as a report to the English Secretary of State, one of the members of the government giving moral support to the undertaking.

Thomas Yong was born in 1579, in the parish of St. Peter's, Cornhill, in the city of London, of a family, it would seem, of the higher sort of merchants, who had attained, apparently, to some affluence and position. The father, Gregory Yong, who figures in the registers of the parish as "Grocer," with the title "Mr.", significantly respectful in that day, was a native of Bedale, in the north riding of Yorkshire, but early in his career had made his appearance in London, and at the time of his death in 1610 was dwelling at the northwest corner of Leadenhall Street. Captain Yong's elder sister Susanna married Robert Evelyn, of the landed family of the Evelyns of Wotton in Surrey—thus becoming aunt by marriage to the accomplished John Evelyn, the diarist—and the relations of her father's family with the Evelyns, as shown by certain of the Evelyn letters, were intimate.

Of the other facts of Yong's life nothing further has been learned beyond those respecting his American exploring expedition. He is first heard of as the promoter of this enterprise in 1633, when as a man of the mature age of fifty-four, possessing, it is presumed, wealth and leisure, he petitioned Charles I. for full powers to equip and lead, without expense to the Crown, but in its behalf, an expedition to America for the discovery, occupation, and exploitation of uninhabited lands. With the support of the group of Catholic[1] sympathizers influential at court in those days of the personal government of the King, his request received favorable consideration, and a royal commission, in which he is mentioned as of London, gentleman, was issued, in September, 1633, granting him authority to carry out his proposals.

In company with his nephew Robert Evelyn, jr. (b. 1606), who served him as lieutenant, and with a cosmographer and a surgeon, he sailed from England with two vessels in May, 1634. He reached Virginia early in July and during the repairing of one of his leaky ships and the building of a shallop, remained for over two weeks at Jamestown as the guest of Governor Sir John Harvey. While in Virginia he talked with leaders on both sides of the controversy between William Claiborne and Lord Baltimore over the conflicting claims of Virginia and Maryland to Kent Island, and wrote what seems to be a fair report of the situation. This report, with an account of his journey, he sent in a letter from Jamestown, dated July 13, 1634, to Sir Toby Matthew, one of his Catholic patrons about the English court.[2] His expressed sympathies, however, are for Lord Baltimore, who was another of his Catholic patrons.

On July 20 Captain Yong set sail from Virginia. From that time the story as he tells it of his experiences in the Delaware can be followed in the text and notes until after the middle of October. He then sent Lieutenant Evelyn to England, by way of Virginia, with this report, along with a letter, dated October 20, 1634, written from Charles River—he so

[1] Although Yong was so closely associated with Catholics in his undertaking, no evidence has been found to support the intimations of some writers that he was himself a Catholic and the agent for the promotion of a scheme of Catholic settlements in America.

[2] See *Narratives of Early Maryland*, in this series, pp. 47–61.

named the Delaware in honor of the King—in which he states
that despite the obstructing falls of the river, he determines
"against the next summer to build a vessell, which he will"
launch above the falls and "goe up to the Lakes," whence he
hopes "to find a way that leadeth into that Mediterranean
Sea. . . . From the lake I judge that it cannot be lesse than 150
or 200 leagues to our North Ocean, and from thence I purpose
to discover the mouths thereof which discharge both into the
North and South Seas." He adds that he will undergo all
hazards and dangers and will "be at much charge for the service of his Matie and honor of my country."

Evelyn returned to England and in the latter part of
May of the following year, 1635, sailed again for America in
the ship *Plain Joan* to join his uncle, it is stated, upon "special
and very important service." How much further exploration
was made in the Delaware is not clear but apparently that
field was soon abandoned for northern New England. In
1636, according to Samuel Maverick, Yong and his companions
went up the Kennebec River, bent upon discovery. "By cary-
ing their canoes some few times" they "came into Canada
River very near" Quebec, "where by the French Captain
Young was taken, and carried for France but his Company
returned safe." Here Yong disappears from history.

Lieutenant Robert Evelyn, the nephew, whose elder
brother Captain George Evelyn (b. 1593) had gone out to
Maryland in 1636, seems to have appeared in Virginia in the
latter part of the same year, and in 1637 was made surveyor-
general and a councillor of that province. In the ensuing year
he was a member of the Maryland assembly, probably residing
with his brother, who had served for a few months early in the
year as commander of Kent Island, and had a plantation at
Piney Point in his manor of Evelynton on the Potomac. In
1641, under the title of *Directions for Adventurers* (reprinted
in chapter III. of Plantagenet's *New Albion*, in 1648), was pub-

lished his description of the Delaware, in which he supplements somewhat his uncle's account and states that a draft of the region as supplied by him had been incorporated in a printed map of New England. In 1642 he was appointed commander of the Maryland forces at Piscataway against the Indians, and represented St. George's Hundred in the assembly.

The original manuscript of Yong's Relation, and the two accompanying letters of which mention has been made, are in the Virginia State Library at Richmond. The papers were purchased at the sale of the collection of the late Samuel L. M. Barlow, of New York City, who obtained them in the Aspinwall papers, once for the most part in the possession of George Chalmers, the historian. They are simple unassuming statements, and believed to be in every way reliable. They were first published in P. C. J. Weston's *Documents connected with the History of South Carolina* (London, 1856), pp. 25–60; again in 1871 in the *Collections of the Massachusetts Historical Society*, fourth series, IX. 117–131, and then (in 1876) reprinted in *Fund Publication No.* 9 of the Maryland Historical Society, pp. 300–312. The present issue has been collated with the original manuscript.

A. C. M.

RELATION OF CAPTAIN THOMAS YONG, 1634

A breife Relation of a voyage lately made by me Captayne Thomas Yong, since my departure from Virginia, upon a discovery, which I humbly present to the Right Ho^{ble} Sr Francis Windebanke, knight, Principall Secretary of State to his Matie.[1]

THE particulars of all occurrents, that happened unto mee, from my departure out of England till my arrivall in Virginia; and likewise, what passed while I was there; I sent in a Relation to Sr Tobie Matthew,[2] entreating him to present it to yor Hono^r; wch I presume, is already come to yor handes; And therefore I omitt to trouble yor honor, wth a second repetition thereof, and now only intend humbly to give yor honor account of such thinges, as since that time have passed in my voyage.

As soone as I had stopped the leakes of my ship, and finished my shallopp, I sett sayle from Virginia, the 20th of July, coasting along the Coast from Virginia to the Northward, faire by the shoare, and the 24th of the same month, I made that great Bay, wherein I purposed at my departure from England, to make triall for the Passage. I came to an Anchor that night in the mouth of the Bay and the next morning, I entered the same. This Bay is in the mouth thereof 6 leagues broad, and hath in the entrance thereof 12 fathome water. When I was gott into the Bay, I came to an anchor, and sent my Leiuitennant in my shallop ashore, on the Southwest part of the Bay, to see if he could speake with any of the Natives, and to learne what he could of them, concerning this Bay, and the course thereof, who after he had spent most part of the day in searching up and downe, for the Natives, returned towards night, without speaking wth any of them. The next

---

[1] Sir Francis Windebank (1582–1646), Secretary of State, of Catholic inclinations. Later he was forced to leave England.

[2] Sir Tobie Matthew (1577–1655), English courtier, diplomatist, and writer, in religion a Roman Catholic.

morning, being the 26, I sayled some tenne leagues higher up into the Bay, and then came to an Anchor, and agayne sent out my shallopp, to see if I could meet wth any of those natives; but they returned as they did the day before, without speaking with any of them.   The 27 in the morning I weighed to proceed yet further into the Bay and after I had passed some 7 leagues up the Bay, my shallop being then on head of me, espied certayne Indians on the West side of the Bay, to whome they made presently, but the Indians made away from them, as soon as they came neere the shoare; soe I sayled along in the middest of the Bay, and they coasted along by the shoare, till about two in the afternoone; and then there came an Indian running along the shoare, and called to my shallop; The shallop presently made towards him, who stayed till theire arrivall, but would not come aboard, wherefore they landed, and went to him, to whome presently also came three or foure more.   At last they perswaded one of them to goe aboard my ship, and so they brought him to mee.   I entertained him curteously, and gave him buiscuit to eat, and strong water to drinke, but the water he seemed not to rellish well.   I also gave him some trifles, as knives and beades and a hatchett, of which he was wonderfull glad.   Then I began to enquire of him, (by my Interpreter, who understood that language) now farr the sea ran, who answered me that not farre above that place I should meet with fresh water, and that the River ranne up very farre into the land, but that he had never bene at the head thereof.   He told me further that the people of that River were at warre with a certaine Nation called the Minquaos, who had killed many of them, destroyed their corne, and burned their houses; insomuch as that the Inhabitants had wholy left that side of the River, which was next to their enimies, and had retired themselves on the other side farre up into the woods, the better to secure themselves from their enimies.   He also told me that not long since there had bene a ship there, and described the people to me, and by his description, I found they were Hollanders, who had bene there trading for furrs; Towards night he desired to be sett on shoare, which accordingly I commanded to be done.   The next day being the 28, there came aboard of my ship an Indian, with a Canoa with store of Eeles, whereof I bought some for a

knife and a hatchett, and whilest I was discoursing with him
concerning the River, for now I was entered into the mouth
thereof, on a suddayne he fell into a great passion of feare and
trembling; I wondered what the matter was, and comforted
him, and bad him feare nothing, he then shewed me a Canoa,
a good way of, making towards the ship, in which, he said,
were some of the Minquaos and that they were enimies to him,
and to his Nation, and had already killed many of them, and
that they would kill him also, if they saw him, and therefore
he desired me to hide him from them; I told him, I would
defend him, and that they should not hurt him, and that if
they should dare to offer him any violence, I then would kill
them, he seemed very glad to heare me say so, and gave me
thankes, but yet was very earnest to be hid from them, saying,
that if they saw him, they would watch for him ashore, and
there murther him, then I caused him to be putt into a cabbin,
betweene deckes, where he could not be seene. The Minquaos
rowed directly to my ship, and as soone as they gott neere her,
they made signes for a Rope, which was cast out to them,
with which they made fast their Canoa, and presently came
aboard without any difficultie. Our Interpreter understood
but only some few words of their language, so as wee were
forced for the most part to gather their meaning by signes the
best wee could. They told us, they were Minquaos, and that
one of them was a king, (for soe all the Indians call them, who
are most eminent among themselves, and they are in nature of
Captaynes or Governors of the rest, and have power of life and
death, of warre and peace, over their subjects, Some have
1000, some 500, some more, some lesse) and made signes to
us, that they were lately come from warre with the other Indians, whome they had overcome, and slayne some of them,
and cutt downe their corne, (which is of the same kind with the
corne of Virginia which they commonly call Maiz). They
brought a good quantitie of greene eares thereof with them, and
some they presented to mee, and others they roasted and eate
themselves. I used them curteously, and gave them each of
them a hatchett, a pipe, a knife, and a paire of sizers, for which
they were very thankfull to mee, and then desired to see my
trucke,[1] whereof I shewed them samples. The King desired

---

[1] Articles of barter.

some of my cloath, but having nothing to give me in exchange thereof, I gave him two small peices, one of redd and the other of blew.   They made signes to us, that about 10 dayes (as wee thought, but wee were mistaken for they meant weekes, as wee perceaved afterwards), they would come to us agayne, and bring with them great store of trucke of beavers and ottors, and therefore they desired to know where wee would bee; soe I told them that about that time I would send my shallop to meet them there, soe they departed, and as soone as they were gone, I called for the Indian who all this time lay hid in my cabbin, who stayed aboard of me till night, and then departed a contrary way to that which the Minquaos went, promising to be with me the next day.   Some two days after I being then gotten some tenne leagues up the River there came to the shoare side 5 or 6 Indians, and haled us.   I sent my boate for them; when they were arrived, they told me they came to see me from a king, who lived not farre of, and that if I pleased to morrow he would come and visitt mee.   I answered them, he should be welcome, and so after they had stayed awhile, and refreshed themselves aboard my shippe, they departed.   The next day wee expected him but he came not, soe wee departed up a little higher up the River, and on the second of August this king came aboard us about noone, accompanied with 40 or 60 Indians.   After he had sate still awhile, which they are wont to doe upon the ground, he then told mee I was welcome into the Countrey, and that he came to see me with desire to make peace with me, in regard he understood by an Indian that I was a good man, and that I had preserved him from the Minquaos, who would otherwise have slayne him, and withall asked, if wee had any trucke. He also presented mee with two Otters skinnes, and some greene eares of corne, excusing himself that he had no better present for me, in regard the Minquaos had lately harrowed his countrey, and carried much beaver from him and his sub-jects, and that the rest they had trucked away to the Hol-landers, who had lately bene there.   I told him that I was sent thither by a great king in Europe, namely the king of England, and that I came thither to discover that Countrey and to make peace with them, if they desired to imbrace it and that if they would soe do, I would defend them from their enimies, he

was very joyfull to hear this, and desired me to tarry two
dayes there, for he would bring thither another king, who was
his father in law, to make peace with mee, and another king
also who was his neighbour, and the proprietor of that part of
the River, wherein I then rode. I condiscended[1] with him to
stay two dayes. In the meane time, I tooke possession of the
countrey, for his Matie, and there sett up his Maties armes
upon a tree, which was performed with solemnities usuall in
that kind. I enquired of this king how farre this River ranne
up into the Countrey, and whither it were navigable or no, he
told me it ranne a great way up, and that I might goe with
my shippe, till I came to a certaine place, where the rockes[2]
ranne cleane crosse the River, and that there he thought I
could not goe over with my great Canoas, (for soe they call all
vessells that swimme upon the water). I then desired him
to lend me a pilott to goe up to that place, which he most
willingly granted. I presented him with a Coate, a hatchett,
and a knife, wherewith he was very well contented, and so
after he had stayd some 4 or 5 houres he tooke his leave. About
some 3 or foure dayes after, this king returned to me, and in
company with him two other kings, whome I mentioned before, with whome I also made peace. Of the old king I enquired if he had ever bene at the head of the River, he answered me no, but that he had heard that the River ranne
farre up into the land, and that some few dayes journey
beyond the rockes of which I spake before there was a moun-
tainous countrey where there were great store of Elkes and
that before the warr with the Minquaos, they were wont to
goe thither to hunt them, but he said that neither he himself
nor any of his people had ever bene further then those mountaines. These kings prayed me that I would do them the
curtesie to stay foure or five dayes with them, because they
were certainly informed, that the Minquaos would within that
time passe over the River to assault them, wherefore they
desired me not to suffer them to passe over. I told them I
would at their request stay five dayes, and that I would labour
to procure them peace, and that if their enimies refused the
same that then I would joyne with them against them, and

---

[1] Agreed.
[2] The Falls of Delaware, at what is now Trenton, New Jersey.

I would lend them souldiers to goe to warre in company with them, and that I would also, if occasion were, invade the Minquaos within their owne countrey, upon this condition, that they shall renounce all trade or alliance with all other persons, save only his Maties Ministers and subjects, and that they shall be wholy dependant on him, of which they were very joyfull and accepted the conditions and soe wee made a solemne peace, they not long after departed, and it was spread all over the River, that I had made peace with them, and that I was a just man, and would defend them against their enimies the Minquaos. Upon the report heer of some three dayes after, there came to me messengers with a present from two other kings, who lived in a lesser River,[1] which falleth into this great River, somewhat neerer the rockes. They told me that their kings desired to make peace with me, according as the other kings their neighbours had done, and that they had some Beaver and Otter skinnes, which they would trucke with me for such commodities as I had. I sent them word that some three days after I would come up to the mouth of that River, where I would desire them to meet mee, and that I would entreat one of those messengers to stay with me, till I were ready to goe, whome I would send to them as soon as I· was arrived, and one of them presently offered himself to stay with mee. When the five dayes were expired I sent to the former kings, to let them understand that now ı had tarried five days expecting the Minquaos and that seeing they came not, I had sent my shallop to seeke them out, but it was returned without any notice of them, and therefore that I thought they were not in the River, wherefore now I would goe up higher into the River to meet with the other kings, whither if they had occasion they should send to mee, and I would send to assist them, desiring them withall to send me a pilot to carrie me to the Rockes. They sent me word they were sorry I was departing from them, neverthelesse they hoped I would shortly returne thither againe, and that if they had occasion they would send to mee, and moreover one of them sent me his Brother in company of my messenger, and commanded him to goe up along with me, and to attend mee, and remayne with me till my returne thither againe, which he

---

[1] Possibly the Schuylkill River.

did accordingly.   As soone as my messengers were come backe,
I sett forward and arrived at the mouth of the said River, and
not long after I was come to an anchor, about 8 of the clocke
in the evening, came the two kings aboard of mee, attended
only with some foure or 5 of their principall men, for the rest
of their company in regard it was night, I desired them to leave
on shoare, till the morning.   I entertained them aboard all
night, and in the morning early being the 23 of August, the
rest of their company came aboard.   I gave each of them a
present, as I had done to the other kings, which when they had
receaved, first the ancient king, and afterward the yonger,
called together all their people, and made to them a long ora-
tion to this purpose.   That wee were a good people.   That
wee were just.   That wee were ready to defend the oppressed
from the crueltie of their neighbours.   That wee were loving
people, as a testimony whereof they shewed the presents I had
given them.   That wee had brought thither such things as
they stood in need of, for which wee desired only Beaver and
Otter skinnes, whereof they had to spare.   That therefore
they comanded them to trade lovingly and freely with our
people, that they should be carefull that no injuries were either
privately or publikely done to them.   That they should use
them as friends and Brothers, and that for me in particular
they should honor and esteeme of me as a Brother of their
kings, and that they should be carefull to carrie themselves
dutifully towards mee, with a great deale more complement,
then I expresse.   This being done my company and the Indians fell a trucking, while these two kings entered into the
same league with me, which the former had done, and then
towards evening the elder king went ashore, the yonger
remayning aboard with mee.   Thither also came two other
neighboring kinges, with whom also I made peace.   Heere also
was the first place, where some of their weomen came aboard
our shippes, and heere during the space of five dayes that wee
tarried we had continually store of Indians aboard us.   One
night about one of the clock in the night, there rose an alarme
amongst the Indians that lay ashore, that the Minquaos were
come upon them; the yonger king was then aboard my ship,
who desired me to receave his people aboard till the morning,
which I did, setting a good guard upon them and disarming

them. In the morning I found this to proceed of nothing else
but their pollicie to trie whether, if occasion were, I would really assist them or no. But howsoever the king gave me
great thankes for my love to him and his people. After I had
stayed there some five dayes, I departed towards the head of
the River, and many Indians as I passed along came aboard
my shippe, with such commodities as they had, some with
furrs, some with victualls. On the 29 of August I had gotten
up with my shippe as far as I could goe with her for now the
water beganne to be shoaly, so I came to an anchor, neere to
the dwelling of one of the principall kings of this Countrey, who
that same night hearing that I was come to his Countrey, came
aboard of me to visitt me, with whome also I made peace as
with the former. This king and his Brother are the greatest
Travaylors that I mett among all the Indians, in the River,
for they have bene by land at the lower fort of Hudsons River,
and likewise very farre up the River, beyond the rockes, I
spake of. On the first of September I sent my leiuetennant
in my shallop up to the Rockes, both to sound the water as he
went, and likewise to trie whether my boates would passe
those rockes or no. The Hollanders of Hudsons River having
gotten some intelligence of our being heere by the Indians,
who in some places live not above a dayes journey from them,
overtooke me heere within sixe houres after I had sent away
my leiuetennant to the rockes. They came to an Anchor close
by me. I sent my boate presently aboard them to know what
they were, and from whence they came, and to bring the
master to mee, who soone after came together with his Marchant in their owne boate. When they were come aboard of
me, I sent for them into my cabbin, and asked them what
they made heere, they answered mee they came to trade as
formerly they had done. I asked them if they had any comis-
sion from his Matie to trade in the River or no, they answered
they had none from the King of England, but from the Governor of new Netherlands they had, to which I replyed that
I knew no such Governor, nor no such place as new Netherlands. I told them that this Country did belong to the crowne
of England, as well by ancient discovery as likewise by possession lawfully taken, and that his Matie was now pleased to
make more ample discovery of this River, and of other places

also, where he would erect Collonies, and that I was therefore
sent hither with a Royall Commission under the great Seale
to take possession heereof. I perceaved by their countenance
that this newes strooke them could at heart, and after a little
pawse they answered me, that they had traded in this River
heeretofore. I then replyed that therein they had done his
Matie and his subjects the greater injurie, for supposing, as
some of the Dutch pretended, that they had by his Maties
leave traded and planted in Hudsons River, yet ought they
not to usurpe upon other trades and Countreyes of his Maties
without his leave, and since that he is now pleased to make
use of this River, either for himself, or his subjects, it would be
good manners in them to desist. Then they desired to see my
Commission, which I shewed them, and after they had read it,
and considered well thereof, apprehending the power I had, if
they should trade without licence, to make them prize, they
desired me to give them a Copie thereof. I answered them
that it was not the custome of England for his Maties Ministers
to give Copies of their Commissions, they then desired to know
how I would proceed with them, which they hoped would be
the better in regard they knew not of my commission, I told
them I would let them know that heereafter, when my leiuetennant was returned which perhaps would be the next
morning.

The next day my leiuetennant being returned, I sent for
the Hollanders to dine with me, and this day I spent in making them wellcome, and after dinner one of their company
dranke to me saying, Heere Governor of the South River, (for
soe they call this) I drinke to you and indeed confesse your
Commission is much better then ours, how say you Copeman[1]
(who is the head marchant) said he is it not. To whome
the Copeman answered yes indeede, I have not seene a larger
Commission. The next day about 8 of the clocke I sent for
them to give them an answerre which was this. That in regard they were subjects to so ancient allies of my Prince, and
that they were neighbours heere, and since they had carried
themselves civilly, I had used them with all curtesy, that I
might lawfully use. That since I had also shewed them my
commission, I made no question but that they knew suffi-

[1] Dutch *Koopman*, (pron. Copeman), merchant,

ciently well what they had to doe, neverthelesse, I was willing
they might stay at Anchor two dayes longer, to provide themselves of whatsoever they should need, and that I would not
suffer any thing to be taken from them during their stay.
They then asked me if I would command them to be gone, I
answered I command you not to be gone, but you may looke
into my Commission, and there you may see whether it be
lawfull for you to vizitt or trade into any places I shall pos-
sesse, where upon they read over the second time that part
of the Commission, and then they answered they would be
gone, but they desired a note under my hand for their discharge, unto their Governor, to shew the cause why they returned without trading.   I answered it was not the custome of
England and that they had no need of any such note, since
they had seene the Commission under the great Seale, and that
I could not beleeve but that their Governor would both creditt
and be satisfied with their Relation.   Soe they parted civilly
though very sadly from mee.   Before the time of two dayes
was expired, they weighed Anchor and went downe the River,
I sent my Leiuetennant in my pinnace to see them cleare of
the River, and to watch them least they should doe me ill
offices with the Indians, in their way homewards.   In their
going downe they sometimes went aboard of one another after
the manner of the Sea, and the Merchant of the Ship upon
some discourse said, that if they had bene in possession at my
arrivall they would not have removed, for all my Commission,
and not long after he said I would we were in possession of it
agayne, yet if the West India Company had been ruled by me,
they had planted this River, rather than Hudsons River, and
whilest my Leiuetennant commended Hudsons River, for a good
place, he replyed, yea so it is, but this is better, and further
said were I sure we should loose this River, I would tell you
something that would please you.   I gave my leiuetennant
order that after he had watched these Hollanders out of the
Bay he should then goe, and discover all along the Coast, as
farre as Hudson's River and so on towards Cape Cod, to see
if there were any probability of a passage through.   Hee accordingly discovered along the coast as farre as Hudsons
River, where he was overtaken with foule weather, and contrary windes, where he endured the stormes till he was forced

by the incommodiousnes of his vessell, and want of victualls to returne. In this voyage he lost two men who were killed by the Indians, but found nothing worthy of particular Relation.

As soone as he was returned I sent him presently up once more to the falls to trie whether he could passe those rockes at a spring tide, which before he could not doe in a neap tide, but it was then also impassable with any great boate, wherefore he returned backe to mee agayne. When he saw he could not passe over the rockes, he went up the River side some five miles above the rockes, to see whither the River were passable or no, who informeth me [it] is deepe and likely to runne very farre up into the Countrey. Heere also is the Brother of the king of Mohigon, who is the uppermost king that wee have mett with who relateth that he hath bene in a Canoa 20 dayes journey up the River, above the rockes which[1] he describeth to runne northwest and westnorthwest, that he was sent thither by his brother to a king of his Alliance, and that there he heard that this River some five dayes journey higher issucth from a great Lake, he saith further that four days journey from this River, over certayne mountaines there is a great mediterranean sea and he offereth to goe him self along in person the next sommer with myself or my leiuetennant to shew us the same, he saith further that about two dayes journey above the falls or rocks, the River divides itself into two branches, the one whereof is this wherein wee are, and the other trendeth towards Hudsons River, and that the farther you goe up the River the broader.

I beseech y^r honor give me leave by the way to give you a short relation of the commodities[2] and scituation of this River. This River dischargeth itself into a great Bay in the North part of Virginia, in 39 and almost a half of latitude. The river is broad and deepe, and is not inferior to any in the North of America, and a ship of 300 Tonnes may saile up within three leagues of the rockes. The River aboundeth with beavers, otters, and other meaner furrs, which are not only taken upon the bankes of the mayne River, but likewise in other lesser rivers which discharge themselves into the

---

[1] *I. e.*, the river.
[2] Advantages or good qualities.

greater, whereof I thinke few Rivers of America have more or
more pleasant. The people are for the most part very well
proportioned, well featured, gentle, tractable and docible.
The land is very good and fruitfull and withall very healthfull.
The soyle is sandy and produceth divers sorts of fruites, especially grapes, which grow wild in great quantity, of which
I have eaten sixe severall sorts, some of them as good as they
are ordinarily in Italy, or Spaine; and were they replanted I
thinke they whould be farre better. Heere also growes the
fruite which in Italy they call lazarroli,[1] plumms, divers sorts
of berries and divers other fruites not knowne in Europe.
The climate is much like that of Italy and all sorts of fruites
of that Countrey will thrive heere exceedingly. The earth
being fruitefull is covered over with woods and stately timber,
except only in those places, where the Indians had planted
their corne. The Countrey is very well replenished, with deere
and in some places store of Elkes. The low grounds of which
there is great quantitie excellent for meadowes and full of
Beaver and Otter. The quantity of fowle is so great as can
hardly be beleeved, wee tooke at one time 48 partriches together, as they crossed the river, chased by wild hawkes.
I myselfe sprang in two houres 5 or 6 covies in walking of a
mile. there are infinit number of wild pidgeons, black birds,
Turkeyes, Swans, wild geese, ducks, Teales, widgins, brants,
herons, cranes etc. of which there is so great aboundance, as
that the Rivers and creekes are covered with them in winter.
Of fish heere is plentie, but especially sturgeon all the sommer
time, which are in such aboundance in the upper parts of the
River, as that great benefitt might be raysed by setting up a
fishing for them, for in the spring and beginning of summer
the weather is so temperate, that they will keepe very well.
Heere are also great store of wild hops yet exellent good and
as faire as those in England, heere are also divers other things
which with industrie will prove exellent good commodities,

---

[1] Lazarola or lazzerola, _i. e._, the azarole or Neapolitan medlar (Crataegus
azarolus), a fruit-bearing shrub allied to the white thorn. "At this spot [on the
south side of Christiana Creek, opposite the site of Fort Christina] there are many
medlar trees which bear good fruit from which one [Jan] Jaquet, who does not
live far from there, makes good brandy or spirits, which we tasted and found
even better than French brandy" (In 1679; _Journal of Dankers and Sluyter_, p. 188).

and for my part I am confident that this River is the most healthfull, fruitefull and commodious River in all the North of America, to be planted.

Hither also very lately came the Hollanders a second time, sent hither by the Governor of the Dutch plantation, with a Commission to plant and trade heere, but after much discourse to and fro, they have publikely declared, that if the king of England please to ownc this River, they will obey, and they humbly desire that he will declare to them their limitts in these parts of America, which they will also observe.

FROM THE "ACCOUNT OF THE SWEDISH
CHURCHES IN NEW SWEDEN," BY REV-
EREND ISRAEL ACRELIUS, 1759

INTRODUCTION

In 1638 the Swedes, impelled by the spirit of territorial and commercial expansion aroused under their late King, the great and victorious Gustavus Adolphus, founded the colony of New Sweden, thus planting the first permanent white settlement on the Delaware. This foundation was laid under the personal direction of Peter Minuit, the first governor, at Fort Christina, on a creek of the same name, where the present city of Wilmington, Delaware, now stands. Thence, during the next decade, especially under the vigorous rule of the warrior Governor Printz, who arrived in 1643, a thin fringe of settlement in the form of forts and trading posts—barely a dozen in all—with a population at no time exceeding a few hundred souls, was extended, mainly on the western shore, about thirty-five miles up and down the river between the sites of Philadelphia and Elsinborough, New Jersey, and not more than three or four miles inland.

The Swedish government supported the enterprise through the medium of a trading company organized, under the inspiration of certain Dutch promoters, on the model of the Dutch and English trading corporations. The Indian fur trade, along with the lesser traffic in Virginia and Maryland tobacco, was the chief business of the colony, and for the most part sustained the somewhat dilatory and wavering interest of the people at home. The colonists gave some attention to tobacco culture and grazing, and occasionally raised small crops of grain, but the evidence thus far available shows that they had no particular success in agriculture; frequently they were largely dependent upon their English and Dutch neighbors for necessary provisions.

53

The Dutch, who in 1623 had erected Fort Nassau on the eastern shore of the river near the present Gloucester, New Jersey, claimed the Delaware region as part of New Netherland, and protested from time to time against the Swedish occupation. Vigorous action, however, was delayed on account of the close political and economic relations between the two mother countries, Sweden as the great Protestant power in the Thirty Years' War aiding the Netherlands, and the Netherlands, in turn, favoring Swedish shipping and trade. After the Treaty of Westphalia of 1648, these conditions were changed. The Swedes having made a rapid commercial development came into effective competition with the Dutch. The Dutch, with their political independence conceded by Spain as well by the other leading powers of Europe, now sought to curb this dangerous northern rival. They built other forts on the Delaware. In 1655, the Dutch Governor, Peter Stuyvesant, from New Amsterdam, attacked New Sweden. Swedish rule was brought to an end and the Delaware became once more in fact a part of New Netherland. It so remained until the English conquest of New Netherland in 1664.

The details of the history of New Sweden, as recounted by the Swedish historian, the Reverend Israel Acrelius, may be followed in the extracts from his work hereafter presented.

Born in 1714 in Österåker, in Roslagen, near Stockholm, Sweden, Acrelius was educated at the University of Upsala and ordained as a Lutheran clergyman in 1743. In 1749 he was sent out from Sweden as provost of the Swedish congregations on the Delaware. He took up his residence at Christina, now Wilmington, as pastor of the Old Swedes' Church, and thence made periodical visits to the other churches. After an efficient service of seven years he went back to Europe, and during the winter of 1756–1757 devoted himself to study in England. He then returned to Sweden, received a pension from the King, and retired to the living of Fellingsbro, in Westerås, near Stockholm. There he completed his history which he had begun in America, and died in 1800.

His book, a quarto of xx+534 pages, published at Stockholm in 1759, is written in Swedish and bears the title *Beskrifning om de Swenska Församlingars forna och närwarande Tilstånd uti det så kallade Nya Swerige* which in English is "Description of the Former and Present State of the Swedish Churches, in the so-called New Sweden."

Of the eight parts into which the work is divided, parts I., II., and III., comprising the first third of the book, form a history of the respective Swedish, Dutch, and English governments in the Pennsylvania and Delaware region up to and including Acrelius's residence there in the middle years of the eighteenth century. The remaining two-thirds of the work are devoted to a full account of the Swedish church on the Delaware for the same period.

Although writing a century after the Swedish régime on the Delaware, Acrelius had the advantage over later historians of a certain intimacy with his subject, not simply by reason of nearness to the earlier period, but because of his knowledge of the topography of the field concerned and the information obtained in religious visits among surviving families of the colonists of New Sweden. On the whole he made careful and intelligent use of some of the chief original sources, a few of which are not now available. Some errors, it is true, have crept in; parts of the book are antiquated, in the light of modern research; and the writer's views, especially with respect to the Dutch, are obviously colored by his Swedish sympathies. Nevertheless, the work has independent value and interest. Such of its shortcomings as have been observed in the present text are pointed out in the notes.

The whole of the book was translated and edited by the Reverend William M. Reynolds, and published in 1874, in the *Memoirs of the Historical Society of Pennsylvania*, volume XI.

Our extracts are from this translation, pp. 20–29, 43–61, and 85–87, as revised by Dr. Amandus Johnson, of the University of Pennsylvania, from the Swedish of the original edition, pages 5–16, 36–55, and 85–88. The text thus selected and here printed is confined to the three chapters constituting Part I. "Of the Swedish Administration." All of Chapter I., "Of the First Arrival of the Swedes, under Commander Menewe [Minuit]," is given, excepting a few introductory pages on America in general. Of Chapter II., "The Administration under Governor Printz," a few sections are omitted. Only the references to the Swedish Church are chosen from the latter part of Chapter III., "The Administration of Director-General Rising." Thus this eighteenth-century narrative serves in the main to fill gaps in those records which are more strictly contemporary in their origin.

A. C. M.

FROM THE "ACCOUNT OF THE SWEDISH CHURCHES IN NEW SWEDEN," BY REVEREND ISRAEL ACRELIUS, 1759

[CHAPTER I.] 3. *The Entrance of the Hollanders into North America.*

ABOUT the same time the Hollanders undertook to explore these American harbors. They took a fancy to the shores of the bay called by the Indians Menahados, and the river Mohaan. Henry Hudson, an Englishman in the service of the Holland East India Company, had first discovered those places, and called the bay after himself, Hudson's Bay. The East India Company, in the year 1608, sold its right to the country, which it based upon its priority of discovery, to some Hollanders. These obtained from the States General an exclusive privilege to the country, and took the name of "The West India Company of Amsterdam." In the year 1610 they began to traffic with the Indians, and in the year 1613 they built a trading post at the place now called Albany, and in the following year placed some cannon there. Samuel Argall, the governor of Virginia, drove them out in 1618, but King James I. gave them permission to remain, that their ships might obtain water there in their voyages to Brazil.[1] From that time until 1623, when the West India Company obtained its charter,[2] their trade with the Indians was conducted entirely on shipboard, and they made no attempts to build any house or fortress until 1629.[3] Now, whether it was done with or without the permission of England, the town of New Amsterdam was built and fortified, as also the place Aurania, Orange, now called Albany, having since had three general-governors, one after the other. But that was not enough. They wished

---

[1] This is legendary.
[2] The Dutch West India Company was chartered in 1621.
[3] They built a fort at Albany as early as 1615.

to extend their power to the river Delaware also, and erected on its shores two or three small forts, which were, however, immediately destroyed by the natives of the country.

4. *Arrangements in Sweden for a Colony.*

It now came in order for Sweden also to take part in this gain. William Usselinx,[1] a Hollander, born at Antwerp in Brabant, presented himself to King Gustaf Adolph, and laid before him a proposition for a Trading Company, to be established for Sweden, and to extend [its operations] to Asia, Africa, and Magellan's Land, [with the assurance] that this would be a great source of revenue to the kingdom. Authority was given him to carry out so important a project; and thereupon a contract of trade was drawn up, under which the Company was to unite, and subscribe it. Usselinx published his explanation of this contract, wherein he also particularly made the country on the Delaware known as to its fertility, convenience, and all its imaginable advantages. To strengthen the matter, a charter was secured for the Company, and especially for Usselinx, who was granted a royalty of one thousandth part upon all articles bought or sold by the Company.

5. *The Execution of the Project.*

The great king, whose zeal for the honor of God was not less ardent than for the welfare of his subjects, availed himself of this opportunity to extend Christian doctrine among the heathen, as well as to establish his own power in other parts of the world. To this end he sent forth letters patent, dated at Stockholm, on the 2d of July, 1626, wherein all, both high and low, were invited to contribute something to the Company, according to their means. The work was continued in the Diet of the following year, 1627, when the estates of the

---

[1] Willem Usselinx (1567–*c*. 1647), the founder of the Dutch West India Company and of the Swedish South Company, was a native of Antwerp. He received a business education in Antwerp and spent several years abroad in Spain, Portugal, and the Azores, returning to Holland about 1591, a wealthy man. From 1600 until his death he was engaged in the promotion of great projects and plans of colonization and trade.

realm gave their assent, and confirmed the measure. Those who took part in this Company were: His Majesty's mother, the Queen Dowager Christina, the Prince John Casimir, the Royal Council, the most distinguished of the nobility, the highest officers of the army, the bishops and other clergymen, together with the burgomasters and aldermen of the cities, as well as a large number of the people generally. The time fixed for paying in the subscriptions was the 1st of May of the following year (1628). For the management and working of the plan there were appointed an admiral, vice-admiral, chapman, under-chapman, assistants, and commissaries, together with soldiers and officers.

6. *Renewal of these Plans.*

But when these arrangements were now in full progress and advertised everywhere, the German war and the King's death occurred, which caused this important work to be laid aside. The Trading Company was dissolved, its subscriptions nullified, and the whole project was about to die with the King. But just as it appeared to be at its end, it received new life. Another Hollander, by the name of Peter Menewe,[1] sometimes called Menuet, made his appearance in Sweden. He had been in Dutch service in America, where he became involved in difficulties with the officers of their Company, in consequence of which he was recalled home and dismissed from their service. But he was not discouraged by this, went over to Sweden, and renewed the representations which Usselinx had formerly made in regard to the excellence of the country, and the advantages that might be derived from it.

[1] Peter Minuit (1580–1638), the first governor of New Sweden, brought over the initial Swedish expedition to the Delaware in 1638, built Fort Christina at the site of Wilmington, Delaware, and thus began the first permanent white settlement on that river. Born of Huguenot parents at Wesel in western Germany, he went over to New Netherland in 1626 as third Director General. Apparently his rule was successful but he was recalled in 1631. Becoming concerned in the Swedish plans of expansion he suggested to Chancellor Oxenstierna and to Spiring the first plan for the settlement of the Delaware, proposing the name New Sweden. On his way home from the new colony he was lost in a storm near the island of St. Christopher in the West Indies. See Amandus Johnson, *Swedish Settlements*, pp. 93–117, 182–186, 191–192, 684–685.

7. *Under Queen Christina.*

Queen Christina, who succeeded her royal father in the government, was glad to have the project thus renewed. The royal chancellor, Count Axel Oxenstierna, understood well how to put it in operation. He took the West India Trading Company into his own hands, as its president, and encouraged other wealthy noblemen to take shares in it. King Charles I. of England had also, in the year 1634, upon representations made to him by John Oxenstierna, at that time Swedish ambassador in London, renounced,[1] in favor of the Swedes, all claims and pretensions which the English had to that country, growing out of their rights as its first discoverers. Hence everything seemed to be settled upon a firm foundation, and all earnestness was employed [in the prosecution of the plans for a colony].

8. *Menewe's Outward Journey.*

As a good beginning the first colony was sent off, and Peter Menewe was placed over it, as being best acquainted in those regions. They set sail from Gothenburg in a ship-of-war, called the *Key of Calmar,* followed by a smaller vessel, bearing the name of the *Bird Griffin,* both laden with people, provisions, ammunition, and merchandise suitable for traffic and gifts to the Indians. The ships successfully reached their place of destination. The high expectations which our emigrants had conceived of that new land agreed exactly with the first views which they had of it. They made their first landing on the bay or entrance to the river Poutaxat,[2] which they called the river of New Sweden, and the place where they landed they called Paradise Point.[3]

9. *Purchase of Land.*

A purchase of land was immediately made from the Indians, and it was determined that the land on the western side

---

[1] No records confirming this have been found.
[2] Evidently the South (later Delaware) Bay and River.
[3] A little south of the present Murderkill Creek, in Kent County, Delaware.

of the river, from the entrance called Cape Inlopen, or Hinlopen,[1] all the way up to the fall called Santickan[2] and then all the country inland, as much as was desired, should belong to the Swedish crown forever.[3] Posts were driven into the ground as landmarks, which were still seen in their places sixty years afterwards. A deed was drawn up for the land thus purchased. This was written in Dutch, because no Swede was yet able to interpret the language of the heathen. The Indians subscribed their hands and marks. The writing was sent home to Sweden, to be preserved in the royal archives. Måns Kling[4] was the surveyor. He laid out the land and made a map of the whole river, with its tributaries, creeks, and capes, which was sent to the royal archives in Sweden. Their clergyman was Reorus Torkillus[5] of East Gothland.

10. *Christina the First Place of Abode.*

The first abode of the newly arrived emigrants was at a place called by the Indians Hopokahacking. There, in the year 1638, Peter Menuet built a fortress, which he named Fort Christina,[6] after the reigning queen of Sweden. This place, situated upon the west side of the river, was probably chosen so as to be out of the way of the Hollanders, who wished to usurp the eastern shore—a measure of prudence, until the arrival of a greater force from Sweden. The fort was built

[1] Henlopen.

[2] The Falls of Delaware at what is now Trenton.

[3] The north and south bounds of this first purchase from the Indians by Minuit in 1638 extended only from Christina Creek to the Schuylkill.

[4] Måns Nilsson Kling, who is frequently mentioned in these narratives, came over in the first expedition to New Sweden in 1638 and was the commander of Fort Christina until 1640, when he returned to Sweden. He came back to the colony as lieutenant the following year. Later he was stationed at the fort near the mouth of the Schuylkill River where he continued until his final return to Sweden in 1648.

[5] Rev. Reorus Torkillus (1608–1643), a native of Mölndal, near Gothenburg, Sweden, attended school at Lidköping and Skara. He was a lecturer at the high school of Gothenburg and chaplain to the superintendent. He arrived with the second expedition in 1640, conducting services in Fort Christina, thus becoming not only the first minister in New Sweden, but the first Lutheran pastor in the present United States. See Amandus Johnson, *Swedish Settlements.* p. 697.

[6] Now Wilmington, Delaware.

upon an eligible site, not far from the mouth of the creek, so as to secure them the navigable water of the Maniquas, which was afterwards called Christina Kihl, or Creek.

11. *The Country Empty and Unoccupied.*

The country was unoccupied and free from the Hollanders. They had had two or three forts on the river—Fort Nassau, where Gloucester now stands, and another at Horekihl, down on the bay. But both of these were entirely destroyed by the Americans, and their people driven away. The following extract from the *History of the New Netherland,* which Adrian van der Donck published in the year 1655, with the license and privilege as well of the States General as of the West India Company, will serve as proof of this:

The place is called Hore-kihl, but why so called we know not. But this is certain, that many years back, before the English and the Swedes came hither, it was taken up and settled as a colony by Hollanders, the arms of the States being at the same time set up in brass. These arms having been pulled down by the villany of the Indians, the commissary there resident demanded that the head of the perpetrator should be delivered to him. The Indians, unable to free themselves in any other way, brought him the head, which was accepted as a sufficient atonement. But some time afterwards, when we were at work in the fields, and unsuspicious of danger, the Indians came as friends, distributed themselves according to the number of the Hollanders [at the various plantations]; fell upon them and completely exterminated them. Thus was the colony exterminated, though sealed with blood, and dearly enough purchased.

12. *The Hollanders Protest.*

Notwithstanding all this the Hollanders believed that they had the best right to the Delaware River, yea, a better right than the Indians themselves. It was their object to secure at least all the land lying between said river and their New Amsterdam, where was their power, and which country they immediately called "The New Netherlands." But as their forces were still too weak, they always kept one or another of their people upon the east side of the river to watch any one who might visit the country. As soon, therefore, as Menuet landed with his Swedish company, notice of the fact was given to the Dutch Director-General in New Amsterdam. He waited for some time, until he could ascertain Menuet's purpose; but when it appeared that a fortress was being erected for the Swedes, the following protest arrived:

THURSDAY, May 6, 1638.

I, William Kieft, Director-General of the New Netherlands, residing upon the island of Manhattan, in the Fort Amsterdam, under the government subject to the High and Mighty States General of the United Netherlands, and the West India Company, chartered by the Council Chamber in Amsterdam, make known to you, Peter Menuet, who style yourself Commander in the service of Her Royal Majesty, the Queen of Sweden, that the whole South River of the New Netherlands, both above and below, has already, for many years, been our property, occupied by our forts, and sealed with our blood; which was also done when you were a servant in the New Netherlands, and you are, therefore, well aware of this. But whereas you have now come between our forts to build a fortress to our injury and prejudice, which we shall never permit; as we are also assured that Her Royal Majesty of Sweden has never given you authority to build forts upon our rivers and coasts, nor to settle people on the land, nor to traffic in peltries, nor to undertake anything to our injury: We do, therefore, protest against all the injury to property, and all the evil consequences of bloodshed, uproar, and wrong which our Trading Company may thus suffer: And that we shall protect our rights in such manner as we may find most advisable.

Then follows the [usual] conclusion.

13. *Another Proof of this.*

In his history of the New Netherlands, at the place already cited, Adrian van der Donck likewise relates how protest was made against the building of Fort Christina, but there also he gives evidence that the strength of the Hollanders in the river on the first arrival of the Swedes consisted almost entirely in great words. He says:

On the river lies, first, Maniqua's Kihl, where the Swedes have built Fort Christina, where large ships can load and unload at the shore.   There is another place on the river called Schulkihl, which is also navigable.   That, also, was formerly under the control of the Hollanders, but is now mostly under the government of the Swedes.   In that river [Delaware] there are various islands and other places formerly belonging to the Hollanders, whose name they still bear, which sufficiently shows that the river belongs to the Hollanders, and not to the Swedes.   Their very commencement will convict them.   For in the year 1638 one Minnewits, who had formerly acted as Director for the Trading Company at Manhatans, came into the river in the ship *Key of Colmar*, and the yacht called the *Bird Griffin*.   He gave out to the Hollander, Mr. van der Nederhorst, the agent of the West India Company in the South River, that he was on a voyage to the West India islands, and that he was staying there only to take in wood and water.   Whereupon said Hollander allowed him to go free.   But, some time after, some of our people going thither found him still there, and he had planted a garden, and the plants were growing in it.   In astonishment we asked the reasons for such procedure, and if he intended to stay there?   He tried to escape from answering by various excuses, and gave us thus no information.   The third time they found them occupied with building a fort.   Then we saw their purpose.   As soon as he was informed of it, Director Kieft protested against it, but in vain.

14. *Peter Hollendare Menewe's Successor.*

Thus Peter Menuet made a good beginning for the settle-ment of the Swedish colony in America.   He guarded his little fort for over three years,[1] and the Hollanders neither at-tempted, nor were able to overthrow it.   After some years of faithful service he died at Christina.[1]   In his place followed Peter Hollendare, a native Swede, who did not remain at the head of its affairs more than a year and a half.[2]   He returned home, to Sweden, and was a major at Skepsholm, in Stock-holm, in the year 1655.

[1] These are errors; Minuit remained only a few months in New Sweden and died the same year, 1638, in the West Indies on his return voyage to Sweden.

[2] Peter Hollender Ridder, the second governor of New Sweden, 1640-1643. See *post*, p. 98.

CHAPTER II

The Administration under Governor Printz.

1. *The Second Swedish Colony.*

The second emigration took place under Lieutenant-Colonel John Printz, who went out with the appointment of Governor of New Sweden. He had a grant of four hundred rix-dollars[1] for his travelling expenses, and one thousand two hundred dollars, silver money, as his annual salary. The Company was invested with the exclusive privilege of importing tobacco into Sweden, although that article was even then regarded as unnecessary and injurious, although indispensable since the establishment of the bad habit of its use. Upon the same occasion was also sent out Magister John Campanius Holm,[2] who was invited by His Excellency, Member of the Royal Council and Admiral, Claes Flemming, to become the government chaplain, and watch over the Swedish congregation.

The ship on which they sailed was called the *Fama*. It went from Stockholm to Gothenburg, and there took in its freight. Along with this went two other ships of the line, the *Swan* and the *Charitas*, laden with people and other necessaries. During the period of Governor Printz ships came to the colony at three different times. The first ship was the *Black Cat*, with ammunition, and merchandise for the Indians. Next the ship *Swan*, a second time, with emigrants, in the year 1647. Again two [other] ships, the *Key* and the *Lamp*.[3] During these times the clergymen, Mr. Lawrence Charles Lockenius[4] and Mr. Israel Holgh, were sent out to the colony.

5. *Intrusion of the Hollanders.*

The Hollanders intruded upon the Swedes in their traffic with the Indians, and Printz, therefore, sought to keep them under. In the name of the High and Mighty States General

[1] About $500, United States currency, or nearly $2,500 in an equivalent value of our time; the Swedish riksdaler being equal to about $1.25 at that period and about five times as much now.   [2] See *post*, p. 110, note 2.

[3] No *Lamp* is known and the order of the ships is incorrect.

[4] Rev. Lars Carlsson Lock.   See *post*, p. 150.

and of the West India Company, under which all their transactions were carried on, they had never bought as much as a
foot's breadth of land; but from time to time sent in some
private persons, to treat with the heathen on their own account, and thus tried to find out how the Swedes would like it.
In the year 1646 came one Thomas Broen with a permit from
Peter Stuyvesant, the Holland Director at New Amsterdam,
to settle himself at Mantas Huck,[1] on the other side of the bay,
directly opposite Tenakongh. This permit he showed to
Governor Printz, and desired his aid in the building of his
abode. The Governor promised this upon condition that he
would place himself under the Swedish government. But
when he saw beneath this the trick of the Hollanders, he himself bought of the Indians the land from Mantas Huck to Narraticon's, or Raccoon's Kihl,[2] and raised upon it a post to
which the Swedish coat-of-arms was affixed, whereby the plan
of the Hollanders was frustrated for the time.

6. *Further about this Matter.*

Andries Hudde, appointed commandant *ad interim* at Fort
Nassau on October 12, 1645, protested in writing against
Printz's land-purchase of September 8, 1646, and gave information of the same to the Director, Peter Stuyvesant, namely,
that Governor Printz sought to procure for himself all the
land east of the river also; that if he could make himself master
of both sides, it was probable that he would export annually
thirty or forty thousand beaver skins. Now, as the Holland
Company's treasury was entirely empty, and the Hollanders
saw that they had no time to lose, they resorted to another
plan. Some freemen—Simon Ruth, Cornelius Marizen, Peter
Hermansson, Andries Hudde, Alexander Boyer, and David
Davids—united together and purchased of the Indians a piece
of land extending from Ancocus Kihl[3] to Tenakongh Island,[4]
another place higher up on the river than where the Governor

---

[1] Mantes, or Mantua Hook, on the east side of the Delaware, a long half
league below Fort Nassau, but above Tinicum.
[2] Raccoon Creek, in New Jersey, opposite Marcus Hook, in Pennsylvania.
[3] Now Rancocas Creek, New Jersey.
[4] This island is near the present Burlington, New Jersey

had his residence, and also took a title therefor; but with the reservation that if the Company wished to purchase it for themselves for the same amount, they would renounce their claim. Governor Printz protested against this as an unbecoming proceeding, which protest also Hudde sent over to New Amsterdam. Peter Stuyvesant, in his answer, complains of their inability to maintain their rights, and promises money to buy all the land from Narraticon's Kihl [1] to the bay, which, however, was never done.

7. *The Hollanders' Purchase of Land, and Building of Fort Casimir.*

Governor Printz had blocked up the passage of the Hollanders to Fort Nassau by water, but they devised another method of evading his superior power. They entered into a treaty with the Indians for the land which lies between Maniqua's or Minqua's Kihl and the river, as far as Bombe's Huck or Bambo Hook [2] (Canarosse), and concluded the purchase on July 19, 1651. That agreement was the only one which had yet been made in the name of the States General and the West India Company. But by that they bought the land which the Minquesses had already, in Menewe's time, sold to the Swedes, and it is therefore unreasonable to believe that the true owners of the land subscribed that bill of sale. Immediately after this Fort Casimir [3] was built at Sandhuk. Governor Printz protested strongly against it; but either he had not the means of hindering it, or had not time for it, and so the matter rested.

8. *The Injury Remedied by the Building of Elfsborg.*

To remedy the injury which the Hollanders inflicted by Fort Casimir, Governor Printz erected upon the place called Wootsessung Sing another Swedish fort, [which he called] Elfsborg,[4] one Swedish mile below Sandhuk, and two miles be-

---

[1] Narraticon's Kill, now Raccoon Creek, New Jersey.
[2] Bombay Hook.   [3] Now New Castle, Delaware.
[4] Fort Nya Elfsborg was built by the Swedes in 1643, eight years before the Dutch built Fort Casimir.

low Christina, [but] on the eastern shore, from which that district of country was in former times, and even now is, called Elsingborg. From this was fired a Swedish salute upon the arrival of Swedish ships. But its principal object was to search the Holland ships which came before it, and (which stuck very hard in their maw) to make them lower their flag. The fort was afterwards abandoned by the Swedes and destroyed, as it was almost impossible to live there on account of the gnats (*myggor*); whence it was for some time called Myggenborg.

9. *Other Forts.*

Besides these there were Fort Korsholm,[1] at Passäyunk, where the commander, Sven Schute,[2] had his residence. Manäyungh,[3] on the Skörkihl, or Skulkihl, [was] a fine little fort of logs, having sand and stones filled in between the woodwork, and surrounded by palisades, four Swedish miles [4] from Christina, eastwardly. Mecoponacka, Upland [5] [was] two Swedish miles from Christina, and one mile from Gothenburg, upon the river shore, a level plain, with some houses and a fort.

10. *Other Places.*

Other places were only well known, and not fortified. Chinsessing,[6] a place upon the Schuylkill, where five families of freemen dwelt together in houses two stories high, built of whitenut tree, which was at that time regarded as the best material for building houses, but in later times was altogether

---

[1] Fort Nya Korsholm (1647–1653) was not at Passayunk but on the present Province or Fisher's Island, to the west of the mouth of the Schuylkill River.

[2] Sven Skute. See *post*, p. 112, note 1.

[3] Another name for Fort Nya Korsholm or its site.

[4] About twenty-seven English miles, a Swedish mile being slightly more than six and a half English miles.

[5] Now Chester, Pennsylvania, about thirteen English miles from Christina, but rather less than half a Swedish mile—say three English miles—from New Gothenburg, or Fort Nya Göteborg, on Tinicum Island.

[6] Kingsessing, the district about the creek of that name, also at a later time, at least, called Minquas Kill or Creek, a western affluent of the Schuylkill, near the mouth of the river. Wasa or Nya Wasa (c. 1645) was on the north side of this creek.

disapproved of. Karakung [1] [had] the watermill,[2] which the
Governor had built for the people, which was the first in the
country. Chamassung,[3] also called Finland, a district where
the Finns dwelt by the waterside, and Neaman's Kihl,[4] one
and a quarter miles from Christina. Manathaan,[5] or Cooper's
Island, was an island below Fort Christina, so called by a
cooper, who dwelt there with two Hollanders, and made casks,
or wooden vessels and small boats. Techoherassi [6]—Olof
Stillé's place—Gripsholm,[7] Nya Wasa,[8] etc., which are marked
upon the oldest maps, were places laid out and planned, but
did not get established under the Swedish administration.[9]

11. To what Land the Swedes had a Right, partly by Purchase and partly by Agreement.

The land on the west side of the river, which the Swedes
had purchased of the heathen, already in Menewe's time, and
afterwards under Governor Printz, or had acquired a right to
by agreement, stretched from Cape Hinlopen to the Falls of
the Delaware, and thence westward to the Great Fall in the
river Susquehanna, near the mouth of the Conewaga Creek.[10]

[1] Karakong, now Cobbs Creek.

[2] Mölndal, or the Swedes mill, on the Karakong Kill, or present Cobbs
Creek, was erected in 1645 and was the first water mill within the limits of Pennsylvania or Delaware. Its site may still be seen at the rocks on the east bank of
the stream near the Blue Bell Inn on the road from Philadelphia to Darby.

[3] Chammassungh or Finland, where the Finns dwelt, was on the west side
of the Delaware River, between the present Marcus Hook in Pennsylvania and
the mouth of Naaman's Creek just over the circular state line in Delaware.

[4] Now Naaman's Creek; about eight English miles from Christina.

[5] Now called Cherry Island Marsh, but no longer an island.

[6] On the Delaware at the north side of the present Ridley Creek, now Eddystone Borough.

[7] Thought to be a corruption of Korsholm (Fort Nya Korsholm); it first
appears on Visscher's (a Dutch) map of about 1655.

[8] On Minquas Kill or Kingsessing Creek, a western affluent of the Schuylkill
near the mouth of the river.

[9] These places were established by the Swedes.

[10] It is doubtful if the Swedes purchased land from the Indians thus far from
the Delaware. The Great Falls of Susquehanna River or Conewago Falls
are a manifestation of the river's cleavage of the South Mountain range, the
southeastern wall of the Great Valley of Pennsylvania and Virginia. They begin
on a line directly opposite the mouth of Conewago Creek, the boundary between

These Indians were called, by Europeans in general, Delawares, but within a circle of eighteen miles [1] around the Swedes, there were ten or eleven separate tribes, each having its own *Sackheman*, or king. Among these were especially the Minesinkos,[2] the Mynkusses, or Minequesses,[3] upon the so-called Maniquas, or Minqua's Kihl (Christina), with whom the Swedes formed a special friendship. These extended twelve Swedish miles [4] into the interior of the country, on to the Conestoga and the Susquehanna, where they had a fort [5] which was a square surrounded by palisades, with some iron pieces on a hill, and some houses within it. But some of them were with the Swedes every day, who also, once or twice in a year, made a journey up into the country among the Minequesses, with their wares for sale. The road was very difficult, over sharp gray stones, morasses, hills, and streams, which can still be very well seen by those who travel between Christina and Lancaster.

the present Lancaster and Dauphin counties, on the east side of the river, and extend about three-quarters of a mile down the river, not quite so far as the mouth of the other Conewago Creek in York County on the west side of the river. The total descent of the falls is fifteen feet.

[1] If Swedish miles are implied the distance would be 118 English miles.

[2] The Minsi or Minisinks, a sub-tribe of the Lenni Lenape or Delawares, occupied the northern region of the Delaware River with its affluent, the Lehigh River. The Swedish activity did not reach into this region.

[3] The Minquas Indians were not regular inhabitants of the Delaware River and the Minquas Kill or Christina Creek, as Acrelius indicates. They were of Iroquoian stock, as previously stated, living in the lower Susquehanna Valley and to the northwest and from time to time held the Lenni Lenape, or Delaware River Indians in subjection, travelling at intervals from the Susquehanna to the Delaware for hunting and fishing, for war or for trade with the whites. See *ante*, p. 23, and *post*, p. 103.

[4] About seventy-eight English miles.

[5] The important fort of the White Minquas or Susquehanna Indians during the Swedish and Dutch régime on the Delaware, was on the west side of Susquehanna River, near the present Mount Wolf, York County, Pennsylvania, at the south side of the mouth of Conewago Creek, just below the stoppage of navigation by the Great Falls. The "present" fort of the Susquehanna Indians is depicted at the above place as a group of wigwams in a circular stockade, on Augustine Herrman's map, of 1670. Doubtless it was from this fort that the Great Trading Path of the Minquas led across what is now Lancaster, Chester and Delaware counties to Kingsessing Creek or the Upper Minquas Kill at Schuylkill River. Another fort of these Indians was lower down the Susquehanna on the east bank, on the north side of Octoraro Creek, in Cecil County, Maryland.

12. *Proof of this.*

The old Indians still remember the treaties which their forefathers made with the Swedes, as also how far they were disposed to open their land to them. Of this it may serve as evidence to introduce the following extract from the minutes of the treaty made in Lancaster:

THE COURT-HOUSE IN LANCASTER,
June 26, 1744, P. M.

Present.—Hon. George Thomas, Esq., Lieutenant-Governor of Pennsylvania, etc.; the Hon. Commissioners of Virginia; the Hon. Commissioners of Maryland; the Deputies of the Six Nations of Indians. Conrad Weiser, Interpreter.

Canasatego, the Indians' spokesman, spoke as follows:

Brother, the Governor of Maryland: When you spoke of the condition of the country yesterday, you went back to old times, and told us you had been in possession of the province of Maryland above one hundred years. But what is one hundred years in comparison to the length of time since our claim began?—since we came up out of this ground? For we must tell you that, long before one hundred years, our ancestors came out of this ground, and their children have remained here ever since. You came out of the ground in a country which lies on the other side of the big lake; there you have claim, but here you must allow us to be your elder brethren, and the lands to belong to us long before you knew anything of them. It is true that, about one hundred years ago, a German[1] ship came hither and brought with them various articles, such as awls, knives, hatchets, guns, and many other things, which they gave us. And when they had taught us to use these things, and we saw what kind of a people they were, we were so well pleased with them that we tied their ships to the bushes on the shore. And afterwards, liking them still better, and the more the longer they stayed with us, thinking that the bushes were too weak, we changed the place of the rope, and fastened it to the trees. And as the trees might be overthrown by a storm, or fall down of themselves, (for the friendship we had for them) we again changed the place of the rope, and bound it to a very strong cliff. Here the Interpreter[2]

---

[1] "The Dutch came here in a ship" is the version in the official report in the published *Colonial Records of Pennsylvania*, IV.

[2] At this point Acrelius has omitted a bit of the speech which is supplied from the official *Colonial Records of Pennsylvania*, IV., as follows: "[here the interpreter explained that they meant the Oneida country.] And not content with this, for their further security, we removed the rope to the big mountains."

said, They mean the land of Onondago.   There we fastened it very securely, and rolled wampum around it.   For still greater security, we stood upon the wampum, and sat upon it to guard it, and to prevent all injury, and we took the greatest care to keep it uninjured for all time.   As long as that stood, the newly-arrived Germans[1] recognized our right to the country, and from time to time urged us to give them portions of our land, and that they might enter into a union and treaty with us, and become one people with us.[2]

That this is more correctly said of the Swedes than of the Hollanders can be inferred from this, that the Hollanders never made such a purchase from them as to include their whole country, which the Swedes did; yet the English are rather disposed to explain this in favor of the Hollanders. The savages regarded both the Swedes and Hollanders, being Europeans, as one people, and looked upon their quarrels as disagreements between private families.

13. *How Purchases of Land were made from the Heathen.*

Purchases of land from the savages were made in this way: Both parties set their names and marks under the purchase-contract.   Two witnesses were also taken from among the Christians.   When these made their oath that they were present at the transaction, and had seen the payment made, then the purchase was valid.   If the kings or chiefs of the Indians signed such an agreement in the presence of a number of their people, then it was legitimate on their side.   In former times they were quite faithful, although oaths were not customary among them.   But it was not so in later times, after they had had more intercourse with Christians.   Payments were made in awls, needles, scissors, knives, axes, guns, powder and balls, together with blankets of frieze or felt, which they wrap around themselves.   One blanket suffices for their dress. The same wares they purchased for themselves, for their skins of beavers, raccoons, sables, gray foxes, wildcats, lynxes, bears, and deer.

[1] Dutch, according to *Colonial Records*, IV.
[2] Acrelius omits the remainder of the speech.

14. *The Indians a Dissatisfied People.*

It is true the savages sold their lands at a low rate, but
they were a discontented people, who, at no great intervals,
must have new gifts of encouragement, if their friendship was
to remain firm. Such they always have been, and still are.
As they regarded the Swedes and the Hollanders as one people,
it was all the same to them which of them had their land, provided only that they frequently got bribes. Three years after
Governor Printz's arrival, as gifts were withheld, and Swedish
ships came but seldom, the Indians murmured that they did
not receive more, and that the Swedes had no more goods for
their traffic. Then there came out a rumor that the savages
had a mind to fall upon and exterminate them. This went so
far that in the year 1654 their *sackkeman* sent out his son,
called his elders together, and had a consultation as to what
was to be done. But as they regarded the Swedes as a warlike people, who had better not be irritated, as also that they
had dealt justly with them, and were shortly expecting other
ships with costly wares, they therefore laid aside all hostile
thoughts, and confirmed anew their former friendship.

15. *They frequently visited the Swedes.*

After the Christians came in, and the savages gave over
their country to them, the latter withdrew farther into the
forests in the interior of the country. But it was their habit
and custom, at certain times of the year, to come forth in
great numbers to visit the Swedes, and trade with them.
That was done for the most part after they had planted their
maize, namely, in the month of June, and so they remained
for some time of the summer, when they gathered wild pease,
which grew along the river, and dried them. These pease, in
their language, were called *Tachy*. The Indians were not
troublesome, as in the meantime they supported themselves
by fishing and hunting, which custom they kept until within
fifty years since. These tribes were the Delawares and Myn-
quesses, or Minnesinks, who called the Swedes their brothers.
Sometimes there came with them some of that race which
the Swedes called Flatheads, for their heads were flat on the

crown. These were dangerous, and murdered people, when
they found anyone alone in the woods. They first struck the
person on the head, so that he either died or swooned, after
which they took off the skin of the head, after which some
persons might revive again. That is called scalping, and is
still in use among all the American Indians, and the skin of
the head is called a scalp, which is their usual token of victory.
An old Swedish woman, called the mother of Lars Buré, living
at Chinsessing,[1] had the misfortune to be scalped in this manner, yet lived many years thereafter, and became the mother
of several children. No hair grew on her head again, except
short down. On their account the people were compelled to
live close together, as also to have stories on their houses provided with loop-holes.[2] By their intercourse with the savages
the Swedes became well acquainted with the Indian language,
and there are still a few of the older ones who express themselves quite well in it. The savages stayed much with Olof
Stille at Techoheraffi, and were very fond of the old man; but
they made a monster of his thick black beard, from which also
they gave him a special name.[3]

16. *Governor Printz chastises the Hollanders, and searches their Ships.*

Governor Printz, for some time, played the master in the
river of New Sweden, and held the Hollanders under him, although he did not exterminate them. Adrian van der Donck,
in the passage before cited, testifies how he chastised them at
Fort Elfsborg:

The Swedish governor, thinking that now is the right time,
has built a fort called Elsingborg. There he holds a high hand
over each and all, even over the vessels of our Trading Company,

[1] Kingsessing.

[2] Apparently blockhouses.

[3] Olof or Olle Stillé, millwright, of Techoheraffi, at the mouth of Olle Stillé's
Kill, now Ridley Creek, at the present borough of Eddystone, Pennsylvania, was
a native of Roslagen, in the parish of Länna, and Penningsby Court, in Sweden,
and came over in 1641. His descendant the late Charles J. Stillé was provost
of the University of Pennsylvania, and president of the Historical Society of
Pennsylvania.

and all those who sail up into the South River, compelling them to strike their flags, without exception. He sends two men on board to inquire where they come from. Which is scarcely better than searching us, to which we expect it will come at last. We cannot understand what right those people, the Swedes, have to act so; or how the officers of another power, as these give themselves out to be with full powers, can take upon themselves such high authority over another people's lands and wares, which they have so long had in possession, and sealed with their own blood: especially as we hold it by a charter.

17. *Causes the Arms of the States General to be torn down.*

The Holland commander had erected the arms of the States General upon the shore of the river, but the Swedish Governor ordered them to be torn down. A Swedish lieutenant was bold enough to perform this errand at Santhickan, now the town of Trenton, where the falls of the river are. When the Hollanders asked him, "How dare you do such a thing?" he answered, "If the very standard of the States General stood there, it would be treated in the same manner." This was done on September 8, 1646.

Adrian van der Donck refers to this in the passage before cited, where he says:

A further proof: Above Maghchachansie or Mechakanzjiåå, at Santhickan, the arms of their High Mightinesses were erected, in consequence of Director Kieft's orders, as a token that the river and all its parts belonged to the dominion, and were the property of the States. But what advantage had we from this? Nothing else than shame, and a diminution of our honor. For the Swedes, in their intolerable haughtiness, threw them down, and now, whilst we keep quiet, they think that they have performed a manly deed. Although we have protested against that and various other trespasses, they regard it no more than as if a crow should fly over their heads. If the Swedish Governor gets reinforcements in time, we should have more to fear from him than from the English, or any of their governors. That is in brief what relates to the Swedes, whereof the Company's servants could give fuller information, to whose journals and documents we appeal.

18. *The Swedes and Hollanders unite in driving out the English.*

However jealous the Hollanders were of the Swedes for the advantages which they thus gained, and however they contended with each other for these things, yet they were united as often as it came to shutting the English out of the river. Already in those times the Englishman sought to settle himself on those coasts, and had so far a claim to it as the western shore was regarded as the rear of Virginia, although the times then gave him the best right who had the most strength. The year before Governor Printz landed, the English had fortified a place upon the Schulkihl, to drive out whom the commissary at Fort Nassau received the following orders:

May 22, 1642.

Instructions for Jan Jansson Ilpendam, *commissary of the West India Company, how to conduct himself upon the South River of the Netherlands:*

So soon as the sloops *Real* and *S. Martin* arrive, he, the said Jan Jansson Ilpendam, shall repair to both or either of the said sloops (and, if he finds it necessary, he shall collect as great a force as he is able), and go into the Schulkihl, to the place which the English have lately taken possession of, and immediately land there, and demand their orders, and by what authority they undertake to rob us of our land and trade. If they have no royal authority, which expressly commands them to set themselves down upon our boundaries, or a copy of the same, he shall compel them, in a polite manner, to remove, so that no blood may be shed. If they refuse this, he shall take them in custody, and convey them on board the sloops, and in other respects see to it that he may maintain the supremacy, and protect the honor of their High Mightinesses, as also of the Most Honorable the West India Company. When the English are either taken or driven away, he shall completely demolish the place. The said Jan Jansson shall also see to it that the English are not injured in their property, of which a full inventory shall be made out in their presence. Done in our Council in the Fort of Amsterdam, and given as aforesaid.

19. *Proof thereof.*

That the Swedes at such occasions gave assistance [to the Dutch] and probably did the most [for its accomplishment], is also testified by Adrian van der Donck in the place often referred to, although he is greatly mistaken as to the situation of the place.

There lies another creek on the eastern shore, three miles down below the mouth of the river, called Varckens Kihl, where some English settled, but Director Kieft drove them away, and protested against them, being in part supported by the Swedes; for they had both agreed to drive the English away (page 39).   The English have, at various times, and in various places, striven to master that river, to which they insist that they have the best right.   This has thus far been prevented by protests and forcible expulsion, well knowing that if we allow them to establish themselves, the river will be lost, or we shall be put to great inconvenience, as they will swarm into it in great crowds.   It is given out as certain, that many English families are now on their way thither.   But if they once get a firm footing, it will soon be all over with both Hollanders and Swedes; at all events, we shall lose part [of the land], if reinforcements are not speedily sent.

20. *The Weakness of the Hollanders.*

It now seems that it may be reasonably concluded that the strength of the Hollanders in the river was considerable, seeing that they could effect so much; but these movements did not mean much.   A few unarmed English families might be driven out of the country by a small force.   On the contrary, they neither drove any trade at that time, nor had they any military force, which reflected the least honor on the commandant.

21. *Proof of this.*

The commandant and commissary, Jan Jansson Ilpendam, who commanded at Fort Nassau, was, on October 12, 1646, called to New Amsterdam, to render an account of goods which he had on hand, for both the West India Company and some private persons.   Andries Hudde was sent to Fort Nassau to examine his books, and return such goods as were unnecessary, but was himself to remain as commandant until further orders, and repair the fort that same year.   The magazine was in no better condition than that Ilpendam in his account specifies [the receipt of] only two bales of Harlem cloth, and two beaver-skins, which he had on hand during his time, and that was all that he was now to account for.

22. *Further Proof.*

Neither could that command have been of much honor or revenue. Andries Hudde, who had been appointed as commander *ad interim* at Fort Nassau, petitioned the Governor and his Council in New Amsterdam, on December 31, 1654, that he might be employed as schoolmaster for New Amsterdam, but the matter was referred to the preachers and their consistory. A singular change from commander to schoolmaster! But neither would that take shape, for in the year 1660 he was secretary to the Governor at Altona [Christina], and at the same time sexton of the church.

23. *The Maintenance of the Budget.*

The support of the Governor and of the garrison amounted annually to twenty-six hundred and nineteen rix-dollars,[1] to be drawn from the excise on tobacco in Sweden, and as the income from this did not amount to so much, the Crown's third of all confiscated tobacco was added to it, as also the fines for the offence. If any loss occurred in the management, it was to be made up out of the department of the excise. All the merchandise which was brought from Holland to Gothenburg, to be shipped to New Sweden, together with all the tobacco and peltries from New Sweden, were to go free of duty. But the tobacco which the Company imported from Holland was to be subject to a duty.

24. *Governor Printz returns Home, and leaves the Administration to John Papegoija.*

Governor Printz indeed saw the weakness of the Hollanders, but prudence suggested to him doubts as to how long that might continue, and what might follow thereafter. He looked

[1] About $3,273 United States currency, in values of that period, or about $15,368 now.

upon New Amsterdam as a place from which a sudden thundering and lightning might burst forth. No doubt he was strong enough to drive the Hollanders out of the river, but how he was afterwards to preserve his advantages he did not know. He had not for a long time had a message from home. The reinforcements which he expected were delayed until his hope turned into despair. Neither were the Indians a people to be much relied upon. As long as the Swedes had anything that they wanted, everything was well; but without that, murmurs and misunderstandings were heard. Some persons were sent home to Sweden with representations in regard to the existing state of affairs, together with complaints concerning the intrusions by his neighbors, among whom the old Skutë [1] was one. But Governor Printz was afraid that he should have to wait too long; he had not patience to wait for either answer or reinforcement, and therefore, in the year 1652, returned home to Sweden, after he had been in the country ten years. In his place he appointed his son-in-law, Mr. John Papegoija, as Vice-Governor. . . . .

CHAPTER III. 18. *The Fortune of the Priesthood.*

The Christian work which had been aimed at by the sending out of five ministers, at the same time received a lamentable check. The Rev. Reorus Torkillus, of East Gothland, who came over with Commandant Menewe, ended his days in Fort Christina, on September 7, 1643. The Rev. John Campanius Holmensis remained no longer than six years, during which time, however, he was very zealous in learning the nature of the country and the language of the heathen, and since he had much intercourse with the wild people, therefore a tradition is still circulated that he travelled up into the interior among them, and so went by land home to Sweden. From his journal, it is seen that he sailed from Elfsborg, in New Sweden, on May 18, and reached Stockholm on July 3, 1648, an uncommonly quick voyage. The Rev. Israel Holgh and Mr. Peter [2] followed some years after. Mr. Lars Lock was the only one who remained in the country, and took care of the poor and scattered

---

[1] Swen Skute.　　　　　[2] Rev. Peter Hjort.

Swedes, preaching at Tenakong and Fort Christina until the day of his death, in the year 1688.

19. *The Fortune of the Tenacon Church.*

Vice-Governor John Papegoija's wife was a daughter of Governor Printz. She lived for many years in the country, residing upon her father's estate at Tenacongh, and preferred calling herself Armegot Printz rather than Madame Papegoija. They still tell of the lady at Tenacong, how haughty she was, and how she oppressed the poor when she was in prosperity, although it is uncertain whether or not she deserved these reproaches. It is, however, true that she, for a considerable time before her return to Sweden, enjoyed a pension from the Holland government. It is reported that, out of contempt for the Swedes, she sold along with her farm the church which was built upon it, as also the bell, to a Hollander. However that may be, they had to buy their bell back again by two days' reaping in harvest time, after Madame Armegot had gone away. The church was used without hindrance until 1700. Perhaps the bell was not excepted in the bill of sale, although the following obligation was given:

Copy.   LAUS DEO, May 24, 1673.

I, the undersigned, Armegot Printz, acknowledge to have transferred to the congregation of the adherents of the Augsburg Confession in this place, the bell that has been on Tennakong, that they may do therewith what pleases them, and promise to keep them free from all claims that are made. Before the undersigned witnesses. Given as above.

ARMEGOT PRINTZ.

His mark,
    P. K.
PETER KOCK.
His mark,
    ⋈
JONAS NILSSON.

The English, during these changes, had not forgotten their pretensions to the country, but were in the way of coming to an understanding with Sweden in regard to the trade with

America, which now, by the intervention of the Hollanders, was entirely broken off. Finally it came to pass that the Crown of Sweden had to relinquish its West India trade entirely to the English, from which it can be concluded that they did not at that time think of leaving the Hollanders much longer upon the Delaware. In like manner, also, arrangements for peace were made with the Republic of Holland, after which no Swedish flag was ever again seen upon the coast of America, and it is a question, whether or not Sweden was ever given satisfaction for the losses she suffered on the Delaware.

AFFIDAVIT OF FOUR MEN FROM THE *KEY OF CALMAR*, 1638

INTRODUCTION

THIS graphic bit of narrative, the sailors' own tale of how the first Swedish expedition arrived in Christina Creek, and how the Indians ceded their land to the newcomers, was sworn to before an Amsterdam notary in the same year, 1638, and is prime historical evidence. The original manuscript, which is a German translation of the Dutch original made at the same time and signed by the same notary, was found in the Kammararkiv (Archives of the Exchequer) in Stockholm, Sweden, by Dr. Amandus Johnson, who translated it. It is here printed for the first time in translation, but a facsimile of the original German manuscript is given in Dr. Johnson's *Swedish Settlements*, between pp. 184 and 185.

Of the four men of the *Key of Calmar* making this report, two were Dutchmen. The one, Michell Simonssen, the mate, "a fine honest man, well acquainted with the coast of North America from previous voyages," was from Zaandam; the other, Peter Johanssen, the upper boatswain, was from the Beemster. The gunner, Johan Joachimssen, was also probably Dutch. Jacob Evertssen Sandelin, the second mate, was a Scotchman, and later figures in New Sweden as the mate of the ship *Charitas* on the third expedition to the colony in 1641–1642. About 1644 he seems to have come into a ship of his own, called the *Scotch Dutchman*, in which he traded to New Amsterdam, bringing a large cargo of goods to Governor Printz in 1645.

A. C. M.

AFFIDAVIT OF FOUR MEN FROM THE *KEY OF CALMAR*, 1638

BE it known by the contents of this open instrument, to everyone, especially however to him whose business it is to know, that on the 29th of December, in the year sixteen hundred and thirty-eight, appeared personally in the presence of the witnesses named below, before me Peter Ruttens, the residing public notary in the city of Amsterdam, admitted and sworn by the Supreme Court in Holland, the mate Michell Simonss., from Sardam,[1] about the age of fifty-four years; the gunner Johan Joachimss., about the age of thirty years; the second mate, Jacob Evertss. Sandelin from Scotland, about the age of thirty-eight years; the upper boatswain, Peter Johanss., from the Bemster,[2] about the age of twenty-seven years; all four of whom, in the abovementioned respective capacities, have lately served on the ship called the *Key of Calmar*, and have come with her from West India to this country. And the testimony was produced [at the instance of Peter Spiring][3] that the abovementioned mate, together with the director Peter Minuit, the skipper Johan von de Water and the former upper boatswain Andress Lucassen and still other officers of the ship's-council, were on this ship, and an examination was made by order of the honorable Mr. Peter Spiring, Lord of Norsholm, financial councillor of the worshipful crown of Sweden, and resident of the same in the Hague, and [the above witnesses] have on their manly word and on their con-

---

[1] Zaandam in Holland, a town about six miles northwest of Amsterdam.

[2] Beemster, a town twelve miles north of Amsterdam, in Holland, in the midst of a district called the Beemster, formerly a lake, which by 1612 was reclaimed from the sea largely through the active interest of Willem Usselinx, later the leader in the initial steps of the New Sweden movement.

[3] Peter Spiring Silfverkrona (d. 1652), son of a wealthy Dutch merchant, went into the service of the Swedish government. In 1635 he was sent as a representative of Swedish interests to Holland. See Amandus Johnson, *Swedish Settlements,* pp. 695–696, and *passim.*

science without and by the confirmation of a sworn oath, affirmed it to be true [as here related].   And at first the above mentioned Michell Simonss. and Johan Joachimss. related in what manner they, in this now ending year, sailed on the abovementioned ship so far into the South River that they came to and by another river, the Minquas Kil,[1] which they also in like manner sailed into.   And they made their presence known with all kinds of signs, both by the firing of cannon and otherwise, and also sailed several miles into the same [Minquas] river, and went into the country, but neither found nor observed any sign or vestige of Christian people.   Neither did they meet nor see any Christian people; whereupon the above-mentioned Director Peter Minuit requested and caused the nations or people to whom the land really belonged to come before him, whom he then asked, if they wished to sell the river, with all the land lying about there, as many days' journeys as he would request.   This they agreed to with the common consent of the nations.   The parties were therefore agreed with one another, and thereupon, on the twenty-ninth of March of the above year, appeared and presented themselves before the abovementioned ship's council, in the name of their nations or people, five *Sachems* or princes, by the name of Mattahorn,[2] Mitot Schemingh,[3] Eru Packen, Mahamen, and Chiton, some being present [on behalf] of the Ermewormahi,[4] the others on behalf of the Mante [5] and Minqua [6] nations. And these sachems or princes, at the same time and place, in the presence of the whole ship's council and hence also of the two first-named witnesses, ceded, transported, and transferred

[1] Now Christina Creek.

[2] Mattahorn, also Amattahorn, possibly of the Delaware Indians of the sub-tribe of the Ermewarmoki mentioned below, who is said to have sold land at the Schuylkill to the Dutchman Arent Corsen in 1633, granted land at the Sandhook, later Fort Casimir, to Stuvyesant in 1651.

[3] Mitotschemingh or Mitasemint was a chief mentioned in several land transactions with the Dutch and Swedes.   He was dead by July, 1651.

[4] The Ermewarmoki, also called Eriwoms, Arwames, Ermomex, and Armeomecks, apparently a tribe of the Lenni Lenape or Delaware River Indians located near the present Gloucester, New Jersey.

[5] The Mantes of the Delaware or Lenni Lenape tribes were doubtless located on or near the Mantes Kill, the present Mantua Creek, New Jersey, nearly opposite Tinicum Island.

[6] The Minquas or Susquehanna Indians.

all the land, as many days' journeys on all places and parts of the river as they requested; upwards and on both sides. Because, however, they did not understand our language, the abovementioned Andress Lucassen, who had before this lived long in the country and who knew their language, translated the same into their speech. Thereupon they all unanimously with one another declared in what manner they transported, ceded, and transferred the said land with all its jurisdiction, sovereignty, and rights to the Swedish Florida Company [1] under the protection and patronage of the most illustrious and most mighty Princess and Virgin Christina, elected Queen of the Swedes, Goths and Wends. At the same time they acknowledged that they, to their satisfaction, were paid and fully compensated for it by good and proper merchandise, which was delivered and given to them in the personal presence of the abovementioned witnesses and of others of the [ship's] council. The two first-mentioned witnesses and attestors affirm that they have heard and seen all this, and were present as witnesses. Thus the abovementioned Jacob Evertss. Sandelin attests that he with the often-mentioned director himself had [gone] up the Minquas Kill, and also journeyed several miles into the country; but they had nowhere seen nor observed any sign or vestige of Christian people. And he further deposes and says, together and in company with the abovementioned upper boatswain Peter Johanss., that both of them and the rest of the ship's people, all together, saw the princes of the abovementioned nations enter the cabin of their ship, whereupon they heard and understood that the said princes had ceded and transferred the land in the above-described manner. And thereupon they give testimony, and all four with one another affirm that, after the completion of the said ceding and transference, followed the erection of the arms of Her Illustrious Majesty of Sweden, accompanied by the firing of cannon and other solemn ceremonies, in the presence of said sachems or princes, and the country was called New Sweden. Then a fort was built on the bank of the river, and the same river was given the name of the Elb-River [2] under

---

[1] *I. e.*, the New Sweden Company, founded in 1637 for trade on the South or Delaware River.

[2] Now Christina Creek.

other solemnities; the fort, however, was called Christina. Here the attestors, closing this account of theirs, after the relation perseveringly insisted in its veracity and hence that it was to be considered as true. They also offered to confirm the same with an oath of grace before me the aforesaid notary. Accordingly, permission was granted to the exhibitor [Peter Spiring], to use and to make, concerning this, one or more open documents in due form, when and wherever it is proper, which in part has been done in this city of Amsterdam, in the lodging and writing-room of my office, in the sight and presence of the honest Cornelius Vignois and David de Willet, called in for this purpose as credible witnesses.

Attested, upon request, by the abovementioned.

P. RUTTENS, *Nots. Pub.*

1639.

REPORT OF GOVERNOR JOHAN PRINTZ,
1644

INTRODUCTION

THIS report, like the other Swedish narratives that follow, is an orderly official statement, and thoroughly reliable. The Swedish original is strongly and clearly expressed; it contains fewer of the Dutch and other foreign words found in Rising's reports, and the sentences are shorter and less involved than in most similar contemporary documents. The author, Johan Printz, governor of New Sweden, had spent only a little over a year on the Delaware, yet he had secured a firm grasp of the situation, and he affords us an intimate view of the problems and conditions of the colony at the end of its first six years of existence.

Johan Printz was born in Bottnaryd in Småland, in the southern part of Sweden, in 1592. He received a liberal education in the universities of Rostock, Greifswald, Leipzig, Wittenberg, and Jena. After an adventurous youthful career in Germany and Italy, and in the armies of France and Austria, he returned to Sweden in 1625. Entering the Swedish army he saw service in the German campaigns, and in 1638 was raised to the rank of lieutenant-colonel. Forced to surrender the Saxon city of Chemnitz in 1640, he was removed from his command. Receiving knighthood, in November, 1642, at the age of fifty, he sailed for America with his family, to assume the governorship of New Sweden.

Arriving in the colony in February, 1643, he established his household on Tinicum Island and made that the capital. For the next ten years he ruled the Delaware with the strong arm of the soldier, maintained the supremacy of the Swedish crown against the Dutch and English, extended the bounds of the colony, carried on the Indian trade, and in general, seems to have governed in the manner best suited to the rough frontier conditions. Under him New Sweden saw its best days. Physically he was a huge man, weighing over four hundred pounds; the Indians called him the "big tub." His hospitable side, as we have seen, is depicted in the pages of De Vries.

In 1653, dissatisfied with the outlook for the colony, Printz returned home. In 1658 he was made commander of the castle of Jönköping, in southern Sweden, and in the following year governor of Jönköpingslän, where he died in 1663. Further references to him may be obtained in Johnson's *Swedish Settlements*, especially pp. 688–690.

The original manuscripts of this report, two in number, one in Swedish and the other in German translation, both signed by Printz, are in the Riksarkiv (Royal Archives) at Stockholm. The Swedish manuscript, which is defective in parts, has been printed with some omissions in the appendix of Claes Theodor Odhner's Swedish book, *Kolonien Nya Sveriges Grundläggning* (The Founding of the Colony of New Sweden), 1637–1640, (Stockholm, 1876), pp. 27–36. Our text is a translation by Dr. Amandus Johnson from Odhner in comparison with transcripts of the Swedish and German manuscripts in the collection of the Historical Society of Pennsylvania, the defective parts of the Swedish being supplied from the German transcript. The brief portion relating to Sir Edward Plowden, as translated by Dr. Gregory B. Keen, has been previously published in the *Pennsylvania Magazine of History*, VII. 50–51 (1883), and in Justin Winsor's *Narrative and Critical History of America*, III. 456–460 (1884); the list of colonists and of the dead is printed in Johnson's *Swedish Settlements*, pp. 700–709. The remainder of the report is now published for the first time in English.

A. C. M.

REPORT OF GOVERNOR JOHAN PRINTZ,
1644

*Relation to the Noble West India Company in Old Sweden[1]
sent out of New Sweden on June 11, Anno 1644.*

1. THE ship *Fama* arrived here in New Sweden at Fort
Christina the 11th of March, and is now sent away in the name
of God on the 11th[2] of June. The reason for this long delay
has especially been this, that we have this past year not had
any special cargoes and therefore no returns to send home
again, but now the trade went well with the savages, [and we
delayed in order] that the ship might not go back again empty,
and that the goods which now were bought might not lie for
years and days and be eaten and destroyed by moths, mice,
and other vermin (which are very plentiful and destructive)
but be sent over with the ship as now has happened. God
grant hereto luck and His gracious blessing, that the ship,
goods, and people may arrive well preserved and in a right
time at the place to which they are destined, etc.

2. The goods sent from Sweden are safely delivered, as the
receipt shows, except a good deal of the linen, and the stockings, which are moulded and entirely ruined, as the skipper
and his people have seen, yet the abovementioned articles were
not (as one observes) ruined on the ship, but in Gothenburg
in a cellar or in some other damp house, where they were care-
lessly allowed to stand. And this loss, due to Timon von
Schotting,[3] can be searched and examined there through him,
who is more able to write about it than I am, and ought to be
held to account for so considerable a loss.

3. Timon von Schotting has also forgotten to put the price

---

[1] Or, the New Sweden Company.

[2] Really sailed about July 20. *Cf.* Printz's next report for 1647, *post*, p. 120.

[3] Timon van Schotting (1603–1674), a native of Flanders, at the age of about
twenty-four accompanied his father to Sweden, settling at Gothenburg, appar-

on the articles, which he has now sent here, which was done last year, and always used to be done. And it ought not to be otherwise, in order that one may know how to make up the bill for each one of those, who are later discharged, and what amount they have received here, and that it may then be subtracted from their salary on their return home. But probably this is done with a purpose, in order that, as it happened last year, both the proof and the price of all kinds of goods should be sent back again. And to this paragraph also belongs the remark that one ought not to give to the wives or authorized representatives of these people [in Sweden] anything on their salaries before they have been informed from here how much they have received, because part of them have spent so much money during their sickness that they have very little to claim, or nothing at all.

4. The returns which it has been possible to bring together in a hurry are herewith sent over, namely, whole beavers, 1300, one-third-part beavers, 538, half-beavers, 299, and one-fourth-part beavers, 5, total, small and large beavers altogether, 2142 pieces. The tobacco which is now sent over makes all together 20467 *lbs*. And how the trade has progressed here in the last year as well as now, since the ship was here, the commissary's account and written relation will fully show. And it is necessary that we have ships here again next December with all sorts of cargoes, according to the specifications enclosed. If this does not happen the Company will in the future suffer no less damage than it suffered in the past year, which cannot be repaired with 20,000 florins. One does not send the beavers now as formerly and as happened before my time, all mixed, large and small together, but, both to prevent fraud and also on account of the customs collector, each kind, as has been said, is packed and strongly sealed by itself, according to which the commissary, both now and hereafter, ought and shall make his account. In the same manner it can also be seen from the bills that [15476] *lbs.*[1] of the tobacco

---

ently in mercantile business. In 1639 he was appointed factor for the New Sweden Company, and served until 1645 when he was compelled to resign for negligence in office. Later he became burgrave of Gothenburg, and died there. See Amandus Johnson, *Swedish Settlements*, especially p. 695.

[1] See Amandus Johnson, *Swedish Settlements*, pp. 317, 318.

is Virginian tobacco, bought for 6 and 7 stivers [1] a pound. The rest [4991] *lbs.* were planted here in New Sweden, one part by our English at Varken's Kil, one part by our Swedish freemen, for which we have paid eight stivers a pound; the reasons for giving our own more than the strangers are, first, that one would make them in the beginning more industrious; secondly, in order that people, both of our own nation and strangers, may in larger numbers come here and settle under Her Royal Majesty. When the land, with the help of God, has thus been populated, then one could easily regain the damage which is not very large; yet I have presented this as well as all other things to the Honorable Company's gracious consideration. But our Swedish freemen request humbly that they may be allowed to send their tobacco to old Sweden, where it can be sold to the Company with greater advantage than here.

5. God grant success to the Caribbean trade, and we hope in case it is rightly administered and faithfully managed that it will become a large means for the continuation of this work. Thus the tobacco trade was last year made free in Virginia to all strangers by the payment of toll; if we had here suitable goods which could be taken to Virginia then one could yearly bring from there a considerable quantity of tobacco with our sloops and increase the supply of the same on the arrival of our ships, and twice as good tobacco for as good a bargain, I suppose, as can be obtained from Cribitz,[2] and the toll be paid at the residence seat Kekathan,[3] 50 [4] miles up in the river. But we could have a good deal of tobacco from Heckemak [5] yearly and would not need to give toll, but we could arrange with the merchants that they pay the duty, which they can do with practically nothing.

6. Of the people twenty-five have died during the year at

[1] About 16 cents then or about 80 cents now, the *stiver* equalling about 2 cents then, or 10 cents now.

[2] The Caribbees or Lesser Antilles in the West Indies.

[3] Kecoughtan, on the James River, in Virginia, near Hampton and Old Point Comfort.

[4] *I. e.,* apparently, fifty German miles or two hundred and thirty English miles from Fort Christina or the Swedish settlements to Kecoughtan in Virginia.

[5] Accomac, near the end of the Eastern Shore of Virginia, in what is now Northampton County.

different places, as the daily register shows—twelve laborers, eight soldiers, two freemen, two women.[1] The others who are preserved, officers and common people, have no longer any desire to remain here, but since I have caused some provisions to be bought from the English and Dutch sloops and given it to them on their request as part of their salary, they have had better health and have become more willing and have allowed themselves to be persuaded to remain here yet for some time. One observes indeed that it is more for the harm than for the benefit of the Company to give to the people here a part of their salary from those goods which have been bought to be used in trade, from which sum the gain will be subtracted at home, yet rather than that the people should leave, as has now happened, I have at all events thought it more advisable to preserve the people than to look upon the small gain; one sees that the amount and the damage are moderate and will not become in the end altogether too great. But if Her Royal Majesty and the Honorable Company should graciously decide to erect a trading-place and a shop with all sorts of provisions, small wares, cloth, and other goods, placing over it a wise and faithful man, who would have both that and other provisions under his charge and in his care, from which they could be given on their salary as much as each one should request, then the people could month after month be paid out of the gains alone, and the Honorable Company would probably retain the capital and a large part of the profit for its benefit, for everything is fearfully dear here. One barrel of malt, Swedish measure, is worth seven, yes even eight, rix-dollars, a pound of hops, half a rix-dollar, a pound of pork ten stivers, a pound of butter ten stivers, a barrel of grain six rix-dollars, which here could be sown, brewed, and baked and then sold for the highest price to the people. For one barrel of meat I have paid to the English 135 florins, which makes 54 rix-dollars; in short everything is expensive.

7. I planted last year maize all over, thinking, according to the representations of Peter Hollander,[2] to receive yearly

[1] Add, to make 25, the preacher, Rev. Reorus Torkillus.

[2] Peter Hollender Ridder (1607-1691), the second governor (1640-1643) of New Sweden, succeeding Peter Minuit, was of Dutch or German origin, but had entered the Swedish service as early as 1635, being employed by the Admiralty in various capacities in Finland and Sweden. He arrived in the colony with the

food for nine men from the planting of one man, but I received, as well on the one place as on the other, from the work of nine men hardly a year's nourishment for one man. Immediately I sent the sloop to Manathans[1] and caused to be bought there for the company seven oxen, one cow, and [75][2] bushels of winter rye. And although they arrived a little late in the year yet I have caused three places to be sown with rye, also a little barley in the spring. It looks very fine. In addition to this, maize can be bought cheaply from the savages here in the river, so that I hope that the nourishment of the people shall not be so expensive hereafter as it has been before. And therefore I have appointed the people to plant tobacco on all places and have engaged a special master or tobacco planter for a monthly wage of 35 florins;[3] who made good proof of his competence last year. How this will turn out will depend on God and the weather; one must hope, with the help of God, for the best. But as concerns salt-making, oil manufactories, whale-catching, minerals, or silk worms, I must report that I have not been able to find an opportunity for these things, as is reported in my former letters.

8. The places which we now possess and occupy are: 1. Elfsborg, which now (especially on the one side) is so secure that there is no need to fear any attack (if it is not entirely too severe); 2. Christina; 3. Tinnakongh; these two places are also in like manner made so strong that those who are therein need not fear for any savages, even if they were several thousands; 4. Upland; 5. Schylenkyll;[4] these two places are now open, yet strong wooden houses are built upon them with small stone-cannon. In the Schylenkyll there have now been bought, since we received a cargo, three hundred beavers for the Honorable Company, yet with such discretion that the Hollanders

second expedition, in 1640. Upon his return to Sweden he was advanced in the naval service from lieutenant to captain and to major, finally in 1663 receiving the command of the castle of Viborg in Finland. See Amandus Johnson, *Swedish Settlements*, pp. 691–692.

[1] Manhattan, or New Amsterdam.

[2] See Amandus Johnson, *Swedish Settlements*, p. 313.

[3] About $17 United States currency in values of that period, or about $87 in terms of present day values; the *florin*, a Dutch coin, being equal to about 50 cents at that time, or about $2.25 to-day.

[4] Evidently Wasa, or Nya Wasa, at Kingsessing.

are not in any manner offended, and although they do not gladly see us here, but always protest and in the meantime loosen the tongue, yet they have nevertheless since I came here kept and yet keep with us good friendship, especially their commander in Manathans, Willem Kiefft, who often and in most cases, when he has been able, has written to me and advised me about what has happened in Sweden, Holland, and other European places. He reminded me indeed in the beginning in his letters about the pretension of the Dutch West India Company to this entire river, but since I answered him with as good reasons as I could and knew how, he has now for a time relieved me of this protesting. Now a new commander is about to arrive and in that case probably a new action may follow. But how hard the Puritans [1] have lain upon my neck and yet do lay can be seen from the acts which are enclosed here. I believe that I shall hardly get rid of them in a peaceful manner because they have sneaked into New Netherland also with their Pharisean practices. Now they are so strong there that they have chased the Hollanders from that place called Fort River,[2] and now keep it with violence although it

---

[1] Printz had difficulties with New Haven as well as Boston Puritans. The people from New Haven, who in 1641 had made a settlement on the Varkens Kill, now Salem Creek, New Jersey, under the leadership of the agent, George Lamberton, secured yet another location higher up the Delaware River, at the eastern terminus of the great trading path of the Minquas Indians, from the Susquehanna Valley and beyond, so as to participate in the valuable beaver trade with them. There in 1642, on the present Fisher's or Province Island at the south side of the mouth of the Schuylkill River, as Dr. Amandus Johnson makes clear in his *Swedish Settlements*, p. 213, the New Englanders built a blockhouse, the first edifice definitely recorded as erected within the present limits of Philadelphia. Both the Dutch and the Swedes vainly protested against this competition, and finally the Dutch descended upon the place, burned the blockhouse and adjacent dwellings, and carried the settlers to New Amsterdam. Lamberton escaped with his vessel, but later was tried in the Swedish court at Fort Christina. In 1647 the Swedes built Fort Nya Korsholm (1647–1653) on the site of this devastated English post.

The Boston Puritans who caused Printz some anxiety, were a company of merchants interested in promoting the search for the inland lake where the beavers were supposed to be plentiful. Believing that this lake might be reached from the upper waters of the Delaware, in the early summer of 1644 they sent an expedition to the river under William Aspenwall. In spite of Printz's suspicions, he was allowed to pass the Swedish forts but was halted by the Dutch at Fort Nassau and obliged to return to Boston.

[2] Connecticut River.

is the land of the Hollanders. And now neither protest nor good words will avail, but if the Hollanders wish to obtain the place again it must be done with other and stronger means. I look at least a hundred times a day in this mirror, God knows with what meditation, for I am here alone and there are hardly thirty men, of all that are here, upon whom I can rely in such cases.

In a like manner I have also in my former writings spoken about the English knight,[1] how he last year wished to go from Heckemak[2] in Virginia to Kikathans[3] with a bark and his people, about sixteen persons, and when they came into the Virginian bay[4] the skipper, who had conspired beforehand with the knight's people to destroy him, took his course, not towards Kikathanss but to Cape Henry. When they had passed this place and had come close to an island in the big ocean called Smeed's[5] Island, they counselled together how they should kill him and they found it advisable not to kill him with their own hands but to put him on the said island without clothes and guns, where there were no people nor any other animals but where only wolves and bears lived, which they also did, but two young pages of the nobility, whom the knight had brought up and who did not know of this conspiracy, when they saw the misfortune of their master, threw themselves out of the bark into the sea and swam ashore and remained with their master. On the fourth day after that an English sloop sailed near by Smeed's Island, so that these young pages could call to it. This sloop took the knight (who

[1] Sir Edmund Plowden (d. 1659), knight, a Catholic, of Wansted, Hampshire, England, second son of Francis Plowden, of Plowden, Herefordshire, is "the English knight" whose misadventures are here related by Governor Printz. Having received a patent, in 1634, from the viceroy of Ireland, under Charles I.— with vague and inconsistent bounds and without the necessary great seal of England—for a great domain on both sides of the Delaware, called New Albion, the Earl Palatine of New Albion, as he styled himself, had come over to America to try to secure his claim. Befriended by Governor Berkeley, he made Virginia his base of operations, staying with his people apparently at Accomac on the Eastern Shore, in present Northampton County. From here at intervals during the next six years he engaged in hazardous cruising vainly seeking to induce the dislodgment of Printz and the Swedes. His means failing, and his followers deserting him, he went back to England to return no more.

[2] Accomac.   [3] Kecoughton.   [4] Chesapeake Bay.
[5] Smith's Island at Cape Charles, off the end of the Eastern Shore of Virginia.

was half dead and black as earth) on board and brought him to Haakemak where he recovered again. But the people belonging to the knight, and the bark, came to our Fort Elfsborgh on May 6, 1643, and asked for ships to Old England. Then I asked for their passport and whence they came, and since I immediately observed that they were not right in their designs I took them with me (with their own consent, however) to Christina in order to buy flour and other provisions from them, and I examined them until a servant maid (who had been employed as washerwoman by the knight) confessed and betrayed them. Then I caused all the goods they had on hand to be inventoried in their presence, and I kept the people prisoners until the same English sloop which had saved the knight arrived here with the knight's letter, written not only to me but to all the governors and commanders of the whole coast from Florida northwards. Then I delivered the people unto him, bark and goods all together, according to the inventory, and he paid me my expenses, which amounted to 425 rixdollars. The principal men among these traitors the knight has caused to be shot, but he himself is yet in Virginia and (as he represents) is expecting ships and people out of Ireland and England. He gives free commission to all sloops and barks which come from there to trade here in the river with the savages, but I have not allowed any one to pass by and will not do it, until I receive a command and order from Her Royal Majesty, my Most Gracious Queen.

The savages here in West India set themselves up against the Christians in one place after another. The Hollanders have fought the whole year with the savages around Manathans, as they are still doing, and although they have chased them from the one place to the other, yet the Hollanders have lost more than a thousand men at it and the company has received so great a damage from it that (as they themselves admit) it cannot be repaired with a few barrels of gold. In Virginia more than a thousand savages banded themselves together about six weeks ago and attacked and fearfully murdered over six hundred Christians. The Marylanders have also suffered great damage from the Minquas and have lost two cannon and some people. Our savages also become very proud here in the river. I have told them the whole year that we shall receive much people with our ships, but three days after the ship arrived and they observed that there was only one ship and no people they fell in between Tinnakungh and Uplandh and murdered a man and a woman on their bed, and they killed a few days afterwards two soldiers and a servant. When their commanders found out that I drew the people together in order to prevent a future and a greater damage, then they feared and came together from all places excusing themselves in the highest manner, and said that this had happened without their knowledge, and asked for peace, which was granted them on the following conditions: that in case they hereafter practised the smallest hostilities against our people then we would not let a soul of them live, upon which they gave their writing and all their sachems signed their names to it and (according to their custom) gave us twenty beavers and some sewant[1] and we presented them with a piece of cloth. But yet they do not trust us and we trust them much less.

Nothing would be better than that a couple of hundred soldiers should be sent here and kept here until we broke the necks of all of them in the river, especially since we have no beaver trade with them but only the maize trade. They are a lot of poor rascals. Then each one could be secure here at his work, and feed and nourish himself unmolested without their maize, and also we could take possession of the places (which are the most fruitful) that the savages now possess; and then, when we have not only bought this river but also won it with the sword, then no one whether he be Hollander or Englishman could pretend in any manner to this place either now or in coming times, but we should then have the beaver trade with the black and white Minquas[2] alone, four

---

[1] Wampum.

[2] These Indians were by race and language of Iroquoian stock. There were two divisions, the Black Minquas and the White Minquas. Black Minquas, also called the Black Indians, believed to be the ancient Eries, or *Nation du Chat* (Cat People) of the Jesuit *Relations* and the Utchowig ("like a wild cat") of John Smith's map of 1608, had their general habitat in western Pennsylvania, in the beaver region of the Allegheny River and its affluents, between Lake Erie and the Allegheny Mountains. "The beavers," wrote Van der Donck in his *New Netherland* of 1655, "are mostly taken far inland, there being very few of them near the settlements—particularly by the black Minquas, who

times as good as we have had it, now or at any past time.
And if there is some delay in this matter it must nevertheless
in the end come to this and it cannot be avoided; the sooner
the better, before they do us more harm.   They are not to be
trusted, as both example and our own experience show, but if
I should receive a couple of hundred good soldiers and in addition necessary means and good officers, then with the help of
God not a single savage would be allowed to live in this river.
Then one would have a passage free from here unto Manathans,
which lies at a distance of three small days' journeys from here
across the country, beginning at Zachikans.[1]

9. The Honorable Company is also not ignorant of the
fact that if *sevant* is not always on hand here, together with the
other cargoes for the savages, it is difficult to trade with the
savages; but half or at least the one-third part of the cargoes
must be sold for *sevant* (which also does not happen without

are thus named because they wear a black badge on their breast and not because
they are really black." Augustine Herrman, a dweller near the Elk River in Maryland as early as 1660, and an excellent authority, writing in 1670, calls the Ohio or
its northern branch the Allegheny River, "the Black Mincquaas River," and states
that the Black Minquas were accustomed to trade to the Delaware River by a
water route which led, according to his description, from the Conemaugh River
by the short portage over the Allegheny Mountains to the Juniata River, and
thence down the Susquehanna River. The Swedes also, in their turn, made
visits from their settlements on the Delaware to the Minquas country, even to the
remote wilderness of the Black Minquas, in 1646, especially, when Huygen and
Van Dyck with eight soldiers, as may be observed above, penetrated the Minquas
land a distance of fifty German, or two hundred and thirty English miles, which
would bring them to the Allegheny River about fifteen miles northeast of the site
of Pittsburgh. The Swedes had no "trade or intercourse with any Indians farther
in the interior than with the black and white Minquesser," writes Lindeström, in
1654, in his manuscript journal ("Geographia," in H. S. P.), "who don't know
the limit of the country, although their nation or tribe has occupied the country
such a length of time." The Jesuit *Relations* report the practical extermination of
the Eries by the Iroquois proper in 1654–1655, yet as late as 1662 the White
Minquas were expecting the assistance against the Iroquois, of "800 black Minquas," "200 of this nation" having already arrived.

The White, True, or Southern Minquas, known to the Virginians and Marylanders as Susquehannas, or Susquehannocks, and to the French as Andastes,
occupied the lower Susquehanna River Valley and the country at the head of
Chesapeake Bay. After prolonged conflict with the Iroquois they were driven
from the Susquehanna to the Potomac, and in 1675 were almost wiped out by the
English.

[1] At the Falls of Delaware, now Trenton, New Jersey.

profit to the Company). Now, as has been stated, our savages are poor, so that one can secure from them only little or hardly any *sevant*, hence we must buy *sevant* from Manathans and of the North English,[1] where *sevant* is made, and it can be bought cheaply there from the savages. If we now had among the North English or at Manathans a faithful man stationed year out and year in, who could buy up *sevant* for us there so that *sevant* would not be lacking here in the river for the Swedish trade, the Company would have yearly a great profit. Likewise one can secure beavers for gold and rix-dollars in Manathans as well as here in the river of the Dutch freemen, at the rate of seven florins apiece for the good ones, and the small profit would help to increase the capital at home without noticeable cost.

10. We have not been able to put into execution our plans concerning the keel-boat which we had in mind to build here, the reason being that two of the carpenters have been sick almost the whole year and one man alone has not been able to do such heavy work. Then the savages set a fire on the island in the night and burnt part of the material which had been sawed and cut for the boat. Yet the one carpenter who has been well has not been idle. He has built two fine gates, one at Elfsborgh the other one at Tinnakungh. But since the carpenters have recovered somewhat they have built two beautiful large boats, one to be at Elfsborg, the other at Christina, and they have likewise repaired and made ready both sloops. No pains shall be spared hereafter, to have them accomplish whatever they can. But the cordage, which was sent here for the keel-boat, since we do not need it so soon, would be good merchandise to sell for beavers and tobacco, but I do not know the price, therefore I have sold, for a test, a piece of it weighing 597 pounds, according to Holland weight, for 26 beavers, less two florins, paying seven florins apiece, or nine stivers a pound, according to Holland weight. I will not sell any more before I have been informed if I have done well or ill in this.

11. And since I often receive Latin letters from different places concerning this work and I can not properly do otherwise than to answer them in the same language, in which I now do not find myself very competent, but when need so re-

[1] The New Englanders.

quires I must sit and laboriously collect together an epistle, and when it at last is accomplished it is only patchwork, especially since I have more often for the last twenty-seven years had the musket and the pistol in my hands than Tacitus and Cicero, I therefore humbly request that a man may be sent over to me who is not only able to prepare the mentioned writing but could also give good counsel and when it was necessary could be sent to foreign places.

12. It seems to me that it would not yet be advisable to recall Commissioner Hindrik Hügen[1] and to appoint Carl Johansson[2] to receive the cargoes and the trade, this for several reasons, but mostly on account of the language of the savages. But Hindrich Hugen has a Holland servant[3] who knows the savage languages and understands well how to carry on the trade. If the said boy could remain here together with Carl Johansson for the sake of the trade, then Hindrich Hugen could probably be recalled from here. Hindrich Hughen does not like to miss the servant (because he is his relative), but if the Honorable Company should find it convenient to command this with the arrival of the next ship, then indeed Hindrich Hugen will be satisfied, especially since he himself desires to leave here and will in no case remain longer than until the arrival of the next ship.

13. And since I sent home in 1643 not only a list of the people but also described the condition and opportunities of each and every one with the humble request to be informed what difference there was between the free people and those

---

[1] Hendrick Huygen, a relative of Peter Minuit, was from Wesel, on the lower Rhine, in Germany. He came over with the first expedition in 1638 and on the departure of Minuit was left in charge of the civil and economic affairs of the colony. From the arrival of Governor Printz in 1643 and the establishment of the seat of government on Tinicum Island Huygen, as chief commissary, had the care of the stores of the colony deposited there. In 1646 he and Sergeant van Dyck penetrated the wilderness to the Minquas country to the westward, and induced further trade between the Indians and the Swedes. Returning to Sweden with Governor Printz in 1654, he brought out the last Swedish expedition, arriving in 1656 after the Dutch conquest. He then entered the Dutch service, settling on Tinicum Island, where he seems to have continued until 1663.

[2] Mentioned in Printz's later report of 1647 as the bookkeeper who had been sent over on account of some difficulty which had occurred at Kexholm, in Finland.

[3] Gotfred Hermansson or Gotfred Hermer (Harmer), a kinsman of Hendrick Huygen.

who had been sent here on account of crimes, how long each
one of the criminals should serve here for his crime and when
his time was past how he should either be sent from here or
be kept here with salary and clothes, likewise what should be
done with the free people who in nowise wish to remain here,
and in like manner a part of the freemen, Finns, and others
(especially those who have their wives in old Sweden) desire
to leave, and since it is difficult for me to dispose both in this
and other cases without orders, I now as before humbly ask
that I may be informed about it.

14. I will not omit humbly to relate that when the emis-
saries of the Hollanders and English arrive here on (as they
imagine) missions of great consequence, concerning this work,
they expect to receive a considerable entertainment, and are
not ashamed to speak about it themselves, that they wish to
be treated in a princely manner. There are also other expenses,[1] occasioned by the visits of merchants, with whom we
trade, and of others, and we do not know who is to pay for
such expenses. Therefore we have until now been as econom-
ical as we could, yet have caused each one to be treated and
entertained according to his rank. And we have used for
this purpose the extra income, namely sixty beavers which the
English paid as recognition, and twenty-one beavers which
the savages presented at the peace-treaty. This, however, is
not sufficient, as the bills show. I therefore humbly request
that this in like manner may be taken into consideration and
decided for my information.

15. The cattle, seven oxen and one cow (which I referred
to in paragraph 7) were bought in Manatans for the Honorable
Company, as the bill of the commissary shows, for [146][2]
florins, and although they are quite large beasts, yet when one
adds the expense to it, it is very dear. But it is impossible to
colonize the land without cattle. I ask humbly that I may
be informed how this matter shall be conducted hereafter,
and on what conditions the freemen shall be supplied with
cattle by the Honorable Company. The rye and barley, which

---

[1] The Swedish copy is defective here, so that the translator has been compelled to use the German translation for the rest of this and the next paragraph.

[2] I. e., 124 florins for the oxen and 22 florins for the cow. Johnson, *Swedish
Settlements*, p. 313.

were sown here in the autumn and spring, stand, as has been remarked, in very fine condition, and I hope to be able to sow so much, that the Company's people and soldiers who are now here may, with the help of God, have their nourishment for the coming year. We should indeed have been able to sow more in the fall if the oxen had not come here too late.

16. In my former relation under date of April 13, 1643, and in paragraph 23, I humbly requested information concerning the privileges of the nobility and the common people who take up land here in New Sweden each one according to his quota, how they and their descendants should own, enjoy, use, and keep it. Also in paragraph 26 I asked how I should conduct myself in the river against the Hollanders, who usurp to themselves all authority and advantage to such a large degree, as Her Royal Majesty my Most Gracious Queen can see from the enclosed resolution of Commander Kieft. They trade and traffic freely and will not even lower their flags and sails before the flags and forts of Her Royal Majesty, but one must remind them of it with a couple of cannon. All this I can easily forbid them to do at our fort Elfsborg, but not before I have received complete orders from Her Royal Majesty and the Honorable Company.

17. The expenses, which I had on account of the knight's people, being paid by my own means, as I have mentioned in paragraph 8, amounted to 425 rix-dollars, mostly paid me in tobacco. I have also bought some for cash from a Virginian merchant, and part of it I caused to be planted myself, so that the total amounts to 7300 *lbs.*, in twenty-eight hogsheads, which I do not send to any other place (I will add), than to the Honorable Company, with the humble expectation and reliance that the Honorable Gentlemen will agree to it, and allow it for my profit, especially since my expenses here are so great, that I indeed can not defray them with twice my salary. I will gladly do my faithful service for the furtherance of this work as far as the grace of God and my understanding will allow.

18. And as I have, here in New Sweden, in the short time since I came here and with this small and weak people, begun to lay the foundation, which I hope to continue during the time that remains for me here and to bring it so far that Her Royal Majesty shall get so strong a foothold here in New Sweden that (in case the means will not be lacking) it will in-

crease more and more as time goes on through God's gracious help and will be incorporated as an everlasting property under Her Royal Majesty and the Swedish Crown, so I have likewise, in as good manner as I could, tried to oppose the pretensions of the Hollanders and the Puritans and the other Englishmen in this place and brought it so far that they suffer us now among themselves and have no more special foundation according to which they can act, or are able to stand by their former pretensions, but correspond and trade with us and do our will and bring to us what we ask for, we hoping that they in the future will not press so hard, but to be contented with what has passed.   It is therefore my humble prayer and request that when this my term of three years is over I may be relieved and allowed to return again to Her Royal Majesty my Most Gracious Queen and my Fatherland, especially since I am no longer young and since the greatest part of my days have been hard and toilsome.   Yet I do not desire to withdraw myself in any manner from the service of Her Royal Majesty and the Fatherland, but I desire gladly to serve Her Royal Majesty and the Fatherland under other circumstances as long as I am able and as I live.   I hope that, with God's help, the one who succeeds me will have less toil than I have had.

19. The things which have been written for with this ship I have not referred to among the articles here, but have caused a special list to be made of them, and will allow it to remain this time with what has been referred to here.   Only this I yet once again humbly repeat, that I might receive at least a hundred soldiers on account of the arrows of the savages, also twelve-, six-, four- and three-pound cannon-balls, more powder and lead.   And this is thus ended, in humility.   Dated at Christina. June 20, 1644.

JOHAN PRINTZ,
manu propria.

P. S.   One should not let it pass unnoticed that the Hollanders at Manathans have this year had a privateer with ten cannon and 40 men in the sea between Spanniola[1] and Cribitz,[2] which has twice brought four Spanish prizes to Menathans this last year, worth (as they themselves admit) over 50,000

[1] The island of Hispaniola or Santo Domingo, in the West Indies.
[2] The Caribbees or Lesser Antilles.

rix-dollars, and since we are situated nearer to the Spanish places than they are, we have therefore much better opportunity for such an advantage.   We have here also, when need should demand it, a clean entrance and good ports as well as sufficient opportunity to provision the ship, year in and year out; and the booty, which God would grant, our ships could yearly bring away with the return cargo.   The privateer could remain in these places as long as God would see fit to preserve it.   It must be a well-fitted ship, manned with good people, and if one should be compelled to have a Holland skipper and mate, yet a Swedish captain should be in command to prevent fraud, for when skipper Adrian cruised about here for a few months with the sloop the *Grip*, it was for his own profit (as his acquaintances . . . admit and say).[1]

[List of the Colonists.]

List of all that people which is now in New Sweden, how they are distributed in all places and plantations, as specified below, for the year 1644.

⌊ˡ⌉

At Fort Christina.

The officers:

Johann Paapegaia   1
The commissary Hindrich Hugenn   1
The pastor Mr. Johann Campanius[2]   1

[1] MSS. defective.

[2] Rev. John Campanius Holm. (1601–1683), a native of Stockholm, had received his theological training at the University of Upsala, and had served as chaplain to the Swedish legation of Russia, as schoolmaster at Norrtälje, near Stockholm, and as preceptor and clergyman at the orphans' home of Stockholm. He arrived in New Sweden in 1643 with Governor Printz and remained more than five years acting as minister to the colonists and as missionary to the Indians.   In 1646 he consecrated a Lutheran Church on Tinicum Island, the first house of worship erected within the present limits of Pennsylvania.   Having learned the Indian language, he began in this same year the translation of Luther's catechism into the idiom of the Lenni Lenape or Delaware Indians, a work which later he completed in Sweden.   Upon his return in 1648 he was for a short time preacher to the Admiralty on the island of Skeppsholm in Stockholm; then in 1649 was made rector of Frösthult and Hernevi, where he continued the remainder of life.   See Amandus Johnson, *Swedish Settlements*, pp. 372–374, 678–679.   Holm. is an abbreviation of Holmiensis, meaning, " of Stockholm."

The barber Mr. Hanns 1
The trumpeter Erich Andersonn 1
The constable Matz Hansonn 1
The blacksmith Mr. Hanns 1
The marshal-provost Johan Oluffzonn 1

The following people employed by the Company plant to-
  bacco on the plantation at Christina:
Knut Mårthensonn 1
Perr Gunnersonn Rambo 1
Mårthenn Göttersson 1
Lars Andersonn Ulff 1
Månns Andersonn 1
Lars Kåckin 1
Svänn Gunnersonn 1
Mårthenn Glaasere 1
Joenn Torsonn 1
Oluff Torsonn 1
Anders the Carpenter 1

The following are carpenters on the island:
Claas Claasonn 1
Tommas the Carpenter 1

The following are appointed to be on the sloop continually:
The skipper Andress 1
Lars Tommesonn 1
Bengt Torsonn 1

The laborers listed below make tobacco casks and other
  cooper's articles:
Lauriss the Cooper 1
Lukass Personn 1

The swineherd:
Anders Minck with his son ⎱
Claas Andersonn   ⎰ 2

The boy who herds the cattle:
Swenn Swensson 1

The miller, who is continually at the mill:
Anders Dreyer 1

The servant of Com. Hindrick Hugen:
Gååtfreedh Hermansonn   1

Soldiers at Christina:
Erich Tåått 1
Mårthen Hansonn 1
Lars Jacobsonn 1
                                        ———
                                        34

[II]

At Fort Elfsborg.
Officers:
Lieutenant Swänn Skuuta[1] 1
The watchmaster Gregorius van Dicke[2] 1
The gunner Johann Matzonn 1
The drummer Swänn Andersonn 1

Common soldiers:
Nicklaus Bock 1
Johann Gustaffzonn 1
Petter Meyer 1
Isack vann Eissenn 1
Constantinos Grönebergh 1
Petter Jochim 1
Anders Joensonn 1

[1] Sven Skute, who next to the Governor was the foremost military leader in the later history of New Sweden, is first mentioned in this report of Governor Printz in 1644 as lieutenant in command of Fort Elfsborg. In 1648 he successfully opposed the settlement of the Dutch on the Schuylkill. Returning to Sweden in 1650 he reported the condition of the colony before the Queen and Council in 1652. The next year he was engaged in enlisting soldiers and securing emigrants for another expedition to New Sweden. Receiving the commission of captain he came over with the expedition of 1654. Landing with his soldiers at the Dutch Fort Casimir, he captured the stronghold for the Swedes, its name being changed to Fort Trinity (Trefaldighets Fort). At the Dutch conquest of New Sweden in 1655 he surrendered the fort to Stuyvesant, but continued to reside on the Delaware, being mentioned by the Dutch in 1658 as holding the position under them of captain of the Swedes.

[2] Gregorius van Dyck came over in the second expedition to New Sweden, in 1640. In 1646 he accompanied Commissary Hendrick Huygen in penetrating the wilderness to the west, as far as the country of the Minquas, and inducing trade between the Indians and the Swedes.

Bengt Hindrichsonn 1
Anders Andersonn 1
Jacob Swensonn 1
Walle Looer 1
Joenn the Tailor 1
Knut Liliehöck 1
                                        ——
                                        17

[III]

At the Skyllerkill [*Plantation*].
Officers:
Lieut. Månns Klingh 1

The working-people, who plant tobacco on the planta-
    tion in the Skyllerkill:
Påfvell Jonsonn 1
Swenn Larsonn 1
Hindrich Matzonn 1
Matz Pipere 1
Ambrosius Erichsonn 1
Anders Daalbo 1
Päder Kåck 1
                                        ——
                                         8

[IV]

At the Upland [*Plantation*].
Officers:
Päder Liliehöck 1
Elias the Tobaccoplanter 1
Mickell Nilsonn the Blacksmith 1

The following laborers plant tobacco on the plantation at
    Upland:
Hindrich Matzonn 1
Matz Hansonn 1
Iffwer Hindersson 1
Johann Andersonn 1
Hanns Månsonn 1
Eskill Larsonn 1

Lars Biör[n]sonn 1
Bertill Eskilsonn 1
Johann Erichson 1
Jacob Spaniol 1
Cleme[n]t Jörensonn 1
                                         ___
                                         14

[V]

At Tinnakumgh

Officers:
Governor Johann Printz 1

Placed over the provisions and accounts:
Carll Johansonn 1
The secretary Knut Personn 1
The gunsmith Master Niklaus 1

The gunner, in charge of the small copper cannon on Tinna-
    kungh:
Swenn Waass 1

The soldiers who daily follow, travel [with], and serve the
    governor:
Elias Gyllenngrenn 1
Hanns Lüneburger 1
Jörann Snöhuitt 1
Lars Andersonn 1
Anders Andersonn 1
Nils Anderssonn 1
Johann Andersonn 1
Månns Nilsonn 1

The laboring-people, who are appointed to cut hay for the
    cattle, and also in the meantime to follow the
    governor in the little sloop:
Anders Bonde 1
Perr Andersonn 1
Antoni Swart 1
Oloff Erichsonn 1
                                         ___
                                         17

The following have died in New Sweden in 1643, 1644.

Officers:

Sept. 7, 1643, the preacher Mr. Regardh[1] at Kirstina   1
July 18, 1643, the corporal Carll Håckensonn at Elfzborg   1

Soldiers:

June 10, 1643, Mickell Kyrssner at Kirstina . . .   1
July   3, 1643, Måns Larsonn at Elfzborgh   1
 "   5, 1643, Erich Hindersonn at Kirstina . . .   1
Aug. [3], 1643, Rutkiert the German at Kirstina . .   1
Nov. [?], 1643, Johenn Hartman at Tennakungh . .   1
March 4, 1643, the following soldiers were killed by
the savages between Kirstina and Elfzborgh:
Mårthenn Bagge   1
Mårthen the Finn   1

The following laborers of the Company have died:
July 9, 1643, the freeman Jönns Påfvelsonn at Uplandh   1
 " 10, "   Carll Marckusonn at Elfzborg   1
 " 12, "   Mårthenn Biör[n]sonn at Uplandh   1
 " 29, "   Matz Jörensonn at Kirstina .   1
 " 30, "   Joen Isacksonn at Elfzborgh   1
 " 31, "   the peasant Per Mickellsonn at Elfzborgh   1
 " 31, "   the peasant Larss Andersonn from Ålandh
at Elfzborgh   1
Aug. 13, "   [the peasant?] Påfvel Påfvelson at Elfzborgh   1
 " 14, "   Jacob Tommesson at Kirstina   1
 " 30, "   Peder Oloffzon from Giefle at
Elfzborgh   1
 " 31, "   Joen Jerpe at Elfzborgh . .   1
Dec. 10, "   Zachriss Andersonn at Kirstina   1
 " 11, "   Påfwell Personn at the Skyllerkill   1

[1] Rev. Reorus Torkillus, the first preacher among the Swedes and the first
Lutheran clergyman to serve in America. See Amandus Johnson, *Swedish
Settlements*, p. 697.

March 1, 1644, the freeman called Johann the Finn was
drowned at Uplanndh   1
"   7,   "   an Englishman, with a Swedish wife, was
murdered by the savages   2
"   4,   "   Giert Elekenn, killed by the savages between Fort Kirstina and Elfzborgh . . .   1

The following return home to Sweden:

Officers:

Christer Boije   1
The preacher Mr. Israell[1]   1
The barber Mr. Zim[2]   1

Soldiers:

Esbiörn Mårthensonn   1
Påfvell Smaal   1
    Total   121
Dated, Christina, June 20, 1644.

JOHEN PRINTZ.

[1] Rev. Israel Fluviander.   [2] Timon Stidden, barber-surgeon.

REPORT OF GOVERNOR JOHAN PRINTZ,
1647

INTRODUCTION

For the greater part of the interval of three years between the writing of the preceding and of the present report by Governor Printz, the colony of New Sweden had been allowed to shift for itself, the people at home being largely occupied in a war with the Danes. Yet, in spite of these handicaps, the work of the settlement, it will be observed, made a fair degree of progress.

This report exists in two manuscript forms, in Swedish, as signed by Printz. They are in the Riksarkiv (Royal Archives) in Stockholm. Three transcripts of these are in the collection of the Historical Society of Pennsylvania, one of each being used in a translation made by Dr. Gregory B. Keen, published in the *Pennsylvania Magazine of History*, VII. 271–281 (1883). The translation, as revised by Dr. Amandus Johnson from these transcripts, is here reproduced.

A. C. M.

REPORT OF GOVERNOR JOHAN PRINTZ,
1647

*Report to the Right Honorable West India Company in Old
Sweden, sent from New Sweden, February 20, 1647.*

1. FROM June 20, in the year 1644, when the vessel *Fama*
went from hence, to October 1, 1646, when the vessel *Haij*[1]
arrived, two years and four months elapsed; and the whole of
this time we received no letters, either from the Kingdom or
from Holland. This last vessel was four months on the way,
losing her sails, topmasts, and other implements, and fared
very badly. The master of the ship, the mate, and all the
people, except one man, were sick; so that, according to their
report, they would have despaired, if they had not reached
land when they did. Not until the month of December was
the vessel in repair, and the people recovered; and, the winter
commencing at the same time, they were obliged to stay here
until the ice broke up. Now, however, on the subscribed date,
the ship is dispatched with 24,177 pounds[2] of tobacco, in 101
casks, of which 6,920 pounds were planted in New Sweden, and
17,257 pounds were purchased. May God Almighty grant her
a happy passage home!

2. The cargo has been safely delivered, according to the
invoice accompanying it from Peter Trotzig, excepting eight
kettles, one plank, three axes, and fourteen ells of frieze wanting in the measure; fourteen pairs of stockings and 180 ells of
frieze were ruined on shipboard; likewise, part of the Norren-
berg goods were much rusted, which (except what the commissary has received to sell amongst the savages) are to be
sent at the very first opportunity to North England[3] for sale.

3. Concerning the improvements of the country: (1) Fort
Elfsborgh has been tolerably well fortified. (2) Fort Christina, which was very much decayed, has been repaired from

[1] *Shark.*   [2] Swedish pounds.   [3] New England.

top to bottom. (3) The Fort in Skylenkÿll, called Kårsholm is pretty nearly ready. We are filling and working at it every day. So that, if we had people, ammunition, and other necessary resources, we should certainly not only be in a position to maintain ourselves in the said places, but also be enabled to settle and fortify other fine sites. Again, 28 freemen are settled, and part of them provided with oxen and cows, so that they already begin to prosper; but women are wanting. Many more people are willing to settle, but we cannot spare them on account of the places wanting them. The country is very well suited for all sorts of cultivation; also for whale fishery and wine, if some one was here who understood the business. Mines of silver and gold may possibly be discovered, but nobody here has any knowledge about such things. The Hollanders boast that three years ago they found a gold mine between Manathans and here, not in any place purchased by us, but nearer to New Sweden than to New Netherland. Hitherto, however, they have not got any gold out of it. There is no appearance here of salt, or of silkworms, because the winter is sometimes so sharp, that I never felt it more severe in the northern parts of Sweden.

4. The people have all the time been in good health; only two men and two small children have died. The reason that so many people died in the year 1643 was that they had then to begin to work, and but little to eat. But afterward we gave them, besides their regular rations, board to apply on their wages, and they have done well from it. Still, all of them wish to be released, except the freemen. And it cannot be otherwise. If the people willingly emigrating should be compelled to stay against their will, no others would desire to come here. The whole number of men, women, boys, girls, and children now living here is 183 souls, according to the annexed roll.

5. In the year 1645, November 25, between ten and eleven o'clock, the gunner Swen Wass, set Fort New Gothenburg on fire; in a short time all was lamentably burnt down, and not the least thing saved, except the barn. The people escaped naked and destitute. The winter immediately set in, bitterly cold; the river and the creeks froze up; and nobody was able to get near us (because New Gothenburg is surrounded by

water). The sharpness of the winter lasted far into the month
of March; so that, if some rye and corn had not been unthreshed, I myself and all the people with me on the island
would have starved to death. But God maintained us with
that small quantity of provision until we got the grain from
the field and were again relieved. By this sad accident the
loss of the Company, testified by the annexed roll, is 4000 rix-
dollars. The above-mentioned Swen Wass who caused the
fire, I have brought to court, and caused him to be tried and
sentenced; so I have sent him home in irons, with the vessel,
accompanied by the whole record concerning him, submissively committing and referring the execution of the verdict
to the pleasure of Her Royal Majesty and the Right Honorable
Company.

6. Again, I have caused a church to be built in New Gothenburg, decorating it according to our Swedish fashion, so far
as our resources and means would allow. Also in the same
place I have rebuilt a storehouse, for the provisions and as
many cargoes as may be sold there on the Company's behalf.
Further, to prejudice the trade of the Hollanders, I have built
a fine house (called Wasa)[1] on the other side of Kårsholm, by
the road of the Minquas,[2] so strong that four or five men, well
provided with guns, balls, and powder, will be able to defend
themselves there against the savages; seven freemen, sturdy
fellows, have settled in that place. Again, a quarter of a
mile[3] higher up, by the said Minquas' road, I have built another
strong house, five freemen settling there. This place I have
called Möndal,[4] building there a watermill, which runs the
whole year, to the great advantage of the country, particularly
as the windmill, formerly here, before I came, would never
work, and was good for nothing. Now, when the great traders,
the Minquas, travel to the Dutch trading-place or house, Nas-

[1] So named for the royal family of Sweden.

[2] The Great Trading Path of the Minquas Indians led from the Susquehanna
River, doubtless from the White Minquas or Susquehanna Fort on the west side
of the river at the mouth of Conewago Creek, York County, just below the stoppage of navigation at the Great Falls, across Lancaster, Chester, and Delaware
counties to Kingsessing Creek or the Upper Minquas Kill at Schuylkill River.

[3] About one and two-thirds English miles.

[4] On the present Cobbs Creek near the Blue Bell Inn on the road from
Darby to Philadelphia.

sau,[1] they are obliged to pass by those two places, which (please God) hereafter shall be provided with cargoes.

7. Concerning trade, in the year 1644, when the ship *Fama* went from here, there was very little of the cargo left in store; and, as we have been without merchandise ever since, not only has the Right Honorable Company suffered the great damage of losing 8000 or 9000 beavers, which have passed out of our hands, but also the Hollanders have drawn the principal traders (the White and Black Minquas) from us; and we shall be able only with great difficulty to regain them. But as soon as this vessel[2] arrived I dispatched Commissary Hindrik Hughen, with the watchmaster Gregorius van Dyk and eight soldiers, to the country of the Minquas, fifty German miles[3] from hence, offering them all sorts of presents, by which means they were induced to negotiate, and we received assurance from them that they would trade with us as before, especially as the commissary promised them to give more than the Hollanders. Whether they keep their word will be seen in the future.

8. It is of the utmost necessity for us to see how we can get rid of the Dutch from the river, for they oppose us on every side: (1) They destroy our trade everywhere. (2) They strengthen the savages with guns, shot, and powder, publicly trading with these against the edict of all Christians. (3) They stir up the savages to attack us, which, but for our prudence, would already have happened. (4) They begin to buy land from the savages within our boundaries, which we had purchased already eight years ago, and have the impudence here and there to erect the seal of the West India Company, calling it their arms; moreover, they give New Sweden the name of New Netherland, and are not ashamed to build their houses there, as can be learned more at length from the Dutch Governor's letter, here annexed, and from my answer to it; in

---

[1] The Dutch Fort Nassau (1623–1651), near the mouth of Big Timber Creek, in the present Gloucester County, New Jersey.

[2] The *Haij*.

[3] About two hundred and thirty English miles. It is given as five German miles (or about twenty-three English miles) in one transcript, but that seems an error. In 1648 the Swedes carried goods from Fort Christina thirty German miles (about one hundred and thirty-eight English miles) into the country of the Minquas.

short, they appropriate to themselves alone every right, hoist high their own flags, and would surely not pay the least attention to Her Majesty's flags and forts, were they not reminded by a couple of cannon. So that if they are not kept out of the river, either by mutual agreement or other means, they will disturb our whole work. The better to accomplish this intention of theirs, some of the Hollanders have entirely quitted the Christians, resorting to the Minquas, behaving with much more unseemliness than the savages themselves. I have several times written to their Governor about all these improprieties, and also caused their arms to be cut down, but it did not make any difference: they see very well that we are weak; and, with no earnestness on our side, their malice against us increases more and more. And all the people, who are doing this mischief, are merely Dutch freemen, provided with their Governor's passport, and trading on their own account, paying duties therefor, the Company itself not trading at all, and deriving very little advantage from this. As to the English Puritans, with whom I had most to do at first, I have at last been able, with the authority of Her Majesty, to drive them from hence; and they have not been heard from for a long time, except that one Captain Clerk[1] was sent here last year, from North England, to try to settle a few hundred families under Her Majesty's flag, which I, in a civil way, refused, referring the matter to Her Majesty's further resolution.

9. The commissary's report will show our provisions and state here in New Sweden. It is a pity that for a long time we have had very little traffic and profit, while the expenses and the wages are the same. Still, could we get rid of the Hollanders, and be left alone in our trade, by successive cargoes the loss would be easily repaired in a short time. What profit we have derived from foreign cargoes, besides our own, can be seen in the commissary's account; I think it may be about 10,000 rix-dollars.

10. The cattle roll will give information about the offspring; the two head of cattle which were here before me, and the three I brought with me. It shows they have increased to ten in all, that the purchased cattle are fourteen oxen and one cow, and that one part is divided amongst the freemen, and

---

[1] Not identified.

the other part is in the use of the Company. And, whereas the freemen need cattle as the principal instrument for the cultivation of the land, I intend next May to buy some in Virginia, particularly as the Governor there has written to me, also offering his assistance in other ways.

11. I have caused the barge to be fully constructed, so that the hull is ready and floating on the water; but the completion of the work must be postponed until the arrival of a more skilled carpenter, the young men here declaring they do not know enough to finish it. Again, we want a good engineer, house-carpenter, mason, brickmaker, potter, cooper, skilful gun- and locksmiths, and blacksmiths, a chamois-dresser, tanner, tailor, shoemaker, ropemaker, wheelwright, and executioner; all these are of great necessity here, and, above all, a good number of unmarried women for our unmarried freemen and others, besides a good many families for cultivating the land, able officers and soldiers, as well as cannon and ammunition, for the defence of the forts and the country. And, when the Hollanders and other nations are aware that Her Royal Majesty has such a royal earnestness in this behalf, I think they will be careful, because when I came here, four years ago, they immediately abandoned the bad intentions they had formerly exercised against our people, but afterward, since so little has been done for the affair, they have once more grown overbearing.

12. The savages in Virginia, New Netherland, and North England have made peace with the Christians, and our own savages have been quiet ever since. Thus, if the Hollanders were not here, we should soon be on good terms with them; but the savages now have war amongst themselves, more to the prejudice than to the advantage of the beaver-trade.

13. As before stated the officers, as well as the common soldiers, not settled in the country and not yet willing to settle, want to be released; particularly Commissary Hindrik Hugen, whom I myself now, for the third time, have with great difficulty persuaded to stay until the arrival of the next ship; he ought to be replaced by a very able commissary. Again, the minister Magister Johan Campanius wishes to be dismissed, and we need at least two clergymen in the places already settled. Again, the freemen desire to know something about

their privileges, for themelves and their descendants; likewise
the criminals, how long they must serve for their crimes; as to
all which I humbly asked to be informed more circumstantially
in my former Reports of 1643 and 1644.

14. Whereas a letter from Postmaster-General Johan Beijer,
dated Stockholm, March 17, 1645, apprises me that the vessels *Calmar Nyckel* and *Fama* had arrived in Holland, and
that my Report was lost on the way (if this really be the fact),
I only recapitulate herein what goods were sent home in return by the *Fama*, annexing a copy of Captain Peter Påwel-
son's receipt for the said goods. These were: 1300 whole
beavers, 299 half-beavers, 537 third-parts of beavers—great
and small together, 2136 beavers; again, tobacco, 20,467 *lbs.*
in 77 hogsheads; again, my own tobacco, which partly I received in payment from foreigners, and partly I planted myself, 7200 *lbs.* in 28 hogsheads, sent home to the shareholders
in Sweden, that they may either reimburse me at eight stivers
a pound, or graciously allow me to sell it elsewhere.

15. In the sixth paragraph of my above-mentioned Report,
sent from here in 1644, I mentioned the necessity of erecting
a trading-house for various kinds of merchandise, namely, for
clothing, shoes, different sorts of stuffs, linen cloth, thread,
silk, fine and coarse cloth, divers colors for dyeing, buttons,
Leyden ribbons, hats, belts, swords, tanned leather, etc. Those
goods are very vendible here, and in Virginia and New England, and can be sold at a profit of 100 per cent. The house
is also needed for all sorts of provisions, both for our own
people, and for foreigners. A judicious and faithful man,
however, must be put over it and all provisions, who may
give each of our people what he wants, on account of wages.
Thus the people can be paid every month entirely out of the
profit, without the Right Honorable Company's diminishing
its principal, but perhaps making money, everything here
being extremely dear: for example, one barrel of malt (Swedish
measure) costs seven to eight rix-dollars, one pound of hops
half a rix-dollar, one pound of pork ten stivers, one barrel of
corn six rix-dollars, which last could be sown in this country,
brewed, baked, and afterwards sold to the people with advantage; I have paid 54 rix-dollars to the English for one barrel
of beef: in short, everything is dear.

16. In the ninth paragraph of my above-mentioned Report I also spoke about the *zewandt* trade in North England, and said that a trusty man ought to be sent to purchase *zewandt* for us there, because it can be had cheap in that country, while here we are obliged to pay to the English and Hollanders a double price in good beavers, and yet we cannot always get it. It is not possible to keep up the Indian trade by means of cargoes only, because the savages always want *zewandt* besides, this being their money.

Again, I have several times before solicited a learned and able man: first, to attend to the judicial business, sometimes very intricate cases occurring, in which it is difficult, and never ought to be, that one and the same person appear in the court as plaintiff as well as judge; and, secondly, to act as secretary, especially in the Latin language, for many times it has happened (as is proved by the annexed paper) that I have received Latin letters from all parts; these it would be well to answer in Latin, as really I have done as best I could, but I submissively entreat if it is possible, for the future, to be released from such work through the assistance, as above stated, of a competent person.

17. I have caused some waterfalls to be examined suitable as a site for saw-mills, below the dam by the newly built gristmill, as well as in three other places, where there is plenty of oak. But we want a man who can superintend the saw-mill; also, windlasses and blades for saws. If such saw-mills were erected (which might easily be done), every year we might cut and make ready a goodly quantity of planks, besides making compass and pipe timber, which could be very advantageously bartered in the Flemish Islands for wine, which might be either carried to the Kingdom, or sold in Virginia for tobacco. But for this purpose a proper vessel ought to be kept here by the year, which at times could cruise to the West Indies, and by this means the country could be annually provided with victuals.

18. If we are able to renew our friendly relations with the White and Black Minquas (as we are assured and may hope we shall), the trade with these will commence next April, and continue the whole summer until fall. Our present cargo may be sold during that time; therefore, it will be a matter of

necessity, to be provided with new cargoes next November, and about that time we may be able (with God's help) to have on hand a great deal of goods for the return cargo.

19. In the fourteenth paragraph of my former Report I submissively asked in what way the extra entertainment of foreign guests coming here shall be paid. We have in such things been as sparing as possible; however, the amount of the disbursement increases more and more, and the accidental revenues which are collected here and which have been assigned for this use will in no wise suffice.

20. The freemen already settled want to be paid the rest of their wages; and, whereas their intention is to continue to cultivate the land with that money, I think it advisable to pay them for the good of the country, and as an example for others. But their wives and relations in the old country should not be allowed to draw any of their wages, unless these can show the account from here, because every day we are obliged to give them more or less, according to their wants, and some are already fully paid.

21. The bookkeeper, Carl Johansson, who chanced to get into a misfortune in Kiexholm,[1] and for that reason was sent over to New Sweden, has been here six years, and has behaved very well the whole time. Three years ago I not only appointed him to take care of the stores, but also trusted him to receive and revise the commissary's monthly accounts, paying him ten rix-dollars a month as wages (to be ratified graciously by the Right Honorable Company), which service he in like manner has ever since faithfully performed. Now his submissive request is, by Her Royal Majesty's and the Right Honorable Company's favor, to be allowed to go home to the Kingdom for a while, with the next ship, to stay as long as it may please Her Royal Majesty, to settle his affairs there. His purpose for the future is to serve Her Royal Majesty and the Right Honorable Company willingly and faithfully, to the best of his ability, so long as he shall live, either here in New Sweden, or wheresoever else he may be assigned to duty.

22. Again, I humbly repeat the eighteenth paragraph of my last Report, purporting how I for a great while (namely

---

[1] Kexholm, a small town of Finland, fifty miles northeast of Viborg, on the west shore of Lake Ladoga.

twenty-eight years) have been in the service of my dear native
country, constantly accompanying her armies to the field, and
now have served in New Sweden one year and seven months
beyond my prescribed term and brought everything into such
order that Her Royal Majesty has obtained a strong footing
here and that the work does not require anything but sufficient
means, to be continued with greater success. Thus (with
God's help) this country will forever be subject to Her Royal
Majesty, who sent us here, maintained us among all the surrounding provinces, and brought the trade into good condition, and satisfactory relation with that of our neighbors, insomuch that, if means fail not, they will remain satisfied with
what has happened. Wherefore, my humble request to Her
Royal Majesty and their Right Honorable Excellencies now
is, that I be relieved, if possible, and sent home by the next
ship to my beloved native land. Yet, I in no wise withdraw
myself from the service of Her Royal Majesty and my native
country, but I am desirous of doing duty on other occasions,
seeking approval in nothing but for faithful service of Her
Royal Majesty and my country, in accordance with my duty,
so long as I shall live. My successor here (with God's help)
will see and comprehend the diligence I have applied in everything, agreeably to my obligation.

23. The officers and soldiers here have frequently solicited
that a faithful and proper man be sent home to the Kingdom,
not only for the purpose of giving an oral account of the whole
enterprise here, but also to procure an answer to the individual
communications they have sent over. Not thinking it proper
to refuse them this, I have deputed for that business the noble
and valiant Johan Papegåja, hoping that he will both humbly
deliver a good report to Her Royal Majesty and the Right
Honorable Lords, and faithfully and diligently do his best in
everything intrusted to him for the good of this work. Given
at New Gothenburg, February 20. 1647.

JOHAN PRINTZ.

REPORT OF GOVERNOR JOHAN RISING,
1654

INTRODUCTION

THIS report, which is addressed to the newly established Swedish Commercial College in whose hands the direction of the affairs of New Sweden, through the chartered company, had recently been placed, was written by Johan Classon Rising, the last governor of the colony, barely two months after his coming to the Delaware. Governor Printz had departed in the fall of 1653. Rising on his arrival, the following May, found the settlements in a discouraged and sadly depleted condition. No word had come from Sweden for nearly six years and the population had dwindled by desertions to Maryland and Virginia, and by other causes, to less than a hundred persons. Rising brought with him an accession of over two hundred settlers, and soon infused new life into the languishing colony. Despite the adverse circumstances he writes in a hopeful constructive spirit, describing the situation; and with an eye trained under the influences of the new Swedish commercial development, he points out the industrial possibilities of the Delaware.

Johan Classon Rising was born in 1617 in Risinge, Östergötlandslän, in south central Sweden. After courses at the gymnasium at Linköping in Sweden and at the universities of Upsala and Leyden, he travelled with the aid of the Swedish government and certain patrons among the nobility, through many of the countries of Europe for purposes of culture and for special information with respect to commerce and trade. In these subjects he became a foremost authority, and from 1651 to 1653 held the office of secretary of the Commercial

College of Sweden. He wrote the first treatise on trade and economics ever compiled in Sweden, a large part of the materials having been collected and partly arranged by the autumn of 1653. Receiving knighthood, being then in his thirty-seventh year, he set out from Sweden early in 1654, to take up his duties in New Sweden.

His first act was, before landing, to cause the seizure of the offensive Dutch Fort Casimir (now New Castle), which the energetic Stuyvesant, as one of the first steps in his campaign of aggression against the Swedes, had erected in 1651, just below Fort Christina. Of the subjugation of the Dutch settlers at Casimir to Swedish rule, of the Indian relations, of the vainly-hoped-for succor from the Fatherland, and of the further events and progress of the colony, as well as finally of the Dutch conquest of New Sweden—all may be read in full detail as chronicled by Rising himself in this and the two succeeding reports.

After the surrender, Rising and the other officials, the soldiers, and such colonists as were unwilling to become Dutch subjects, were taken back to Europe. Rising after some wanderings returned to Sweden, but led a precarious existence in devotion to the continuance of his great work on commerce. He died in poverty at Stockholm in 1672. See Johnson's *Swedish Settlements* for a more detailed life.

His reports, and a manuscript journal for the period 1654–1655, extending over the greater part of his American experience, are replete with succinct and accurate information, plainly and clearly expressed, constituting the most valuable sources for the history of New Sweden under his administration.

A contemporary manuscript copy of this report in Swedish is in the Riksarkiv (Royal Archives), in Stockholm. It was printed in Swedish at Stockholm, in 1878, in the appendix of Professor Carl K. S. Sprinchorn's *Kolonien Nya Sveriges*

Historia (History of the Colony of New Sweden), pp. 92–102, and is now published for the first time in English from a translation of Sprinchorn's text made by Dr. Amandus Johnson.

A. C. M.

REPORT OF GOVERNOR JOHAN RISING,
1654

MOST honorable Count, honorable gentlemen, powerful benefactors, and friendly patrons.

Although it can well be seen from the diary, which I now send over, how our long journey hither proceeded, and also what our condition is here now, nevertheless I have thought it necessary to relate certain things more at length to the Royal College,[1] in order that Your Excellency and Lordships, observing from it our disadvantages, may be able through your good directions, to dispatch to us here all needed succor, so that this highly-profitable work may not, after so good a beginning, receive any set-back or henceforth lack necessary assistance, but that everything, as time goes on, may be aided in a becoming manner. And although, indeed, several difficulties have befallen us, ever since we came here, bringing with us a lot of sick and weak people, finding before us an empty country, disturbed partly by despondency, partly by mutiny and desertion; nevertheless, God be praised, we still prosper. The people are now recovering. Would to God that we had provisions for them, now and during the winter. We are awaiting some provisions from the Fatherland and some with our sloop, which is daily expected from N. England; some also from the savages and other neighbors, until, God willing, we are able to harvest the crops of one or two years. Then we hope to be able to get along, as far as food is concerned. The mutiny here is now fully suppressed; but still there is some smoke after the fire. I hope that good discipline and vigilance will prevent all such disturbances.

As to the government of the country, I am able to report that I have, according to Her Royal Majesty's most gracious orders and the desire of the College, taken as assistants the good men whom I found suitable thereto, since I found that

[1] The then recently established Royal Commercial College.

the Governor had departed from here. These assistants are Captain Sven Scuthe[1] and Lieutenant Johan Pappegoija,[2] with whose counsel and co-operation I have managed everything, which has so far been done here. I expect a complete gracious regulation by the next ship, according to which I will live and direct myself submissively in all obedience, and all respect for the faithful service of my Most Gracious Sovereign and the advantage of the Fatherland; which will be dearer to me than any of my own profit or reputation, whatever hereafter may be ordained by my Gracious Sovereign for the government of this work.

Meantime I would desire that full authority might as soon as possible be given here in judicial matters, in higher and lower trials (especially in order to put down the mutiny); and that for this purpose an executioner with sword be sent here. Through this, much disorder would be prevented, which otherwise might hereafter break out through secret plots.

The greater part of the colonists indeed complain of the severity with which they claim to have been treated by Governor Printzen.[3] But many of them may have caused him much trouble, therefore I handle the case as moderately as I can. I could not refuse to hear the matter in the court, and then I requested them to draw up their complaints themselves. This they did later and I herewith send them over. Since Governor Printzen is now there himself, he is able, in the proper place, to answer them and explain himself.

Meantime, I shall exert myself so to direct things here in that matter that neither our Swedes, nor the Hollanders dwelling here, nor others, can rightly complain of injustice in legal proceedings. If a law-reader could be sent here, it would be desirable. It might for this purpose be ordained that all the fines, which are here imposed, should be divided into three parts, one-third for the accuser (with which a fiscal under the name of substitute could be paid), the second third for the

[1] Sven Skute.

[2] Johan Papegoja arrived in New Sweden in 1643 where he was married about 1645 to Armegot, daughter of Governor Johan Printz. On his return to Sweden he became a captain in the navy, about 1661. About 1667 he was advanced to major. He lived at Ramstorp, where he owned an estate. Amandus Johnson, *Swedish Settlements*, especially pp. 686–687.

[3] *I. e.*, Printz, *en* being the Swedish definite article.

court, and the third third for the government, for the payment of the law-reader, the support of the poor, or other such things.

As to the culture and improvement of this country, I will pass this over briefly, since it is known to Your Countly Excellency[1] already, what splendid advantages this river has and what conveniences this land possesses (which I have caused to be mapped, as well as it could be done in a hurry, all the way from the bay even up to the falls, by one A. Hudden),[2] wherefore it is well worth while, in order to get this land into some state of prosperity, to employ a liberal expenditure, which later would pay itself a thousand fold. For both goods and blood are often spent on land which cannot by far be compared with this. Wherefore should one not risk expense of money and goods, without bloodshed (as we have reason to hope), since we now, God be praised, have free opportunity to settle it, and so to fortify it against all attack, that it, by the help of God, will endure, and later, in case of need, will give good assistance to the Fatherland, and be a jewel in the royal crown, if only succor can now early be sent here? And at the same time this advantage is also to be expected, that our sailors thereby will become trained for the sea, our ships put into motion, the inhabitants here and there animated to trade, our trade so extended, that all the good designs which might be entertained for the improvement of commerce will be carried out, and ship-building and navigation be thereby increased.

I will leave it to a more suitable time to discuss, how our commerce to Africa and America, yes, into the West and

[1] Count Eric Oxenstierna was president of the college.

[2] Andries Hudde came to New Amsterdam with Governor Kieft in 1638. For some years he acted as surveyor there. In 1645 he was sent to the Delaware River, where he was actively concerned in upholding Dutch interests, and served as commissary, first at Fort Nassau, 1645–1651, then at Fort Casimir, 1651–1654. After the capture of Fort Casimir in the latter year he was employed by Rising, as stated, in making a map of the Delaware River, his compensation from the Governor, according to the notes of Dr. Amandus Johnson, being twenty florins for "some maps of the river and other drawings." Hudde promised to remain with the Swedes but soon slipped away to New Amsterdam. After the Dutch conquest in 1655 he was made surveyor and secretary and later commander at New Amstel. He died in 1663 at Appoquiminy in Maryland whither he had gone to settle.

East-Sea[1] can be combined, through good means, for the great increase of navigation, and the great utility of our dear Fatherland, which then could seize the advantage derived from the goods which come into the East-Sea—and much of that in the West Sea—but this belongs to its proper time and place. But as far as time and convenience allow I will here use all diligence, that as much of this land as possible may first be cleared and planted by our colonists, since very little has been sown this year. For the continuation of this work, I have an advantage in this, that a part of the old freemen have requested new lands, being encouraged thereto by the freedoms which Her Royal Majesty has now given, and have wished to transfer their cleared land to the new-comers; but no new-comers have means to redeem them, therefore I intend to buy them for the Company (payment for only the clearing being understood), and then set young freemen upon them, lend them oxen for working their lands, give them grain for seeding, and each year take one-half of the grain from the field, and give them cows for half of the increase, on condition that if the cow dies before the Company gets any increase from her then the tenant must pay for her. By this means they are immediately and imperceptibly brought under a reasonable tax. So, if this gets started, they will both clear the land and supply it with cattle, and also give the Company a good income, so that it seems to me (with all deference) in this case, that it could not be taken into better use, without any hazard, inconvenience or cost. It also seems to be more necessary at this time to settle the land along the river itself, than up in the creeks. Therefore I intend to put most of this people between Trinity[2] and Christina, near which place a large piece of land ought to be taken up for the property of the Company, and it were good to provide that this should not be alienated. Hereafter it would be well worth while to settle Christina Kill, in order that one might be the more secure against Virginia, and be-

[1] North Sea and Baltic Sea.

[2] Fort Trinity or Sandhoeck, now New Castle, Delaware. The place experienced several changes of name just after the middle of the seventeenth century, as follows: Fort Casimir, so named on its founding by the Dutch, in 1651; Fort Trinity, upon its seizure by the Swedes in 1654; New Amstel, in 1656, upon the Dutch conquest of New Sweden, in 1655; New Castle, in 1664, upon the English conquest of New Netherland.

sides to carry on trade with them, making a passage from their river[1] into the said kill, by which we could bring the Virginian goods here and store them, and load our ships with them for a return cargo. If we could buy Sakakitqz[2] and Amisackan[3] from the Minquas, then this could well be brought about, and we could also carry on the best trade with them [the Minquas] there. And the Englishman, referred to, Mr. Ringoldh,[4] presented it to me and exhorted us thereto, yet probably more for the purpose of discovering our intention about it than because the English would gladly see it accomplished; still the sooner it were done the better. In this said kill and near here there are some water-falls; and at the most important one, called the great fall,[5] many waterworks could be placed, for the great benefit of the Company. About this I will use all zeal, as far as is possible with this people and at this time, intending, as soon as everything is harvested and sown, to construct there a good dam, with all the ability of the country, and then a flour-mill, a saw-mill, and a chamois-dressing mill; wherefore it would be good that this fall were not given away nor alienated. But the others are of small value.

Apoquenema Kill,[6] below Trinity, which runs nearest the English river,[7] would also be well worth occupying at the first opportunity, also the Hornkill,[8] since the savages now at this time and before this have often requested this of us; otherwise their mind will cool, and probably the English[9] who are

---

[1] Elk River.

[2] *I. e.*, Chakahilque or Chakakatique Fall. See *post*, p. 159, note 3.

[3] *I. e.*, Amisackan Fall. See *post, ibid.*

[4] Thomas Ringgold (b. 1610), one of the county commissioners, resided on his plantation of 1,200 acres, called "Huntingfield," on a creek of that name flowing into Rockhall Creek, on the northeastern part of the Chesapeake in Kent County, Maryland.

[5] Apparently in Christina Creek, although the great fall in the Brandywine may be the one referred to.

[6] Appoquinimink Creek, in Kent County, Delaware.

[7] The present Bohemia River, in Maryland, a branch of Elk River, which is an affluent of the northeastern part of Chesapeake Bay. From its head waters to those of Appoquinimink Creek in Delaware, was the shortest and usual portage path between the Chesapeake and the Delaware.

[8] The Hoorn or Hoere Kill, now Lewes Creek, Delaware.

[9] Of Maryland and Virginia.

now beginning some trade from their own river in this direction, will slip in there, which it would indeed be well to forestall. What other districts there may be in the river, which now call for settlement into large estates, yea, even princedoms, Mr. Pappegoija will probably be able to tell, who has good knowledge about it, and who now returns home for the service of the Company and to report concerning our condition.

And since cattle are very necessary for agriculture, therefore I will use all possible diligence in securing some here for the people. And it is sure that if a cargo were here of shoes, stockings, linen stuff, etc., then we could get as many cattle from Virginia as we wish, and could obtain them for a good price, and give them out or sell them to the freemen with advantage. The fisheries we shall gradually (God granting grace and success) practise and carry on with diligence, for there are sturgeon and other fish in the river, but in the creeks there are eel, salmon, thickhead and striped bass in the bay, and outside the bay the codfish and other kinds,—provided only that a few good fishermen with all sorts of implements were sent here.

With brewery and distillery and alehouses and well-fitted inns there would be a good profit for the company to be made, provided only we in the beginning had a number of liquors on hand and provided an order were made that on all foreign drinks a duty about equal to their value should be paid, according as might be found necessary here for moderation, but that if the importers sold their drinks to the Company they should not pay more than two per cent.

N. B. It is better to grant a free import, but afterwards to collect double excise, of which the buyer and the seller should each pay half to the magistrates.

We will also in the future see what advantage can be had from woods and timber, with planks and clapboards, pipestaves, etc., with which a profitable trade could be carried on in the Caribbee Islands and our own ships could be loaded from here, which now, on account of the sickness of the people and because it is not now the season for cutting logs, could not be accomplished.

What advantage various trades could bring here into the country is self-evident, especially if one could make all kinds of things from these good trees, which could be sold to advantage. Besides timber-cutters, we need some one who can burn tar and make shoemaker's wax, which is here an expensive article; also a soap-maker, since we have a potash-burner with us. Besides this there are other materials of the land, which could be taken up and manufactured, as saltpeter, for which we have a good man who can seek for it, and if we could here establish powder-mills it would bring us great profit. A powder-mill we could cause to be built on the abovementioned stream, but we should wish that skilled masters and people should be sent here. Of blacksmiths (aside from gunsmiths) we have enough for our needs, as well as cordwainers and leatherdressers, tailors, skinners, swordmakers, glass makers, masons, house-carpenters, etc. But we have need of pottery-makers, brick-makers, lime-burners, cabinet makers, wooden-basin makers and wooden-plate turners, shoemakers and tanners. An assayer would be needed here. He ought to take the proofs and send them home as soon as the works had been started, in order that the neighbors, who have always tried to get up a copper mine, might not gain possession of one, but that strict orders should be given about it. For here are surely to be found many of the best minerals in the country. A French hat-maker could do much good here; also a wine-grower and a bird-catcher who could capture geese and ducks in nets on the low places in spring and fall, since these birds come here by thousands in the fall and spring. Also, if some Dutch farmers could be brought here and settled on the company's own land it would be very useful, and more such things.

Upon these and other considerations, it does not seem unwise to lay out a town here at Christina and to place there a good deal of the abovementioned or other laborers, as it is most convenient to establish staple and resident places. To this end I have already caused the field adjoining Christina to be divided into lots by Lindeströhm[1] and he has made a plan

---

[1] Peter Mårtensson Lindeström (d. 1691) was educated in the University of Upsala, where he specialized in mathematics and the art of fortification. In 1654 he went out to New Sweden as engineer, remaining until 1655. On his return to Sweden he secured the position of engineer of fortifications. His final settlement was at Brosäter, Sweden. In his later years while bedridden he

of it, which he in humility sends home, and we intend (God granting success) to build houses there in the autumn. And here are suitable places for establishing towns, trading-places and villages, as the time shall give opportunity, but there is now, besides Christina, also Sandhook or Trinity, where there are about 22 houses built by the Hollanders.

Concerning the trade, it can be said, that it would be the most important thing in the country, if we only had enough cargo to draw the beaver trade to us from the Minquas and from the Black Minquas, which buy up both our ordinary cargo and also silk and satin cloth, hats and other things; likewise the trade of the Maquas[1] and other surrounding savages could now be drawn to us, since the Dutch formerly used to buy up yearly at Fort Orange[2] from fifty to sixty thousand beavers, and the English are not loved by these savages nor are they accustomed to carry on trade with them. In addition it is thought that the English are about to attack Manathes.[3] Wherefore if the work would be taken hold of with power this trade, which is of great importance, could be drawn here into the river, since no Christian nation is in better credit with the savages than we now are. But in case such a large trade could not yet be brought about, we should indeed get along with the common trade with the Minquas and with our own river savages.[4] The other sources of income in the country, such as agriculture, logging and handicraft, would, besides this, next unto the help of God, well support us. Specifications of the necessary cargoes, I send enclosed herewith, for which we shall be able to buy up from our near Christian neighbors good return cargoes as well as cattle and victuals for the people and the preparation of the ships.

This cargo which we now have brought with us cannot be used for much else at this time than to enlist and hold the savages in good friendship and for the buying of provisions and necessaries, without which we could not subsist here; also to pay the old and newly enlisted people, and to pay the old

wrote his valuable *Geographica*, an unpublished manuscript in the Swedish archives, which contains his maps of the Delaware, and of the American colonies for the period of his visit. Amandus Johnson, *Swedish Settlements*, pp. 682–683.

[1] Mohawks.   [2] Now Albany, New York.
[3] Manhattan or New Amsterdam.   [4] The Lenni Lenape, or Delawares.

debts of the Company (which are now presented) and, lastly, to build forts and necessary houses, which are few here, so that, besides that I and the others hardly have room here, a good many of the workmen have been compelled to go idle on account of lack of houses. But although there cannot follow a complete gain from this ship's cargo (and probably not from the next coming ship) on account of the many expenses which now in the beginning must be made as a foundation, yet if now an early succor follows upon this, and continues all along, these preparations will not be found fruitless in the future. Accurate accounts shall be kept for everything, and it will be rightly handled, as far as is in my power and understanding. No other return of goods can be sent from here at this time, except only this that it can be reported that the country and the river, as far as is possible, have been taken into our possession.

Concerning any navigation which we can carry on from here I am not able to report, for until we receive some ships here we have, so to say, our hands and feet tied, and must see with regret how this beautiful ship, which Governor Printzen has caused to be built, must lie without employment in its place. It is well built; only a few things are to be changed and finished. Wherefore, a ship's carpenter would be greatly needed, and P. Trotzigh or H. Hügen might be able to secure Claes the Carpenter from Holland, the same who built this ship. The ropes which we have brought with us are preserved in the store-house on Tinnakonck and are very good, but almost too large for this ship. If, however, we had smaller vessels they would be serviceable for us to sail to the neighboring countries as well as in the river, in the bay, and outside, for fishing purposes.

A wise and faithful merchant such as Hindrich Hügen has been reported to have been, is much needed, as also a bookkeeper. Jacob Svensson[1] is now almost the only one whom

---

[1] Jacob Svensson came over with Governor Printz in 1643 and was stationed as a common soldier at Fort Elfsborg. He was a gunner at Fort Christina in 1649 and later served as assistant commissary of the colony for some years, procuring supplies from New England, notably in personal visits with a sloop in 1653 and 1654. He also was an Indian interpreter. Upon the Dutch conquest he became an ensign of New Netherland.

we can use, but we are always having to send him to the surrounding places, for our necessaries and on other commissions.
And he is not yet returned from N. England, but we await
him every day with the sloop, if Stuffwesandh[1] shall not by ill
luck intercept him on the way, which he has threatened, yet
we hope that he will get through. I have, therefore, had no
one who has been able to carry on any trade in the storehouse,
nor has as yet any savage arrived with goods. Therefore, we
have no goods to send home with the ship *Eagle* for the Company, but we hope to be able to do it better another time,
when our affairs can be brought into better working order. I
have indeed used all my diligence to secure some freight homeward for the ship, as well in Virginia as at Manathans, but it
could not be done. And since I was instructed by Your
Excellency and the worthy College[2] to seek in Gothenburg for
some good men who would venture their goods hither on the
ship to begin a trade with, I did my best, but found no one
who had any suitable cargo in store, or who dared to risk it.
Since then I have got a quantity of Virginian tobacco on credit
from an Englishman, Mr. Allerton,[3] on the condition that it
be paid for at the next arrival of cargo, but at a high price;
wherefore I would submissively and humbly request that the
Honorable College would let me enjoy the favor which it has

[1] Petrus Stuyvesant (1602–1672), the capable and energetic but tyrannical
last Dutch governor of New Netherland (1647–1664), and the conqueror of New
Sweden, was a Frieslander, the son of a clergyman. Trained in the military service, he lost his leg in an unsuccessful encounter of the Dutch with the Portuguese on the island of St. Martin, in 1644, while he was governor of the Dutch
colony of Curaçao, in the West Indies. After the English conquest of New
Netherland in 1664, he was summoned to account in Holland, but soon returned
to spend his later days in New York.

[2] The Royal Commercial College.

[3] Isaac Allerton (c. 1588–1658), one of the commercial leaders of the New
World of that day, was a native of England, removed to Leyden in Holland and
in 1620 came over with the Pilgrims in the *Mayflower* to Plymouth in New England. After service as deputy-governor, and as agent for the Plymouth Colony in
several visits to England, he engaged in fishing and trading ventures with his
vessels on the upper New England coast. Later he removed to New Amsterdam
and finally as early as 1646 to New Haven. His chief warehouses seem to have
been in New Amsterdam whence his vessels traded to Massachusetts Bay, Delaware Bay, Virginia, and Barbados. He made several personal trading visits to
the Swedes and Dutch on the Delaware, as early as 1644. In July, 1651, he witnessed an Indian deed at Fort Nassau.

granted to others, namely, that I might be allowed to bring
the abovementioned tobacco into Gothenburg free of duty
and freight, since many would be encouraged thereby to risk
their ship[s] and goods for the increase of the trade in the
river; for which I dare to have a sure hope, especially since the
ship in any case would have to go from here empty. I should
be found to acknowledge this privilege with all faithful service.

The moderate duty which has been placed here as well as
the other favorable conditions for those who wish to trade
here or to settle and live under the protection of Her Royal
Majesty, will without doubt draw many here, if only the matter
can be pushed forward and brought into effect. Yet it seems
(without question) that it would be best if the said duty should
be so favorable that all Swedish ships should pay only two
per cent. on outgoing and incoming goods and all strangers
four to six per cent., except on provisions, which, for a time,
in the beginning, might be brought in free, save that all liquors,
which are not sold or brought for the good and need of the
Company, might pay about as much as the wine costs. And
if any ship should arrive here with a cargo and then should
not sell it all, that it might in that case not pay any duty on
that which was not sold here. But whatever else could be of
service here in that regard, is all referred to the Honorable
College, either to have it drawn up, or to give power to establish such ordinances here as might be best for the furtherance
of the trade or the advantage of the Company; then they would
here be diligently observed and put into execution.

Our military affairs and defense are managed in general
like the others, but Captain Skuthe has to give account for
the ammunition, shot, and guns, and he is especially now engaged to fortify Fort Trinity, which is as a key to the river.
And if the office of commandant for the military forces should
be given to anyone, he is considered a much more suitable
man than Hans Amundsson;[1] and the greatest part of those

---

[1] Hans Amundsson—the news having not yet reached Governor Rising—had
died at Porto Rico, on July 2, 1654, just eleven days prior to the writing of Rising's report. Amundsson had been the commander of the ill-fated expedition of
1649, which had been shipwrecked, and maltreated by the Spanish and French
in the West Indies. He met his death while coming over on his second voyage
to recover his claims in Porto Rico and then to settle on lands granted to him on
the Schuylkill.

serving here have said that they will leave the service if such
a one as the latter shall get the command, which I only mention in passing. It seems proper that the military force and
all other things should be kept under one direction and not
be split up, on account of the evil consequences, which in this
matter may follow out of jealousy.

Cannon, iron as well as brass cannon, are here greatly
needed by us, as well for service on the sea as on the forts,
especially for the defense of the river at Trinity, where the
cannon which the Hollanders left are mostly useless, and we
do not know whether Her Royal Majesty will give them the
cannons back again with everything else found in the fort
or not. We have therefore borrowed four fourteen-pounders
from the ship and placed them in an entrenchment before the
fort, the better to sweep the river straight across. At Christina other guns are also needed, for most of the old ones are
useless. We need a large quantity of powder and bullets,
lead and other ammunition. Muskets and guns we have
enough at this time, but good French fusils are much more
used here in the country and in addition bags of leather with
three or four compartments, in which one could place cart-
ridges; these are many times better in the rain in the woods
than bandeliers and match-lock muskets, and they are much
sought after by the savages. We also intend to put flint-locks
on a large number of our muskets.

Whatever the Company's finances and property may be
here in the country I will use all diligence to list carefully and
will cause it to be valued approximately as soon as I can secure
any suitable man for it, as for instance land, cleared and un-
cleared, woods, streams, fishing-waters, fortresses, buildings,
equipments, implements, boats, ships, mills, cargoes for trade
and for return voyages, grain, cattle, goods and provisions,
ammunition and guns, and especially the means by which the
Company can gain some income, also a list of those who wish
to buy land and property from the Company, and a list of the
lands which have been rented for half of the crops or which
have been forfeited for non-payment of taxes. I would also
present an account of the industries, namely [*stenckerÿ ?*], of
the powder and saltpeter manufactories, of the saw-mills and
logging, of breweries and taverns, of the mill toll, of tanneries

and shoemakers and leatherdressers and other such things,
also concerning dues on Swedish and foreign shipping, etc.
Good and suitable men for this purpose are much needed
by us.

I also humbly request that the visits which here must daily
be received may be provided for either by a certain appropri-
ation by the Company or otherwise according to reasonable
allowances.

It is also very necessary, in order to avoid much trouble
out here, that no donations be given or any land assigned to
anyone, unless he occupies it effectively or settles it himself,
or in this either serves the crown or the Company.   Otherwise,
much confusion will result from the fact, that the land of the
Company is given away or land which in reality belongs to
the savage sachems, as for example, Marikens Point.[1] This
land, together with Finland [2] (on which about five or six freemen of the Company have until this been living), I intend now
to buy from them for the Company, the improvements only
being compensated for, as also Printztorp,[3] all the way up
to Upland's Kill.[4]   Hans Amundsson has received Her Royal
Majesty's patent for the piece of land which now for the first
time last Sunday was given to the Swedes, in exchange for
gifts, by the sachem Peminacka as the rightful owner.   The
sachem Ahopameck also gave to us all the land which Captain
Scute had received in donation, only excepting for himself half
of the Schuylkill and the land called Passayungh.[5]   It would
therefore be advisable to give authority out here to encourage
such donations and to reserve that which ought not to be
divided, either because such land might be found necessary for
the uses of the Company or of the country; and all donations
not accompanied by a proper certificate should be held back.
I have therefore not been able to give a certificate to Captain
Scuthe both because the greatest number of the Company's

[1] Now Marcus Hook, Pennsylvania.

[2] Finland or Chammassungh, between the present Marcus Hook in Pennsylvania and the mouth of Naamans Creek in northern Delaware.

[3] Printztorp, on the Delaware, on the south side of Upland Kill, now Chester
Creek, just over the creek from Upland, later Chester.

[4] Now Chester Creek.

[5] On the east side of the Schuylkill River near the Delaware, within the
present city of Philadelphia.

freemen dwell on that land and also because the savages have only lately presented the land to me, and lastly because I have no authorization from the Honorable Company, but am awaiting one concerning it. For the same reasons a certificate cannot be given to Hans Amundsson. At least it seems that one should withhold that which the freemen have occupied, and that it might now, this year, be taken under the Company's management together with Printztorp, to which the Company has a good claim, as is to be seen from the documents of the freemen presented herewith.

The pretensions which the English and the Dutch have to this river will fall of themselves, when a complete settlement is made here, especially since our own people have secured for themselves from the rightful owners the first right, and since occupation has followed upon this, although the work has stopped for a time. The Virginians who were here requested to be allowed to buy land and plant colonies. I said that I could not now allow it, since I had no orders. And I do not know whether it is advisable, since we are still so weak, for in N. Netherland the English have thus bought and borrowed land from the Hollanders with the result that they have later pressed them out. But whether or not a man may be allowed to do this on his written oath to Her Majesty's service and the good of the land, I submit to the Honorable College. It would be very well for us to have a good man on our side in Virginia who could settle his servants here. But as to any stranger who wishes to buy land and to settle here I will honor the express orders and permission concerning this from Her Royal Majesty and the College.

Concerning our people I can say that they are, (God be praised), mostly well, and altogether three hundred and seventy souls, and the Swedes were only seventy when we arrived here. The old people largely remain (a number of old men go home again); one of them is better than any of the new-comers, who are weak and a good part of them lazy and unwilling Finns. The best men went away from here with the Governor, of whom a great number would gladly have remained here who at this time could have done much good, which now must stand undone until a more proper time.

Lastly, as to our church affairs, we are indeed in need of a learned priest, although we now have three of them, namely, Matthias Nertunius,[1] who indeed is the best one, and Laurentius Caroli Lock,[2] who has been here before, and is accused of mutiny, wherefore I have intended to send him home to defend and free himself, but he is now become very ill. The third one is Peter Laurentii Hiort[3] and he is both materially and spiritually a poor priest. He is stationed in Trinity Fort.

If now [the land at] Upland[4] which belongs to the Company, and is large enough for the sowing of twenty or thirty bushels of grain, might be given to the parsonage for Nertunius, together with the small houses there, it would be very well; then he would need no other salary from the Company. If one could obtain willingly from the people tithes of grain and cattle, half of them could be assigned for the salary of the ministers, the other part for the maintenance of schools and church buildings. In addition a piece of land should be set aside for the maintenance of the poor and the education of young children, with revenues and some part of the confiscations, that might be made and of alms and other things, concerning which orders are awaited. Priestly vestments, an altar painting, and two or three bells would also be very serviceable here, if we could receive them by the next ship.

This is what I have considered to be the most important to present, this and everything that could serve for the build-

---

[1] Rev. Matthias Nertunius, a man of education, came over to New Sweden in 1653 and remained until the conquest by the Dutch in 1655, when he returned home with Rising and was made pastor of a parish in Helsingland. Amandus Johnson, *Swedish Settlements*, p. 685.

[2] Rev. Lars Carlsson Lock (d. 1688), a native of Finland, for forty years Lutheran pastor of the Swedes on the Delaware, came over with the seventh expedition in 1647, relieving the Rev. Johan Campanius of his pastorate. After the Dutch conquest of New Sweden he was the sole pastor among the Swedes, officiating, alternately, in the church at Tinicum, in Fort Christina, and, from 1667, at Crane Hook, Delaware, until the arrival of Fabritius, in 1677, after which he confined his services to Crane Hook.

[3] Rev. Peter Laurentii Hiort (d. 1704) arrived with the expedition of 1654, and returned to Sweden the following year with Governor Rising, after the Dutch conquest, and became associate minister in Wimmerby and Pelarne, Sweden.

[4] Now Chester.

ing up of the land being submitted to Your Excellency and Their Lordships.   I remain always

Your Excellency's and Their Lordships'
faithful and obedient servant,
JOHAN RISING.

From Fort Christina in New Sweden, July 13, Anno 1654.

REPORT OF GOVERNOR JOHAN RISING,
1655

INTRODUCTION

NOTWITHSTANDING the threatening dangers from whites and red men, Rising, emboldened by the hope of relief from home, writes with much of the same optimism in this second report, which is dated nearly a year after the first one.

The text of the report is from a contemporary manuscript copy in Swedish in the Kammararkiv (Archives of the Exchequer) in Stockholm, found by Dr. Amandus Johnson, and is now published, for the first time, in English translation by him. The Swedish text, edited by him, has been published (1910) in *German American Annals*, viii. 87–93, 288.

A. C. M.

REPORT OF GOVERNOR JOHAN RISING,
1655

Honorable Count, Most Gracious Master and Mighty Patron,
Honorable High, Noble, and Well-born Lords:

AFTER I had sent a relation a year ago with the ship *Örn*[1] concerning the condition of this country and necessary means for its advancement, I also reported last fall about various things, among others concerning the prize [made of] the *Gyllennhaÿ*[2] by Stuvesand in Manathas and sent the letter through Mr. Lord[3] in Harford to Ben. Bonell[4] in London. I will now also humbly report concerning our present condition, namely, that everything is still in a fairly good state and especially since all here have the sure hope that a good succor from the Fatherland will soon relieve and comfort us, especially through Your Excellency and the assistance of the High Lords.[5]

If the people were not animated by this hope, there would be danger that a part of them would go beyond their limits, or that indeed a large number of them would desert from here, not only because many necessaries are lacking, but also because both the savages and the Christians keep us in alarm. Our neighbors the Renappi[6] threaten not only to kill our people in the land and ruin them, before we can become stronger and

---

[1] *Eagle.* [2] *Golden Shark.*

[3] Captain Richard Lord (c. 1611–1662) went from Massachusetts to Hartford, Connecticut, in 1638 and was one of the most energetic and efficient men in the latter colony. He held various public offices and was a commander in the Indian wars. He made trading voyages to New Sweden as early as July, 1643, and was also there in 1654 and 1655, in June of the latter year being present at the treaty made by the Swedes with the Minquas Indians at Fort Christina.

[4] Benjamin Bonnell, an Englishman, had been sent from Sweden to London in 1651 to look after Swedish interests in England. Previously he had lived in Amsterdam as a merchant, had spent about twenty years in Spain and Portugal, and in 1625 had gone to Sweden to engage in glass manufacture. In 1640 he had received the appointment of factor of the New Sweden Company at Stockholm. Amandus Johnson, *Swedish Settlements*, especially pp. 676–677.

[5] Of the College of Commerce. [6] Lenape.

prevent such things, but also to destroy even the trade, both
with the Minques and the other savage nations, as well as
with the Christians. We must daily buy their friendship with
presents, for they are and continue to be hostile, and worse
than they have been hitherto. If they buy anything here,
they wish to get half on credit, and then pay with difficulty.
They run to the Minques, and there they buy beavers and elk-
skins, etc., for our goods, and then they proceed before our
eyes to Manathas, where the traders can pay more for them
than we do, because more ships and more goods arrive there.
Yet we associate with them to a certain extent, and they are
fond of us, because we do not do them any harm or act hostile
towards them. Otherwise, they would indeed ruin our cattle,
yes probably the people on the land, as they vex them daily
and take away whatever they can. Last winter one of them
killed a woman not far from here and robbed what there was.
Later indeed they promised that they would make amends for
it, but have not as yet given more than ten fathoms of *sevan*.

Then the English draw our people to themselves over to
Virginia (Saverne)[1] as much as they are able and keep those
who deserted thither last year. They largely ruin our trade
with the Minques, especially Scarboroug,[2] who gives them 7
to 8 *lbs.* of powder for one beaver, where we are accustomed
to give at the highest from 3 to 4 *lbs.* and cannot give over 5
lbs. except at a loss. During Easter-time two more freemen
deserted, leaving their children and wives behind, and probably many were about to run, if I had not presented to them
so seriously their proper duties, assuring them that the English would certainly at a later time deliver these up to us and
that they would be condemned here and be killed in the sight

[1] Severn River at Annapolis, Maryland.

[2] Edmund Scarborough or Scarburgh (d. 1670-1671) was not only the leading planter and merchant of the Eastern Shore of Virginia but one of the principal figures in seventeenth century Virginia. He resided in Accomac County,
at Occahannock, on the north side of a creek of that name flowing into Chesapeake Bay and dividing Accomac from Northampton County. He acquired a
large property by planting and trading, his vessels venturing as far as Delaware
River and New Amsterdam. He was not only concerned in the fur trade, but
had salt works, and in 1662 was employing nine shoemakers. He served as
sheriff and justice of the county court, was speaker of the House of Burgesses
in 1645, and was made surveyor general of Virginia in 1655.

of everyone.   I keep a close watch on those worthy of suspicion.

The Hollanders at Manathes likewise hinder us as much as they can, and threaten strongly that Stufvesand, when he returns from W. India and Curacos, where he went last fall with three ships (among which the G[yllene] Haye was one) will come here and capture Fort Casimir, which we now call Trinity. But if he comes we will see to it that he is received in the manner of S. Martens[1] (where he lost one of his legs), and we are in no wise afraid about this.   But the savages alarm our people with it, the savages being thus informed by the Hollanders, when they come to Manathes.   It accomplishes, however, God be praised, very little against us.

The N. English bring us our provisions, but we have had the disadvantage in this trade.   Those of New Haven (indeed the whole republic of the N. England, as may be seen by the enclosed copy of their letter) lay claim stoutly to a large part of this country (concerning which I also wrote and reported last fall); and last spring they had about a hundred men ready to come here to take possession of it.   But they gave up their design in the hope that the English would capture Cuba, Hispaniola, etc., whither then a good many of them intended to transport themselves.[2]   And the factor Elsvic[3] had a conference with Mr. Croutier,[4] vice-governor in N. Haven, last spring in Manathes, where he had gone, sent there as though he intended to go back to Sweden, to secure some provisions for us; and he then gave him so good reasons and answers that I have not considered it worth while to answer them before Your Lordly Excellency and the directors please to send orders to me.   My humble idea would be that a good keel-boat

---

[1] Governor Stuyvesant lost his leg in 1644, in an engagement with the Portuguese on the island of St. Martins, in the West Indies.

[2] See Frank Strong, "A Forgotten Danger to the New England Colonies," Annual Report of the American Historical Association, 1898, pp. 77–94.

[3] Hendrick Elswick, originally a Lübeck merchant, removed to Stockholm, and in 1654 was sent over to serve as factor of New Sweden.   He returned to Sweden in 1656.   Amandus Johnson, Swedish Settlements, 491–526.

[4] Stephen Goodyear (d. 1658), deputy governor of New Haven, had been a London merchant.   From New Haven he engaged extensively in foreign commerce, sometimes in company with Governor Eaton and others.   In 1654 he was sent to Delaware Bay to treat with the Swedes about the New Haven settlement near present Salem Creek, New Jersey.

ought to be kept at Rieten Island [1] with cannon to keep out one or another party, who wish to come in with force, and it would be a good means to prevent injustice when power should be needed; yet it would seem best to come to some sort of an agreement with them, for it seems indeed that they will never quit their pretensions, especially since Governor Eaton[2] has contributed most to the English colony and plantation here in the river.

All this alarms us indeed somewhat, but it is borne in upon us that we are placed here just as on a theatre; and if we receive succor we will with the help of God play our part according to our power as well as the other nations do according to theirs. But now we lack power for so large a design, where such a splendid land and river now stand open for us at this time, and which could be planted and secured with a reasonable expense. The Minques, who are yet faithful to us and call themselves our protectors, were recently here and presented me with a very beautiful piece of land [3] beyond (*utom*) the

[1] Reedy Island.

[2] Theophilus Eaton (*c.* 1591–1658), the first Governor of New Haven, was a native of Stony Stratford, Oxfordshire, England. He had been an agent in Denmark and a successful London merchant before his coming to New Haven, in 1637. He was the leader in the governmental as well as in the commercial affairs of his colony. He was one of the largest investors in the New Haven settlement at the Varkens Kill on the Delaware.

[3] Governor Rising in his unpublished manuscript journal states, that in 1655 "they [the chiefs] . . . on behalf of the entire council of the Minquas and their united nations presented to us Swedes all the land which is located on the east side of (*wydh*) the Virginia River (called Elk River in English), all [the way] from the beginning of the Chakakitque-fall all the [way] unto the ends of Amisackan-fall; a land . . . of choice soil and endowed with beautiful fresh rivers, so that many thousand families, who might settle there, can find nourishment." Another Swedish manuscript, of 1667, says that "the warlike Minquas presented to us two beautiful rivers and land situated near their limits, called Cheakakitquate and Amihakan 22 Dutch miles in length and 12 [Dutch] miles in width." The piece of land thus secured from the Indians extended apparently from the "fall line" on Big Elk Creek in Cecil County, Maryland, well up into Pennsylvania. Chakahilque or Chakakitque Fall was possibly the first stoppage of navigation at what is now the town of Elkton, Cecil County. Amisackan Fall may have been in a creek of nearly the same name entering Cobbs Creek, in Philadelphia County, Pennsylvania.

English river, namely, all the way from Chakahilque to Amisackan, which we have long desired, and it is said to be very
suitable for drawing to us the trade with the Minques, likewise the tobacco trade from Virginia, and for making a staple
here in Christina. Jacob Swensson has accomplished this
with them, and has done good service this year and is entirely
indispensable in the country. But the Minques stipulated
that we should soon build there and keep there all sorts of
cargoes for as good price as others give them and have blacksmiths and artisans for [the mending of] their guns. All this
I promised them, when our ships arrive.

All such could be placed in good condition with moderate
resources, and it would be possible now to do more with one
or a half barrel of gold than could be done in the future with
millions, when other nations have put their foot there. If
succor now is long delayed, then our affairs will have a short
end and we shall all be ruined among so many jealous people
and persecutors, for we sit here already as though we had
hands and feet tied. The newly built ship lies in its place and
rots. Our sloop is leaking and has been drawn up on the land
for lack of timber, and our good intentions of erecting useful
manufactories in the country, namely, saw-mills, powder-mills,
timbering and logging, brick-making, etc., have not been carried out. Our trade is lessening and is already very small,
and it is unspeakably hard to supply all this people with food
and clothes in a desert, yet if they lack anything they are immediately disposed to run away from here. If large succors
do not come soon we shall miss all our credit and respect with
the savage nations, who will on that account insult us and do
us harm. The Christians will also do us more harm than good,
for we sit here as a beam in the eye unto them, and this work
cannot be carried on with little succor sent at long intervals,
for in that case it is as it was in the beginning, lost expense and
work, and in the end it will all go to ruin.

But on the other hand, as has been said before, our courage
among ourselves and our reputation among the others are sustained by the belief that we shall indeed receive a complete
succor, for we assure ourselves that Your Noble Highness and
the Well-born Lords will not allow their work to go to pieces,
which can become so great. And if now in the beginning a

half barrel of gold should be employed as a capital, then the land (with God's blessing) would be improved to the value of many barrels of gold, and would bring in fifty per cent. when it has become well established, as the factor Elswic will humbly represent in his proposal.   Then the people here would cultivate the land with pleasure.   Sweden would be freed from many indolent people, who in this place would have to work or starve.   Much goods would be produced and a good profit would be derived from them.   Many skilled workmen would get work and sustenance here and there, and increase the supply of manufactured goods; our sailors would become experienced, our ships and our commerce, and also the building of ships, would increase, trade and produce would develop, and our own goods and the profits of them would remain in our own hands and not be chased into the purses of strangers, as often happens.   Indeed, if it could be advanced so far that shipping and commerce could be instituted here in N. Sweden, then a good part of the West Indian merchandise could be stored here and be brought back with our ships for much better price than now happens, especially if our ships would take the proper course to these coasts (according to the course which the English sail from England) which can be accomplished at the most in five to ten weeks, and in this manner they sail in a cold climate and thus lose less people from heat and sickness, and lose less time, have less expense, and indeed run less risk than is the case with our ships, which come hither by way of the Canaries and Caribbean Islands, and thus sail on the W. Indian coast, a course many hundred miles longer than hither to the North English[1] or these coasts.

Moreover, all the cargoes needed here, concerning which Your Excellency and High-born Lords have already been informed, can also be made up from the supplies of the Company at home in Sweden; and since linen, fine and coarse, can be bought for a cheap price, and wadmal[2] and hards[3] also, then it would be well if it would be continued a hundredfold, for there would be a splendid gain to be secured from these goods from every country, especially here in America,

---

[1] *I. e.*, New Englanders.   [2] A kind of coarse woolen cloth.
[3] The coarser parts of flax or hemp separated in hackling, a coarse fabric being made therefrom.

since there is no linen either in the North or in the South.
And we wish with the next ship one or two barrels of good
flax-seed, and the same amount of hemp-seed, since the
former is entirely ruined. If now through the Grace of God
and the assistance of Your Excellency and the Well-born
Lords this river could be brought into a prosperous condition,
then the Fatherland could be supplied from here with tobacco,
calmus, sassafras, sugar, figs and other goods, and our ships
could be supplied with provisions homeward, which would
save much expense, if the ships could bring more freight.
All this I suggest in all humility and good intention, well
knowing that the good knowledge of Your Excellency and
your regard for the whole work will support me as well as the
others.

And as we have been compelled for the sustenance of the
people to buy provisions and other goods from the above mentioned Richard Lord, merchant in Harfort in New England,
and we have not in this predicament had means with which
to pay him, therefore we have jointly found no other counsel
to satisfy him than that we should draw a draft on the Commercial College as our principals amounting to [2196½]¹ rix-
dollars, humbly requesting that said draft might be paid to
him, (iron necessity has compelled us to this), and we hope
that it will be easier for the Company to pay there, for he as
well as all the English do not take beavers in any other way
than by the pound, which is an unspeakable injury to us; the
same also with the elk-skins and deer-skins. We hope the
draft can be paid without any loss. The bills for this will be
sent over at the first opportunity as well as the draft.

Last year we should have been in lack of bread and provisions if he had not come to our rescue; we could not have
subsisted with so many poor people in a desert country among
so many enemies. He offers every good thing to us, promises
to bring us sheep of the English breed, bees, fruit trees, and
other things for the good of this colony, barley and grain for
seed of every kind, and gives directions concerning plantations
and our trade and where we can bring lumbering and other
things to a good condition. He also says that he will place
his brother here under Her Royal Majesty's authority.

¹ Amandus Johnson, *Swedish Settlements*, p. 530.

He has also promised to send our letters to Holland and therefore I address these to P. Trotzigh[1] in Amsterdam, requesting humbly that Your Excellency and the Well-born Lords would also send our letters the same way, that Trotzigh may send them to London to the correspondent of Lord. Then they will be delivered safely into our hands, especially if the envelope shall be addressed to him as follows: "To the Hounorable Richart Lord, Marcht. ath Hareforth i Niew England." And I would regard it as the greatest benefaction if I could at least receive letters and news, what we have to expect for the advancement of our work, and how things stand at home. In this manner we could write twice a year and receive letters twice, and be sure of receiving them, for otherwise they will be intercepted.

Further, as to what concerns us here in the country, [I can report] that we are in good courage, and each one does his best, and there is not one in the country who has not been put to his work. We now hope for a complete and early assistance as well as a good success in our undertaking, and we have this year cleared more land, and occupied as much again as there ever was in the country, and have planted it all with maize, so that the Company should be relieved for the year from furnishing rations for the people, since they can obtain their own. We have also good hope that the Fatherland will supply a capital for it liberally since, with God's help, it will be rewarded with gain. The sum which the factor Elswic has secured in P.[orto] Rico to be paid in Spain for the loss of the ship *Katt*, will also help to increase this. The original documents concerning the transaction are still lying here and he will give a report about it. He is an indispensable man here, and does his work with diligence and faithfulness. For here are as many who will scatter, as there are who will hold things together, so that I had with difficulty striven to keep things together before his arrival. May God help and grant that

[1] Peter Trotzig, a native of Sweden, removed to Amsterdam and was a merchant there. In 1642 he became agent of the Swedish government and in 1661 commissary, his duties including the hiring of Dutch sailors, officers, and skilled laborers for the Swedish service, the purchasing of ships and the like. As factor of the New Sweden Company in Holland he purchased many of the cargoes sent to the Delaware. About 1666 he returned to Sweden. Amandus Johnson, *Swedish Settlements,* especially p. 697.

good people may come over, whereby the madness and excesses of some of those who are now here might be remedied. And at this time a few [law] cases could not be tried, because our small power will not allow that the cases be fully examined into and the punishment executed, especially since the door of flight stands open.

Here at Christina the people are building houses as far as they are able and six or eight lots are now occupied. I expect that when more people come there will be more buildings, in the form of a city, where it seems best to place the staple town, since a port can be made and the place can be fortified against attack, so that ships can lie there in the winter away from the ice of the spring, and at no other place in the river. Fort Christina was built up last autumn with good ramparts of turf, on two sides where it had mostly fallen down. In the spring it was surrounded by palisades, so that one can dwell there securely against the attacks of the savages. Yet one side is greatly dilapidated, which like the forementioned is made of turf. This I have it in mind to mend as soon as the hay and the grain have been harvested, with which the people are now occupied. Commandant Schute is diligently working on Fort Trinity, where already two bastions with the curtain are ready, as also a fine rampart on the water side in front of the fort. He is hurrying the work forward with speed.

The Hollanders dwelling there who took the oath are now gone off to Manathans, two or three weeks ago. Yet they have been compelled to pay 14 days' work each upon the said Fort Trinity, of which I according to the agreement could not relieve them, and they were out of their element here in the river. The land is now practically clear of the Hollanders. It would be well if the same thing could be said of the English, concerning whom I am awaiting orders as well as concerning other things which should be regulated for us, as for example concerning the rule of the country, its improvement and progress.

Regarding these I have indeed made some ordinances according to the commission given to me by the College of Commerce and have had them examined and discussed by the principal men here in the country, but I have not published them before, God willing, a further supply of people shall arrive here. And we especially await ordinance concerning the donations, about which I have written before, and which without further orders will cause much bad confusion here, the basis and organization of the trade, the freedoms of the inhabitants, when and how they can in the future be taxed, and other things.

Skilled workmen would be very useful to us, especially the following which are now needed—saltpeter-makers and powder-makers, ship-carpenters and house-carpenters, those who understand how to cut all kinds of timber (yet we expect to obtain them best from New England), cabinet-makers, brick-makers, potters (for here is very beautiful clay of every kind, red as bolus[?], white to whitewash houses with, as good as lime, yellow, blue, etc.), and clay workers, millwrights, gardeners, and hop-garden masters, etc., which I have enumerated before.

Whatever else may be found necessary for the advancement of this country according to the desire and pleasure of Your Noble Countly Excellency and Well-born Lords expressed in the memorial, this I shall and will strive to do and to accomplish according to my small ability with all faithfulness and diligence and I remain ever,

Your Noble Countly Excellency's and Well-born Lordships'
faithful and most humble servant,
JOHAN RISINGH.

Dated, Christina in New Sweden,
June 14, Anno 1655, in greatest haste.[1]

[1] It was received by the Commercial College in Stockholm on Nov. 15, 1655.

RELATION OF THE SURRENDER OF NEW
SWEDEN, BY GOVERNOR JOHAN CLASON
RISING, 1655

INTRODUCTION

An cighteenth-century manuscript copy of this report in Swedish is in the library of the University of Upsala, Sweden. It was first published in Swedish, at Upsala, in 1825, by Carl David Arfwedson, in the appendix of his Latin dissertation, *De Colonia Nova Suecia* (Concerning the Colony of New Sweden), pp. 23–30. It was again printed, in a translation by George P. Marsh, in the *Collections of the New York Historical Society*, second series, I. 443–448 (1841); and thence reprinted in Samuel Hazard's *Annals of Pennsylvania* (1850) and in *Pennsylvania Archives*, second series, V. (1890), pp. 239–244. The version in the *Collections* is the basis of the present text, as collated and revised from Arfwedson by Dr. Amandus Johnson.

A Dutch account of the same episode, the absorption of New Sweden into New Netherland, will be found in another volume of this series, *Narratives of New Netherland*, pp. 279–286.   A. C. M.

RELATION OF THE SURRENDER OF NEW SWEDEN, BY GOVERNOR JOHAN CLASON RISING, 1655

Relation concerning the unexpected and hostile Attack on the Swedish Colony in Nova Suecia, by the Dutch, under the Command of P. Stuyvesant, Governor of the New Netherlands, wherefore the Faithful Subjects of His Royal Majesty of Sweden,[1] who have endured such Violence, do most humbly appeal to His Royal Majesty's Most Gracious Shelter and Protection, to the Intent that they may be sustained and indemnified for the Wrongs and Injuries which they have suffered.

In the year 1655, on the 30th day of August, the Dutch from the North River, where Manhattan or New Amsterdam is situated, with seven ships or vessels, under command of the said P. Stüvesant, having on board 600 or 700 men, arrived in the South River, where N[ova] Suecia lieth, and anchored before the fortress of Elfsborg, which then lay in ruins; the next day, they passed Fort Casimir, and bringing to a little above, they landed, and immediately summoned Swen Sküthe, who was in command, to surrender the fort, enforcing their summons both with menaces and persuasion; and proceeded to throw up some works. And although some time before this, when we learned from the savages that the Dutch were about to assail us, we had caused Fort Casimir to be supplied with men and munitions to the best of our ability, and had drawn up a resolution in writing to defend the fort in case the Dutch should attack it, ordering Captain Schütte, the commandant, to send on board their ships, when they approached, and demand of them whether they came as friends, and in any case

[1] King Charles X. Gustavus, who had succeeded Queen Christina upon the latter's abdication in 1654.

to warn them not to run by the said fort, upon pain of being fired upon, (which in such case they could not reckon an act of hostility); but if they were minded to treat with us as friends concerning our territory and boundaries, he should compliment them with a Swedish national salute, and assure them that we were well disposed to a fast friendship; nevertheless, Captain Swen Schüte not only suffered the Dutch ships to pass the fort without remonstrance or firing a gun, whereby they gained the command both of the fort and of the whole river, and cut off the communication between the forts, by posting troops between them, as high up as Christina Kill, but also surrendered the fort to Stüvesant by a disadvantageous capitulation, in which he forgot to stipulate a place to which he, with his people and effects, might retire; he also subscribed the capitulation, not in the fort or in any indifferent place, but on board a Dutch ship. So Stüvesant detained the people, and transported most of them to Manahatans, whereby we were greatly reduced in strength and left destitute, and not even knowing as yet that Fort Casimir had so suddenly fallen into the enemy's hands, we had sent thither in the mean time, September 1, nine or ten of our best freemen to strengthen the garrison. This detachment, when they had crossed Christina Kill betimes in the morning, found the Dutch posted there, who immediately attacked them, fifty or sixty men strong, and summoned them to surrender; but they put themselves in posture of defence, and after a skirmish with the Dutch, were all taken prisoners, except two, who retreated to the boat, the Dutch firing many shots after them, but without hitting. Upon this we fired upon the Dutch from the sconce, with a gun, whereupon they retired into the woods, and afterwards treated harshly and cruelly such of our people as fell into their hands.

The same day the factor Hendr. Elzvii [1] was sent down from Fort Christina to Stüvesant to obtain an explanation of his arrival and intention, and to dissuade him from further hostilities, as we could not be persuaded that he seriously purposed to disturb us in the lawful dominions of His Royal Majesty and our principals. But as Stüvesant had so cheaply obtained possession of Fort Casimir, whither we before had

[1] Hendrick Elswick.

sent our best soldiers, thus depriving ourselves in a great measure both of men and munitions, he would give Elzvii no satisfaction, but claimed the whole river and all our territory, and had well nigh detained Elzvii as a spy. When we learned this we collected all the people we could for the defence of Fort Christina, and labored with all our might, by night and by day, on ramparts and gabions. The next day, being September 2, the Dutch shewed themselves in considerable strength on the upper bank of Christina Kill, but seemed to undertake nothing special. On the morning of the 3d, they hoisted a flag on our shallop, which lay drawn up on the beach, and appeared to be about establishing themselves in a house. We therefore sent over Lieutenant Swen Höök,[1] with a drummer, to find out what they purposed, for what cause they posted themselves there, and for what we should hold them. When he had nearly crossed the creek, he asked them from the boat, whether he might freely go to them? They answered yes; and whether, after discharging his commission, he might freely return? to which also they answered yes, as we could all hear in Fort Christina, and can bear witness accordingly. So the drummer rowed the boat to the shore, without beat of drum, because the lieutenant already had their parole, and knowing no cause of hostility, he supposed this ceremony to be unnecessary. They then both went on shore, and an officer met them, and conducted them some distance to a house, where the enemy had already taken up a position. The Dutch then sent our lieutenant down to Stüvesant, pretending that he was a spy, and Stüvesant arrested him and threw him into the ship's hold, but Captain Fridr. Könich detained the drummer and his drum in his own custody, and thus they treated our messengers, contrary to the laws and customs of all civilized nations.

On the night of the 4th they had planted gabions about the house on the opposite bank of Christina Kill, above [the fort], and afterwards threw up a battery under cover of them, and entrenched themselves there. Some of our people inter-

---

[1] Sven Höök came over from Sweden in the ship *Haÿ*, in 1653, and served as lieutenant in the colony. After the Dutch conquest he returned to Sweden and entered the navy, in 1658 commanding the vessel *Postryttarens*. Amandus Johnson, *Swedish Settlements*, pp. 596, *et seq.*, 681.

preted all this as indicating the purpose of the Dutch to be to claim and hold all our territory up to the creek, and to construct a fort there, not yet believing that they would, in contempt of public peace, and without any known cause, commence hostilities against us, until they had set up some claim, or promulgated some protest against us, whereas up to this time we had received from them neither message nor letter assigning any manner of cause or complaint.

On the 5th, the Dutch ships went up to Third Hook[1] where they landed their men, who then passed over to Timber Island,[2] and thence over the great falls[3] and so invested Fort Christina on all sides. They brought their ships into the mouth of the creek, and planted their great guns on the western side of the fort, and when we burnt a little powder in a couple of pieces to scale them, they fired several shots over our heads from Timber Island, where they had also taken post in a house, and announced to us, that they had taken up a position on the west side, by regular volleys. We continued to prepare ourselves to make the best defence which our strength would allow, if we should be attacked, for we were not yet satisfied what the Dutch intended; but in a short time an Indian came in to us with a letter from Stüvesant, in which he arrogantly demanded the surrender of the whole river, and required me and all the Swedes either to evacuate the country, or to remain there under Dutch protection, threatening with the consequences in case of refusal. Hereto I answered briefly, by letter, that, since so strange a demand was sent by him to me, I would reply by special messengers, and sent him my answer by the same Indian. We then held a general council of war, as to what should be done, if the Dutch assaulted us by storm or battery; and it was determined that we should in any case maintain the defensive, and make the best resistance we could, but should not commence or provoke hostilities, on account of our weakness and want of supplies; that we should wait until they fired upon us, or began to storm the works, and then de-

---

[1] An elevated piece of firm land on the north side of Brandywine Creek, below the railroad bridge in Wilmington, Delaware.

[2] Timber Island, on the north-east side of the Brandywine Creek, near Fort Christina.

[3] Of Brandywine Creek, at present Wilmington, Delaware.

fend ourselves as long as we could, and leave the consequences to be redressed in the future by our gracious superiors.

The Dutch now began to encroach upon us more and more every day. They killed our cattle, goats, swine and poultry, broke open houses, pillaged the people outside the sconce of their property, and higher up the river they plundered many, and stripped them to the skin. At Gothenburg they robbed Mr. Papegoija's wife of all she had, with many others, who had collected their property together in the Hall there. They daily continued to advance their approaches to Fort Christina, (which was a small and feeble work, and lay upon low ground, and could be commanded from the surrounding heights), and threw up two batteries besides those on the opposite bank and on Timber Island, and hoisted their flags on all of them, as well as on our ship in Fish Creek,[1] all which hostile acts, injuries, and insults we were, to our great mortification, compelled to witness and suffer, being unable to resist them, by reason of our want of men and of powder, whereof our supply scarcely sufficed for a single round for our guns. Notwithstanding all this, we still trusted that they would at length be persuaded to hear reason, and accordingly on the 7th we sent messengers down to Stüvesant at Fort Casimir, with a written commission, whereby we sought to dissuade him from further hostilities, protesting against his invasion and disturbance of our proper territory without cause assigned, or declaration denying, as far as they could, our right of possession in the river; also suggesting to him the displeasure of our respective sovereigns, and other consequences of great moment which would ensue; that we were determined to defend our rights to the utmost of our strength, and that he must answer for all consequences, and finally required him to cease hostilities, and to retire with his people from Fort Christina. But all this availed nothing with him, and on the contrary he persisted in his claim to the whole river, and would listen to no terms of accommodation, declaring that such were his orders, and that those who had given them might answer for the consequences. He then wrote me a letter on the 9th, in which he anticipates all terms of accommodation, will not allow that we have any rights to the said river, seeks to refute our argu-

[1] Now Brandywine Creek, near the site of Fort Christina.

ments, and styles our possession a usurpation, and so interprets every point to his own advantage.

As we still determined to maintain our own defence, and abide the result, the enemy continued to carry on their approaches day and night, and with our little force of about thirty men we could make no sorties, or prevent him from gaining positions from which he could command the sconce so completely, that there was not a spot on the ramparts where a man could stand in security, and as he now daily advanced his works, and summoned us to capitulate, with threats of giving no quarter, our men proposed to us to go out and try to bring Stüvesant to reason, both on account of our want of supplies, and the advanced condition of the enemy's works, and especially because our provisions were scanty and would soon be exhausted. Besides, our few and hastily collected people were getting worn out, partly sick, and partly ill disposed, and some had deserted.—From these considerations, and the fear of a mutiny, it was agreed, that I and Elzvii should go out the next day and hold a parley with Stüvesant, and endeavor to restrain him from forcible measures, and to bring him to reason. We accordingly went out for this purpose on the 13th, and Stüvesant and Nicatius de Sylle[1] met us between the sconce and their most advanced work. We solemnly protested against his procedure and his hostile conduct, and replied verbally to his last mentioned letter, confirmed our title with the best arguments we could, and held a long discussion with them; but all this produced no impression upon them, and they maintained their first ground, and insisted upon the surrender of Fort Christina and the whole river; to which we replied that we would defend ourselves to the last and would await them, clearly showing them that they were unjustly invading our possessions, and declaring that we would appeal to our government to redress our wrongs, and protect our rights thus forcibly trenched upon,

[1] Nicasius de Sille (b. 1610), a member of the council of New Netherland, ranking next to Stuyvesant in the expedition, was a native of Arnheim, in the eastern part of the Netherlands, his father being a native of Namur, in Belgium. He had served as advocate to the court of Holland, and as captain in the forces of the States General. He came to New Netherlands in 1653 and was actively concerned in the governmental affairs of the colony until 1660.

and so we went back to the sconce, exhorted our men to a manly defence, and encouraged them as well as we were able.

As soon as the Dutch had nearly completed their works, they brought the guns of all their batteries to bear upon us, and on the 14th instant, formally summoned Fort Christina, with harsh menaces, by a drummer and a messenger, to capitulate within twenty-four hours. We then assembled a general council of the whole garrison, and it was found to be their unanimous opinion, that inasmuch as we had not sufficient strength for our defence, (the Dutch having completed their works against the sconce, and neither the sconce nor the garrison being able to stand an assault), and were in want both of powder and other munitions, and had no hope of relief, therefore they were all of opinion, that we should make the best terms we could obtain with the Dutch; all which may be seen by the documents. So the next day we announced to the enemy, that we would consider their summons within the time prescribed, and being now reduced, by our want of supplies and weak condition, to yield to the violence practised upon us, we concluded a capitulation with Stüvesant, as may be found by the original among the documents, and surrendered Fort Christina to him on the 15th instant, stipulating that the guns and all the effects belonging to the crown or the Company should be restored by the Dutch, according to the inventory, upon demand, and reserving the restitution of our sovereign's rights in time and manner fitting; providing also, that the Dutch should freely transport to Sweden both us, and as many Swedes as chose to accompany us, for we held it better that the people should be restored to their Fatherland's service than to leave them there in misery, without the necessaries of life, in which case they would have entered the service of the Dutch or English, and never again advantaged their country.

THE EPISTLE OF PENN, LAWRIE, AND LUCAS, RESPECTING WEST JERSEY, 1676

INTRODUCTION

THE preceding narratives have to do with the Dutch and Swedish period. The narratives that follow concern the English period alone. The two groups differ, moreover, in that while the accounts in the first group are mainly official reports addressed to superior authority with no intent of publication, those of the second were contemporaneously put into print, for the most part to attract European immigrants to the shores of the Delaware—an object which they accomplished with great success.

In the two decades that intervene between the two parts thus defined, the region of the Delaware had experienced some extensions of settlement and had come under the successive control of two great rival powers. During nearly the whole of the first decade the Dutch held sway. Then the English, with their revival of interest in trade and colonization after the Restoration, which resulted in endeavors to deprive the Dutch of their commercial supremacy and of their American opportunities, began war, in 1664, and seized New Netherland. This acquisition supplied the one link hitherto missing in the chain of England's American colonies. The Delaware region, along with the remainder of New Netherland, acquired by the English, was transferred by their king, Charles II., to his brother, James, duke of York.

Of the Duke's tenure and government, of his grants of territory, and of the later sub-grants with their tedious and involved recitals, the essentials for our purpose may be found in the succeeding pages. Let it suffice here to state that the large portion of the English conquest on the east side of the

Delaware, the moiety of New Jersey called West New Jersey, came as a trust into the hands of three eminent members of the persecuted sect of English Quakers (the joint authors of this *Epistle*): and it is this territory that is the theme of their disquisition as here reprinted.

The Quakers, whose leaders for years had been on the lookout for a home of refuge in the New World, first became directly concerned in the founding of colonies there in the year 1673–1674, when two of their number, John Fenwick and Edward Byllynge, old Cromwellian soldiers in England, purchased this tract of West New Jersey. A dispute as to the land arising between Fenwick and Byllynge, the foremost of all Quakers was called in as arbiter. This was William Penn, son of the Duke's favorite admiral in the Dutch War, and the future Founder of Pennsylvania, who thus made his first entry into the field of American colonization.

"The present difference between thee and E. B. fills the hearts of Friends with grief," wrote Penn to Fenwick. "I took care to hide the pretences on both hands as to the original of the thing, because it reflects on you both and which is worse on the truth" [*i. e.*, on the profession of Quakerism]. Fenwick endeavored to evade the award, but finally submitted to it. Byllynge accepted his allotment, but meeting business reverses, was compelled for the satisfaction of his creditors to convey his rights (February 14, 1675) to the above-mentioned trustees, William Penn and two creditors, Gawen Lawrie and Nicholas Lucas.

Fenwick, also, notwithstanding extensive sales of his share of the land, fell into debt and had to lease those parts yet unsold to two other Quakers, Eldridge and Warner, as security for money borrowed. They in turn conveyed their claim to Penn, Lawrie, and Lucas, so that the latter secured control of practically the whole of West New Jersey. In 1675 Fenwick brought over the initial Quaker colony in the ship *Griffin*, and planted

Salem, the first permanent English settlement on the east side of the Delaware.

Gawen Lawrie has been ascribed to Hertfordshire, but in 1676–1677 he is mentioned as a merchant of King's Court, Lombard Street, London. In 1684 he came over with his family to East New Jersey as Deputy Governor, and took up his residence at Elizabethtown. There he died in the fall of 1687. He wrote several accounts of East New Jersey. Nicholas Lucas was a maulster, of Hertford, suffering persecution in that town for his Quaker belief as early as 1658. In 1664 he was the joint author of a Quaker tract and in the same year was confined in Hertford jail, under sentence of banishment, being kept there for eight years.

The *Epistle* may be accepted as a careful statement of the facts. Judging especially from the use of the first person under the tenth heading, it was evidently composed in large part by Penn himself, although the other two men doubtless had a hand in the draft. It is mentioned in Joseph Smith's *Catalogue of Friends' Books* (1867), volume II., p. 295, as a broadside, with no title, dated 1676. It was reprinted in 1775 in Samuel Smith's *History of New Jersey* (Burlington, N. J.), pp. 88–91. Our text is from Smith's book. It also appears in Robert Proud's *History of Pennsylvania*, I. 141–142 (1797), and in *New Jersey Archives* I. 231–235 (1880).

A. C. M.

THE EPISTLE OF PENN, LAWRIE, AND LUCAS, RESPECTING WEST JERSEY, 1676

Dear friends and brethren,

IN the pure love and precious fellowship of our Lord Jesus Christ, we very dearly salute you: Forasmuch as there was a paper printed several months since, entitled, *The description of New-West-Jersey,*[1] in the which our names were mentioned as trustees for one undivided moiety of the said province:[2] And because it is alledged that some, partly on this account, and others apprehending, that the paper by the manner of its expression came from the body of friends,[3] as a religious society of people, and not from particulars,[4] have through these mistakes, weakly concluded that the said description in matter and form might be writ, printed and recommended on purpose to prompt and allure people, to dis-settle and transplant themselves, as it's also by some alledged: And because that we are informed, that several have on that account, taken encouragement and resolution to transplant themselves and families to the said province; and lest any of them (as is feared by some) should go out of a curious and unsettled mind, and others to shun the testimony of the blessed cross of Jesus, of which several weighty friends have a godly jealousy upon their spirits; lest an unwarrantable forwardness should act or hurry any beside or beyond the wisdom and counsel of the lord, or the freedom of his light and spirit in their own hearts, and not upon good and weighty grounds: It truly laid hard upon us, to let friends know how the matter stands; which we shall endeavor to do with all clearness and fidelity.

1. That there is such a province as New-Jersey, is certain.
2. That it is reputed of those who have lived and have

---

[1] *The Description of the Province of West-Jersey* is mentioned in Joseph Smith's *Catalogue of Friends' Books*, II. (1867), 295, as a large broadside [*c.* 1676].

[2] *I. e.,* of the province of New Jersey.

[3] Or Quakers.   [4] Individuals.

travelled in that country, to be wholesome of air and fruitful of soil, and capable of sea trade, is also certain; and it is not right in any to despise or dispraise it, or disswade those that find freedom from the Lord, and necessity put them on going.

3. That the duke of York[1] sold it to those called lord Berkeley, baron of Stratton, and sir George Carteret, equally to be divided between them, is also certain.

4. One moiety or half part[2] of the said province, being the right of the said lord Berkeley, was sold by him to John Fenwick, in trust[3] for Edward Byllinge,[4] and his assigns.

5. Forasmuch as E. B. (after William Penn had ended the difference[5] between the said Edward Byllinge and John Fenwick) was willing to present his interest in the said province to his creditors, as all that he had left him, towards their satisfaction, he desired William Penn (though every way unconcerned) and Gawen Lawrie, and Nicholas Lucas, two of his creditors, to be trustees for performance of the same; and because several of his creditors, particularly and very importunately, pressed William Penn to accept of the trust for their sakes and security; we did all of us comply with those and the like requests, and accepted of the trust.

6. Upon this we became trustees for one moiety of the said province, yet undivided: And after no little labor, trouble and cost, a division was obtained between the said sir George Carteret and us, as trustees: The country is situated and bounded as is expressed in the printed description.

7. This now divided moiety is to be cast into one hundred parts, lots, or proprieties; ten of which upon the agreement made betwixt E. Byllinge and J. Fenwick, were settled and conveyed unto J. Fenwick, his executors and assigns, with a

---

[1] James, duke of York, who received the grant of New Jersey from his brother Charles II. in 1664, at the time of the English conquest of New Netherland, reconveyed it the same year to his two favorites, John lord Berkeley and Sir George Carteret.

[2] West New Jersey. The sale, for £1,000, took place March 18, 1673/4.

[3] As later alleged.

[4] Edward Byllynge (p. 1684–1685), a Quaker brewer of Westminster, and a former Cromwellian soldier.

[5] Fenwick and Byllynge disputing the title to West New Jersey, William Penn had been called in as arbiter. Fenwick, then, February 10, 1674/5, relinquished to Byllynge's assignees nine-tenths of his purchase for £400.

considerable sum of money, by way of satisfaction for what he became concerned in the purchase from the said lord Berkely, and by him[1] afterwards conveyed to John Edridge and Edmond Warner, their heirs and assigns.

8. The ninety parts remaining are exposed to sale, on the behalf of the creditors of the said E. B. And forasmuch as several friends[2] are concerned as creditors, as well as others, and the disposal of so great a part of this country being in our hands; we did in real tenderness and regard to friends, and especially to the poor and necessitous, make friends the first offer; that if any of them, though particularly those that being low in the world, and under trials about a comfortable livelihood for themselves and families, should be desirous of dealing for any part or parcel thereof, that they might have the refusal.

9. This was the real and honest intent of our hearts, and not to prompt or allure any out of their places, either by the credit our names might have with our people throughout the nation, or by representing the thing otherwise than it is in itself.

As for the printed paper sometime since set forth by the creditors, as a description of that province; we say as to two passages in it, they are not so clearly and safely worded as ought to have been; particularly, in seeming to limit the winter season to so short a time; when on further information, we hear it is sometime longer and sometime shorter than therein expressed; and the last clause relating to liberty of conscience, we would not have any to think, that it is promised or intended to maintain the liberty of the exercise of religion by force and arms; though we shall never consent to any the least violence on conscience; yet it was never designed to encourage any to expect by force of arms to have liberty of conscience fenced against invaders thereof.

[1] John Fenwick, after his settlement with Byllynge, having sold over 100,000 acres of land to about fifty purchasers, Fenwick leased all his unsold tenth, July 17–19, 1675, for 1,000 years to Eldridge and Warner as security for money borrowed. Eldridge and Warner shortly after conveyed the same to Penn, Lawrie, and Lucas. John Edridge, or Eldridge, Quaker, was a tanner of Gravel Lane, St. Paul's Shadwell, county Middlesex, in 1676. Edmond Warner (d. 1683), also a Quaker, was a citizen and poulterer of London, and is said to have come over to Pennsylvania with his family as early as 1683.

[2] Quakers.

10. And be it known unto you all, in the name and fear of Almighty God, his glory and honour, power and wisdom, truth and kingdom, is dearer to us than all visible things; and as our eye has been single, and our heart sincere to the living God, in this as in other things; so we desire all whom it may concern, that all groundless jealousies may be judged down and watched against, and that all extremes may be avoided on all hands by the power of the Lord; that nothing which hurts or grieves the holy life of truth in any that goes or stays, may be adhered to; nor any provocations given to break precious unity.

This am I, William Penn, moved of the Lord, to write unto you, lest any bring a temptation upon themselves or others; and in offending the Lord, slay their own peace: Blessed are they that can see, and behold him their leader, their orderer, their conductor and preserver, in staying or going: Whose is the earth and the fullness thereof; and the cattle upon a thousand hills. And as we formerly writ, we cannot but repeat our request unto you, that in whomsoever a desire is to be concerned in this intended plantation, such would weigh the thing before the Lord, and not headily or rashly conclude on any such remove; and that they do not offer violence to the tender love of their near kindred and relations; but soberly and conscientiously endeavour to obtain their good wills, the unity of friends where they live; that whether they go or stay, it may be of good favour before the Lord (and good people) from whom only can all heavenly and earthly blessings come. This we thought good to write for the preventing of all misunderstandings, and to declare the real truth of the matter; and so we commend you all to the Lord, who is the watchman of his Israel. We are your friends and brethren,

WILLIAM PENN,
GAWEN LAWRIE,
NICHOLAS LUCAS.

THE PRESENT STATE OF THE COLONY OF WEST-JERSEY, 1681

INTRODUCTION

In the gap of five years from our last document the Quaker settlements of West New Jersey made marked progress. Byllynge's trustees soon effected sales of large tracts of land to two Quaker companies in England, one in southern Yorkshire and contiguous territory and the other in London. Much of the land being resold, the number of proprietors rapidly increased. Preparations for sending over another Quaker colony were then energetically forwarded, in connection with which a thoroughly democratic constitution embodying the Quaker ideals was drawn up in England. This was the famous *Concessions and Agreements of the Proprietors, Freeholders and Inhabitants of West New Jersey*, a document of deep import in American constitutional history. It was signed by Penn, who has been credited with its drafting, and one hundred and fifty other persons representative of the groups mentioned in the title. By this instrument the government was placed in the hands of a board of ten commissioners—to be chosen at first by the proprietors—and in a law-making assembly freely elected by the inhabitants.

The second colony of two hundred persons, bearing this constitution, went over in the ship *Kent* in 1677 and laid the foundations of the town and settlement of Burlington, more than fifty miles up the Delaware from Salem. The Yorkshire and London tracts were located respectively north and south of the new town. Questions having arisen as to the validity of the West New Jersey title, particularly as concerned the power of government, which, it was asserted, had not been included in the original real estate transfer, the commissioners for the first three years managed the affairs of the settlement under authority of Andros, the Duke's governor at New York. Penn, in the meantime, with persistence and skill, finally influenced the Duke to recognize the Quaker title in both the land and government, the latter however being vested solely in Byllynge. It is this reconveyance of the Duke, dated August 6, 1680, that is here announced in *The Present State*. Byllynge, on assuming control, sent over Samuel Jenings as the first Deputy Governor and authorized the call of the Assembly, which met for the first time in November, 1681.

Several hundred more immigrants followed those who came on the *Kent*, and gradually extended the bounds of the two original settlements of Salem and Burlington.

The author of *The Present State* is unknown, but obviously the pamphlet was sent out by the trustees and proprietors. It seems to be a fair and truthful statement of the existing conditions. The original, a single sheet printed on both sides ($11\frac{1}{4} \times 6\frac{3}{4}$ inches), is in the collection of the Historical Society of Pennsylvania. It was published in 1681, probably in London, and was reprinted in 1894, in the *Pennsylvania Magazine*, XVIII. 158–162. The text which follows is from the original.

A. C. M.

THE PRESENT STATE OF THE COLONY OF WEST-JERSEY, 1681

The Present State of the Colony of West-Jersey, in America. September, Anno Dom. 1681.

1. Some few Years since, there were several Printed Papers published, giving Account of this Colony, which gave Encouragement to many Persons to Purchase Lands, and Transport Themselves, Servants, and Families thither, who have settled Themselves in that Colony, upon the Great River of Delaware, and the Creeks and Harbors thereof; and have Built some Towns apt for Trade, with Convenient Ports, where large Ships of Considerable Burthen have already unloaded, especially at Burlington, Scituate about a Hundred and Fifty Miles[1] from the Sea up the said River.

2. And there are also many Families, who have settled Themselves in that Country; some about Husbandry, others have Erected Mills for Grinding Corn, and several other necessary Tradesmen have There settled Themselves in Towns, and in the Country, fit for their Respective Undertakings.

3. The Husband-Men have good Increase, as well in large Cattle and Hoggs; as also, in all such sorts of Grain which grow in England; and the same are Sold at Easie and Reasonable Rates: The Increase of their Corn being considerably Greater than in England; of which they Make good Bread, and Brew good Beer and Ale for their Use. And as for other Provisions, they are Plentiful; as Fish, Fowls, Deer, Pork, Beef, and many Sorts of Fruits; as Grapes, Peaches, Apricocks, Cherryes, and Apples, of which Good Syder is made.

4. The Country also produces Flax and Hemp, which they already Spin and Manufacture into Linnen: They make several Stuffs and Cloath of Wool for Apparrel: They Tan **Leather, Make** Shooes and Hats.

---

[1] Only about a hundred miles.

5. They have also Coopers, Smiths, Carpenters, Brick-layers, Wheel-Wrights, Plow-Wrights, and Mill-Wrights, Ship-Carpenters, and other Trades, which work upon what the Country produces for Manufacturies.

6. For the Soyl it is Good, and capable to produce any thing that England doth: [and] the Yearly Increase is far Greater. The Air Temperate and Healthy; Winter not so long as is in England: Few Natives in the Country; but those that are, are very Peaceable, Useful, and Serviceable to the English Inhabitants.

7. There are many Creeks and Bayes adjoining, and belonging to Delaware-River, beside other Rivers and Creeks along the Sea-shore, which are Navigable.

8. For Minerals within the Earth, they have not had Time to search; only, there are Iron-Mines,—and a Furnace, and Forging Mill already set up in East-Jersey, where they Make Iron.

9. Their Houses are some Built of Brick, some of Timber, Plaister'd and Ceil'd, as in England: So that they have Matterials within the Country, to set Themselves at work, and to make all manner of Conveniency for Humane Life: And what they do not Spend, or have to Spare, they sell to their Neighbours, and Transport the Rest to the other American-Plantations.

10. There is variety of Trees in the Country, and many of them; as Oak, Cedar, Chesnut, Wallnut, Mulberry, etc. and several sorts that are not in England.

11. For the Title of the said Colony, it stands thus: Some Years since, the King granted under the Great Seal of England, unto the Duke of York, His Heirs and Assigns, several Tracts of Land in America, (in which Jersey is included) with full Power of Government, making Laws, Peace, War, and all other Things whatsoever, for Settling and Governing the same. The Duke of York, (in Affirmation of former Grants and Conveyances thereof) by Conveyance Inrolled in the High-Court of Chancery, Grants and Conveys the Whole Colony of West-Jersey, with all Lands, Rivers, Bayes, Creeks, Royalties, and Priviledges thereunto belonging, unto William Pen, Gawen Lawry, and Nicholas Lucas, In Trust for Edward Billinge, His Heirs and Assigns for ever: And by like Convey-

ance, the said Duke Granted the Power of Government of the said West-Jersey unto the said Edward Billinge, His Deputy or Deputyes, Commissioner or Commissioners, for Governing and Settling the said West-Jersey; And that in as full and ample Manner, to all Intents and Purposes, as the same was Granted to Him by the King.[1] All which Laws and Settlements are, and are to be Made and Done with the Consent and Approbation of the Proprietors and Free-holders thereof. So that, neither Customs, Charge, Imposition, nor any other Services or Taxes whatsoever, are to be Imposed upon the Inhabitants, but by their own Consent in a Free and General-Assembly of the Proprietors and Free-Holders of the said Colony; which Assembly is to meet once every Year.

12. There is likewise Certain Provision made for the Liberty of Conscience, in Matters of Religion, that all Persons living Peaceably, may injoy the Benefit of the Religious Exercise thereof, without any Molestation whatsoever.

13. The Method laid down for Sale and Division of the Country of West-Jersey, is by Proprieties, (that is to say) One Propriety contains the Hundredth Part of the Whole Country: Of which Proprieties, many are already Sold, and disposed of to Purchasers; and several of the same remains yet to be Sold. In each of these Hundred Parts or Proprieties, the Quantity of Acres, cannot be absolutely Ascertain'd; but its generally judged to be Twenty Thousand Acres, and upwards; but some have accounted each Propriety to contain much more. And if any Person be not minded to deal for a Whole Propriety; Two, Four, Six, Eight, or more, may joyn in the Purchase thereof; There being Land enough in one of these Proprieties for many Families.

14. The Dividing, and Laying out the Land, is done by Commissioners appointed upon the Place. And there is a large Tract of Land, containing above Sixty English Miles, lying along the River of Delaware, taken up, and Bought of

[1] The validity of the grant of Charles II. to his brother the Duke of York having been questioned because of the Dutch reconquest of 1673, Charles II. issued a new patent to the Duke for the region including New Jersey, June 29, 1674. The Duke, then, August 6, 1680, confirmed West New Jersey to Penn, Lawrie, and Lucas, also specifically empowering Byllynge with its government, a prerogative which, it was held, had not accompanied the grant of Berkeley to Fenwick, March 18, 1673/4.

the Natives: The Commissioners lay out (at present) about
Five or Six Thousand Acres of Land for a Propriety out of
this Tract, as People come over that have Bought: By which
Means, the People settle near together, for their Conveniency
of Trade and Commerce.   And when this Tract of Land is all
Settled, then it's intended to take up another Tract of Land,
and proceed in the same Method; and so in like manner to
continue, until the Whole Country is Divided.   And the said
Commissioners, for dividing the same, are to be Chosen by the
General-Assembly of the Colony, with Approbation of the Governor, or His Deputy, upon the Place.

15. As for the Deeds or Conveyances, signed, or to be
signed by Edward [Billinge] and His Trustees, they were at
first drawn up by able Counsellors at Law, and are [all] after
one manner: So that, every Purchaser hath alike Priviledge.

16. For Transportation of Passengers to West-Jersey, Ships
set Sail from London generally Once in Three Months, sometimes in Two Months: The Master gives Notice Six Weeks
(or more) of his Going before-hand.

17. The Price for every Passenger, (that is to say) for Men
and Women, Meat, Drink, and Passage, with a Chest, is Five
Pounds sterling per Head: For Children of Twelve Years of
Age, and under, Fifty Shillings per Head; Sucking Children,
Nothing: For Goods, Forty Shillings a Tun Freight, to be
Landed at Burlington, or elsewhere upon Delaware-River.

18. Sometimes, ships go from Dublin, sometimes from
Hull: But if any Persons, to the Number of Thirty, or more,
in Scotland or Ireland, desiring to be taken in There, the Ship-
Master will take them in at Leith, Dundee, or Aberdeen on the
East, and at Aire on the West of Scotland, and at Dublin
or Waterford in Ireland; so as they order some Person in London, to agree, and give Security for so many Passengers to be
ready at the Time and Place agreed upon, to be taken Aboard,
with Account how many Tun of Goods they intend to Ship.
And the Commodities fit to be carryed to New-Jersey, are such
as are usually carryed to Virginia, New-York, or Mary-land.

19. Thus far it is thought meet (in short) to inform all
Persons, to whose Hands the several former Printed Papers
and Testimonies concerning New-Jersey may not come: But
if any Desire to have further Information, there are several

Letters from Persons settled in West Jersey to their Friends in England, lately Printed, and are to be had at Benjamine Clarks, in George-Yard in Lumbord-Street, London; and Robert Turners, at Dublin in Ireland; David Falkner, at Edinburgh; Hugh Woods, at Hamilton; John Cowey's, at Aberdeen in Scotland.   And for such who desire to be Purchasers of Land in West-Jersey, or to be satisfyed concerning any thing relating thereto, they may Repair or Write to Thomas Rudyard,[2] in the afore-said George-Yard in Lumbard-Street; where they may be further Treated with therein; where, it's doubted not, but they will have Full Satisfaction both as to the Holding, Division, Concessions, and Settlements of the said New Jersey.

[1] *An Abstract or Abbreviation of some Few of the Many (Later and Former) Testimonys from the Inhabitants of New-Jersey and other Eminent Persons who have Wrote particularly concerning that Place. London, Printed by Thomas Milbourn, in the Year 1681. Pp. 32, quarto (John Carter Brown Library).*

[2] Thomas Rudyard (d. about 1692), a lawyer, of George Yard, Lombard Street, London, originally from the town of Rudyard, in Staffordshire, had been concerned in the famous trial of the Quakers, William Penn and William Mead, in London in 1670.   It was in his office that William Penn's first deeds granting Pennsylvania lands were drawn up and signed.   He became one of the New Jersey proprietors, and in 1682 went over as Deputy Governor of East Jersey, serving until the close of 1685, when he set out for Barbados.

SOME ACCOUNT OF THE PROVINCE OF
PENNSILVANIA, BY WILLIAM PENN, 1681

INTRODUCTION

THE founding of the province of Pennsylvania by William Penn was the direct result of his active participation—beginning, as we have seen, in 1675—in the management of the affairs of the New Jersey settlements. He had thus become fully acquainted with the conditions and possibilities not only of the latter region but of the whole domain of the English America of that day, and particularly of that portion of it contiguous to West New Jersey on the west side of the Delaware. A keen desire (evolved under the influence of his Quaker viewpoint and experiences from a germinating idea, as he tells us, of his youthful days at Oxford University), had grown up in him to plant in the New World a colony all his own, where he might exemplify his altruistic ideals of the government and development of such a settlement and establish a democracy, under his paternal care, which while essentially Quaker in character, would nevertheless attract other desirable European immigrants seeking religious freedom and economic opportunity. Along with these great purposes, but subordinate to them, William Penn as an Englishman of rank and influence in the realm, with the traditions of his class, had also a concern for his material interests and for the perpetuity of an estate for his family.

The realization of his dream of a Quaker commonwealth was made practically possible through a claim of £16,000, which as his father's heir he held against the crown. He could rely also upon the sincere friendship of the royal brothers. Having vainly sought the direct recovery of the debt, he now made this loss to his estate, as he phrases it, the basis of a petition to King Charles, in June, 1680, requesting the grant of the Pennsylvania tract. The King's favor brought the desired result, and on March 4, 1681, the charter, after going through the usual stages of preparation, received the royal signature and Penn was duly vested with a great domain nearly as large as England itself.

Early the next month Penn appointed his cousin William Markham to serve as Deputy Governor of Pennsylvania and sent him over with instructions to call a council, to receive the allegiance of the people, to settle boundaries, to survey and distribute lands, and to keep the peace. Markham arrived there about the latter part of June, 1681, and assumed control of the government, which he administered until Penn himself came over.

Penn in the meantime began energetically the exploitation of his new province, giving chief attention to the preparation of *Some Account of the Province of Pennsilvania* (a folio of [2] +10 pages). This was the first of his series of immigration pamphlets in the interest of his project. He did not seek to entice intending settlers by misleading accounts, as did some promoters of early—not to speak of later—American emigration, but with that scrupulous regard for true statement that characterized Quaker writings, he was careful in this as in other similar publications to present the simple facts without exaggeration. Having as yet no personal knowledge of America, his data for the parts of his work relating to it were acquired at second hand, yet before issuing the pamphlet he first took the precaution to read it, as he states in a letter of April 12, 1681, "to Traders, Planters, and Shipmasters, that know those parts, and finally to the most eminent Friends, hereway [London], and so [it] comes forth. I have foreborne pains and allurement, and writt truth." Published in London, early in April, as it would seem from the above letter, *Some Account* was immediately issued on the Continent, under the direction of Penn's Pennsylvania agent there, the learned and well-to-do merchant, Benjamin Furley, an English Quaker, resident in Rotterdam. Two such editions appeared, one in Dutch at Rotterdam (a quarto of 24 pages), and the other in German at Amsterdam (a quarto of 31 pages). To these translations was added Penn's letter to the burgomaster and council of the city of Emden, dated London, December 14, 1674, and originally printed in Dutch in 1675. The German edition contains an additional short explanation or glossary, covering three pages, of some of the English words retained in the translation. The pamphlet in its respective forms was widely circulated among those most likely to respond to it, especially in those communities and countries where Penn had travelled or was known, notably in England, Ireland and Wales, and in Holland and Germany, and it had considerable influence in inducing the emigration that followed.

Some Account was reprinted in Samuel Hazard's *Register of Pennsylvania*, I. 305–308, (May 17, 1828), with the omission of the abstract of the charter, and also, but with less fullness, in his *Annals of Pennsylvania* (1850), pp. 505–513. It was again reprinted, without the abstract, in Thompson Westcott's *History of Philadelphia (Sunday Dispatch*, Philadelphia, 1867), chapter XVII. The complete text is here reprinted for the first time, it is believed, in English, from an original copy of the book in the collection of the Historical Society of Pennsylvania.

A. C. M.

SOME ACCOUNT OF THE PROVINCE OF PENNSILVANIA, BY WILLIAM PENN, 1681

Some account of the province of Pennsilvania in America;
Lately Granted under the Great Seal of England to William
Penn, etc. Together with Priviledges and Powers necessary
to the well-governing thereof. Made publick for the Infor-
mation of such as are or may be disposed to Transport
themselves or Servants into those Parts.
London: Printed, and Sold by Benjamin Clark Bookseller in
George-Yard, Lombard-street, 1681.

SINCE (by the good providence of God) a Country in America is fallen to my lot, I thought it not less my Duty than my honest Interest to give some publick notice of it to the World, that those of our own, or other Nations, that are inclin'd to Transport themselves or Families beyond the Seas, may find another Country added to their choice, that if they shall happen to like the Place, Conditions and Constitutions, (so far as the present Infancy of things will allow us any prospect) they may, if they please, fix with me in the Province hereafter describ'd. But before I come to treat of my particular Concernment, I shall take leave to say something of the benefit of Plantations or Colonies in general, to obviate a common Objection.

Colonies then are the Seeds of Nations begun and nourished by the care of wise and populous Countries; as conceiving them best for the increase of Humane Stock, and beneficial for Commerce.

Some of the wisest men in History have justly taken their Fame from this Design and Service: We read of the Reputation given on this account to Moses, Joshua and Caleb in Scripture-Records; and what Renown the Greek story yields to Lycurgus, Theseus, and those Greeks that Planted many parts of Asia: Nor is the Roman account wanting of instances to the Credit of that People; They had a Romulus, a Numa Pompilius; and not only reduc'd, but moraliz'd the Manners of the Nations they subjected; so that they may have been rather said to conquer their Barbarity than Them.

Nor did any of these ever dream it was the way of decreasing their People or Wealth: For the cause of the decay of any of those States or Empires was not their Plantations, but their Luxury and corruption of Manners: For when they grew to neglect their ancient Discipline, that maintained and rewarded Virtue and Industry, and addicted themselves to Pleasure and Effeminacy, they debas'd their Spirits and debauch'd their Morals, from whence Ruine did never fail to follow to any People: With Justice therefore I deny the vulgar Opinion against Plantations, That They weaken England; they have manifestly inrich'd, and so strengthened her; Which I briefly evidence thus.

1st. Those that go into a Foreign Plantation, their Industry there is worth more than if they stay'd at home, the Product of their Labour being in Commodities of a superiour Nature to those of this Country. For Instance; What is an improved Acre in Jamaica or Barbadoes worth to an improved Acre in England? We know 'tis threetimes the value, and the product of it comes for England, and is usually paid for in English Growth and Manufacture. Nay, Virginia shews that an ordinary Industry in one man produces Three thousand pound weight of Tobacco and Twenty Barrels of Corn yearly: He feeds himself, and brings as much of Commodity into England besides as being return'd in the Growth and Workmanship of this Countrey, is much more than he could have spent here: Let it also be remembred, that the Three thousand weight of Tobacco brings in Three thousand Two-pences by way of Custom to the King, which makes Twenty five Pounds; An extraordinary Profit.

2dly. More being produc'd and imported than we can spend here, we Export it to other Countries in Europe, which brings in Money, or the Growth of those Countries, which is the same thing; And this is the Advantage of the English-Merchants and Seamen.

3dly. Such as could not only not marry here, but hardly live and allow themselves Cloaths, do marry there, and bestow thrice more in all Necessaries and Conveniencies (and not a little in Ornamental things too) for themselves, their Wives and Children, both as to Apparel and Household-stuff; which coming out of England, I say 'tis impossible that England should not be a considerable Gainer.

4thly. But let it be consider'd, That the Plantations imploy many hundreds of Shipping, and many thousands of Seamen; which must be in divers respects an Advantage to England, being an Island, and by Nature fitted for Navigation above any Countrey in Europe. This is followed by other depending Trades, as Shipwrights, Carpenters, Sawyers, Hewers, Trunnel-makers, Joyners, Slopsellers, Dry-salters, Iron-workers, the Eastland-Merchants,[1] Timber-sellers, and Victuallers, with many more Trades which hang upon Navigation: So that we may easily see the Objection (That Colonies or Plantations hurt England) is at least of no strength, especially if we consider how many thousand Blacks and Indians are also accommodated with Cloaths and many sorts of Tools and Utensils from England, and that their Labour is mostly brought hither, which adds Wealth and People to the English Dominions. But 'tis further said, They injure England, in that they draw away too many of the people; for we are not so populous in the Countries as formerly: I say there are other reasons for that.

1st. Country-People are so extremely addicted to put their Children into Gentlemens Service, or send them to Towns to learn Trades, that Husbandry is neglected; and after a soft and delicate Usage there, they are for ever unfitted for the Labour of a Farming Life.

2dly. The Pride of the Age in its Attendance and Retinue is so gross and universal, that where a man of 1000*l.* a year formerly kept but four or five Servants, he now keeps more than twice the number; He must have a Gentleman to wait upon him in his Chambers, a Coach-man, a Groom or two, a Butler, a Man-Cook, a Gardner, two or three Lacques, it may be an Huntsman, and a Faulkner,[2] the Wife a Gentlewoman, and Maids accordingly: This was not known by our Ancestors of like Quality. This hinders the Plough and the Dairy, from

---

[1] Merchants engaged in the Baltic trade.
[2] Falconer.

whence they are taken, and instead of keeping People to Manly-labour, they are effeminated by a lazy and luxurious Living; But which is worse, these people rarely marry, tho' many of them do worse; but if they do, 'tis when they are in Age; And the reason is clear, because their usual Keeping at their Masters is too great and costly for them with a Family at their own Charge, and they scarcely know how to live lower; so that too many of them chuse rather to vend their Lusts at an evil Ordinary than honestly Marry and Work: The excess and sloth of the Age not allowing of Marriage and the Charge that follows; all which hinders the increase of our People. If Men, they often turn either Souldiers, or Gamesters, or Highway-men. If Women, They too frequently dress themselves for a bad market, rather than know the Dairy again, or honestly return to Labour, whereby it happens that both the Stock of the Nation decays and the Issue is corrupted.

3dly. Of old time the Nobility and Gentry spent their Estates in the Country, and that kept the people in it; and their Servants married and sate at easie Rents under their Masters favour, which peopled the place: Now the Great men (too much loving the Town and resorting to London) draw many people thither to attend them, who either don't marry; or if they do, they pine away their small gains in some petty Shop; for there are so many, they prey upon one another.

4thly. The Country being thus neglected, and no due Ballance kept between Trade and Husbandry, City and Country, the poor Country-man takes double Toil, and cannot (for want of hands) dress and manure his Land to the Advantage it formerly yielded him, yet must he pay the old Rents, which occasions Servants, and such Children as go not to Trades, to continue single, at least all their youthful time, which also obstructs the increase of our people.

5thly. The decay of some Country-manufactures (where no Provision is made to supply the people with a new way of living) causes the more Industrious to go abroad to seek their Bread in other Countries, and gives the lazy an occasion to loiter and beg or do worse, by which means the Land swarms with Beggars: Formerly 'twas rare to find any asking Alms but the Maimed, or Blind, or very Aged; now thousands of

both Sexes run up and down, both City and Country, that are
sound and youthful, and able to work, with false Pretences
and Certificates; nor is there any care taken to imploy or deter
such Vagrants, which weakens the Country, as to People and
Labour.

To which let me add, that the great Debauchery in this
Kingdom has not only rendred many unfruitful when married,
but they live not out half their time, through Excesses, which
might be prevented by a vigorous execution of our good Laws
against corruption of manners.   These and the like evils are
the true grounds of the decay of our People in the Country, to
say nothing of Plague and Wars: Towns and Cities cannot complain of the decay of People, being more replenish'd than ever,
especially London, which with reason helps the Country-man
to this Objection.   And though some do go to the Plantations,
yet numbering the Parishes in England, and computing how
many live more than die, and are born than buried, there goes
not over to all the Plantations a fourth part of the yearly increase of the People.   And when they are there, they are not
(as I said before) lost to England, since they furnish them with
much Cloaths, Houshold-stuff, Tools, and the like necessaries,
and that in greater quantities than here their condition could
have needed, or they could have bought, being there well to
pass, that were but low here, if not poor; and now Masters of
Families too, when here they had none, and could hardly keep
themselves; and very often it happens that some of them, after
their Industry and Success there have made them wealthy,
they return and empty their Riches into England; one in this
capacity being able to buy out twenty of what he was when he
went over.

This much to justifie the Credit and Benefit of Plantations;
wherein I have not sought to speak my Interest, but my Judgment; and I dare venture the success of it with all sober and
considering men.   I shall now proceed to give some account
of my own concern.

1st. I shall say what may be necessary of the Place or
Province.

2dly. Touch upon the Constitutions.

3dly. Lay down the Conditions.

4thly. Give my sense what persons will be fit to go.

5thly. What Utensils, Furniture and Commodities are fit to carry with them, with the charge of the voyage, and what is first to be done and expected there for some time.

And *lastly*, I shall give an Abstract of the Grant by Letters Patents under the Great Seal of England, that an account may be given of the Estate and Power granted to me thereby.

I. *Something of the Place.*

The Place lies 600 miles nearer the Sun than England; for England begins at the 50th Degree and ten minutes of North Latitude, and this Place begins at fourty, which is about the Latitude of Naples in Italy, or Mompellier[1] in France.   I shall say little in its praise, to excite desires in any, whatever I could truly write as to the Soil, Air and Water: This shall satisfie me, that by the Blessing of God, and the honesty and industry of Man, it may be a good and fruitful Land.

For Navigation it is said to have two conveniencies; the one by lying Ninescore miles upon Delaware River; that is to say, about three-score and ten miles, before we come to the Falls,[2] where a Vessel of Two hundred Tuns may Sail, (and some Creeks and small Harbours in that distance, where Ships may come nearer than the River into the Country) and above the Falls, for Sloops and Boats, as I am informed, to the extent of the Patent.   The other convenience is through Chesapeak-Bay.

For Timber and other Wood there is variety for the use of man.

For Fowl, Fish, and Wild-Deer, they are reported to be plentiful in those Parts.   Our English Provision is likewise now to be had there at reasonable Rates.   The Commodities that the Country is thought to be capable of, are Silk, Flax, Hemp, Wine, Sider, Woad, Madder, Liquorish, Tobacco, Pot-ashes, and Iron, and it does actually produce Hides, Tallow, Pipe-staves, Beef, Pork, Sheep, Wool, Corn, as Wheat, Barly, Ry, and also Furs, as your Peltree, Mincks, Racoons, Martins, and such like; store of Furs which is to be found among the Indians, that are profitable Commodities in Europe.

The way of trading in those Countries is thus: they send to the Southern Plantations Corn, Beef, Pork, Fish and Pipe-

---

[1] Montpellier.   [2] Now Trenton, New Jersey.

staves, and take their Growth and bring for England, and return with English Goods to their own Country. Their Furs they bring for England, and either sell them here, or carry them out again to other parts of Europe, where they will yield a better price: And for those that will follow Merchandize and Navigation there is conveniency, and Timber sufficient for Shipping.

II. *The Constitutions.*

For the Constitutions of the Country, the Patent shows, first, That the People and Governour have a Legislative Power, so that no Law can be made, nor Money raised, but by the Peoples Consent.

2dly. That the Rights and Freedoms of England (the best and largest in Europe) shall be in force there.

3dly. That making no Law against Allegiance (which should we, 'twere by the Law of England void of it self that moment) we may Enact what Laws we please for the good prosperity and security of the said Province.

4thly. That so soon as any are ingaged with me, we shall begin a Scheam or Draught together, such as shall give ample Testimony of my sincere Inclinations to encourage Planters, and settle a free, just and industrious Colony there.

III. *The Conditions.*

My Conditions will relate to three sorts of People: 1st. Those that will buy: 2dly. Those that take up Land upon Rent: 3dly. Servants. To the first, the Shares I sell shall be certain as to number of Acres; that is to say, every one shall contain Five thousand Acres, free from any Indian incumbrance, the price a hundred pounds, and for the Quit-rent but one English shilling or the value of it yearly for a hundred Acres; and the said Quit-Rent not to begin to be paid till 1684. To the second sort, that take up Land upon Rent, they shall have liberty so to do, paying yearly one peny per Acre, not exceeding Two hundred Acres. To the third sort, to wit, Servants that are carried over, Fifty Acres shall be allowed to the Master for every Head, and Fifty Acres to every Servant when their time is expired. And because some engage with me that

may not be disposed to go, it were very advisable **for every**
three Adventurers to send an Overseer with their Servants,
which would well pay the Cost.

The Divident may be thus; if the persons concern'd please,
a Tract of Land shall be survey'd; say Fifty thousand Acres
to a hundred Adventurers; in which some of the best shall be
set out for Towns or Cities; and there shall be so much Ground
allotted to each in those Towns as may maintain some Cattel
and produce some Corn; then the remainder of the fifty thousand Acres shall be shar'd among the said Adventurers (casting
up the Barren for Commons, and allowing for the same) whereby every Adventurer will have a considerable quantity of
Land together; likewise every one a proportion by a Navigable
River, and then backward into the Country. The manner of
divident I shall not be strict in; we can but speak roughly of
the matter here; but let men skilful in Plantations be consulted, and I shall leave it to the majority of votes among the
Adventurers when it shall please God we come there, how to
fix it to their own content.

IV. *These persons that providence seems to have most fitted
for Plantations are,*

1st. Industrious Husbandmen and Day-Labourers, that
are hardly able (with extreme Labour) to maintain their
Families and portion their Children.

2dly. Laborious Handicrafts, especially Carpenters, Masons, Smiths, Weavers, Taylors, Tanners, Shoemakers, Shipwrights, etc. where they may be spared or are low in the
World: And as they shall want no encouragement, so their
Labour is worth more there than here, and there provision
cheaper.

3dly. A Plantation seems a fit place for those Ingenious
Spirits that being low in the World, are much clogg'd and
oppress'd about a Livelyhood, for the means of subsisting
being easie there, they may have time and opportunity to
gratify their inclinations, and thereby improve Science and
help Nurseries of people.

4thly. A fourth sort of men to whom a Plantation would
be proper. takes in those that are younger Brothers of small

Inheritances; yet because they would live in sight of their Kindred in some proportion to their Quality, and can't do it without a labour that looks like Farming, their condition is too strait for them; and if married, their Children are often too numerous for the Estate, and are frequently bred up to no Trades, but are a kind of Hangers on or Retainers to the elder Brothers Table and Charity: which is a mischief, as in it self to be lamented, so here to be remedied; For Land they have for next to nothing, which with moderate Labour produces plenty of all things necessary for Life, and such an increase as by Traffique may supply them with all conveniencies.

Lastly, There are another sort of persons, not only fit for, but necessary in Plantations, and that is, Men of universal Spirits, that have an eye to the Good of Posterity, and that both understand and delight to promote good Discipline and just Government among a plain and well intending people; such persons may find Room in Colonies for their good Counsel and Contrivance, who are shut out from being of much use or service to great Nations under settl'd Customs: These men deserve much esteem, and would be harken'd to. Doubtless 'twas this (as I observ'd before) that put some of the famous Greeks and Romans upon Transplanting and Regulating Colonies of People in divers parts of the World; whose Names, for giving so great proof of their Wisdom, Virtue, Labour and Constancy, are with Justice honourably delivered down by story to the praise of our own times; though the World, after all its higher pretences of Religion, barbarously errs from their excellent Example.

V. *The Journey and it's Appurtenances, and what is to be done there at first coming.*

Next let us see, What is fit for the Journey and Place, when there, and also what may be the Charge of the Voyage, and what is to be expected and done there at first. That such as incline to go, may not be to seek here, or brought under any disappointments there. The Goods fit to take with them for use, or sell for profit, are all sorts of Apparel and Utensils for Husbandry and Building and Household Stuff. And because I know how much People are apt to fancy things beyond what they are, and that Immaginations are great flatterers of the minds of Men; To the end that none may delude themselves, with an expectation of an Immediate Amendment of their Conditions, so soon as it shall please God they Arrive there; I would have them understand, That they must look for a Winter before a Summer comes; and they must be willing to be two or three years without some of the conveniences they enjoy at home; And yet I must needs say that America is another thing then it was at the first Plantation of Virginia and New-England: For there is better Accommodation, and English Provisions are to be had at easier rates: However, I am inclin'd to set down particulars, as near as those inform me, that know the Place, and have been Planters both in that and in the Neighbouring Colonys.

1st. The passage will come for Masters and Mistresses at most to 6 Pounds a Head, for Servants Five Pounds a Head, and for Children under Seven years of Age Fifty Shillings, except they Suck, then nothing.

Next being by the mercy of God, safely Arrived in September or October, two Men may clear as much Ground by Spring (when they set the Corn of that Country) as will bring in that time twelve month Forty Barrels, which amounts to two Hundred Bushels, which makes Twenty Five quarters of Corn. So that the first year they must buy Corn, which is usually very plentiful. They may so soon as they come, buy Cows, more or less, as they want, or are able, which are to be had at easy rates. For Swine, they are plentiful and cheap; these will quickly Increase to a Stock. So that after the first year, what with the Poorer sort, sometimes labouring to others, and the more able Fishing, Fowling, and sometime Buying; They may do very well, till their own Stocks are sufficient to supply them, and their Families, which will quickly be and to spare, if they follow the English Husbandry, as they do in New-England, and New-York; and get Winter Fodder for their Stock.

VI. and Lastly, *An Abstract of the Patent granted by the king To William Penn, etc. The Fourth of March,* 168¼.

I. WE do Give and Grant (upon divers considerations) to William Penn his Heirs and Assigns for ever all that Tract of Land in America with all Islands thereunto belonging That is to say from the beginning of the fortieth degree of North Latitude unto the forty third Degree of North Latitude whose Eastern bounds from twelve English Miles above New Castle (alias Delaware Town) runs all along upon the side of Delaware River.

II. Free and undisturb'd use and passage into and out of all Harbours Bays Waters Rivers Isles and Inlets belonging to or leading to the same Together with the Soyl Fields Woods Underwoods Mountains Hills Fenns Isles Lakes Rivers Waters Rivulets Bays and Inlets Scituate in or belonging unto the Limits and Bounds aforesaid Together with all sorts of Fish Mines Mettles, etc. To have and to hold to the only behoof of the said William Penn his Heirs and Assigns for ever To be holden of us as of our Castle of Windsor in free and common soccage paying only two Beaver Skins yearly.

III. And of our further Grace we have thought it fit to erect and we do hereby erect the aforesaid Countrey and Islands into a Province and Seigniory and do call it Pennsilvania and so from henceforth we will have it call'd.

IV. That reposing special confidence in the wisdom and justice of the said William Penn we do grant to him and his Heirs and their Deputies for the good and happy Government thereof to ordain and enact and under his and their Seals to publish any Laws whatever for the publick uses of the said Province by and with the Advice and Approbation of the Free-holders of the said Countrey or their delegates so as they be not repugnant to the Law of this Realm and to the Faith and Allegiance due unto us by the legal Government thereof.

V. Full power to the said William Penn, etc., to appoint Judges Leiutenants Justices Magistrates and Officers for what causes so-ever and with what Power and in such Form as to him seems convenient Also to be able to Pardon and Abolish Crimes and Offences and to do all and every other thing that to the compleat Establishment of Justice unto Courts and Tribunals forms of Judicature and manner of proceedings do belong And our pleasure is and so we enjoyn and require that such Laws and Proceedings shall be most absolute and avuilable in Law and that all the Leige People of us Heirs and Successors inviolably keep the same in those parts saving to us final appeals.

VI. That the Laws for regulating Property as well for the discent of Lands as enjoyment of Goods and Chattels and likewise as to Felonies shall be the same there as here in England until they shall be altered by the said William Penn his Heirs or Assigns and by the Freemen of the said Province or their Delegates or Deputies or the greater part of them.

VII. Furthermore that this new Colony may the more happily encrease by the multitude of People resorting thither therefore we for us our Heirs and Successors do hereby grant License to all the leige People present and future of us, etc. (excepting such as shall be specially forbidden) to Transport themselves and Families into the said Countrey there to Inhabit and Plant for the publick and their private Good.

VIII. Liberty to Transport what Goods or Commodities are not forbidden paying here the legal Customs due to us, etc.

IX. Power to divide the Countrey into Counties Hundreds and Towns to Incorporate Towns and Burroughs and Burroughs into Cities to make Fairs and Markets with convenient Priviledges according to the merit of the Inhabitants or the fitness of the place And to do all other thing or things touching the Premises which to the said William Penn his Heirs or Assigns shall seem meet and requisite albeit they be such as of their own nature might otherwise require a more special commandment and warrant then in these presents is express'd.

X. Liberty to Import the Growth or Manufactures of that Province into England paying here the legal duty.

XI. Power to erect Posts Harbours Creeks Havens Keys and other places for Merchandizes with such Jurisdictions and Priviledges as to the said William Penn, etc., shall seem expedient.

XII. Not to break the Acts of Navigation neither Governour nor Inhabitants upon the penaltys contained in the said Acts.

XIII. Not to be in League with any Prince or Countrey that is in War against us our Heirs and Successors.

XIV. Power of safety and defence in such way and manner as to the said William Penn, etc., seems meet.

XV. Full power to Assign Alien Grant Demise or Enfeoff of the premises so many and such parts and parcels to those that are willing to purchase the same as the said William Penn thinks fit to have and to hold to them the said Persons their Heirs or Successors in fee Simple or fee Tail or for term of Life or Lives or years to be held of the said William Penn, etc., as of the said Seigniory of Windsor by such services Customs and Rents as shall seem fit to the said William Penn his Heirs and Assigns and not immediately of us our Heirs or Successors and that the said Persons may take the premisses or any Parcel thereof of the said William Penn, etc., and the same hold to themselves their Heirs and Assigns the Statute Quia emptores Terrarum in any wise notwithstanding.

XVI. We give and grant License to any of those Persons to whom the said William Penn, etc., has granted any Estate of Inheritance as aforesaid with the consent of the said William Penn to erect any parcel of Lands within the said Province into Mannors to hold Courts Barron and view of Franckepledge, etc., by Themselves or Stewards.

XVII. Power to those Persons to Grant to others the same Tenures in fee Simple or otherwise to be held of the said Mannors respectively and upon all further Alienations the Land to be held of the Mannor that it held of before the Alienation.

XVIII. We do covenant and Grant to and with the said William Penn his Heirs and Assigns that we will not set or make any Custom or other Taxation upon the Inhabitants of the said Province upon Lands Houses Goods Chattels or Merchandizes except with the consent of the Inhabitants and Governour.

XIX. A charge that no Officers nor Ministers of us our Heirs and Successors do presume at any time to attempt any thing to the contrary of the premisses or in any sort withstand the same but that they be at all times aiding to the said William Penn and his Heirs and to the Inhabitants and Merchants their Factors and Assigns in the full use and benefit of this our Charter.

XX. And if any doubts or questions shall hereafter arise about the true sense or meaning of any Word Clause or Sentence contained in this our Charter We will ordain and command that at all times and in all things such Interpretation be made thereof and allowed in any of our Courts whatsoever as shall be adjudged most advantageous and favourable unto the

said William Penn his Heirs and Assigns so as it be not against
the Faith and Allegiance due to us our Heirs and Successors.
In witness whereof we have caused our Letters to
be made Patents. Witness our self at Westminster, etc.

To conclude, I desire all my dear Country-Folks, who may
be inclin'd to go into those Parts, to consider seriously the premises, as well the present inconveniences, as future ease and
Plenty, that so none may move rashly or from a fickle but
solid mind, having above all things, an Eye to the providence
of God, in the disposal of themselves. And I would further
advise all such at least, to have the permission, if not the good
liking of their near Relations, for that is both Natural, and a
Duty Incumbent upon all; and by this means will natural
affection be preserved, and a friendly and profitable correspondence be maintained between them. In all which I beseech Almighty God to direct us, that his blessing may attend
our honest endeavour, and then the Consequence of all our
undertaking will turn to the Glory of his great Name, and the
true happiness of us and our Posterity. Amen.

WILLIAM PENN.

POSTSCRIPT.

Whoever are desirous to be concern'd with Me in this
Province, they may be treated with and further Satisfied, at
Philip Fords[1] in Bow-lane in Cheapside, and at Thomas Rud-
yards or Benjamin Clarks in George Yard in Lumbard-street.

THE END.

[1] Philip Ford, Penn's steward, who later brought the Founder into financial
difficulties.

LETTER FROM WILLIAM PENN TO THE COMMITTEE OF THE FREE SOCIETY OF TRADERS, 1683

INTRODUCTION

WILLIAM PENN had been an extraordinarily busy man in the two years prior to the writing of this *Letter* By July, 1681, his plans for the sale and settlement of his Pennsylvania lands, as foreshadowed in *Some Account,* having been more fully developed, were published on the 11th of that month under the caption *Conditions and Concessions.* With the issue of the latter document, which may be regarded as a form of contract between Penn and those who were to join in his enterprise, the sale of lands began. Journeying between the two great English cities of that day, London and Bristol, Penn, in the next three months, disposed of over 300,000 acres of unlocated lands in amounts of from 10,000 to 250 acres, to about 250 persons. These grantees, who were called First Purchasers, with special privileges as to the choice of allotment, were largely well-to-do Quakers of southern England. Two-thirds of the territory sold was about equally divided between purchasers in London and Bristol, the other third being taken chiefly in some of the intervening counties.

In October, 1681, the Proprietor sent over three commissioners to assist Governor Markham in the work of organizing the colony, especially with respect to the laying out of grants of land and to the choice of a site for the capital city. Along with the commissioners went Penn's advance-guard of immigrants, one group sailing from London in the ship *John and Sarah,* and the other from Bristol in the *Factor.*

The Free Society of Traders in Pennsylvania, the land and trading company, to which the present *Letter* is addressed, and of which great things were vainly expected, was incorporated

219

by Penn in March, 1682.   In the following month he sent over
the surveyor general, Thomas Holme, who laid out Philadelphia that summer.   The same month witnessed the completion
and signing of the elaborate Frame of Government, the famous first constitution of Pennsylvania, to which were appended certain laws agreed upon in England.

All these activities in the furtherance of the undertaking
delayed the Proprietor's visit to his new province.   He was
unable to depart until August, 1682.   At that time the roll
of First Purchasers, as kept in the London office, was closed;
more than 600,000 acres of land had thus far been sold.   Just
before sailing Penn once more prevailed upon his old friend
the Duke of York to make him another American grant, that
of the Three Lower Counties of Delaware.

It was on October 28, 1682, that William Penn first stepped
upon American soil.   On that day amidst the joyful acclama-
tions of the inhabitants he disembarked from the good ship
Welcome at New Castle and received turf, twig, and water,
symbols of his feudal possession of the country.   After devoting
several weeks to affairs at Upland (Chester), New Castle, and
his rapidly rising city of Philadelphia, he journeyed to New
York and paid his respects to the officials of government there.
From December 4 to 7 he sat with the first legislative assembly
at Chester.   A series of important measures known as the
Great Law, including the code of laws agreed upon in England,
and embodying Penn's ideas and principles, was enacted, thus
laying broadly and deeply the constitutional foundations of
the Province.   The boundaries between Pennsylvania and
Maryland, which were long to be a bone of contention, were the
subject of a conference between Penn and Lord Baltimore, in
Maryland, during the latter part of December, and again at
New Castle in the following May.   Early in March, 1683, as one
of the proprietors, Penn met for a few days with the council of
East New Jersey.   He then attended, in Philadelphia, the ses-

sions of the second assembly of Pennsylvania, and at the instance of that body issued a second Frame or Constitution, which lessened the number of representatives in the council and assembly.

Penn's first residence was at Chester, but with the development of the capital town he took up his abode in a house which had been especially erected for him there; he made occasional visits, however, to Pennsbury, a country-seat he was establishing on the shores of the Delaware in Bucks County.

The movement of population to Pennsylvania under Penn was truly remarkable; in no previous period had it reached such proportions. Beginning with the spring of 1682 a steady stream of immigration had set in. More than thirty ships bringing to the province several thousand settlers arrived in the next twelve months, so that in a little while the older inhabitants of Swedish and Dutch origin were far outnumbered. A fringe of settlement, in some instances reaching several miles into the interior, notably along the tributary rivers and creeks, now extended, at the date of this *Letter*, along the Delaware from Lewes to above the Falls. The majority of the newcomers were English Quakers; but an initial wedge of Welsh settlement, which in the general advance was destined in after years to cleave the English area of population in twain, had found lodgment west of the falls of the Schuylkill.

This *Letter*, which is in Penn's characteristic, descriptive style, is very properly regarded as the most important and interesting of his series of Pennsylvania pamphlets. He had but recently returned from a general tour of his dominions and he had also been much occupied for some months in treating with the Indians for their lands. He was thus fully informed by personal observation of the events and conditions which he here so faithfully and vividly chronicles.

The original draft of the *Letter* is still preserved in the collection of the Historical Society of Pennsylvania. This manu-

script is a folio of thirty pages, of which twenty-three pages
(pp. 3–24 and 29–30) are in the handwriting of Penn himself;
the first part (pp. 1–2) and the latter part (pp. 25–27) are in
two other hands. The *Letter* was published the same year in
which it was written, 1683, in London (a folio of ten pages),
apparently in two editions, since to one copy is appended a
list of property-owners in the city of Philadelphia, with numbers affixed to the names designating the lots on the accompanying plan of the city.[1] The next year, 1684, the *Letter* was published in three continental languages: in Dutch as *Missive van
William Penn*[2] (two editions), at Amsterdam; in German,[3]
as a translation of the latter, included in *Beschreibung der in
America neu-erfundenen Provinz Pensylvanien*, issued at Hamburg; and in French, as translated with the other pieces of
Beschreibung, under the title, *Recüeil de Diverses pieces concernant la Pensylvanie*,[4] printed at the Hague.

Reprints of the *Letter*—in some instances not in full—have
appeared in Richard Blome's *Present State of his Majesty's
Isles and Territories in America* (London, 1687), pp. 91–111;
the *Works of William Penn* (London editions, 1726, 1771,
1782, 1825); Edward Rack, *Caspipina's Letters* (Bath and
London, 1777), I. 154–209; Robert Proud's *History of Pennsylvania* (Philadelphia, 1797), I. 246–264; Thomas Clarkson's
Memoirs of William Penn (London, 1813), I. 375–406; Samuel
Hazard's *Register of Pennsylvania* (Philadelphia, 1828), I. 433–

[1] A copy of this plan may be seen in the New York Public Library.
[2] A contemporary manuscript copy in Dutch from the Könneken manuscripts of the Ministerial Archives at Lübeck, Germany, is reproduced in facsimile,
at pp. 10–19 of Julius F. Sachse's *Letters Relating to the Settlement of Germantown* (Philadelphia, 1903).
[3] Another early German translation in manuscript was found by Professor
Marion Dexter Learned, in 1909, in the Royal Privy Archives in Munich, and
printed by him in *German American Annals*, new series, VIII. 51–75, (March
and April, 1910); also by Emil Heuser in *Pennsylvanien im 17. Jahrhundert
und die ausgewanderten Pfälzer in England* (Neustadt a. H., 1910).
[4] See English translation by Samuel W. Pennypacker in *Pennsylvania
Magazine*, VI. 311–328 (1882).

437; Samuel M. Janney's *Life of William Penn* (Philadelphia, 1852), pp. 227–238; Thompson Westcott's *History of Philadelphia (Sunday Dispatch)* chapter xxv.; and *Old South Leaflets*, no. 171. A facsimile of the original English edition of 1683 was produced by James Coleman, of London, in 1881, and from this the text which follows is taken.

A. C. M.

LETTER FROM WILLIAM PENN TO THE COMMITTEE OF THE FREE SOCIETY OF TRADERS, 1683

A Letter from William Penn, Proprietary and Governour of Pennsylvania in America, to the Committee of the Free Society of Traders of that Province, residing in London.

Containing a General Description of the said Province, its Soil, Air, Water, Seasons and Produce, both Natural and Artificial, and the good Encrease thereof, of the Natives or Aborigines, their Language, Customs and Manners, Diet, Houses or Wigwams, Liberality, easie way of Living, Physick, Burial, Religion, Sacrifices and Cantico, Festivals, Government, and their order in Council upon Treaties for Land, etc., their Justice upon Evil Doers, of the first Planters, the Dutch, etc., and the present Condition and Settlement of the said Province, and Courts of Justice, etc.

To which is added, An Account of the City of Philadelphia, newly laid out, its Scituation between two Navigable Rivers, Delaware and Skulkill, with a Portraiture or Plat-form thereof, wherein the Purchasers Lots are distinguished by certain Numbers inserted, directing to a Catalogue of the said Purchasors Names, and the Prosperous and Advantagious Settlements of the Society aforesaid, within the said City and Country, etc.

Printed and Sold by Andrew Sowle,[1] *at the Crooked-Billet in Holloway-Lane in Shoreditch, and at several Stationers in London,* 1683.

[1] Andrew Sowle (1628–1695) was the Quaker printer and bookseller in London for the Friends of England. He had just removed in this year, 1683, to the above location from his old shop in Devonshire New Building, without Bishopsgate. Upon his retirement in 1691 his daughter, Tacie Sowle, carried on the business. Another daughter, Elizabeth, married her father's apprentice, William Bradford (1663–1752), who brought his wife over to Pennsylvania, and in 1685 established his printing-press in Philadelphia, the first in America south of New England and north of Mexico.

My Kind Friends;

The Kindness of yours by the Ship *Thomas and Anne*, doth much oblige me; for by it I perceive the Interest you take in my Health and Reputation, and the prosperous Beginnings of this Province, which you are so kind as to think may much depend upon them. In return of which, I have sent you a long Letter, and yet containing as brief an Account of My self, and the Affairs of this Province, as I have been able to make.

In the first place, I take notice of the News you sent me, whereby I find some Persons have had so little Wit, and so much Malice, as to report my Death, and to mend the matter, dead a Jesuit too. One might have reasonably hop'd, that this Distance, like Death, would have been a protection against Spite and Envy; and indeed, Absence being a kind of Death, ought alike to secure the Name of the Absent as the Dead; because they are equally unable as such to defend themselves: But they that intend Mischief, do not use to follow good Rules to effect it. However, to the great Sorrow and Shame of the Inventors, I am still Alive, and No Jesuit, and I thank God, very well: And without Injustice to the Authors of this, I may venture to infer, That they that wilfully and falsly Report, would have been glad it had been So. But I perceive, many frivolous and Idle Stories have been Invented since my Departure from England, which perhaps at this time are no more Alive, than I am Dead.

But if I have been Unkindly used by some I left behind me, I found Love and Respect enough where I came; an universal kind Welcome, every sort in their way. For here are some of several Nations, as well as divers Judgments: Nor were the Natives wanting in this, for their Kings, Queens and Great Men both visited and presented me; to whom I made suitable Returns, etc.

For the Province, the general Condition of it take as followeth.

I. The Country it self in its Soyl, Air, Water, Seasons and Produce both Natural and Artificial is not to be despised. The Land containeth divers sorts of Earth, as Sand Yellow and Black, Poor and Rich: also Gravel both Loomy and Dusty; and in some places a fast fat Earth, like to our best Vales in England, especially by Inland Brooks and Rivers, God in his Wisdom having ordered it so, that the Advantages of the Country are divided, the Back-Lands being generally three to one Richer than those that lie by Navigable Waters. We have much of another Soyl, and that is a black Hasel Mould, upon a Stony or Rocky bottom.

II. The Air is sweet and clear, the Heavens serene, like the South-parts of France, rarely Overcast; and as the Woods come by numbers of People to be more clear'd, that it self will Refine.

III. The Waters are generally good, for the Rivers and Brooks have mostly Gravel and Stony Bottoms, and in Number hardly credible. We have also Mineral Waters, that operate in the same manner with Barnet[1] and North-hall,[2] not two Miles from Philadelphia.

IV. For the Seasons of the Year, having by God's goodness now lived over the Coldest and Hottest, that the Oldest Liver in the Province can remember, I can say something to an English Understanding.

1st, Of the Fall, for then I came in: I found it from the 24th of October, to the beginning of December, as we have it usually in England in September, or rather like an English mild Spring. From December to the beginning of the Moneth called March, we had sharp Frosty Weather; not foul, thick, black Weather, as our North-East Winds bring with them in England; but a Skie as clear as in Summer, and the Air dry, cold, piercing and hungry; yet I remember not, that I wore more Clothes than in England. The reason of this Cold is given from the great Lakes that are fed by the Fountains of Canada. The Winter before was as mild, scarce any Ice at all; while this for a few dayes Froze up our great River Delaware. From that Moneth to the Moneth called June, we enjoy'd a sweet Spring, no Gusts, but gentle Showers, and a fine Skie. Yet this I observe, that the Winds here as there, are more Inconstant Spring and Fall, upon that turn of Nature, than in Summer or Winter. From thence to this present

---

[1] Chipping Barnet, or High Barnet, a town in Hertfordshire, eleven miles north of London, having on the town common a mineral spring, the water of which contains a considerable portion of calcareous glauber, with a small portion of sea salt.

[2] Northaw, in Hertfordshire, about four miles northeast of Chipping Barnet, has a fine saline spring, formerly much resorted to.

Moneth, which endeth the Summer (commonly speaking) we have had extraordinary Heats, yet mitigated sometimes by Cool Breezese. The Wind that ruleth the Summer-season, is the South-West; but Spring, Fall and Winter, 'tis rare to want the wholesome North Wester seven dayes together: And whatever Mists, Fogs or Vapours foul the Heavens by Easterly or Southerly Winds, in two Hours time are blown away; the one is alwayes followed by the other: A Remedy that seems to have a peculiar Providence in it to the Inhabitants; the multitude of Trees, yet standing, being liable to retain Mists and Vapours, and yet not one quarter so thick as I expected.

V. The Natural Produce of the Country, of Vegetables, is Trees, Fruits, Plants, Flowers. The Trees of most note are, the black Walnut, Cedar, Cyprus, Chestnut, Poplar, Gumwood, Hickery, Sassafrax, Ash, Beech and Oak of divers sorts, as Red, White and Black; Spanish Chestnut and Swamp, the most durable of all: of All which there is plenty for the use of man.

The Fruits that I find in the Woods, are the White and Black Mulbery, Chestnut, Wallnut, Plumbs, Strawberries, Cranberries, Hurtleberries and Grapes of divers sorts. The great Red Grape (now ripe) called by Ignorance, the Fox-Grape (because of the Relish it hath with unskilful Palates) is in it self an extraordinary Grape, and by Art doubtless may be Cultivated to an excellent Wine, if not so sweet, yet little inferior to the Frontimack, as it is not much unlike in taste, Ruddiness set aside, which in such things, as well as Mankind, differs the case much. There is a white kind of Muskedel, and a little black Grape, like the cluster-Grape of England, not yet so ripe as the other; but they tell me, when Ripe, sweeter, and that they only want skilful Vinerons to make good use of them: I intend to venture on it with my French man[1] this season, who shews some knowledge in those things. Here are also Peaches,

---

[1] Andrew Doz, Penn's French vigneron, with his wife Ann, were among the Huguenot exiles naturalized by royal letters patent at Westminster, London, March 8, 1682. They were brought over to Pennsylvania that same year, and he was placed in charge of Penn's vineyard, on the east bank of the Schuylkill, north of Fairmount, in the manor of Springettsbury, on what is now Lemon Hill, in Fairmount Park, Philadelphia. "Be regardfull to Andrew Doze the french man," writes Penn, in 1685, "he is hott, but I think honest and his wife a pretty

and very good, and in great quantities, not an Indian Plantation without them; but whether naturally here at first, I know not, however one may have them by Bushels for little; they make a pleasant Drink and I think not inferior to any Peach you have in England, except the true Newington. 'Tis disputable with me, whether it be best to fall to Fining the Fruits of the Country, especially the Grape, by the care and skill of Art, or send for forreign Stems and Sets, already good and approved. It seems most reasonable to believe, that not only a thing groweth best, where it naturally grows; but will hardly be equalled by another Species of the same kind, that doth not naturally grow there. But to solve the doubt, I intend, if God give me Life, to try both, and hope the consequence will be as good Wine as any European Countries of the same Latitude do yield.

VI. The Artificial Produce of the Country, is Wheat, Barley, Oats, Rye, Pease, Beans, Squashes, Pumkins, Water-Melons, Mus-Melons, and all Herbs and Roots that our Gardens in England usually bring forth.[1]

VII. Of living Creatures; Fish, Fowl, and the Beasts of the Woods, here are divers sorts, some for Food and Profit, and some for Profit only: For Food as well as Profit, the Elk,

woman in her disposition." The vineyard with 200 acres of land was patented to Doz in 1690, he paying the Proprietor 100 vine cuttings yearly on demand. His grandson, Andrew Doz, was a well-known citizen of Philadelphia. The Vineyard Hill was occupied from 1770 to 1798 by "The Hills," the country mansion of Robert Morris, the Financier of the American Revolution, and later by the Lemon Hill mansion which yet remains.

[1] "Note, that Edward Jones, Son-in-Law to Thomas Wynn, living on the Sckulkil, had with ordinary Cultivation, for one Grain of English Barley, seventy Stalks and Ears of Barley; And 'tis common in this Country from one Bushel sown, to reap forty, often fifty, and sometimes sixty. And three Pecks of Wheat sows an Acre here."

The above foot-note appears in the original text. Dr. Edward Jones (1645–1737), from near Bala, in Merionethshire, Wales, was one of the leaders of the first company of Welsh settlers, which, sailing from Liverpool in the ship *Lyon*, arrived in the Schuylkill River in August, 1682. Their settlements were made on a tract of 5,000 acres of land, stretching from the Falls of the Schuylkill westerly of Merion Meeting House (built 1695), in the present Lower Merion Township, Montgomery County. Dr. Thomas Wynne (died 1692), a native of Caerwys, Flintshire, Wales, came over to Pennsylvania in the ship *Welcome*, with William Penn, in 1682. He was speaker of the first provincial assembly held in Philadelphia.

as big as a small Ox, Deer bigger than ours, Beaver, Racoon, Rabbits, Squirrels, and some eat young Bear, and commend it. Of Fowl of the Land, there is the Turkey (Forty and Fifty Pound weight) which is very great; Phesants, Heath-Birds, Pidgeons and Partridges in abundance. Of the Water, the Swan, Goose, white and gray, Brands, Ducks, Teal, also the Snipe and Curloe, and that in great Numbers; but the Duck and Teal excel, nor so good have I ever eat in other Countries. Of Fish, there is the Sturgeon, Herring, Rock, Shad, Catshead, Sheepshead, Ele, Smelt, Pearch, Roach; and in Inland Rivers, Trout, some say Salmon, above the Falls. Of Shelfish, we have Oysters, Crabbs, Cockles, Concks, and Mushels; some Oysters six Inches long, and one sort of Cockles as big as the Stewing Oysters, they make a rich Broth. The Creatures for Profit only by Skin or Fur, and that are natural to these parts, are the Wild Cat, Panther, Otter, Wolf, Fox, Fisher, Minx, Musk-Rat; and of the Water, the Whale for Oyl, of which we have good store, and two Companies of Whalers, whose Boats are built, will soon begin their Work,[1] which hath the appearance of a considerable Improvement. To say nothing of our reasonable Hopes of good Cod in the Bay.

VIII. We have no want of Horses, and some are very good and shapely enough; two Ships have been freighted to Barbadoes with Horses and Pipe-Staves, since my coming in. Here is also Plenty of Cow-Cattle, and some Sheep; the People Plow mostly with Oxen.

IX. There are divers Plants that not only the Indians tell us, but we have had occasion to prove by Swellings, Burnings, Cuts, etc., that they are of great Virtue, suddenly curing the Patient: and for smell, I have observed several, especially one, the wild Mirtle; the other I know not what to call, but are most fragrant.

X. The Woods are adorned with lovely Flowers, for colour, greatness, figure, and variety: I have seen the Gardens of London best stored with that sort of Beauty, but think they may be improved by our Woods: I have sent a few to a Person of Quality this Year for a tryal.

Thus much of the Country, next of the Natives or Aborigines.

---

[1] The whaling activity centred about the entrance to Delaware Bay.

XI. The *Natives* I shall consider in their Persons, Language, Manners, Religion and Government, with my sence of their Original. For their Persons, they are generally tall, streight, well-built, and of singular Proportion; they tread strong and clever, and mostly walk with a lofty Chin: Of Complexion, Black, but by design, as the Gypsies in England: They grease themselves with Bears-fat clarified, and using no defence against Sun or Weather, their skins must needs be swarthy; Their Eye is little and black, not unlike a straight-look't Jew: The thick Lip and flat Nose, so frequent with the East-Indians and Blacks, are not common to them; for I have seen as comely European-like faces among them of both, as on your side the Sea; and truly an Italian Complexion hath not much more of the White, and the Noses of several of them have as much of the Roman.

XII. Their Language is lofty, yet narrow, but like the Hebrew; in Signification full, like Short-hand in writing; one word serveth in the place of three, and the rest are supplied by the Understanding of the Hearer: Imperfect in their Tenses, wanting in their Moods, Participles, Adverbs, Conjunctions, Interjections: I have made it my business to understand it, that I might not want an Interpreter on any occasion: And I must say, that I know not a Language spoken in Europe, that hath words of more sweetness or greatness, in Accent and Emphasis, than theirs; for Instance, *Octorockon,*[1] *Rancocas,*[2] *Ozicton,*[3] *Shakamacon,*[4] *Poquerim,* all of which are names of Places, and have Grandeur in them: Of words of Sweetness, *Anna,* is Mother, *Issimus,* a Brother, *Netap,* Friend, *usque ozet,* very good; *pone,* Bread, *metse,* eat, *matta,* no, *hatta,* to have, *payo,* to come; *Sepassen,*[5] *Passijon,* the Names of Places;

---

[1] Doubtless Octorara Creek, an eastern affluent of the Susquehanna.

[2] Rancocas Creek, in Burlington County, New Jersey.

[3] Oricton, in Penn's handwriting in the original manuscript, *i. e.*, Orectons, now Biles Island, was near to the Falls of Delaware, and to Penn's country-seat, Pennsbury, in Bucks County.

[4] Shackamaxon, now in Kensington, Philadelphia, where Penn lived in the house of Thomas Fairman, early in 1683, and where he is said to have held treaties with the Indians.

[5] Sepassing Land was the name applied to that part of what is now Bucks County which included Penn's manor and country-seat of Pennsbury.

Tamane,[1] *Secane,*[2] *Menanse, Secatereus,*[3] are the names of Persons. If one ask them for anything they have not, they will answer, *mattá ne hattá,* which to translate is, not I have, instead of I have not.

XIII. Of their Customs and Manners there is much to be said; I will begin with Children. So soon as they are born, they wash them in Water, and while very young, and in cold Weather to chuse, they Plunge them in the Rivers to harden and embolden them. Having wrapt them in a Clout, they lay them on a straight thin Board, a little more than the length and breadth of the Child, and swadle it fast upon the Board to make it straight; wherefore all Indians have flat Heads; and thus they carry them at their Backs. The Children will go very young, at nine Moneths commonly; they wear only a small Clout round their Waste, till they are big; if Boys, they go a Fishing till ripe for the Woods, which is about Fifteen; then they Hunt, and after having given some Proofs of their Manhood, by a good return of Skins, they may Marry, else it is a shame to think of a Wife. The Girls stay with their Mothers, and help to hoe the Ground, plant Corn and carry Burthens; and they do well to use them to that Young, they must do when they are Old; for the Wives are the true Servants of their Husbands: otherwise the Men are very affectionate to them.

XIV. When the Young Women are fit for Marriage, they wear something upon their Heads for an Advertisement, but so as their Faces are hardly to be seen, but when they please: The Age they Marry at, if Women, is about thirteen and fourteen; if Men, seventeen and eighteen; they are rarely elder.

[1] Tamany is the form in the original manuscript draft of the *Letter* in Penn's own handwriting, but other variations, as appearing in Indian deeds and official documents for the period, 1683–1697, are Tamene, Tamine, Tamina, Tamanee, Tamanen, Tamanend, and Taminent. During the above period, to which his authentic history is confined, he was one of the leading chiefs of the Lenni Lenape for the region of Bucks County, Pennsylvania.

[2] Siccane, the form in Penn's hand in the original draft of the *Letter,* but usually Secane. He was one of the two chiefs granting the region between Schuylkill River and Chester Creek to Penn in 1683. In 1685 Penn writes that he sends a cap as a present for "Shikane."

[3] Secatareus, in the original manuscript draft of the *Letter,* in Penn's hand. To "Secetareus," Penn was sending a cap as a present in 1685.

XV. Their Houses are Mats, or Barks of Trees set on Poles, in the fashion of an English Barn, but out of the power of the Winds, for they are hardly higher than a Man; they lie on Reeds or Grass. In Travel they lodge in the Woods about a great Fire, with the Mantle of Duffills they wear by day, wrapt about them, and a few Boughs stuck round them.

XVI. Their Diet is Maze, or Indian Corn, divers ways prepared: sometimes Roasted in the Ashes, sometimes beaten and Boyled with Water, which they call *Homine*; they also make Cakes, not unpleasant to eat: They have likewise several sorts of Beans and Pease that are good Nourishment; and the Woods and Rivers are their Larder.

XVII. If an European comes to see them, or calls for Lodging at their House or *Wigwam* they give him the best place and first cut. If they come to visit us, they salute us with an *Itah* which is as much as to say, Good be to you, and set them down, which is mostly on the Ground close to their Heels, their Legs upright; may be they speak not a word more, but observe all Passages: If you give them any thing to eat or drink, well, for they will not ask; and be it little or much, if it be with Kindness, they are well pleased, else they go away sullen, but say nothing.

XVIII. They are great Concealers of their own Resentments, brought to it, I believe, by the Revenge that hath been practised among them; in either of these, they are not exceeded by the Italians. A Tragical Instance fell out since I came into the Country; A King's Daughter thinking her self slighted by her Husband, in suffering another Woman to lie down between them, rose up, went out, pluck't a Root out of the Ground, and ate it, upon which she immediately dyed; and for which, last Week he made an Offering to her Kindred for Attonement and liberty of Marriage; as two others did to the Kindred of their Wives, that dyed a natural Death: For till Widdowers have done so, they must not marry again. Some of the young Women are said to take undue liberty before Marriage for a Portion; but when marryed, chaste; when with Child, they know their Husbands no more, till delivered; and during their Moneth, they touch no Meat, they eat, but with a Stick, least they should defile it; nor do their Husbands frequent them, till that time be expired.

XIX. But in Liberality they excell, nothing is too good for their friend; give them a fine Gun, Coat, or other thing, it may pass twenty hands, before it sticks; light of Heart, strong Affections, but soon spent; the most merry Creatures that live, Feast and Dance perpetually; they never have much, nor want much: Wealth circulateth like the Blood, all parts partake; and though none shall want what another hath, yet exact Observers of Property. Some Kings have sold, others presented me with several parcels of Land; the Pay or Presents I made them, were not hoarded by the particular Owners, but the neighbouring Kings and their Clans being present when the Goods were brought out, the Parties chiefly concerned consulted, what and to whom they should give them? To every King then, by the hands of a Person for that work appointed, is a proportion sent, so sorted and folded, and with that Gravity, that is admirable. Then that King sub-divideth it in like manner among his Dependents, they hardly leaving themselves an Equal share with one of their Subjects: and be it on such occasions, at Festivals, or at their common Meals, the Kings distribute, and to themselves last. They care for little, because they want but little; and the Reason is, a little contents them: In this they are sufficiently revenged on us; if they are ignorant of our Pleasures, they are also free from our Pains. They are not disquieted with Bills of Lading and Exchange, nor perplexed with Chancery-Suits and Exchequer-Reckonings. We sweat and toil to live; their pleasure feeds them, I mean, their Hunting, Fishing and Fowling, and this Table is spread every where; they eat twice a day, Morning and Evening; their Seats and Table are the Ground. Since the European came into these parts, they are grown great lovers of strong Liquors, Rum especially, and for it exchange the richest of their Skins and Furs: If they are heated with Liquors, they are restless till they have enough to sleep; that is their cry, Some more, and I will go to sleep; but when Drunk, one of the most wretchedst Spectacles in the world.

XX. In sickness impatient to be cured, and for it give any thing, especially for their Children, to whom they are extreamly natural; they drink at those times a *Teran* or Decoction of some Roots in spring Water; and if they eat any flesh, it must be of the Female of any Creature; If they dye, they bury them

with their Apparel, be they Men or Women, and the nearest
of Kin fling in something precious with them, as a token of their
Love: Their Mourning is blacking of their faces, which they
continue for a year; They are choice of the Graves of their
Dead; for least they should be lost by time, and fall to common use, they pick off the Grass that grows upon them, and
heap up the fallen Earth with great care and exactness.

XXI. These poor People are under a dark Night in things
relating to Religion, to be sure, the Tradition of it; yet they
believe a God and Immortality, without the help of Meta-
physicks; for they say, There is a great King that made them,
who dwells in a glorious Country to the Southward of them,
and that the Souls of the good shall go thither, where they shall
live again. Their Worship consists of two parts, Sacrifice and
Cantico. Their Sacrifice is their first Fruits; the first and
fattest Buck they kill, goeth to the fire, where he is all burnt
with a Mournful Ditty of him that performeth the Ceremony,
but with such marvellous Fervency and Labour of Body, that
he will even sweat to a foam. The other part is their *Cantico*,
performed by round-Dances, sometimes Words, sometimes
Songs, then Shouts, two being in the middle that begin, and
by Singing and Drumming on a Board direct the Chorus:
Their Postures in the Dance are very Antick and differing,
but all keep measure. This is done with equal Earnestness and
Labour, but great appearance of Joy. In the Fall, when the
Corn cometh in, they begin to feast one another; there have
been two great Festivals already, to which all come that will:
I was at one my self; their Entertainment was a green Seat
by a Spring, under some shady Trees, and twenty Bucks, with
hot Cakes of new Corn, both Wheat and Beans, which they
make up in a square form, in the leaves of the Stem, and bake
them in the Ashes: And after that they fell to Dance, But
they that go, must carry a small Present in their Money, it
may be six Pence, which is made of the Bone of a Fish; the
black is with them as Gold, the white, Silver; they call it all
Wampum.

XXII. Their Government is by Kings, which they call
Sachema, and those by Succession, but always of the Mothers
side; for Instance, the Children of him that is now King, will
not succeed, but his Brother by the Mother, or the Children

of his Sister, whose Sons (and after them the Children of her Daughters) will reign; for no Woman inherits; the Reason they render for this way of Descent, is, that their Issue may not be spurious.

XXIII. Every King hath his Council, and that consists of all the Old and Wise men of his Nation, which perhaps is two hundred People: nothing of Moment is undertaken, be it War, Peace, Selling of Land or Traffick, without advising with them; and which is more, with the Young Men too. 'Tis admirable to consider, how Powerful the Kings are, and yet how they move by the Breath of their People. I have had occasion to be in Council with them upon Treaties for Land, and to adjust the terms of Trade; their Order is thus: The King sits in the middle of an half Moon, and hath his Council, the Old and Wise on each hand; behind them, or at a little distance, sit the younger Fry, in the same figure. Having consulted and resolved their business, the King ordered one of them to speak to me; he stood up, came to me, and in the Name of his King saluted me, then took me by the hand, and told me, That he was ordered by his King to speak to me, and that now it was not he, but the King that spoke, because what he should say, was the King's mind. He first pray'd me, To excuse them that they had not complyed with me the last time; he feared, there might be some fault in the Interpreter, being neither Indian nor English; besides, it was the Indian Custom to deliberate, and take up much time in Council, before they resolve; and that if the Young People and Owners of the Land had been as ready as he, I had not met with so much delay. Having thus introduced his matter, he fell to the Bounds of the Land they had agreed to dispose of, and the Price, (which now is little and dear, that which would have bought twenty Miles, not buying now two.) During the time that this Person spoke, not a man of them was observed to whisper or smile; the Old, Grave, the Young, Reverend in their Deportment; they do speak little, but fervently, and with Elegancy: I have never seen more natural Sagacity, considering them without the help, (I was agoing to say, the spoil) of Tradition; and he will deserve the Name of Wise, that Outwits them in any Treaty about a thing they understand. When the Purchase was agreed, great Promises past between us of Kindness and good Neighbourhood, and that the Indians and English must live in Love, as long as the Sun gave light. Which done, another made a Speech to the Indians, in the Name of all the *Sachamakers* or Kings, first to tell them what was done; next, to charge and command them, To Love the Christians, and particularly live in Peace with me, and the People under my Government: That many Governours had been in the River, but that no Governour had come himself to live and stay here before; and having now such a one that had treated them well, they should never do him or his any wrong. At every sentence of which they shouted, and said, Amen, in their way.

XXIV. The Justice they have is Pecuniary: In case of any Wrong or evil Fact, be it Murther it self, they Attone by Feasts and Presents of their *Wampon*, which is proportioned to the quality of the Offence or Person injured, or of the Sex they are of: for in case they kill a Woman, they pay double, and the Reason they render, is, That she breedeth Children, which Men cannot do. 'Tis rare that they fall out, if Sober; and if Drunk, they forgive it, saying, It was the Drink, and not the Man, that abused them.

XXV. We have agreed, that in all Differences between us, Six of each side shall end the matter: Don't abuse them, but let them have Justice, and you win them: The worst is, that they are the worse for the Christians, who have propagated their Vices, and yielded them Tradition for ill, and not for good things. But as low an Ebb as they are at, and as glorious as their Condition looks, the Christians have not out-liv'd their sight with all their Pretensions to an higher Manifestation: What good then might not a good People graft, where there is so distinct a Knowledge left between Good and Evil? I beseech God to incline the Hearts of all that come into these parts, to out-live the Knowledge of the Natives, by a fixt Obedience to their greater Knowledge of the Will of God, for it were miserable indeed for us to fall under the just censure of the poor Indian Conscience, while we make profession of things so far transcending.

XXVI. For their Original, I am ready to believe them of the Jewish Race, I mean, of the stock of the Ten Tribes, and that for the following Reasons; first, They were to go to a

Land not planted or known, which to be sure Asia and Africa were, if not Europe; and he that intended that extraordinary Judgment upon them, might make the Passage not uneasie to them, as it is not impossible in it self, from the Easter-most parts of Asia, to the Wester-most of America. In the next place, I find them of like Countenance and their Children of so lively Resemblance, that a man would think himself in Dukes-place[1] or Berry-street[1] in London, when he seeth them. But this is not all, they agree in Rites, they reckon by Moons: they offer their first Fruits, they have a kind of Feast of Tabernacles; they are said to lay their Altar upon twelve Stones; their Mourning a year, Customs of Women, with many things that do not now occur.

So much for the Natives, next the Old Planters will be considered in this Relation, before I come to our Colony, and the Concerns of it.

XXVII. The first Planters in these parts were the Dutch, and soon after them the Sweeds and Finns. The Dutch applied themselves to Traffick, the Sweeds and Finns to Husbandry. There were some Disputes between them some years, the Dutch looking upon them as Intruders upon their Purchase and Possession, which was finally ended in the Surrender made by John Rizeing, the Sweeds Governour, to Peter Styvesant, Governour for the States of Holland, *Anno* 1655.

XXVIII. The Dutch inhabit mostly those parts of the Province, that lie upon or near to the Bay, and the Sweeds the Freshes of the River Delaware. There is no need of giving any Description of them, who are better known there then here; but they are a plain, strong, industrious People, yet have made no great progress in Culture or propagation of fruit-Trees, as if they desired rather to have enough, than Plenty or Traffick. But I presume, the Indians made them the more careless, by furnishing them with the means of Profit, to wit, Skins and Furs, for Rum, and such strong Liquors. They kindly received me, as well as the English, who were few, before the People concerned with me came among them; I must needs commend their Respect to Authority, and kind Behaviour to the English; they do not degenerate from the Old friendship between both Kingdoms. As they are People

---

[1] Then as now these streets were in the centre of a Jewish quarter.

proper and strong of Body, so they have fine Children, and almost every house full; rare to find one of them without three or four Boys, and as many Girls; some six, seven and eight Sons: And I must do them that right, I see few Young men more sober and laborious.

XXIX. The Dutch have a Meeting-place for Religious Worship at New Castle, and the Sweedes three, one at Christina, one at Tenecum,[1] and one at Wicoco, within half a Mile of this Town.

XXX. There rests, that I speak of the Condition we are in, and what Settlement we have made, in which I will be as short as I can; for I fear, and not without reason, that I have tryed your Patience with this long Story. The Country lieth bounded on the East, by the River and Bay of Delaware, and Eastern Sea; it hath the Advantage of many Creeks or Rivers rather, that run into the main River or Bay; some Navigable for great Ships, some for small Craft: Those of most Eminency are Christina, Brandywine, Skilpot,[2] and Skulkill; any one of which have room to lay up the Royal Navy of England, there being from four to eight Fathom Water.

XXXI. The lesser Creeks or Rivers, yet convenient for Sloops and Ketches of good Burthen, are Lewis, Mespilion,[3] Cedar, Dover,[4] Cranbrook,[5] Feversham,[6] and Georges,[7] below, and Chichester,[8] Chester, Toacawny,[9] Pemmapecka, Portquessin, Neshimenck and Pennberry in the Freshes; many lesser that admit Boats and Shallops. Our People are mostly settled upon the upper Rivers, which are pleasant and sweet, and generally bounded with good Land. The Planted part of the Province and Territories is cast into six Counties, Philadelphia, Buckingham,[10] Chester, New Castle, Kent and Sussex,

---

[1] Tinicum Island. Wicaco was the Swedish settlement, at what is now **Front** Street and Washington Avenue, Philadelphia.

[2] Shelpot Creek.   [3] Mispillion Creek.   [4] Now Murderkill Creek.

[5] Now St. Jones Creek, in Kent County, Delaware.

[6] Not definitely identified, but probably between St. Jones and St. Georges Creek, in Kent County, Delaware. Feversham is a place-name in the county of Kent, England, not far from Penn's home in Sussex.

[7] St. Georges Creek.   [8] Now Marcus Creek.

[9] Tacony Creek, Philadelphia County. The next three are Pennypack, Poquessing, and Neshaminy Creeks, respectively.

[10] Bucks County.

containing about Four Thousand Souls. Two General Assemblies have been held, and with such Concord and Dispatch, that they sate but three Weeks, and at least seventy Laws were past without one Dissent in any material thing. But of this more hereafter, being yet Raw and New in our Geer: However, I cannot forget their singular Respect to me in this Infancy of things, who by their own private Expences so early consider'd Mine for the Publick, as to present me with an Impost upon certain Goods Imported and Exported: Which after my Acknowledgements of their Affection, I did as freely Remit to the Province and the Traders to it. And for the well Government of the said Counties, Courts of Justice are establisht in every County, with proper Officers, as Justices, Sheriffs, Clarks, Constables, etc., which Courts are held every two Moneths: But to prevent Law-Suits, there are three Peace-makers chosen by every County-Court, in the nature of common Arbitrators, to hear and end Differences betwixt man and man; and Spring and Fall there is an Orphan's Court in each County, to inspect, and regulate the Affairs of Orphans and Widdows.

XXXII. Philadelphia, the Expectation of those that are concern'd in this Province, is at last laid out to the great Content of those here, that are any wayes Interested therein; The Scituation is a Neck of Land, and lieth between two Navigable Rivers, Delaware and Skulkill, whereby it hath two Fronts upon the Water, each a Mile, and two from River to River. Delaware is a glorious River, but the Skulkill being an hundred Miles Boatable above the Falls, and its Course North-East toward the Fountain of Susquahannah (that tends to the Heart of the Province, and both sides our own) it is like to be a great part of the Settlement of this Age. I say little of the Town it self, because a *Plat-form*[1] will be shewn you by my Agent, in which those who are Purchasers of me, will find their Names and Interests: But this I will say for the good Providence of God, that of all the many Places I have seen in the World, I remember not one better seated; so that it seems to me to have been appointed for a Town, whether we regard the Rivers, or the conveniency of the Coves, Docks, Springs, the

---

[1] The map or plan of Philadelphia made by the surveyor general Thomas Holme, in 1683, and first published the same year at the end of this pamphlet, as *A Portraiture of the City of Philadelphia.*

loftiness and soundness of the Land and the Air, held by the People of these parts to be very good.   It is advanced within less than a Year to about four Score Houses and Cottages, such as they are, where Merchants and Handicrafts, are following their Vocations as fast as they can, while the Country-men are close at their Farms; Some of them got a little Winter-Corn in the Ground last Season, and the generality have had a handsom Summer-Crop, and are preparing for their Winter-Corn.   They reaped their Barley this Year in the Moneth called May; the Wheat in the Moneth following; so that there is time in these parts for another Crop of divers Things before the Winter-Season.   We are daily in hopes of Shipping to add to our Number; for blessed be God, here is both Room and Accommodation for them; the Stories of our Necessity being either the Fear of our Friends, or the Scare-Crows of our Enemies; for the greatest hardship we have suffered, hath been Salt-Meat, which by Fowl in Winter, and Fish in Summer, together with some Poultery, Lamb, Mutton, Veal, and plenty of Venison the best part of the year, hath been made very passable.   I bless God, I am fully satisfied with the Country and Entertainment I can get in it; for I find that particular Content which hath alwayes attended me, where God in his Providence hath made it my place and service to reside.   You cannot imagin, my Station can be at present free of more than ordinary business, and as such, I may say, It is a troublesom Work; but the Method things are putting in, will facilitate the Charge, and give an easier Motion to the Administration of Affairs. However, as it is some mens Duty to plow, some to sow, some to water, and some to reap; so it is the Wisdom as well as Duty of a man, to yield to the mind of Providence, and chearfully, as well as carefully imbrace and follow the Guidance of it.

XXXIII. For your particular Concern, I might entirely refer you to the Letters of the President of the Society;[1] but

---

[1] The Free Society of Traders in Pennsylvania, a joint stock company, which had been planned and discussed in London throughout the year 1681, and of which great results were expected, received a liberal charter from Penn in March, 1682. Over two hundred persons in the British Isles, largely from among those most interested in the new colony, became subscribers to the stock, which had reached £10,000 in June, 1682. A purchase of 20,000 acres of land in the province was made. The first officers were Dr. Nicholas More, of London.

this I will venture to say, Your Provincial Settlements both within and without the Town, for Scituation and Soil, are without Exception; Your City-Lot is an whole Street, and one side of a Street, from River to River, containing near one hundred Acers, not easily valued, which is besides your four hundred Acers in the City Liberties, part of your twenty thousand Acers in the Countery.   Your Tannery hath such plenty of Bark, the Saw-Mill for Timber, the place of the Glass-house so conveniently posted for Water-carriage, the City-Lot for a Dock, and the Whalery[1] for a sound and fruitful Bank, and the Town Lewis by it to help your People, that by Gods blessing the Affairs of the Society will naturally grow in their Reputation and Profit.   I am sure I have not turned my back upon any Offer that tended to its Prosperity; and though I am ill at Projects, I have sometimes put in for a Share with her Officers, to countenance and advance her Interest.   You are already informed what is fit for you further to do, whatsoever tends to the Promotion of Wine, and to the Manufacture of Linnen in these parts, I cannot but wish you to promote it; and the French People are most likely in both respects to answer that design: To that end, I would advise you to send for some

president, at a salary of £150 per annum, John Simcock, of Cheshire, deputy, and James Claypoole, of London, treasurer, the latter two at £100 per annum. These officers removed to Pennsylvania, the president with about fifty servants of the society arriving at Philadelphia in the ship *Geoffrey* in October, 1682. The principal trading house and offices were erected on the Society tract in the infant city, on the west side of Front Street—the main street—near the south side of Dock Creek, and at the foot of Society Hill, so named from the location of the company.   Thence the society's city tract of about one hundred acres extended westerly in a tier of lots from Front Street on the Delaware to the Schuylkill, flanked by Spruce Street on the north and Pine Street on the south.   This main station was the centre for the various activities of the society.   From here whalers went fishing for whales to the entrance of Delaware Bay, preparing their oil and whalebone on the shore near Lewes.   At Frankford a grist-mill and a saw-mill on Tacony Creek, a tannery, brick kilns, and glass-works were conducted.   Cargoes of English goods were brought in and sold at a profit, but collections being difficult, and the officers tending to look after their private affairs to the detriment of those of the society, it suffered severe losses, and in a few years practically went out of business except as an owner of real estate.

[1] "Advise what commodity whale oyl may be with you [in Barbados] for we [the Free Society of Traders] have 24 men fishing in the [Delaware] bay that are like to make a good Voyage."   James Claypool's letter, dated Philadelphia, 10 Mo (December) 2, 1683.

Thousands of Plants out of France, with some able Vinerons, and People of the other Vocation: But because I believe you have been entertained with this and some other profitable Subjects by your President, I shall add no more, but to assure you, that I am heartily inclined to advance your just Interest, and that you will always find me

Your Kind Cordial Friend,

WILLIAM PENN.

Philadelphia, the 16th of the
    6th Moneth, call'd August,
    1683.

A Short Advertisement upon the Scituation and Extent of the City of Philadelphia and the Ensuing Plat-form thereof, by the Surveyor General.[1]

The City of Philadelphia, now extends in Length, from River to River, two Miles, and in Breadth near a Mile; and the Governour, as a further manifestation of his Kindness to the Purchasers, hath freely given them their respective Lots in the City, without defalcation of any their Quantities of purchased Lands; and as its now placed and modelled between two Navigable Rivers upon a Neck of Land, and that Ships may ride in good Anchorage, in six or eight Fathom Water in both Rivers, close to the City, and the Land of the City level, dry and wholsom: such a Scituation is scarce to be parallel'd.

The Model of the City appears by a small Draught now made, and may hereafter, when time permits, be augmented;

---

[1] Captain Thomas Holme (1624–1695), the first surveyor general of Pennsylvania, probably of a gentle Yorkshire family of the name, apparently went over from England to Ireland in Cromwell's army, and by 1655 was living in Limerick. Later he removed to Waterford. By 1657 he had become a Quaker, and subsequently was fined and imprisoned. He was a First Purchaser of 5,000 acres of land in Pennsylvania, and a subscriber to £50 of stock of the Free Society of Traders. Early in 1682, with his commission as surveyor general, he came over to Pennsylvania with his family in the *Amity*, and laid out country lands and the city of Philadelphia, the latter as exhibited in the *Plat-Form* here referred to, published in 1683. By 1686 he had gathered connected surveys of the lands as granted, and compiled an important map of the province, which was sent to London and printed in 1687. He was a member of the first assembly, and of the provincial council.

and because there is not room to express the Purchasers **Names** in the Draught, I have therefore drawn Directions of Reference, by way of Numbers, whereby may be known each mans **Lot** and Place in the City.

The City is so ordered now, by the Governour's Care and Prudence, that it hath a Front to each River, one half at Dela- ware, the other at Skulkill; and though all this cannot make way for small Purchasers to be in the Fronts, yet they are placed in the next Streets, contiguous to each Front, *viz.* all Purchasers of One Thousand Acres, and upwards, have the Fronts, (and the High-street) and to every five Thousand Acres Purchase, in the Front about an Acre, and the smaller Purchasers about half an Acre in the backward Streets; by which means the least hath room enough for House, Garden and small Orchard, to the great Content and Satisfaction of all here concerned.

The City, (as the Model shews) consists of a large Front- street to each River, and a High-street (near the middle) from Front (or River) to Front, of one hundred Foot broad, and a Broad-street in the middle of the City, from side to side, of the like breadth. In the Center of the City is a Square of ten Acres; at each Angle are to be Houses for publick Affairs, as a Meeting-House, Assembly or State-House, Market-House, School-House, and several other Buildings for Publick Con- cerns. There are also in each Quarter of the City a Square of eight Acres, to be for the like Uses, as the Moore-fields[1] in London; and eight Streets, (besides the High-street, that run from Front to Front, and twenty Streets, (besides the Broad- street) that run cross the City, from side to side; all these Streets are of fifty Foot breadth.

In each Number in the Draught, in the Fronts and High- street, are placed the Purchasers of One Thousand Acres, and upwards, to make up five Thousand Acres Lot, both in the said Fronts and High-street) and the Numbers direct to each Lot, and where in the City; so that thereby they may know where their Concerns are therein.

---

[1] Moorfields, a moor or fen without the walls of the old city of London to the north. It was first drained in 1527, laid out into walks in 1606, and first built upon late in the reign of Charles II. The name has now been lost in **Finsbury** Square and adjoining localities.

The Front Lots begin at the South-ends of the Fronts, by the Numbers, and so reach to the North-ends, and end at Number 43.

The High-street Lots begin towards the Fronts, at Number 44, and so reach to the Center.

The lesser Purchasers begin at Number 1, in the second Streets, and so proceed by the Numbers, as in the Draught; the biggest of them being first placed, nearest to the Fronts.

LETTER OF THOMAS PASCHALL, 1683

INTRODUCTION

A BRISTOL pewterer, Thomas Paschall, is the author of this *Letter*. He came over to Pennsylvania as a settler in the summer of 1682 and writes from Philadelphia several months after his arrival. Paschall was a native of Bristol, having been baptized in the great church of St. Mary Redcliffe in 1634. His father William Paschall (*c.* 1608–1670) was also a pewterer by trade and to him the son in 1652, at the age of eighteen, was apprenticed for a term of seven years. In 1661 Thomas Paschall was admitted a freeman of the city, and there he followed his occupation until the time of his migration to America. His account book, containing a number of business transactions in Bristol, along with his copy of *Agricola on Metals*, is still preserved by Philadelphia descendants.[1] Before 1665 he was married to Joanna Sloper, by whom he had at least seven children, as mentioned in the city registers from 1668 to 1682. On May 4 of the latter year his son of the same name was apprenticed to him in Bristol, and on the 22nd of that month the father purchased from William Penn 500 acres of land, to be located in Pennsylvania. Soon after this date Thomas Paschall with his family embarked, probably at the port of Bristol, for the New World, reaching Philadelphia somewhat before early September, 1682.

His land was laid out to him about five miles from the infant town of Philadelphia and west of the Schuylkill River, within the county of Philadelphia, near the present Delaware County line; his land warrant was issued by Governor Mark-

The family of the late Israel W. Morris, of South Eighth Street.

ham, September 13, 1682. What are now Angora and Mount Moriah Cemetery mark respectively its approximate northern and southern limits. He lodged his family in a rented dwelling for the first winter but erected a small house on his land for his servants. About six acres of his purchase, he informs us, were cleared at the time of his writing. His house with its single chimney at one end is depicted on a survey of 1684 as about one and a quarter miles from the Schuylkill, between Mill or Cobbs Creek and its branch Ameaseka Run. It was in the old Blockley Township. Paschallville, which is a little to the south of the site, commemorates the family name. Peter Yocum and other Swedish neighbors lived between Paschall and the river, and it is from them doubtless that he generalizes as to the Swedes.

Thomas Paschall was elected to the provincial assembly of Pennsylvania from Philadelphia County, in 1685 and in 1689. Within a few years after his arrival he had taken up his residence in Philadelphia proper. He is named in the first charter of the city in 1691, as one of the twelve common councillors, and was also holding the same office in 1701, 1704, and 1705. Although he uses the "thee" and "thy" of the Quakers in the first part of the *Letter*, it is thought that he was not a Friend; his children were baptized in parish churches of Bristol and both he and his wife were buried as non-Quakers in the Friends' burial ground in Philadelphia. She died in 1706 and he in 1718. Numerous descendants, some of the name, still remain in and near Philadelphia.

The *Letter* is, to be sure, the raw production of an unlettered tradesman; nevertheless it conveys a true picture of pioneering in the initial months of Penn's colony. It was addressed to a friend at Chippenham, in Wiltshire, about twenty miles east of Bristol. It was first printed as a two-page folio by the Quaker publisher, John Bringhurst, at the Sign of the Book, in Gracechurch Street, London, in 1683. This text is

the one here reproduced. Translations appeared in Dutch[1]
in *Missive van William Penn* (*i. e.*, *Letter to the Free Society of
Traders*), (Amsterdam, 1684), pp. 20–23 of one edition, pp. 25–
28 of the other; in German, in *Beschreibung der in America
neu-erfundenen Provinz Pensylvanien* (Hamburg, 1684), pp.
29–32; and in French in the translation of the latter, under the
title *Recüeil de Diverses pieces concernant la Pensylvanie* (Hague,
1684). In a translation of the *Recüeil* by Samuel W. Pennypacker in the *Pennsylvania Magazine*, VI. 311–328 (1882), the
Paschall Letter emerges once more into English (pp. 323–328)
somewhat smoothed and improved in the order of its arrange-
ment but lacking the quaint crudeness of the original edition.

A. C. M.

[1] Julius F. Sachse's *Letters relating to the Settlement of Germantown* (Philadelphia, 1903; ten copies made) contains a contemporary copy in Low Dutch
script, photographically reproduced, pp. 21–24, from the Könneken manuscript
in the Ministerial Archives of Lübeck, Germany; a shipping notice, which is not
in the original London edition, has been added as a postscript to this version.

LETTER OF THOMAS PASCHALL, 1683

*An Abstract of a letter from Thomas Paskell of Pennsilvania
To his Friend J. J. of Chippenham.*

MY kind love remembred unto Thee, and thy wife, and to all
the rest of thy Family, hoping that you are all in good health,
as through the goodness of God we all are at this present writing, Excepting one of my servants, who was a Carpenter, and
a stout young man, he died on board the Ship, on our Voyage.
I thank God I, and my Wife, have not been sick at all, but continued rather better than in England; and I do not find but
the Country is healthfull, for there was a Ship that came the
same day with us into the river, that lost but one Passenger
in the Voyage, and that was their Doctor, who was ill when he
came on board, and those people that came in since continue
well.   William Penn and those of the Society[1] are arrived.
W. P. is well approved of, he hath been since at New Yorke,
and was extraordinarily entertained, and he behaved himself
as Noble.   Here is a place called Philadelphia, where is a Market kept, as also at Upland.[2]   I was at Bridlington[3]-fair, where
I saw most sorts of goods to be sold, and a great resort of people;
Where I saw English goods sold at very reasonable rates; The
Country is full of goods, Brass and Pewter lieth upon hand,
That which sells best, is Linnen cloath, trading Cloath for the
Indians; I bought Kersey and it doth not sell, Broad Cloath
is wanting, and Perniston,[4] and Iron-potts; and as for the
Swedes, they use but little Iron in Building, for they will build,
and hardly use any other toole but an Ax; They will cut down
a Tree, and cut him off when down, sooner then two men can
saw him, and rend him into planks or what they please; only

---

[1] The Free Society of Traders. See p. 240, n. 1, *supra.*
[2] Chester.   [3] Burlington, New Jersey.
[4] Penistone, a kind of coarse woollen cloth formerly used for garments and
the like, made at Penistone, a small town in the West Riding of Yorkshire,
England.

with the Ax and Wooden wedges, they use no Iron; They are generaly very ingenous people, lives well, they have lived here 40 Years, and have lived much at ease, having great plenty of all sorts of provisions, but then they weer but ordinarily Cloathd; but since the English came, they have gotten fine Cloaths, and are going proud. Let all people know that have any mind to come hither, that they provide Comfortable things for their passage, and also some provitions to serve them here, for although things are to be had at reasonable rates here, yet it is so far to fetch, that it spends much time, so that it's better to come prcvided for half a Year then to want one day, I thank God we have not wanted, but have fared well beyond what we did in England.

The River is taken up all along, by the Sweads, and Finns and some Dutch, before the English came, near eight score miles, and the Englishmen some of them, buy their Plantations, and get roome by the great River-side, and the rest get into Creeks, and small rivers that run into it, and some go into the Woods seven or eight Miles; Thomas Colborne[1] is three miles in the Woods, he is well to pass, and hath about fourteen Acres of Corne now growing, and hath gotten between 30 and 40 *li.* by his Trade, in this short time. I have hired a House for my Family for the Winter, and I have gotten a little House in my Land for my servants, and have cleared Land about six Acres; and this I can say, I never wisht my self at Bristol again since my departure. I live in the Schoolkill Creek, near Philadelphia, about 100 Miles up the River. Here have been 24 Ships with Passengers within this Year, so that provisions are somewhat hard to come by in some places, though at no dear rate, there is yet enough in the River, but it is far to fetch, and suddainly there will be an Order taken for continuall supply. Now I shall give you an impartial account of the Country as I find it, as followeth. When we came into Delawarebay we saw an infinite number of small fish in sholes, also large fish leaping in the Water; The River is a brave pleasant River as

---

[1] Thomas Coebourn (d. 1698–99), carpenter, Quaker emigrant, from Lamborn Woodlands, Berkshire, England, came over to Pennsylvania early in 1682 and settled on Chester Creek, about three miles northwest of the town of Chester. About 1687 he built a mill—the second on Chester Creek—which gave great offence to the proprietors of the Chester mills farther down the creek.

can be desired, affording divers sorts of fish in great plenty, it's planted all along the Shoare, and in some Creeks, especialy in Pensilvania side, mostly by Sweads, Finns, and Dutch, and now at last, English throng in among them, and have filed all the Rivers and Creeks a great way in the Woods, and have settled about 160 Miles up the great River; some English that are above the falls, have sowed this Year 30 or 40 bushels of Wheat, and have great stocks of Cattel; Most of the Sweads, and Finns are ingeneous people, they speak English, Swead, Finn, Dutch and the Indian; They plant but little Indian corne, nor Tobacco; their Women make most of the Linnen cloath they wear, they Spinn and Weave it and make fine Linnen, and are many of them curious housewives: The people generally eat Rye bread, being approved of best by them, not but that here is good Wheat, for I have eaten as good bread and drank as good drink as ever I did in England, as also very good butter and cheese, as most in England. Here is 3 sorts of Wheat, as Winter, Summer, and Buck Wheat; the Winter Wheat they sow at the fall, the Summer Wheat in March, these two sorts are ripe in June; then having taken in this, they plow the same land, and sow Buck Wheat, which is ripe in September: I have not given above 2s. 6d per skipple,[1] (which is 3 English pecks) for the best Wheat and that in goods which cost little more then half so much in England, here is very good Rye at 2s per skipple, also Barly of 2 sorts, as Winter, and Summer, at 4 Guilders per skipple; also Oats, and 3 sorts of Indian Corne, (two of which sorts they can Malt and make good bear of as of Barley,) at four Guilders per Skiple, a Guilder is four pence halfpenney. I have bought good Beef, Porke, and Mutton at two pence per pound and some cheaper, also Turkeys and Wild-geese at the value of two or three Pound of Shot apeice, and Ducks at one Pound of Shot, or the like value, and in great plenty: here is great store of poultry, but for Curlews, Pidgons, and Phesants, they will hardly bestow a shot upon them. I have Venison of the Indians very cheap, although they formerly sold it as cheap again to the Sweads; I have four Dear for two yards of trading cloath, which cost five shillings, and most times I purchase it cheaper: We had Bearsflesh this fall for little or nothing, it is good food, tasting

---

[1] The Dutch *schepel*.

much like Beef; There have been many Horses sold of late to
Barbadoes, and here is plenty of Rum, Sugar, Ginger, and
Melasses. I was lately at Bridlington-fair,[1] where were a great
resort of people, with Cattle and all sorts of Goods, sold at very
reasonable rates.

Here are Gardens with all sorts of Herbs, and some more
then in England, also Goose-beries and Roasetrees, but what
other Flowers I know not yet: Turnips, Parsnips, and Cabbages, beyond Compare. Here are Peaches in abundance of
three sorts I have seen rott on the Ground, and the Hogs eate
them, they make good Spirits from them, also from Corne and
Cheries, and a sort of wild Plums and Grapes, and most people
have Stills of Copper for that use. Here are Apples, and Pears,
of several sorts, Cheries both Black and Red, and Plums, and
Quinces; in some places Peach Stones grow up to bear in three
Years: the Woods are full of Oakes, many very high and
streight, many of them about two foot through, and some
bigger, but very many less; A Swead will fell twelve of the
bigger in a day; Here are brave Poplar, Beach, Ash, Lyme-
trees, Gum-trees, Hickary-trees, Sasafras, Wallnuts, and Chesnuts, Hazel, and Mullberies: Here growes in the Woods abundance of Wortle-beries or Whorts, Strawberies and Blackberies,
better then in England, as also three sorts of Grapes and
Plums; Here is but few Pine-trees, and Ceder; Here is good
Firestone[2] plenty enough in most places: and the Woods are
full of runs of water. I have lately seen some Salt, very good
to salt meat with, brought by an Indian out of the Woods:
they say there is enough of it: but for Minnerals or Mettals,
I have not seen any, except it be Marcasite,[3] such as they make
Vitriol or Copperis with in England. Here are Beavers, Rackoons, Woolves, Bears, a sort of Lyons, Polecatts, Mushratts,
Elks, Mincks, Squirills of several sorts and other small Creatures, but none of these hurt unless surprised: also Rattle
Snakes and black Snakes, but the Rattle Snaks I have not seen,
though I have rambled the Woods much these three Months,
since the beginning of September. The Indians are very quiet
and peaceable, having their understandings, and qualifications,
and when abused will seek revenge, they live much better since

---

[1] In Marginal note, "New-Jersey."
[2] Iron pyrites.   [3] Iron pyrites.

the English came; getting necessarys as cheap again as formerly, and many of them begin to speake English, I have heard one say *Swead no good, Dutch man no good,* but *Englishman good.* William Penn is settling people in Towns. There are Markets kept in two Towns viz. Philadelphia, being Chiefest, Chester, formerly called Upland. To write of the Seasons of the Year I cannot, but since I came it hath been very pleasant weather. The Land is generally good and yet there is some but ordinary and barren ground. Here are Swamps which the Sweads prize much, and many people will want: And one thing more I shall tell you, I know a man together with two or three more, that have happened upon a piece of Land of some Hundred Acres, that is all cleare, without Trees, Bushes, stumps, that may be Plowed without let, the farther a man goes in the Country the more such Land they find. There is also good Land, full of Large and small Trees, and some good Land, but few Trees on it. The Winter is sharp and the Cattel are hard to keep. The people that come must work and know Country affairs; They must be provided with some provisions for some time in the Country, and also some to help along on Board the Ship. I have more to write, but am shortned in time. *Vale.*

THOMAS PASKELL.

Pennsilvania, the last of January, 168⅔.

London, Printed by John Bringhurst, at the Sign of the Book in Grace-Church-Street. 1683.

A FURTHER ACCOUNT OF THE PROVINCE OF
PENNSYLVANIA, BY WILLIAM PENN, 1685

INTRODUCTION

AFTER an absence of over two years in America William Penn had reached England in October, 1684. He had been called home for the defence of the boundaries of the province against the aggressions of Lord Baltimore and also for intercession on behalf of his persecuted Quaker brethren. The accession of his old friend the Duke of York to the throne of England as James II., in the following February, gave Penn great influence as a courtier and patron at court, and was especially opportune for the furtherance of the two chief objects of his return. These objects he pressed forward most actively. Thus, by October, 1685, only a few days before the writing of *A Further Account*, he obtained a favorable report regarding the Three Lower Counties to which Baltimore laid claim; and a few months later he secured the release of more than 1,200 Quakers, imprisoned as Dissenters.

Of Penn's Pennsylvania pamphlets *A Further Account* ranks next in importance to his *Letter to the Free Society of Traders*, and is really a sequel to the latter. It was written at Worminghurst Place, the Proprietor's country-seat in Sussex, in the south of England, and was printed in 1685, in two editions of small quarto, one of twenty pages and the other of sixteen pages, probably from a London press. A Dutch translation entitled *Tweede Bericht* appeared the same year at Amsterdam. A large portion of the English text was reprinted in Richard Blome's *Present State of His Majesties' Isles and Territories in America* (London, 1687), pp. 122–134; in Thompson Westcott's *History of Philadelphia* (*Sunday Dispatch*, Philadelphia) chapter XXXI., and in William J. Buck's *William Penn in Amer-*

ica (Philadelphia, 1888), pp. 174–180.   It was reprinted in full from the original English editions in the collection of the Historical Society of Pennsylvania, in the *Pennsylvania Magazine*, IX. 68–81 (1885).   It is this text that follows.

A. C. M.

A FURTHER ACCOUNT OF THE PROVINCE OF PENNSYLVANIA, BY WILLIAM PENN, 1685

A Further Account of the Province of Pennsylvania and its Improvements, for the Satisfaction of those that are Adventurers, and enclined to be so.

IT has, I know, been much expected from me that I should give some farther Narrative of those parts of America where I am chiefly interested, and have lately been; having continued there above a Year after my former Relation,[1] and receiving since my return the freshest and fullest Advices of its Progress and Improvement. But as the reason of my coming back was a Difference between the Lord Baltimore and myself, about the Lands of Delaware, in consequence reputed of mighty moment to us, so I wav'd publishing anything that might look in favor of the Country, or inviting to it, whilst it lay under the Discouragement and Disreputation of that Lord's claim and pretences.

But since they are, after many fair and full hearings before the Lords of the Committee for Plantations justly and happily Dismist, and the things agreed; and that the Letters which daily press me from all Parts on the subject of America, are so many and voluminous that to answer them severally were a Task too heavy and repeated to perform, I have thought it most easie to the Enquirer, as well as myself, to make this Account Publick, lest my silence or a more private intimations of things, should disoblige the just inclinations of any to America, and at a time too when an extraordinary Providence seems to favour its Plantation and open a door to Europeans to pass thither. That, then, which is my part to do in this Advertisement is:

First. To Relate our Progress, especially since my last of the month called August, '83.

Secondly. The Capacity of the Place for further Improvement, in order to Trade and Commerce.

[1] *I. e.*, Letter to the Free Society of Traders, *ante.*

Lastly. Which way those that are Adventurers, or incline to be so, may imploy their Money, to a fair and secure Profit; such as shall equally encourage Poor and Rich, which cannot fail of Advancing the Country in consequence.

I. We have had about Ninety Sayl of Ships with Passengers since the beginning of '82, and not one Vessel designed to the Province, through God's mercy, hitherto miscarried.

The Estimate of the People may thus be made: Eighty to each Ship, which comes to Seven Thousand Two Hundred Persons. At least a Thousand there before, with such as from other places in our neighbourhood are since come to settle among us; and I presume the Births at least equal to the Burials; For, having made our first Settlements high in the Freshes of the Rivers, we do not find ourselves subject to those Seasonings that affect some other Countries upon the same Coast.

The People are a Collection of divers Nations in Europe: As, French, Dutch, Germans, Sweeds, Danes, Finns, Scotch, Irish and English; and of the last equal to all the rest: And, which is admirable, not a Reflection on that Account: But as they are of one kind, and in one Place and under One Allegiance, so they live like People of One Country, which Civil Union has had a considerable influence towards the prosperity of that place.

II. Philadelphia, and our intended Metropolis, as I formerly Writ, is two Miles long, and a Mile broad, and at each end it lies that mile upon a Navigable River. The scituation high and dry, yet replenished with running streams. Besides the High Street, that runs in the middle from River to River, and is an hundred foot broad, it has Eight streets more that run the same course, the least of which is fifty foot in breadth. And besides Broad Street, which crosseth the Town in the middle, and is also an hundred foot wide, there are twenty streets more, that run the same course, and are also fifty foot broad. The names of those Streets are mostly taken from the things that Spontaneously grow in the Country, As Vine Street, Mulberry Street, Chestnut Street, Wallnut Street, Strawberry Street, Cranberry Street, Plumb Street, Hickery Street, Pine Street, Oake Street, Beach Street, Ash Street, Popler Street, Sassafrax Street, and the like.

III. I mentioned in my last Account that from my Arrival, in Eighty-two, to the Date thereof, being ten Moneths, we had got up Fourscore Houses at our Town, and that some Villages were settled about it.   From that time to my coming away, which was a Year within a few Weeks, the Town advanced to Three hundred and fifty-seven Houses; divers of them large, well built, with good Cellars, three stories, and some with Balconies.

IV. There is also a fair Key[1] of about three hundred foot square, Built by Samuel Carpenter,[2] to which a ship of five hundred Tuns may lay her broadside, and others intend to follow his example.   We have also a Ropewalk made by B. Wilcox,[3] and cordage for shipping already spun at it.

V. There inhabits most sorts of useful Tradesmen, As Carpenters, Joyners, Bricklayers, Masons, Plasterers, Plumers, Smiths, Glasiers, Taylers, Shoemakers, Butchers, Bakers, Brewers, Glovers, Tanners, Felmongers, Wheelrights, Millrights, Shiprights, Boatrights, Ropemakers, Saylmakers, Blockmakers, Turners, etc.

[1] Samuel Carpenter's wharf, the first in Philadelphia, was built into the Delaware River from his bank lot, which was 204 feet wide, about 100 feet north of Walnut Street, and facing his house and lot on the west side of Front Street. The lot was leased to him by Penn in 1684, for a term of fifty years.

[2] Samuel Carpenter (1647–1714), a native of Horsham, Sussex, England, after the death of his father in 1670 removed to Barbados, and successfully engaged in mercantile pursuits. Having joined the Quakers he suffered severe distraint of his property, and about 1683 migrated to Philadelphia. As a man of considerable capital and of remarkable enterprise he was a very valuable addition in the economic and governmental beginnings of the city and province. He not only erected the first wharf of the city, above Walnut Street, as recounted by Penn, but built stores and was concerned in milling and other undertakings in and near the city. In 1693, his assessable property in the province ranked in value next to that of the Proprietor. Furthermore, he actively participated in governmental affairs, serving as assemblyman, councillor, commissioner of property, treasurer, and finally as deputy governor of the province. The mansion built by him, later called the Slate Roof House, was considered the most suitable for the occupation of Proprietor Penn and his family on the occasion of his second visit to the province, in 1699. "That honest and Valluable man [Samuel Carpenter] whose Industry and Improvements," wrote Isaac Norris, from Philadelphia, in 1705, "has been the Stock whereon much of the Labour and Success of this Country has been Grafted."

[3] Barnabas Wilcox (d. 1690), Quaker, came over from Bristol, England, with his family to Philadelphia in 1682. His rope-walk was then at the north side of the town, running westward from Front to Third, north of Vine Street.

VI. There are Two Markets every Week, and Two Fairs every year. In other places Markets also, as at Chester and New-Castle.

VII. Seven Ordinaries for the Intertainment of Strangers and Workmen, that are not Housekeepers, and a good Meal to be had for sixpence, sterl.

VIII. The hours for Work and Meals to Labourers are fixt, and known by Ring of Bell.

IX. After nine at Night the Officers go the Rounds, and no Person, without very good cause, suffered to be at any Publick House that is not a Lodger.

X. Tho this Town seemed at first contrived for the Purchasers of the first hundred shares, each share consisting of 5000 Acres, yet few going, and that their absence might not Check the Improvement of the Place, and Strangers that flockt to us be thereby Excluded, I added that half of the Town, which lies on the Skulkill, that we might have Room for present and after Commers, that were not of that number, and it hath already had great success to the Improvement of the Place.

XI. Some Vessels have been here Built, and many Boats; and by that means a ready Conveniency for Passage of People and Goods.

XII. Divers Brickerys going on, many Cellars already Ston'd or Brick'd and some Brick Houses going up.

XIII. The Town is well furnish'd with convenient Mills; and what with their Garden Plats (the least half an Acre), the Fish of the River, and their labour, to the Countryman, who begins to pay with the provisions of his own growth, they live Comfortably.

XIV. The Improvement of the place is best measur'd by the advance of Value upon every man's Lot. I will venture to say that the worst Lot in the Town, without any Improvement upon it, is worth four times more than it was when it was lay'd out, and the best forty. And though it seems unequal that the Absent should be thus benefited by the Improvements of those that are upon the place, especially when they have serv'd no Office, run no hazard, nor as yet defray'd any Publick charge, yet this advantage does certainly redound to them, and whoever they are they are great Debtors to the Country; of which I shall now speak more at large.

Of Country Settlements.

1. We do settle in the way of Townships or Villages, each of which contains 5,000 acres, in square, and at least Ten Families; the regulation of the Country being a family to each five hundred Acres. Some Townships have more, where the Interests of the People is less than that quantity, which often falls out.

2. Many that had right to more Land were at first covetous to have their whole quantity without regard to this way of settlement, tho' by such Wilderness vacancies they had ruin'd the Country, and then our interest of course. I had in my view Society, Assistance, Busy Commerce, Instruction of Youth, Government of Peoples manners, Conveniency of Religious Assembling, Encouragement of Mechanicks, distinct and beaten Roads, and it has answered in all those respects, I think, to an Universall Content.

3. Our Townships lie square; generally the Village in the Center; the Houses either opposit, or else opposit to the middle, betwixt two houses over the way, for near neighborhood. We have another Method, that tho the Village be in the Center, yet after a different manner: Five hundred Acres are allotted for the Village, which, among ten families, comes to fifty Acres each: This lies square, and on the outside of the square stand the Houses, with their fifty Acres running back, where ends meeting make the Center of the 500 Acres as they are to the whole. Before the Doors of the Houses lies the high way, and cross it, every man's 450 Acres of Land that makes up his Complement of 500, so that the Conveniency of Neighbourhood is made agreeable with that of the Land.

4. I said nothing in my last of any number of Townships, but there are at least Fifty settled before my leaving those parts, which was in the moneth called August, 1684.

5. I visitted many of them, and found them much advanced in their Improvements. Houses over their heads and Garden plots, Coverts for their Cattle, an encrease of stock, and several Enclosures in Corn, especially the first Commers; and I may say of some Poor men was the beginnings of an Estate; the difference of labouring for themselves and for others, of an Inheritance and a Rack Lease, being never better understood.

Of the Produce of the Earth.

1. The Earth, by God's blessing, has more than answered our expectation; the poorest places in our Judgment producing large Crops of Garden Stuff and Grain. And though our Ground has not generally the symptoms of the fat Necks that lie upon salt Waters in Provinces southern of us, our Grain is thought to excell and our Crops to be as large. We have had the mark of the good Ground amongst us from Thirty to Sixty fold of English Corn.

2. The Land requires less seed: Three pecks of Wheat sow an acre, a Bushel at most, and some have had the increase I have mention'd.

3. Upon Tryal we find that the Corn and Roots that grow in England thrive very well there, as Wheat, Barly, Rye, Oats, Buck-Wheat, Pease, Beans, Cabbages, Turnips, Carrets, Parsnups, Colleflowers, Asparagus, Onions, Charlots, Garlick and Irish Potatos; we have also the Spanish and very good Rice, which do not grow here.

4. Our low lands are excellent for Rape and Hemp and Flax. A Tryal has been made, and of the two last there is a considerable quantity Dress'd Yearly.

5. The Weeds of our Woods feed our Cattle to the Market as well as Dary. I have seen fat Bullocks brought thence to Market before Mid Summer. Our Swamps or Marshes yeeld us course Hay for the Winter.

6. English Grass Seed takes well, which will give us fatting Hay in time. Of this I made an Experiment in my own Court Yard, upon sand that was dug out of my Cellar, with seed that had lain in a Cask open to the weather two Winters and a Summer; I caus'd it to be sown in the beginning of the month called April, and a fortnight before Midsummer it was fit to Mow. It grew very thick: But I ordered it to be fed, being in the nature of a Grass Plott, on purpose to see if the Roots lay firm: And though it had been meer sand, cast out of the Cellar but a Year before, the seed took such Root and held the earth so fast, and fastened itself so well in the Earth, that it held fast and fed like old English Ground. I mention this, to confute the Objections that lie against those Parts, as of that, first, English Grass would not grow; next, not enough to mow;

and, lastly, not firm enough to feed, from the Levity of the Mould.

7. All sorts of English fruits that have been tryed take mighty well for the time: The Peach Excellent on standers, and in great quantities: They sun dry them, and lay them up in lofts, as we do roots here, and stew them with Meat in Winter time. Musmellons and Water Mellons are raised there, with as little care as Pumpkins in England. The Vine especially, prevails, which grows every where; and upon experience of some French People from Rochel and the Isle of Rhee,[1] Good Wine may be made there, especially when the Earth and Stem are fin'd and civiliz'd by culture. We hope that good skill in our most Southern Parts will yield us several of the Straights Commodities, especially Oyle, Dates, Figgs, Almonds, Raisins and Currans.

Of the Produce of our Waters.

1. Mighty Whales roll upon the Coast, near the Mouth of the Bay of Delaware. Eleven caught and workt into Oyl one Season. We justly hope a considerable profit by a Whalery; they being so numerous and the Shore so suitable.

2. Sturgeon play continually in our Rivers in Summer: And though the way of cureing them be not generally known, yet by a Receipt I had of one Collins, that related to the Company of the Royal Fishery, I did so well preserve some, that I had them good there three months of the Summer, and brought some of the same so for England.

3. Alloes,[2] as they call them in France, the Jews Allice, and our Ignorants, Shads, are excellent Fish and of the Bigness of our largest Carp: They are so Plentiful, that Captain Smyth's Overseer at the Skulkil, drew 600 and odd at one Draught; 300 is no wonder; 100 familiarly. They are excellent Pickled or Smokt'd, as well as boyld fresh: They are caught by nets only.

4. Rock are somewhat Rounder and larger, also a whiter fish, little inferior in rellish to our Mallet. We have them almost in the like plenty. These are often Barrell'd like Cod, and not much inferior for their spending. Of both these the

---

[1] Rochelle, France, and the Isle de Ré, just off that city.   [2] Ale wives.

Inhabitants increase their Winter store: These are caught by Nets, Hooks and Speers.

5. The Sheepshead, so called, from the resemblance of its Mouth and Nose to a Sheep, is a fish much preferr'd by some, but they keep in salt Water; they are like a Roach in fashion, but as thick as a Salmon, not so long. We have also the Drum, a large and noble fish, commended equal to the Sheepshead, not unlike to a Newfoundland Cod, but larger of the two. Tis so call'd from a noise it makes in its Belly, when it is taken, resembling a Drum. There are three sorts of them, the Black, Red and Gold colour. The Black is fat in the Spring, the Red in the Fall, and the Gold colour believed to be the Black, grown old, because it is observ'd that young ones of that colour have not been taken. They generally ketch them by Hook and Line, as Cod are, and they save like it, where the People are skilful. There are abundance of lesser fish to be caught of pleasure, but they quit not cost, as those I have mentioned, neither in Magnitude nor Number, except the Herring, which swarm in such shoales that it is hardly Credible; in little Creeks, they almost shovel them up in their tubs. There is the Catfish, or Flathead, Lampry, Eale, Trout, Perch, black and white, Smelt, Sunfish, etc.; also Oysters, Cockles, Cunks, Crabs, Mussles, Mannanoses.

Of Provision in General.

1. It has been often said we were starv'd for want of food; some were apt to suggest their fears, others to insinuate their prejudices, and when this was contradicted, and they assur'd we had plenty, both of Bread, Fish and Flesh, then 'twas objected that we were forc't to fetch it from other places at great Charges: but neither is all this true, tho all the World will think we must either carry Provision with us, or get it of the Neighbourhood till we had gotten Houses over our heads and a little Land in tillage, We fetcht none, nor were we wholly helpt by Neighbours; The Old Inhabitants supplied us with most of the Corn we wanted, and a good share of Pork and Beef: 'tis true New York, New England, and Road Island did with their provisions fetch our Goods and Money, but at such Rates, that some sold for almost what they gave, and

others carried their provisions back, expecting a better Market neerer, which showed no scarcity, and that we were not totally destitute on our own River.   But if my advice be of any Value I would have them to buy still, and not weaken their Herds, by Killing their Young Stock too soon.

2. But the right measure of information must be the proportion of Value of Provisions there, to what they are in more planted and mature Colonies.   Beef is commonly sold at the rate of two pence per Pound; and Pork for two pence half penny; Veal and Mutton at three pence or three pence half penny, that Country mony; an English Shilling going for fifteen pence.   Grain sells by the Bushel; Wheat at four shillings; Rye, and excellent good, at three shillings; Barly, two shillings six pence; Indian Corn, two shillings six pence; Oats, two shillings, in that money still, which in a new Country, where Grain is so much wanted for feed, as for food, cannot be called dear, and especially if we consider the Consumption of the many new Commers.

3. There is so great an encrease of Grain by the dilligent application of People to Husbandry that, within three Years, some Plantations have got Twenty Acres in Corn, some Forty, some Fifty.

4. They are very careful to encrease their stock, and get into Daries as fast as they can.   They already make good Butter and Cheese.   A good Cow and Calf by her side may be worth three pounds sterling, in goods at first Cost.   A pare of Working Oxen, eight pounds: a pare of fat ones, Little more, and a plain Breeding Mare about five pounds sterl.

5. For Fish, it is brought to the Door, both fresh and salt. Six Alloes or Rocks for twelve pence; and salt fish at three fardings per pound, Oysters at 2s. per bushel.

6. Our Drink has been Beer and Punch, made of Rum and Water: Our Beer was mostly made of Molosses, which well boyld, with Sassafras or Pine infused into it, makes very tollerable drink; but now they make Mault, and Mault Drink begins to be common, especially at the Ordinaries and the Houses of the more substantial People.   In our great Town there is an able Man,[1] that has set up a large Brew House, in

[1] William Frampton (d. 1686), Quaker merchant and brewer, justice and provincial councillor, owner of extensive lands in Pennsylvania, had removed

order to furnish the People with good Drink, both there, and up and down the River. Having said this of the Country, for the time I was there, I shall add one of the many Letters that have come to my hand, because brief and full, and that he is known to be a Person of an extraordinary Caution as well as Truth, in what he is wont to Write or Speak:

PHILADELPHIA, the 3d of the 6th month [August] 1685. *Governour.*

Having an opportunity by a Ship from this River, (out of which several have gone this Year) I thought fit to give a short account of proceedings, as to settlements here, and the Improvements both in Town and Country. As to the Country, the Improvements are large, and settlements very throng by way of Townships and Villages. Great inclinations to Planting Orchards, which are easily raised, and some brought to perfection. Much Hayseed sown, and much Planting of Corn this Year, and great produce, said to be, both of Wheat, Rye and Rise; Barly and Oates prove very well, besides Indian Corn and Pease of several sorts; also Kidny Beans and English Pease of several kinds, I have had in my own Ground, with English Roots, Turnaps, Parsnaps, Carrets, Onions, Leeks, Radishes and Cabbidges, with abundance of sorts of Herbs and Flowers. I have but few seeds that have mist except Rosemary seed, and being English might be old. Also I have such plenty of pumpkins, Musmellons, Water Mellons, Squashes, Coshaws, Bucks-hens, Cowcumbers and Simnells of Divers kinds; admired at by new Commers that the Earth should so plentifully cast forth, especially the first Years breaking up; and on that which is counted the Worst Sort of Sandy Land.

from New York to Philadelphia in 1683, and at this time (1685) was living in his house at the west side of Front Street, between Walnut and Spruce streets, on a lot purchased in the early summer of 1684. He had there at his death in 1686 a well-stocked shop of general merchandise. His "great brew-house," built in 1683, was on the next lot to the rear, on the west side of Second Street by the south side of Dock Creek, a plot acquired from Penn in the beginning of the latter year. Here also he had a bake-house and a dwelling-house, the latter evidently his earlier residence, but now rented as an inn; and here in 1685 he erected the brick house hereafter mentioned by Robert Turner. Facing his Front Street residence was his wharf, one of the first three wharves of the city in Delaware River, built on a lot which he bought from the Proprietor in midsummer, 1684.

I am satisfied, and many more, that the Earth is very fertil, and the Lord has done his part, if Man use but a moderate Dilligence. Grapes, Mulberies and many wilde Fruits and natural Plums, in abundance, this year have I seen and eat of. A brave Orchard and Nursery have I planted, and thrive mightily, and Fruit the first Year. I endeavor choice of Fruits and Seeds from many parts; also Hay Seed; and have sowed a field this spring for tryall. First, I burned the leaves, then had it Grub'd, not the Field but the small Roots up, then sowed great and small Clover, with a little old Grass seed, and had it only raked over, not Plowed nor Harrowed, and it grows exceedingly; also for experience I sowed some patches of the same sort in my Garden and Dunged some, and that grows worst. I have planted the Irish Potatoes, and hope to have a brave increase to Transplant next Year. Captain Rapel[1] (the Frenchman) saith he made good Wine of the grapes (of the country) last Year, and Transported some, but intends to make more this Year. Also a French man[2] in this Town intends the same, for Grapes are very Plentiful.

Now as to the Town of Philadelphia it goeth on in Planting and Building to admiration, both in the front and backward, and there are about 600 Houses in 3 years time. And since I built my Brick House,[3] the foundation of which was laid at thy going, which I did design after a good manner to incourage others, and that from building with Wood, it being the first, many take example, and some that built Wooden Houses, are sorry for it: Brick building is said to be as cheap: Bricks are exceeding good, and better than when I built: More Makers fallen in, and Bricks cheaper, they were before at 16 s. English per 1000, and now many brave Brick Houses are going up, with

[1] Captain Gabriel Rappel, a Protestant, from St. Martin, in France, was a fugitive in England in November, 1682, petitioning the Privy Council for liberty to plant in English America. He arrived in the Delaware in 1683, purchasing for the use of a London merchant a plantation of 1,000 acres called the Exchange in Reedy Point Neck, in New Castle County, along with certain live stock and a servant man. He probably conducted this plantation for a few years, and may have made there the wine referred to by Turner.

[2] Possibly Monsieur Jacob Pellison, of Philadelphia.

[3] On his lot at the southwest corner of Front and Mulberry (now Arch) streets.

good Cellars.   Arthur Cook [1] is building him a brave Brick
House near William Frampton's, on the front: For William
Frampton hath since built a good Brick house, by his Brew
house and Bake house, and let the other for an Ordinary.
John Wheeler,[2] from New England, is building a good Brick
house, by the Blew Anchor; and the two[3] Brickmakers a
Double Brick House and Cellars; besides several others going
on: Samuel Carpenter has built another house by his.[4]   I am
Building another Brick house by mine, which is three large
Stories high, besides a good large Brick Cellar under it, of two
Bricks and a half thickness in the wall, and the next story half
under Ground, the Cellar hath an Arched Door for a Vault to
go (under the Street) to the River, and so to bring in goods, or
deliver out.   Humphery Murry,[5] from New York, has built
a large Timber house, with Brick Chimnies.   John Test [6] has
almost finished a good Brick House, and a Bake House of

---

[1] Arthur Cook (d. 1699), speaker of assembly, provincial councillor, and
chief justice, formerly of New Gravel Lane, in St. Paul's Shadwell, London, was
building his brick house on the west side of Front Street below Walnut Street.
By 1697 he had "a most Stately Brick-House," near Frankford, hereafter mentioned by Gabriel Thomas.

[2] John Wheeler (d. 1691), merchant and distiller, ship-owner and trader
with the West Indies and Europe, a resident as early as 1667 of New London,
Connecticut, where he died.   He made only a brief sojourn in Philadelphia,
building his brick house on the west side of Front Street, below Walnut Street,
near the Blue Anchor Inn, on a lot purchased by him from Penn in midsummer,
1684.   This property he sold in 1686 to Edward Shippen, then of Boston, but
later of Philadelphia.

[3] Thomas Smith and Daniel Pegg (d. 1702).

[4] On the west side of Front Street, a hundred feet north of Walnut Street.

[5] Humphrey Morrey (d. 1715–6), was a merchant in New York early in
1684, but by 1685 had become a resident of Philadelphia and had built the
"Timber house" at the southwest corner of Front and Chestnut streets.   He
was the first mayor of Philadelphia (1691–1692) and served as assemblyman
and provincial councillor.   In his will of 1715 he is described as yeoman, of
Cheltenham Township, now Montgomery County.

[6] John Test (d. 1718), a non-Quaker merchant, from London, had probably
come over to West New Jersey with John Fenwick's colony in the Griffin, in 1675.
He was a resident of Upland (Chester) as early as 1677, and as late as 1679.   In
1681 he was made sheriff of Pennsylvania by the court of Upland, and in 1682
the first sheriff of the newly-constituted Philadelphia County.   His brick house
was at the northeast corner of Third and Chestnut streets.   In later life he removed to Darby, and died there as an innkeeper.

Timber; and N. Allen[1] a good house, next to Thomas Wynns,[2] front Lot. John Day[3] a good house, after the London fashion, most Brick, with a large frame of Wood, in the front, for Shop Windows; all these have Belconies. Thomas Smith and Daniel Pege are Partners, and set to making of Brick this Year, and they are very good; also, Pastorus,[4] the German Friend, Agent for the Company at Frankford, with his Dutch[5] People, are preparing to make Brick next year. Samuel Carpenter, is our Lime burner on his Wharf. Brave Lime Stone found here, as the Workmen say, being proved. We build most Houses with Belconies. Lots are much desir'd in the Town, great buying one of another. We are now laying the foundation of a large plain Brick house,[6] for a Meeting House, in the Center,[7] (sixty

---

[1] Nathaniel Allen (d. 1692), Quaker, a cooper of Redcliffe Street, Bristol, England, was one of the three commissioners who preceded Penn to Pennsylvania, in 1681, to lay out Philadelphia and the lands of the First Purchasers. His house was on the west side of Front, above Chestnut Street. He finally settled with his family on his plantation "Allenbury," on the west side of Neshaminy Creek in Bensalem Township, Bucks County.

[2] Dr. Thomas Wynne (1627–1692), Quaker, a native of Bronvedog, parish of Yskewiog, Flintshire, Wales, came over in the ship *Welcome* with William Penn in 1682 and was the first speaker of the assembly of Pennsylvania held in Philadelphia. His lot was on the west side of Front Street, about midway between Chestnut and High (Market) streets.

[3] John Day (d. 1696), carpenter, from the parish of St. Nicholas Cole Abbey, London, his brick house with adjoining orchard being on Front, between Sassafras (now Race) and Mulberry (now Arch) streets.

[4] Francis Daniel Pastorius.

[5] The "Crefelders," from Crefeld, Germany, near the Dutch border. See *post*, p. 393, note 3.

[6] "Our first [Quaker] Meeting-house in the sd City," writes Pastorius, who came in 1683, "was nothing else than a Lodge or Cottage, nailed together of Pine-boards, Imported from New-York, and sold a hundred foot at 10. Shill. And never the less the Lord appeared most powerfully in that Tabernacle of Shittim wood." Learned, *Pastorius*, pp. 212–213.

[7] The Friends' Meeting House in the Centre Square of the city, midway between the Delaware and Schuylkill Rivers, where the City Hall now stands, was built of brick, in 1685–1686, and was used for a time for the more important First-day (Sunday) morning and business meetings of the society. The location being in the midst of the forest some little distance without the town, and its two or three streets along the Delaware, the meeting was not well attended; the Friends preferred to wait for the afternoon meeting at the Bank Meeting House, near at hand, within the town proper; consequently, in a few years the Centre Square meeting was abandoned.

foot long, and about forty foot broad) and hope to have it soon up, many hearts and hands at Work that will do it. A large Meeting House,[1] 50 foot long, and 38 foot broad, also going up, on the front of the River, for an evening Meeting, the work going on apace. Many Towns People setling their liberty Lands. I hope the Society will rub off the Reproaches some have cast upon them. We now begin to gather in some thing of our many great Debts.

I do understand Three Companies for Whale Catching are designed to fish in the River's Mouth, this season, and find through the great Plenty of fish they may begin early. A Fisherman this Year found the way to catch Whiteins in this River, and it's expected many sorts of fish more than hath been yet caught may be taken by the skilful. Fish are in such plenty that many sorts on tryal, have been taken with Nets in the Winter time: The Sweeds laughing at the English for going to try, have since tried themselves. The River so big, and full of several sorts of brave fish, that it is believed, except frozen over, we may catch any time in the Winter. It's a great pity, but two or three experienced Fishermen were here to Ply this River to salt and serve fresh to the Town. A good way to Pickle Sturgion is wanting; such abundance in the River, even before the Town: many are Catcht, Boyld and Eaten. Last Winter great plenty of Dear brought in by the Indians and English from the Country. We are generally very Well and Healthy here, but abundance Dead in Maryland this Summer.

The manufacture of Linnen by the Germans[2] goes on finely, and they make fine Linnen: Samuel Carpenter having been lately there, declares they had gathered one Crop of Flax, and had sowed for the Second and saw it come up well: And they say, might have had forewarder and better, had they had old seed, and not stay'd so long for the Growth of new seed to sow again. And I may believe it, for large hath my experience

---

[1] The Bank Meeting House of the Friends, built in 1685–1686 for the afternoon meetings, was at the north end of the town on the west side of Front Street, then the principal thoroughfare, just above Mulberry (now Arch) Street. This structure was replaced, evidently in 1703, Isaac Norris writing in that year that there was "a new house built in the place where the old bank meeting House Stood."

[2] In Germantown.

been this Years, though in a small peece of Ground, to the admiration of many.

I thought fit to signify this much, knowing thou wouldst be glad to hear of thy People and Provinces welfare; the Lord preserve us all, and make way for thy return, which is much desired, not only by our Friends but all sorts.   I am, etc., thy truly Loving Friend,

ROBERT TURNER.[1]

Of Further Improvements for Trade and Commerce.

These things that we have in prospect for Staples of Trade, are Wine, Linnen, Hemp, Potashes and Whale Oyle; to say nothing of our Provisions for the Islands, our Saw Mills, Sturgeon, some Tobacco, and our Furs and Skins, which of themselves are not contemptible; I might add Iron (perhaps Copper too), for there is much Mine; and it will be granted us that we want no Wood, although I must confess I cannot tell how to help preferring a domestick or self subsistance to a life of much profit, by the extream Toy of forraign Traffick.

Advice to Adventurers how to imploy their Estates, with fair profit.

It is fit now, that I give some Advertisement to Adventurers, which way they may lay out their Money to best advantage, so as it may yield them fair returns, and with content to

---

[1] Robert Turner (1635–1700), one of the wealthiest and most prominent merchants of the Philadelphia of that day, was a native of Cambridge, England; joined the early Quaker movement in Ireland, suffering in consequence fines and imprisonment; acquired large means as a Dublin linen draper; became one of the New Jersey proprietors by the purchase (1) in 1677, with other Irish Friends, of a share of West New Jersey and, (2) in 1681, along with the Earl of Perth, Penn, Barclay, and others, of the whole of East New Jersey.   As a friend of Penn he entered largely into the Pennsylvania enterprise, buying 5000 acres of land in the province and subscribing £500 for stock of the Free Society of Traders.   In 1683 with his family and seventeen servants he came over to Pennsylvania in the ship Lyon and established his residence on his Philadelphia lot at the southwest corner of Front and Mulberry (Arch) streets, where in 1684, as he states, he built the first brick house in the city, as well as a wharf, called Mount Wharf, on his lot facing the river, one of the first three wharves of Philadelphia.   He served as judge, receiver general, commissioner of property, provincial councillor, and as one of the five commissioners governing the province.   In the Keith schism he joined the Keithites.

all concerned, which is the last part of my present task; and
I must needs say so much wanting, that it has perhaps given
some occasion to ignorance and prejudice to run without
mercy, measure or distinction against America, of which Pennsylvania to be sure has had its share.

1. It is agreed on all hands, that the Poor are the Hands
and Feet of the Rich. It is their labour that Improves Countries; and to encourage them, is to promote the real benefit
of the publick. Now as there are abundance of these people
in many parts of Europe, extreamly desirous of going to
America; so the way of helping them thither, or when there,
and the return thereof to the Disbursers, will prove what I
say to be true.

2. There are two sorts, such as are able to transport themselves and Families, but have nothing to begin with there;
and those that want so much as to transport themselves and
Families thither.

3. The first of these may be entertained in this manner.
Say I have 5000 Acres, I will settle Ten Families upon them,
in way of Village, and built each an house, an out house for
Cattle, furnish every Family with Stock, as four Cows, two
Sows, a couple of Mares, and a yoke of Oxen, with a Town
Horse, Bull and Boar; I find them with Tools, and give each
their first Ground-seed. They shall continue Seven Year, or
more, as we agree, at half encrease, being bound to leave the
Houses in repair, and a Garden and Orchard, I paying for the
Trees and at least twenty Acres of Land within Fence and improved to corn and grass; the charge will come to about sixty
pounds English for each Family: At the seven years end, the
Improvement will be worth, as things go now, 120 *l.* besides
the value of the encrease of the Stock, which may be neer as
much more, allowing for casualties; especially, if the People
are honest and careful, or a man be upon the spot himself, or
have an Overseer sometimes to inspect them. The charge in
the whole is 832 *l.* And the value of stock and improvements
2400 *l.* I think I have been modest in my computation. These
Farms are afterwarde fit for Leases at full rent, or how else the
Owner shall please to dispose of them. Also the People will
by this time be skilled in the Country, and well provided to
settle themselves with stock upon their own Land.

4. The other sort of poor people may be very beneficially transported upon these terms: Say I have 5000 Acres I should settle as before, I will give to each Family 100 Acres which in the whole makes 1000; and to each Family thirty pounds English, half in hand, and half there, which in the whole comes to 300 *l.* After four years are expired, in which time they may be easie, and in a good condition, they shall each of them pay five pounds, and so yearly for ever, as a Fee-farm rent; which in the whole comes to 50 *l.* a Year. Thus a man that buys 5000 Acres may secure and settle his 4000 by the gift of one, and in a way that hazard and interest allowed for, amounts to at least ten per cent. upon Land security, besides the value it puts upon the rest of the 5000 Acres. I propose that there be at least two working hands besides the wife; whether son or servant; and that they oblige what they carry; and for further security bind themselves as servants for some time, that they will settle the said land accordingly and when they are once scated their improvements are security for the Rent.

5. There is yet another expedient, and that is, give to ten Families 1000 Acres for ever, at a small acknowledgement, and settle them in way of Village, as afore; by their seating thus, the Land taken up is secured from others, because the method of the Country is answered, and the value such a settlement gives to the rest reserved, is not inconsiderable; I mean, the 4000 Acres; especially that which is Contiguous: For their Children when grown up, and Handicrafts will soon covet to fix next them, and such after settlements to begin at an Improved Rent in Fee, or for long Leases, or small Acknowledgements, and good Improvements, must advance the whole considerably. I conceive any of these methods to issue in a sufficient advantage to Adventurers, and they all give good encouragement to feeble and poor Families.

6. That which is most advisable for People, intended thither, to carry with them, is in short all things relating to Apparel, Building, Housholdstuf, Husbandry, Fowling and Fishing. Some Spice, Spirits and double ear, at first were not a miss: But I advise all to proportion their Estates thus; one-third in Money, and two thirds in Goods. Upon pieces of eight, there will be almost a third gotten, for they go at 6 *s.* and by goods well bought, at least fifty pounds sterl. for every

hundred pounds; so that a man worth 400 *l.* here, is worth
600 *l.* there, without sweating.

Of the Natives.

1. Because many Stories have been prejudicially propagated, as if we were upon ill terms with the Natives, and sometimes, like Jobs Kindred, all cut off but the Messenger that brought the Tidings; I think it requisite to say thus much, that as there never was any such Messenger, so the dead People were alive, at our last advices; so far are we from ill terms with the Natives, that we have liv'd in great friendship. I have made seven Purchasses, and in Pay and Presents they have received at least twelve hundred pounds of me. Our humanity has obliged them so far, that they generally leave their guns at home, when they come to our settlements; they offer us no affront, not so much as to one of our Dogs; and if any of them break our Laws, they submit to be punisht by them: and to this they have tyed themselves by an obligation under their hands. We leave not the least indignity to them unrebukt, nor wrong unsatisfied. Justice gains and aws them. They have some Great Men amongst them, I mean for Wisdom, Truth and Justice. I refer to my former Account about their Laws Manners and Religious Rites.

Of the Government.

The Government is according to the words of the Grant, as near to the English as conveniently may be: In the whole, we aim at Duty to the King, the Preservation of Right to all, the suppression of Vice, and encouragement of Vertue and Arts; with Liberty to all People to worship Almighty God, according to their Faith and Perswasion.

Of the Seasons of Going, and usual time of Passage.

1. The Ships go hence at all times of the Year, it must be acknowledged, that to go so as to arrive at Spring or Fall, is best. For the Summer may be of the hottest, for fresh Commers, and in the Winter, the wind that prevails, is the North West, and that blows off the Coast, so that sometimes it is difficult to enter the Capes.

2. I propose therefore, that Ships go hence about the middle of the moneths call'd February and August, which allowing two moneths for passage reaches time enough to plant in the Spring such things as are carried hence to plant, and in the Fall to get a small Cottage, and clear some Land against the next Spring.   I have made a discovery of about a hundred Miles West, and find those back Lands richer in Soyl, Woods and Fountains, then that by Delaware; especially upon the Sasquehannah River.

3. I must confess I prefer the Fall to come thither, as believing it is more healthy to be followed with Winter then Summer; tho, through the great goodness and mercy of God we have had an extraordinary portion of health, for so new and numerous a Colony, notwithstanding we have not been so regular in time.

4. The Passage is not to be set by any man; for Ships will be quicker and slower, some have been four moneths, and some but one, and as often.   Generally between six and nine weeks.   One year, of four and twenty Sayl, I think, there was not three above nine, and there was one or two under six weeks in passage.

5. To render it more healthy, it is good to keep as much upon Deck as may be; for the Air helps against the offensive smells of a Crowd, and a close place.   Also to scrape often the Cabbins, under the Beds; and either carry store of Rue and Wormwood; and some Rosemary, or often sprinkle Vineger about the Cabbin.   Pitch burnt, is not amiss sometimes against faintness and infectious scents.   I speak my experience for their benefit and direction that may need it.

And because some has urged my coming back, as an argument against the place, and the probability of its improvment; Adding, that I would for that reason never return; I think fit to say, That Next Summer, God willing, I intend to go back, and carry my Family, and the best part of my Personal Estate with me.   And this I do, not only of Duty, but Inclination and Choice.   God will Bless and Prosper poor America.

I shall conclude with this further Notice, that to the end such as are willing to embrace any of the foregoing propositions for the Improvement of Adventurers Estates, may not be discouraged, from an inability to find such Land-Lords, Tennants, Masters and Servants, if they intimate their desires to my friend and Agent Philip Ford, living in Bow-Lane in London, they may in all probability be well accommodated; few of any quality or capacity, designed to the Province, that do not inform him of their inclinations and condition.

Now for you that think of going thither, I have this to say, by way of caution; if an hair of our heads falls not to the ground, without the providence of God, Remember, your Removal is of greater moment. Wherefore have a due reverence and regard to his good Providence, as becomes a People that profess a belief in Providence. Go clear in yourselves, and of all others. Be moderate in Expectation, count on Labour before a Crop, and Cost before Gain, for such persons will best endure difficulties, if they come, and bear the Success, as well as find the Comfort that usually follow such considerate undertakings.

WILLIAM PENN.

Worminghurst Place, 12th }
    of the 10th Month 85.   }

LETTER OF DOCTOR NICHOLAS MORE,
1686

INTRODUCTION

Of the collection of seven letters from Pennsylvania put forth by Penn in the pamphlet here reproduced, the initial one by Dr. Nicholas More, which appears in full, occupying nearly one-half of the space, is of most interest and deservedly gives title to the piece. The other letters, however, although simply in the form of abstracts, contain items of value and—barring that of the Pennsbury gardener—are by men of like prominence in the governmental affairs of the province; but notice of them is reserved for the notes. Attention now is devoted to the writer of the most important letter alone.

Dr. More was a personage. He was not only the first speaker of the provincial assembly, held at Chester in December, 1682, but he has even the greater distinction of being the first (1684-1685) of the long and illustrous line of chief justices of Pennsylvania. In 1686 he was appointed by Penn one of the five commissioners to govern the province. He was, moreover, a great landowner, having in his tenure the manor of Moreland, a tract of 10,000 acres of land in Philadelphia County, adjacent to the Bucks County line. This territory, which now covers the greater part of Moreland Township, Montgomery County, was granted to him as a barony, entitling him to hold a court baron and a court leet and to take view of frankpledge. These feudal privileges, however, he never exercised. Adjoining his manor on the south was his country-seat "Green Spring," located about thirteen miles northeast of the Philadelphia of that day and about a half mile west of the present Somerton. It was here on September 13, 1686, that he wrote his letter and it was here that he obtained the agricultural results he describes.

Concerning Dr. More's parentage and other details of his early life nothing is really known, although the evidence seems to point to origin from an armigerous family. Born about 1638, probably in London, he became a physician of that city, living there until his removal to Pennsylvania. In 1670 he was a resident of the parish of St. Gregory's, London, his marriage occurring that year, in the church of St. Dunstans-in-the-East. His bride, a girl of sixteen, only one half his years, was Mary Hedge, of St. Catherine Coleman, daughter of Samuel Hedge, merchant.

His brother-in-law, Samuel Hedge, had preceded him to America in 1675, as a settler with John Fenwick at Salem in West New Jersey, becoming the husband of the latter's daughter Ann. Doubtless thus early through this relative Dr. More would become familiar with the possibilities of the region of the Delaware and would thus be all the more disposed six years later to take up with Penn's project. At all events, before October, 1681, Dr. More had acquired the title to the 10,000 acres of land, which later was located as his manor of Moreland, and early in 1682 he had subscribed £ 300 to the stock of the Free Society of Traders. Of this company he was made the first president at a salary of £ 150 per annum.

In September, 1682, with his family and fifty servants of the Society, he sailed from London in the ship *Geoffrey* or *Jeffries*, and after a quick passage of nearly a month, reached Pennsylvania about the time of William Penn's arrival. He made his first location on the Society lot in Front Street, Philadelphia, but by the early part of 1684 had given up his office as president, and soon settled upon his plantation of "Green Spring."

Although a man apparently of good abilities he was a non-Quaker, out of sympathy with members of that sect, who then made up the majority of the governing class. After the early part of 1685 he suffered from ill health. He was, besides, a man of a somewhat haughty and arbitrary temper. Those handicaps, for a time at least, made his tenure of office very uncomfortable. In 1685 he fell so much under the displeasure of the assembly that the latter body presented articles of impeachment against him to the council, charging him with "assuming to himselfe an unlimited and unlawful Power." Towards the close of his life he became financially embarrassed and at his death in 1687 his estate was disposed of by the sheriff.

An original copy of the pamphlet, which was printed in London, in 1687, as a quarto of nine pages, is in the John Carter Brown Library at Providence. A reprint, appearing in the *Pennsylvania Magazine*, IV. 445–453 (1880), is the basis of that which follows.

A. C. M.

LETTER OF DOCTOR NICHOLAS MORE,

1686

*A Letter from Doctor More with Passages out of Several Letters
from Persons of Good Credit, Relating to the State and Improvement of the Province of Pennsilvania. Published to
prevent false Reports. Printed in the year 1687.*

The Preface.

Divers false Reports going about Town and Country, to
the Injury of the Province of Pennsilvania, I was prevailed
with by some concerned in that Province, and others that
desire the truth of things, to Publish such of the last Letters
as made mention of the State of the Country; to serve for
answer to the Idle and Unjust Stories that the Malice of some
invent, and the Credulity of others prepare them to receive
against it; which is all the part I take in this present Publication.

WILLIAM PENN.

A Letter from Dr. More.

Honored Governour.

I have seen a Letter from your hand, directed to me, among
many in this Province, which came by Captain Richard Di-
mond:[1] It was in all respect welcome to me, and more particularly, for that you make mention of your coming to us again,
with your Family; a thing so much desired by all in these
parts, and more particularly by my self. But I fear that
Madam Penn should give too much credit to the evil Reports
that I do understand are given out by many Enemies to this
new Colony, as if we were ready to Famish, and that the Land

[1] Captain Richard Diamond, or Dymond, of the parish of Bermondsey,
Surrey, England, master of the ship *Amity*, of London, voyaging to Pennsylvania
in 1682, 1685, and 1686, arrived in Pennsylvania 5 mo. 15th of the latter year.

is so barren, the Climet so hot, that English Grain, Roots and Herbs do not come to Maturity; and what grows, to be little worth. How untrue all these things are you well know; but we that have seen our handy Work, accompanied with God's blessing upon it, since your departure from us, are able to say something more to encourage you to return to us again. You know, that when you went for England, there was an indifferent plenty of most things, and that many hundred Families were clearing of Land to Sow and Plant, as I was also doing; since that, our Lands have been grateful to us, and have begun to reward our Labours by abounding Crops of Corn this Year. But to give you to understand the full of our Condition, with respect to Provision in this Province; we had last Fall, and the Winter, abundance of good fresh Pork in our Market at two Pence half-penny per pound, of this Country Money, which is an English two Pence; Beef at the same rate; the like is this Year; and Butter for six Pence per Pound; Wheat for four Shillings per Bushel; Rye three Shillings; and now all this Summer Wheat is at three Shillings, and three Shillings 6 Pence; Rye at eight Groats, and half a Crown; Indian-Corn seven Groats, and two Shillings this Country Money still; so that there is now some Corn Transported from this River. Doctor Butler has bought two hundred Bushels of Wheat at three Shillings six Pence, to Transport, and several others, so that some Thousands of Bushels are Transported this Season, and when this Crop that now is gathered is Threshed, it is supposed that it will be abundantly cheaper than now it is, for there has been abundance of Corn this Year in every Plantation.

The last year I did plant about twelve Acres of Indian Corn, and when it came off the Ground, I did only cause the Ground to be Harrowed, and upon that I did sow both Wheat and Rye, at which many Laughed, saying, That I could not expect any Corn from what I had sowed, the Land wanting more Labour; yet I had this Year as good Wheat and Rye upon it, as was to be found in any other place, and that very bright Corn. I have had a good Crop of Barley and Oats and whereas my People did not use my Barley well, so that much was shed upon the Ground, I caused it immediately to be Plowed in, and is now growing, keeping a good Colour, and I am in hope of another Crop of Barley, having good Ears tho the Straw be shorter. I did plant an Hopp-Garden this Spring, which is now exceeding full of Hopps, at which all English People admire. Richard Collet [1] and Samuel Carpenter,[2] etc., having had some Fields of Rye the last Summer, and plowed the Stuble in order to sow other Corn, by some Casualty could not sow their Fields; yet have they had considerable Crops of Rye, in the said Fields, by what had been shed on the Ground in Harvest time. I have had seventy Ears of Rye upon one single Root, proceeding from one single Corn; forty five of Wheat: eighty of Oats; ten, twelve and fourteen of Barley out of one Corn: I took the Curiosity to tell one of the twelve Ears from one Grain, and there was in it forty five Grains on that Ear; above three Thousand of Oats from one single Corn, and some I had, that had much more, but it would seem a Romance rather than a Truth, if I should speak what I have seen in these things.

Arnoldus de la Grange[3] hath above a Thousand Bushels of English Grain this year, there is indeed a great increase every

---

[1] Richard Collett (d. 1717), yeoman, of Byberry Township, Philadelphia, a neighbor of Doctor More, was a son of Richard Collett, husbandman, of Binton-on-the-Hill, Gloucestershire, but had lived for a time prior to his emigration in Fenchurch Street, London, as serving man to William Mead.

[2] Samuel Carpenter held land not far from Dr. More.

[3] Arnoldus de la Grange (c. 1650–c. 1694), Labadist, had a considerable tract of land on Christiana Creek in New Castle County, Delaware, where evidently the grain mentioned was raised. Near by on the same stream was a mill owned by him in partnership with two Swedes. Doubtless born of a Huguenot family sometime resident in Holland, he was living with his wife Cornelia née de la Fontaine as a shopkeeper in New York in 1679 when visited by Labadist missionaries who describe him as "dressed up like a great fop as he was." He seems to have made frequent business trips to the Delaware, as early as the later date, holding title to several tracts of land, along with a claim, through an incomplete purchase by his father, to Tinicum Island. In the latter part of 1681, apparently, he located with his family in New Castle, having in that year built a windmill for grinding grain in the town. The following year he was one of the residents of New Castle to welcome William Penn to the new domain on the Proprietor's first landing at the town, and was thereupon constituted one of the justices of the court of New Castle and naturalized. In 1684–1685 he was concerned in the purchase from Augustine Herrman of over 3000 acres of land on Bohemia River in Bohemia Manor in southern Cecil County, Maryland, for the communistic settlement of the Labadists, and by 1692 he was a regular inmate of that community.

where. I had the last year as good Turnops, Carrots and Parsnops as could be expected, and in no wise inferior to those in London, the Parsnops better, and of a great bigness; my Children have found out a way of Rosting them in the Embers, and are as good as Barbadoes-Potatoes, insomuch that it is now become a dish with us. We have had admirable English Pease this Summer; every one here is now persuaded of the fertility of the ground, and goodness of the climate, here being nothing wanting, with industry, that grows in England, and many delicious things, not attainable there; and we have this common advantage above England, that all things grow better, and with less labour. I have planted this Spring a Quickset, of Sixscore Foot long, which grows to admiration; we find as good Thorns as any in the World.

We have had so great abundance of Pigeons this Summer, that we have fed all our Servants with them. A Gentlewoman near the City, which is come into this Province since you went for England (Mrs. Jeffs[1] from Ireland) Cured Sturgion the last year, and I have eaten some this Summer at her House, as good as you can get in London; Some Barbadoes Merchants are treating with her for several Barrels for the Barbadoes, and will give her anything for them. We are wanting of some more good Neighbours to fill up the Country. There is a French Gentleman[2] who made the last Year some Wine of the wild Grapes, which proved admirable good, and far above the best Mader as that you ever tasted, a little higher colour'd. And one thing I must take notice of that we strove to make Vinegar of it, but it is so full of Spirit that it will not easily turn to Vinegar; a certain evidence of its long keeping. Your Vig[n]eron[3] had made a Barrel of the same Wine, resolving to keep it for your Entertainment; I being one day there, and speaking of what I had tasted at Monsieur Pelison's,[2] he shewed me a Barrel, which he said was of the same sort that he had

---

[1] Mary Jeffes (d. 1709), wife of Robert Jeffes. They lived at this time in Frankford or Oxford in a house rented from Thomas Fairman in 1684, shortly after their arrival from Ireland. Later they removed to the Falls, in Bucks County, where he died in 1688. In 1702 she was living in Philadelphia.

[2] Monsieur Jacob Pellison, of Philadelphia, who was legatee of the will of Charles de la Noe, in 1686.

[3] Andrew Doz.

taken a great deal of care to secure from being meddled with,
he tapping the head, it sounded empty, at which the man
was so amased, that he was ready to Faint; afterwards looking about, it had leaked underneath, to about two Quarts;
I tasted it, and it was yet very good Wine, so I left the poor
man much afflicted for his loss.   But I must acquaint you with
one thing, that he having planted some French Vines, the
twenty fourth of March, the last year, the same Vines have
brought forth some Grapes this year, and some of them were
presented to President Lloyd[1] the 28th of July, fully Black
and Ripe, which is a thing unheard of, or very extraordinary.
I thought that this short account of our present State and Condition, and Improvement would not be ill news to you, considering that you know me not forward to put my hand to
Paper slightly; wherefore I hope that your Lady will not
despise what I do here report, as being the very truth of things;
and if I could contribute thereby to her full Satisfaction, I
should have my end, as being willing to see you and her in
this place, where I shall not fear being rebuked for mis-repre-
senting things, I shall conclude,

Governor,

Green-Spring the 13th |
  of September, 1686. |

Your truly affectionate Friend and Servant,
NICHOLAS MORE.

Madame Farmer[2] has found out as good Lime-Stone, on the
School-kill, as any in the World, and is building with it; she

---

[1] Thomas Lloyd (1640–1694), the highest officer in the province, then president of the provincial council, which included the deputy governorship, 1684–1688,
and 1690–1691.   He also served alone as deputy governor, 1691–1693.   Born of
the gentle family of the Lloyds of Dolobran, Montgomeryshire, Wales, he was
graduated with the degree of B. A. from Jesus College, Oxford, in 1661, and became a practising physician.   Joining the Quakers he suffered persecution and
imprisonment.   He brought his family over for settlement in Philadelphia in
1683, on the voyage having the congenial companionship of another university
man, the learned Francis Daniel Pastorius, with whom he conversed in Latin.

[2] Mary Farmar (d. 1687), widow of Major Jasper Farmar (d. 1685).   They
migrated from Arderolaine, County Tipperary, Ireland, to Philadelphia in 1685
and settled on a large tract of 5000 acres of land, on the east side of Schuylkill
River at a place they called Farmars Town, in what is now Whitemarsh Town-

offers to sell ten Thousand Bushels at six Pence the Bushel, upon her Plantation, where there is several considerable Hills, and near to your manner of Springfield.[1]   N. M.

In a Letter from the Governors Steward,[2] Octob. 3, 1686.

The Gardiner is brisk at Work.   The Peach-Trees are much broken down with the weight of Fruit this Year.   All or most of the Plants that came from England grow, (being about four Thousand.)   Cherries are sprung four and five Foot.   Pears, Codlings and Plumbs three or four Foot.   Pears and Apple Grafts, in Country Stocks, and in Thorns, are sprung three and four Foot.   Rasberries, Goosberries, Currans, Quinces, Roses, Walnuts and Figs grow well.   Apricocks from the Stone fourteen or sixteen Inches sprung, since the Month called April. Our Barn, Porch and Shed, are full of Corn this year.

In a Letter from the Governers Gardiner,[3] dated the 14th of the Month, call'd May, 1686.

As for those things I brought with me, it is much for People in England to believe me of the growth of them; some of the Trees and Bulbes are shot in five weeks time, some one Inch, some two, three, four, five, six, seven, yea some a eleven

ship, Montgomery County, Pennsylvania.   The tract, which even yet is among the most important for limestone and lime burning in the vicinity of Philadelphia, is almost the eastern terminus of that underlying belt of limestone that stretches away continuously southwesterly through the Chester Valley of Chester County, and spreads out into the great limestone area of central Lancaster County.

[1] The proprietary manor of Springfield, to the east of the Farmars' tract.

[2] James Harrison (c. 1628–1687), Quaker minister, speaker of assembly, and provincial councillor, had been appointed steward at Pennsbury on Penn's departure from the province in 1684 and held that office until death.   Born near Kendal, Westmoreland, England, he learned the shoemaker's trade, joined the Quakers, became a minister, and travelled in that service all over England, experiencing imprisonment and distraint of property.   Living some years at Stiall Green, Cheshire, he removed, in 1668, to Bolton-in-the-Moors, near Manchester, thence in 1682 migrating with his family by way of Maryland to Pennsylvania and settling in Bucks County between the Falls and Pennsbury House.

[3] James, the second gardener for Pennsbury—Ralph Smith, the first gardener, having died in 1685—was a Scotchman bred in Ireland.   His surname is unknown.   "A good gardner," writes Penn to the steward at Pennsbury in sending James over from England the latter part of 1685, "counted a rare Artist at it, lett him have at least three hands, for he will put things, I hope, in a very good

Inches; some of them not ten days set in the Ground before
they put out Buds.   And seeds do come on apace; for those
Seeds that in England take fourteen days to rise, are up here
in six or seven days.   Pray make agreement with the Bishop
of London's Gardiner or any other that will furnish us with
Trees, Shrubs, Flowers and Seeds, and we will furnish them
from these places; for we have excellent Trees, Shrubs and
Flowers, and Herbs here, which I do not know I ever saw in
any Gardens in England.

*In a Letter from Robert Turner, a Merchant in Philadelphia
and one of the Councel, the 15th of October, 1686.*[1]

I also advise, that, blessed be God, Corn is very cheap this
Season; English Wheat sold here, to carry for New-England
at three Shillings six Pence per Bushel, and much Wheat-
Flower and Bisket for Barbadoes.   Things prosper very well,
and the Earth brings forth its encrease; God grant we may
walk worthy of his Mercies.   Of other Grains, plenty.   As
to the Town, Building goeth on.   John Readman[2] is building
one Brick House for Richard Whitpain,[3] of sixty Foot long,
and fifty six Foot wide.   For the Widow Farmer, another
Brick House.   For Thomas Barker and Samuel Jobson[4] two

method, thou wilt have the tryall of him."   "Thou Knowst his country:" he
adds, "he must be kept to the Seed, for if he be lett up, they want not for head.
The man has lived well."   The gardener was indentured for three years, having
his passage paid, and was to receive a month to himself each year and at the end
of his term £30 and 60 acres of land.

[1] See his previous letter, pp. 268–273, *supra*.

[2] John Redman (d. 1713), bricklayer, of Philadelphia.

[3] Richard Whitpain (c. 1631–1689), Quaker butcher, of St Leonards, East-
cheap, London, remained in London, but his sons John (b. 1663) and Zachariah
(b. 1665) came over to Philadelphia; in 1690 there is mention of "the great house
they Live in."   "Taking into consideration the great expense of Richard Whitpain," writes Penn, in 1687, "to the advancement of the province, and the share he
taketh here (in England) on all occasions for its honour, I can do no less than
recommend to you for public service his great house in Philadelphia, which, being
too big for a private man, would provide you a conveniency above what my cottage affords."   In 1695 the assembly met there.   The house stood on the bank
or bluff on the east side of Front, below Walnut Street.

[4] Thomas Barker (d. 1710), wine merchant, of London, and Samuel Jobson,
fellmonger, of St Mary Magdalen, London, sent over Jacob Chapman to act as
their agent in Pennsylvania, in 1685.

Brick Cellars, and Chimnies for back Kitchings. Thomas Ducket[1] is Building a Brick House at the Skulkil, forty eight Foot long and three Stories high; there are two other Brick Houses to be built this Summer.

In a Letter, of the 2d of October [1686], from David Lloyd,[2] Clerk of the Peace, of the County of Philadelphia.

I shall only add, that five Ships are come in since our arrival, one from Bristol, with 100 Passengers; one from Hull with 160 Passengers; one from New-England for Corn, and two from Barbadoes; all of them, and ours (of above 300 Tun) had their loading here, ours for New-England, and the rest for Barbadoes; and for all this, Wheat (as good, I think, as any in England) is sold at three Shillings six pence per Bushel, this Country Money, and for three Shillings ready Money (which makes two Shillings five pence English Starling) and if God continues his blessing to us, this Province will certainly be the Grainary of America. The Governours Vineyard goes on very well, the Grapes I have tasted of; which in fifteen Months are come to maturity.

---

[1] Thomas Duckett (d. 1699), Quaker minister, a bricklayer, from Wiltshire, England, came over to Philadelphia in 1683 and settled on the west side of the Schuylkill, opposite the town.

[2] David Lloyd (1656–1731), the Welsh Quaker lawyer, destined a few years later to become one of the great lawgivers and agitators for popular rights in the early history of the American colonies, had been a resident of the province but a little more than two months, having arrived with his family at Philadelphia, in the ship *Amity*, from London, July 15, 1686, to take up his duties as attorney general of Pennsylvania. A native of the parish of Manoron, in Montgomeryshire, Wales, he was a kinsman of the most prominent man in the province, Governor Thomas Lloyd. He probably received his legal training at the Inner Temple in London and—so Governor Gookin stated in 1709—"under my Lord Chancellor Jefferies." He lived for some years in Philadelphia and then about 1700 removed to Chester. He was a member of the provincial council, 1695–1700, but accomplished his most important work thereafter as a member of assembly, serving for more than a quarter of a century, frequently as speaker. He was the leader of the popular party in that body, tenaciously contending for the privileges and liberties of the common people in opposition to the proprietary interests as defended by James Logan, the proprietary secretary and agent. To him "liberal government in Pennsylvania," says Pennypacker, "owes more than to any other man among our early lawgivers, unless we except Penn himself." In 1718 he was made chief justice and served until death.

In a Letter, of October last [1686], from Thomas Holmes[1]
Surveyor General.

We have made three Purchases of the Indians, which, added unto the six former Sales they made us, will, I believe, be Land enough for Planters for this Age; they were at first High, and upon their Distances; but when we told them of the Kindness our Governour had always shown them; that the Price we offer'd far exceeded former Rates, and that they offered us the Land before we sought them, they agreed to our last Offer, which is something under three hundred Pounds sterling. The Kings salute our Governour; they hardly ever see any of us, but they ask, with much affection when he will come to them again; we are upon very good terms with them. I intend to send the Draughts for a Map[2] by the first——

In a Letter from James Claypole[3] Merchant in Philadelphia and one of the Councel.

I have never seen brighter and better Corn then in these parts, especially in the County of Chester. Provisions very cheap; Pork at two Pence, and good fat fresh Beef at three half-pence the Pound, in our Market. Fish is plentiful; Corn cheap; Wheat three and six pence a Bushel; Rye half a Crown; Indian Corn two Shillings, of this Money: And it is without

---

[1] For Thomas Holme, see p. 242, note 1.

[2] This was Thomas Holme's well known wall map of Pennsylvania (32½x55 inches), the most important of the early maps of the province, giving the southeastern part with the streams, counties, townships, towns, the individual surveys or plots containing the owners' names and the like. It was engraved by E. Lamb, and published without date in London. But the date was 1687, for William Penn on his way from London to Bristol Fair in September of that year stopped at Marlborough in Wiltshire and exhibited a "Mapp" showing lands in Pennsylvania.

[3] James Claypoole (1634–1687), a native of London, son of a justice and member of Parliament, and brother of John Claypoole, who married Oliver Cromwell's daughter Elizabeth, was a prosperous Quaker merchant. Previous to his migration he had lived in Scots Yard, in Bush Lane, London. Having social, religious, and business relations with William Penn he became actively concerned in the Pennsylvania project from its beginning, purchased 5,000 acres of land in the province, was elected the first treasurer of the Free Society of Traders in 1682, and in the following year came over with his family to settle,

doubt that we shall have as good Wine as France produces. Here is great appearance of a Trade, and if we had small Money for Exchange, we should not want Returns. The Whale-Fishery[1] is considerable; several Companies out to ketch them: There is one caught that its thought will make several hundred Barrels of Oyle. This besides Tobacco and Skins, and Furs, we have for Commerce.

arriving at Philadelphia in the ship *Concord* in October. He located on his lot at the southwest corner of Front and Walnut streets, and during the remaining four years of his life was busily engaged in attending to his duties as treasurer of the Free Society and promoting his private trading enterprises, at the same time holding important public offices as justice of the courts, register general, assembly-man and provincial councillor. His manuscript letter-book (1681–1684), printed in part in the *Pennsylvania Magazine*, X. (1886), is a valuable historical source for the period.

[1] "I have been 3 weeks from home," Claypoole writes from Philadelphia, 2 Mo. (April) 4, 1684, "about 150 miles of [off] whare they take the whales, they took 2 while I was there, they had killed about 12 in all and lost 3 of them and they intend to stay till the end of this month and may expect to gitt 5 or 6 more they fish for the Society [Free Society of Traders] but must be pd. the Markett prise for $\frac{2}{3}$ of the oyle and bone besides some other Charges we are at so we are like to gett no great Matter by it this time, this is the first year of their fishing and they were not provided with Nessesarys in time else they might have made 100lb each man, here being great plenty of whales and very easy to take them here is abundance of Sturgeon and other fish."

A SHORT DESCRIPTION OF PENNSILVANIA.
BY RICHARD FRAME, 1692

INTRODUCTION

In 1692, William Bradford, the Quaker printer, of Philadelphia, published a small quarto (6¾x4⅞ inches) of eight pages entitled *A Short Description of Pennsilvania*. This little book is in verse and is believed to be the first metrical composition printed in Pennsylvania. The only known copy of the work is in the Ridgway Branch of the Library Company of Philadelphia, to which it was bequeathed by Charles A. Poulson some sixty years ago.

An element of uncertainty hangs over the authorship of the verses. The title and last page of the book assign them to one Richard Frame. Yet strange to say a thorough search of all Pennsylvania sources likely to be fruitful of results has failed to reveal a single reference—other than these citations in the book itself—to substantiate the existence of a person of this name here at that time.

It is true that some of the public and many private records for the period have perished or are otherwise defective; nevertheless those that survive are so full and of such a varied character that it is rare indeed to find entries lacking of settlers of even the most humble position. The observing intelligence discernible in this writer would seem to raise him far out of the obscurity of the latter class. The suggestion that the author may have made only a brief sojourn here and so have escaped record or chronicler finds no support from the internal evidence, which indicates an extended acquaintance with the province. This absence of data, then, respecting the presence of Richard Frame raises the question whether this was not an assumed name.

Be that as it may, we are confined to the book itself for

biographical facts as to its author. From it may be deduced the somewhat scanty conjectures that he was a native of England, that he had come to Pennsylvania at the beginning of the Penn era, had actively participated in the felling of the forests and the clearing of the land, and had joined in the pioneer farming of which he writes so familiarly. Despite his manifest defects of education he was a man of sense and good powers of observation. He seems to know whereof he writes, evidently having a personal acquaintance with the settled part of Pennsylvania proper.

His verse, to be sure, falls far short of poetry; it will never find a place in the American Anthology: yet what it lacks in poetical form it makes up in the quaint interest and valuable information of its content. It conveys a truthful and not unpleasing impression of the state of Penn's colony—of its flora, its fauna, products and the like—after a decade of prosperous growth.

Granting that Richard Frame was the author's real name, he may have been related to the family of Fream or Freame of Gloucestershire, England. A Thomas Fream, from Avon, in that county, was a settler in Bucks County, Pennsylvania; his will dated September 5 was probated October 10, 1682, being the first will recorded in Philadelphia. Again, a Robert Freame, of Cirencester, supposed to be Penn's First Purchaser of this name in 1681, was the father of Robert and John Freame, prominent Quakers, of London, in the latter part of the seventeenth century. Both the latter held shares of stock in the Pennsylvania Land Company of London. Thomas Freame, son of Robert, jr., married William Penn's daughter Margaret in 1727 and lived for a time in Pennsylvania.

A Short Description was reprinted in a small edition (118 copies) by Samuel J. Hamilton (Dr. James Slack), at the Oakwood Press, a private press, in 1867, with an introductory letter by Horatio Gates Jones. The present issue is from a careful copy of the unique original book compared by the editor. The title-page is worn and broken in places and the first page of the text has been trimmed so closely for binding that the first one or two letters of each line have been cut off; a tear also appears in the sheet. These defective parts have been supplied in brackets as well as may be from portions of letters remaining, or from the obvious sense. Doubtful words are so indicated.

A. C. M.

A SHORT DESCRIPTION OF PENNSILVANIA,
BY RICHARD FRAME, 1692

A Short Description of Pennsilvania, Or, a Relation What things
are known, enjoyed, and like to be discovered in the said
Province. [Presen(?)]tted as a Token of Good Will [to
the People(?)] of England. By Richard Frame. Printed
and Sold by William Bradford in Philadelphia, 1692.

A short Relation of what things are Known, Enjoyd, and like to
be Discovered in the Province of Pennsilvania.

TO all our Friends that do desire to know,
What Country 'tis we live in, this will show.
Attend to hear the Story I shall tell,
[N]o doubt but you will like this Country well.
We that did leave our Country thought it strange,
[T]hat ever we should make so good Exchange:
[I(?)] think 'tis hard for me for to express,
[H]ow God provideth in a Wilderness,
[*torn*   ]arge a wo[*torn*]
[*torn*] Wolves, and Bears, and Pa[*torn*]
[Fo]xes, Raccoons and Otters dwelleth here,
[Be]side all these the Nimble footed Dear;
[T]he Hare so lightly runs for to escape;
[Y]et here are things of a more stranger shape,
[T]he Female Possum, which I needs must tell ye,
[Is] much admired with her double Belly;
[T]he Belly for her Meat, she hath beside
[A]nother where her Young Ones use to hide.
[O] strange! 'tis hard, I think, for me to name
[T]he Multitudes of Beasts, both Wild and Tame:
[B]evers here are, whose Skins are soft as Silk,
[H]orses to Ride on, Cows to give us Milk,
[Be]sides the Beasts, whose Nature is so Rude,

[To] speak of them, I think I must Conclude.
[Al]so the Flocks of Fowle, and Birds, pray mind,
[The] Swans, and Geese, and Turkyes in their kind,
The Turky-Buzard, and Bald-Eagle high,
Wild Ducks, which in great Companyes do fly;
More sorts of fowle here are, than I need [tell],
Yet here are other things, which do excell.
The Fields, most fruitful, yield such Crops of Wheat,
And other things most excellent to eat.
As Barley, Rye, and other sorts of Grain;
In peace we plow, we sow, and reap again,
Good Indian Corn, which is a larger breed,
It doth our Cattle, Swine and Horses feed,
Buck-Wheat and Oats, beside, good store of Reed,
A plentiful Land, O plentiful indeed,
For Plants, and Roots, and Herbs, wee'l let them be,
To name the Fruit that grows upon each Tree:
The fruit Trees do flourish, and are green,
Where Apples, Peaches, Quinces, Plumbs are seen,
With other Fruits, whose glittering Faces shine.
The Grapes grow plenty on the fruitful Vine:
Wall-Nuts, Chest-Nuts, Hazel-Nuts appear,
These things are plenty with us every Year.
More things I can relate, for all is true,
And yet, not give the Country half his due.
Also, here is of divers sorts of Fish,
So good, so pleasant as a man need wish,
Within our Rivers, swiming to and fro.
Great ones we catch, but small ones let them go.
Here are more things than I can well express,
Strange to be seen in such a Wilderness.
By Day we work, at Night we rest in Peace,
So that each Day our Substance doth increase:
O blessed be his Name, who doth provide
For you, and us, and all the World beside.

The first part that I writ is good indeed,
But yet perhaps the second may exceed:
The Truth in Rhyme, which I do here compose,
It may be spoken thus, as well as Prose:

Therefore unto my words once more attend,
Here are more Properties I shall commend.

The Riches of this Land it is not known,
What in the after Ages may be shown;
My words are true, for here was lately found
Some precious Mettle under-neath the Ground,
The which some men did think was Silver Oar,
Others said Copper, but some think 'tis more.
They say there is a vein of Lead or Tin,
Where choicer Mettle lodgeth further in;
So divers men have divers judgments spent,
And so the matter lies in Argument.
If men would venture for to dig below,
They might get well by it, for ought I know:
Those Treasures in the Earth which hidden be,
They will be good, whoever lives to see.
A certain place here is, where some begun
To try some Mettle, and have made it run,
Wherein was Iron absolutely found,
At once was known about some Forty Pound.

We know no end of this great Tract of Land,
Where divers sorts of Timber Trees doth stand,
As mighty Oaks, also, here's Cedars tall,
And other sorts, 'tis hard to name them all,
The strong Hickery, Locust and lofty Pine,
'Tis strange to see what Providence divine
Hath in the World ordained for to be,
Which those that live at home do never see.

I also give you here to understand
What People first inhabited this Land:
Those that were here before the Sweeds and Fins,
Were Naked Indians, Cloathed with their Skins,
Which can give no account from whence they came;
They have no Records for to shew the same;
But I may think, and others may suppose
What They may be, yet I think few men knows,

Unless they are of Esau's scattered Seed,
Or of some other wild corrupted Breed.
They take no care to plow, nor yet to sow,
Nor how to till their Land they do not know,
Therefore by that we may observe it plain,
That this can hardly be the Seed of Cain;
Some Men did think they were the scattered Jews,
But yet I cannot well believe such News:
They neither do New Moons nor Sabbath keep,
Without much Care they eat, they drink, they sleep;
Their care for Worldly Riches is but light,
By Day they hunt, and down they lie at Night.
Those Infidels that dwelleth in the Wood,
I shall conclude of them so far so good.

You that will seek a Country strange,
    Attend to what is true,
All that are willing to exchange,
    An Old place for a New.
We that our Country did forsake,
    And leave our Native Land,
Will do the best we can to make
    Our Neighbours understand.

Although I have a good intent,
    Yet hardly can express,
How we, through Mercy, were content
    In such a Wilderness.
When we began to clear the Land,
    For room to sow our Seed,
And that our Corn might grow and stand,
    For Food in time of Need,
Then with the Ax, with Might and Strength,
    The Trees so thick and strong,
Yet on each side, such strokes at length,
    We laid them all along.
So when the Trees, that grew so high,
    Were fallen to the ground,
Which we with Fire, most furiously
    To Ashes did Confound,

Then presently we sought for Wood,
    I mean (not Wood to burn,
But for) such Timber, choice and good,
    As fitted well our turn.
A City, and Towns were raised then,
    Wherein we might abide,
Planters also, and Husband-men,
    Had Land enough beside.
The best of Houses then was known,
    To be of Wood and Clay,
But now we build of Brick and Stone,
    Which is a better way.

The Names of Some of our Towns.

Philadelphia, that great Corporation,
Was then, is now our choicest Habitation.
Next unto that there stands the German-Town,
Also, within the Country, up and down,
There's Haverford, where th' Welch-men do abide,
Two Townships more, I think, they have beside:
Here's Bristol, Plymouth,[1] Newtown, here doth stand,
Chester, Springfield, Marple in this Land,
Darby, and other famous Habitations,
Also, a multitude of New Plantations.

The German-Town[2] of which I spoke before,
Which is, at least, in length one Mile and More,
Where lives High-German People, and Low-Dutch,
Whose Trade in weaving Linnin Cloth is much,
There grows the Flax, as also you may know,
That from the same they do divide the Tow;
Their Trade fits well within this Habitation,
We find Convenience for their Occupation.
One Trade brings in imployment for another,
So that we may suppose each Trade a Brother;
From Linnin Rags good Paper doth derive,

[1] Near present Norristown, in Montgomery County.
[2] "A Town of Dutch and German People that have set up the Linnen Manufactory, which weave and make many Hundred Yards of pure fine Linnen Cloath in a Year."—Letter of John Goodson, Philadelphia, 1690.

The first Trade keeps the second Trade alive:
Without the first the second cannot be,
Therefore since these two can so well agree,
Convenience doth approve to place them nigh,
One in the German-Town, 'tother hard by.
A Paper Mill[1] near German-Town doth stand,
So that the Flax, which first springs from the Land,
First Flax, then Yarn, and then they must begin,
To weave the same, which they took pains to spin.
Also, when on our backs it is well [worn],
Some of the same remains Ragged and Torn;
Then of those Rags our Paper it is made,
Which in process of time doth waste and fade:
So what comes from the Earth, appeareth plain,
The same in Time returns to Earth again.

So much for what I have truly Compos'd,
Which is but a part of what may be disclosed,
Concluding of this, and what is behind,
I may tell you more of my Mind;
But in the mean time be content with this same,
Which at present is all from your Friend

RICHARD FRAME.

[1] The first paper-mill in America, erected in 1690, on a branch of Wissahickon Creek, in Germantown, by William Rittinghuysen or Rittenhouse (1644–1708), a Mennonite paper-maker, with the assistance of a company consisting of William Bradford, the first printer of the middle colonies, and the wealthy Philadelphia citizens, Samuel Carpenter, Robert Turner, and Thomas Tresse. Bradford obtained his paper from this mill. Rittenhouse was a native of the principality of Broich, near the city of Mülheim-on-the-Ruhr, Germany, not far from the borders of Holland. His ancestors for generations had been paper-makers at Arnheim. In 1678 he was a resident of Amsterdam; thence he came to New York, and in 1688 to Germantown, where he served as a minister in the Mennonite congregation.

AN HISTORICAL AND GEOGRAPHICAL AC-
COUNT OF PENSILVANIA AND OF WEST-
NEW-JERSEY, BY GABRIEL THOMAS, 1698

INTRODUCTION

THE book here reprinted was the largest and most pretentious that had yet appeared descriptive of the twin provinces on the Delaware. The author was a Welsh yeoman who, having been a pioneer in Penn's colony during the fifteen years of his young manhood, the very period of its rise and development to this time, had returned to the Old World, and in 1697 prepared this account from his experiences and observation. The work was published the following year in London. The first part, which has to do with Pennsylvania, is dedicated to William Penn, and apparently was issued with his knowledge and encouragement, although Penn's recent removal to Bristol and subsequent travels in Ireland doubtless gave him no opportunity to read either the manuscript or proof of the book.

Gabriel Thomas was the author. He had his origin in the extreme southeastern part of Wales, in Monmouthshire, not far from the English border and at no great distance from Bristol. Pontemoil, a little place nestling at the foot of a spur of the Drynos mountains, was his birthplace. There he first saw the light in March, 1661. His parents, Lewis and Grace Thomas, who had lived at the place as early as 1650, were Quakers. One Lewis Thomas, a dissenting Quaker liberated from Monmouth jail in 1671, was probably the father. No further records of Gabriel Thomas in Wales have been found.

In the fall of 1681, being then in his twenty-first year, Gabriel Thomas set out for Pennsylvania, sailing from London with the first company of Penn's emigrants in the ship *John and Sarah*. At Philadelphia, he informs us, "I saw the first Cellar when it was digging for the use of our Gouvernour Will. Penn." His parents with nearly all of their eight children also came over to the province, but the time of their arrival is unknown.   In 1688 two of his sisters were married by the Quaker meeting in Philadelphia, his younger sister Rachel at that time becoming the bride of Thomas Wharton, the founder of the distinguished Philadelphia family of that name.   In the same year the father died, being mentioned in one of the papers of his estate at Philadelphia, as "late of West Jersey" and in another as "late of Philadelphia."   The mother died in Philadelphia in 1694.   The records indicate Thomas's presence in the city in 1692 and in 1693 and that was probably in general his place of residence in Pennsylvania.

Proceeding to London about 1697, being then aged thirty-six, he saw his book through the press and remained there as late as 1702.   In this year he figures in an acrimonious controversy with William Penn.   With the plea, as he states, that his book on Pennsylvania had "proved to the province's great advancement by causing great numbers of people to goe over to those parts," he sought the proprietary post of collector of quit-rents for New Castle County.   Penn failing to meet these expectations, Thomas took sides with Colonel Robert Quarry, judge of admiralty in the middle colonies, in the latter's campaign of aggression against Penn and the government of Pennsylvania, and finally invoked the aid of the British Board of Trade in his endeavors to secure the place.   In his petition to this body Thomas complains that he is now "reduced to great poverty by reason" of Penn's "unjust dealings" and is persecuted because of assistance given to Colonel Quarry.   He then declares that he is ready to appear as evidence for the Crown against Penn.   The incident closes with Penn's response to the board under date of August, 1702, in which he characterizes Thomas as "so beggarly and base a man, that I am sorry to finde time lost upon him."

By 1706 Thomas had come back to America and was living as a yeoman in Sussex County in the present state of Delaware, where he possessed a plantation of about a thousand acres called "Pleasant," located on the north side of Prime Hook Neck. In 1712 he was again a resident of Philadelphia and there he doubtless continued until his death, which occurred in December, 1714, at the age of fifty-three.

Gabriel Thomas, as we have seen, was not only a birth-right Quaker, but he used the Quaker form of speech in his dedication to Penn, and is so named in the records of the British Board of Trade. In later life, however, his membership was discontinued, as both the burial records of the Philadelphia Friends and the manuscript "Beehive," kept by Pastorius, the contemporary German Quaker, enter him as a non-Quaker.

The intent of Thomas's history, like that of our other narratives for this English epoch, was chiefly to incite the movement of European population to the Delaware. The book is written in a simple, descriptive style, but with an undercurrent of playfulness and occasional touches of satire that lend a certain charm and quaint pleasantness to the account. Along with these evidences of the Cymric temperament of the writer is a tendency to exaggerate in some of the passages; these lapses, however, are easily discernible. Where he writes what he himself knows he is in general reliable, but he falls sadly into error with respect to some of the dates and places that are without his own experience. These inaccuracies are corrected in the notes.

An Historical and Geographical Account is a sextodecimo book published in London in 1698. The part dealing with Pennsylvania comprises 8 + 55 pages. The second part concerns West New Jersey, and is inscribed to the proprietors of that province. Although bound up with the first part, it has its own title-page and separate pagination, numbering 11 + 34 pages. A map covering the region of both provinces is included in the volume. A German translation forming part of the Pastorius *Continuatio der Beschreibung der Landschafft*

Pennsylvaniae (2 + 40 pages) was published at Frankfort and Leipzig about 1702. Our text is from a lithographic facsimile of the original London edition, published in New York in 1848 by Henry Austin Brady. The original edition was also reprinted in the *Philadelphia Daily News*, in August and December, 1864, and again by Burrows Brothers of Cleveland, Ohio, in 1903 (pp. 83), with an introduction by Cyrus Townsend Brady.

A. C. M.

AN HISTORICAL AND GEOGRAPHICAL ACCOUNT OF PENSILVANIA AND OF WEST-NEW-JERSEY, BY GABRIEL THOMAS, 1698

An Historical and Geographical Account of the Province and Country of Pensilvania; and of West-New-Jersey in America. The Richness of the Soil, the Sweetness of the Situation the Wholesomness of the Air, the Navigable Rivers, and others, the prodigious Encrease of Corn, the flourishing Condition of the City of Philadelphia, with the stately Buildings, and other Improvements there. The strange Creatures, as Birds, Beasts, Fishes, and Fowls, with the several sorts of Minerals, Purging Waters, and Stones, lately discovered. The Natives, Aborogines, their Language, Religion, Laws, and Customs; The first Planters, the Dutch, Sweeds, and English, with the number of its Inhabitants; As also a Touch upon George Keith's New Religion, in his second Change since he left the Quakers, with a Map of both Countries.

By Gabriel Thomas, who resided there about Fifteen Years. London, Printed for, and Sold by A. Baldwin, at the Oxon Arms in Warwick-Lane, 1698.

The Dedication.

Friend William Penn,

I Here present Thee with a succinct (yet compleat) Account of the late Improvement, and Present State of the Noble Province, and Fertile Countrey of Pensilvania; with the strange things that have been found there, as the Salamander-Stone,[1] and several others, mentioned in this Treatise; discovered since thou camest out of those Parts. I desire Thee to excuse me for addressing to Thee, such a Plain and Peasant-like Piece; yet however homely or coarse it may appear, Thou wilt find here a true and genuine Description of that (once) obscure,

[1] Asbestos.

tho' (now) glorious Place. So considering how generous and
candid a Man Thou art, I know thou wilt bear with my weak
and imperfect Performance, and accept of my good Meaning
and kind Intention, which may encourage me, in time to come,
to add some more Memoirs to this rough Essay of mine. Being
unwilling to tire Thee with any long or tedious Epistle, I take
my Leave of Thee,

(Most Noble and Excellent Governor) and am

Thy hearty Well-wisher, ever ready to
serve Thee on all Occasions, (in
the way of Truth,)

GABRIEL THOMAS.

The Preface.

Reader,

There never having been any fair or full Account given to
the World of Pensilvania, I thought the Curious wou'd be
gratified with an ample Description thereof.

For tho' this Country has made little Noise in Story, or
taken up but small room in Maps, yet thus much with great
Justice may be said of it, that notwithstanding the Difficulties
and Inconveniencies the First English Colonies met with before
they were well settled there, yet the mighty Improvements,
Additions, and Advantages that have been made lately there,
are well worth Communicating to the Publick, and I am sensible
they will be well receiv'd.

The late Tedious, Hazardous, and Expensive War[1] (in
which England, in Conjunction with the Allies was so deeply
engag'd) was without doubt no small Bar or Obstacle to the
Flourishing of this New Country. The great Discouragements
the Traders thither lay under, (together with the frequent
Capture of their Ships out and home, cou'd not chuse but
baulk them in their honest Endeavours, which (now Peace is
restor'd) they may pursue with greater Security and Satisfaction.

Nor is there the least question or doubt to be made, but
this Noble Spot of Earth will thrive exceedingly, and that in a
short time too, and advance considerably to the mighty Ad-

---

[1] Known in the colonies as King William's War, 1689–1697, ending with the
treaty of Ryswick in the latter year.

vantage of the Present and Future Propietors, who have, and are willing to give all due Encouragement to any that shall Transport themselves thither.

I cou'd say much here in Praise of that sweet Tract of Land, but having spoken so largely and particularly thereof in the Book it self, I shall forbear the least mention in this place. Nor will I Anticipate or forestal thee, by presenting thee here with what thou wilt find there, with the greater Satisfaction. And so I bid thee heartily farewel.

GAB. THOMAS.

The History of Pensilvania, etc.

PENSILVANIA lies between the Latitude of Forty and Forty five Degrees;[1] West-Jersey on the East, Virginia on the West, Mary-Land South, and Canada[2] on the North. In Length three hundred, and in Breadth one hundred and eighty Miles.[3]

The Natives, or first Inhabitants of this Country in their Original, are suppos'd by most People to have been of the Ten Scattered Tribes, for they resemble the Jews very much in the Make of their Persons, and Tincture of their Complexions: They observe New Moons, they offer their first Fruits to a *Maneto*, or suppos'd Deity, whereof they have two, one, as they fansie, above (good,) another below (bad,) and have a kind of Feast of Tabernacles, laying their Altars upon Twelve Stones, observe a sort of Mourning twelve Months, Customs of Women, and many other Rites to be toucht (here) rather than

[1] Although several of the boundaries of Pennsylvania were then either not fully determined or in dispute, yet Thomas even for that period had very erroneous and inconsistent notions as to some of them. His absurd extension of the northern boundary to the forty-fifth parallel of north latitude, the present northern line of the state of New York, included the province of New York in Pennsylvania, a claim at no time made by Pennsylvania; while his restriction of the southern boundary of Pennsylvania to the fortieth parallel, as contended by Maryland, left out Philadelphia, which is in 39° 57', and half of the province as then settled, not to speak of the Three Lower Counties of Delaware (now the state of Delaware), at that time constituting a part of Pennsylvania. The present state of Pennsylvania lies between 39° 43' and 42° 15' north latitude.

[2] The province of New York not Canada was on the north.

[3] The present state of Pennsylvania is 307 miles long in its greatest length from east to west, and 177 miles wide from north to south. If "forty-five" is a misprint for "forty-three" Thomas has these directions in mind.

dwelt upon, because they shall be handled more at large at the latter end of this Treatise.

They are very Charitable to one another, the Lame and the Blind (amongst them) living as well as the best; they are also very kind and obliging to the Christians.

The next that came there,[1] were the Dutch, (who call'd the Country New Neitherland) between Fifty and Sixty Years ago, and were the first Planters in those Parts; but they made little or no Improvement, (applying themselves wholly to Trafique in Skins and Furs, which the Indians or Natives furnish'd them with, and which they Barter'd for Rum, Strong Liquors, and Sugar, with others, thereby gaining great Profit) till near the time of the Wars between England and Them, about Thirty or Forty Years ago.

Soon after them came the Swedes[2] and Fins, who apply'd themselves to Husbandry, and were the first Christian People that made any considerable Improvement there.

There were some Disputes between these two Nations some Years, the Dutch looking upon the Swedes as Intruders upon their Purchase and Possession, which was absolutely terminated in the Surrender made by John Rizeing,[3] the Swedes Governour, to Peter Styreant,[4] Governour for the Dutch, in 1655. In the Holland War about the Year 1665,[5] Sir Robert Carr took the Country from the Dutch for the English, and left his Cousin, Captain Carr,[6] Governor of that place; but in a short time after, the Dutch re-took the Country from the English, and kept it in their Possession till the Peace was concluded between the English and them, when the Dutch Surrendered that Country with East and West-Jersey, New-York, (with the whole Countries belonging to that Government) to the English

[1] Evidently here referring not simply to Pennsylvania proper but to the larger Delaware River region which was first occupied by the Dutch at least seventy-five years before 1697, Fort Nassau in New Jersey being built in 1623.

[2] The first Swedish settlement was made at present Wilmington, Delaware, in 1638.

[3] Rising.   [4] Stuyvesant.   [5] 1664.

[6] Captain John Carr accompanied his brother, not his cousin, Sir Robert Carr, on the conquering expedition of the English against the Dutch on the Delaware in 1664 and after the departure of his brother remained in command at New Castle (the new name for the New Amstel of the Dutch), until the reconquest by the Dutch in 1673.

again.[1]   But it remain'd with very little Impovement till the
Year 1681, in which William Penn Esq; had the Country given
him by King Charles the Second, in lieu of Money that was due
to (and signal Service done by) his Father, Sir William Penn,
and from him bore the Name of Pensilvania.

Since that time, the Industrious (nay Indefatigable) Inhab-
itants have built a Noble and Beautiful City, and called it
Philadelphia, which contains above two thousand Houses, all
Inhabited; and most of them Stately, and of Brick, generally
three Stories high, after the Mode in London, and as many
several Families in each.   There are very many Lanes and
Alleys, as first, Huttons-Lane,[2] Morris-Lane,[3] Jones's-Lane,[4]
wherein are very good Buildings; Shorters-Alley,[5] Towers-
Lane,[6] Wallers-Alley,[7] Turners-Lane,[8] Sikes-Alley,[9] and Flowers-
Alley.[10] All these Alleys and Lanes extend from the Front
Street to the Second Street.   There is another Alley in the
Second Street, called Carters-Alley.[11]   There are also besides
these Alleys and Lanes, several fine Squares and Courts within
this Magnificent City, (for so I may justly call it,) As for the
particular Names of the several Streets contained therein, the
Principal are as follows, viz, Walnut-Street, Vine-Street, Mul-
berry-Street,[12] Chesnut-Street, Sassafras-Street,[13] taking their
Names from the abundance of those Trees that formerly grew

[1] In 1674.

[2] The second alley above Walnut Street, Thomas Hooton being owner of an
adjacent lot.

[3] Possibly opposite the bank lot of Anthony Morris (1654–1721), the emigrant,
a rich Quaker brewer, mayor and provincial councillor.

[4] The first alley above High (now Market) Street, running from Front to
Second Street, adjoining a lot of Griffith Jones (d. 1712), a Welshman, one of the
wealthiest citizens.

[5] Not located, but Elizabeth Shorter owned a lot above Chestnut Street.

[6] Ewers Lane, above Chestnut Street, adjoining Robert Ewer's lot.

[7] Not located.

[8] The first below Mulberry (now Arch) Street, adjoining Robert Turner's
property.

[9] May have been opposite the bank lot of Nathaniel Sykes, below Chestnut
Street.

[10] Doubtless named for Enoch Flower, Quaker, who taught the first school in
Philadelphia, in 1683.

[11] The first below Chestnut Street, William Carter owning an adjoining lot
on Second Street.

[12] Now Arch.   [13] Now Race.

there; High-Street,[1] Broad-Street, Delaware-Street, Front-Street, with several of less Note, too tedious to insert here.

It hath in it Three Fairs every Year, and Two Markets every Week, They kill above Twenty Fat Bullocks every Week, in the hottest time in Summer, for their present spending in that City, besides many Sheep, Calves, and Hogs.

This City is Situated between Schoolkill-River and the great River Delaware,[2] which derives its Name from Captain Delaware, who came there pretty early: Ships of Two or Three Hundred Tuns may come up to this City, by either of these two Rivers. Moreover, in this Province are Four Great Market-Towns, *viz*, Chester, the German Town, New-Castle, and Lewis-Town,[3] which are mightily Enlarged in this latter Improvement. Between these Towns, the Water-Men constantly Ply their Wherries;[4] likewise all those Towns have Fairs kept in them, besides there are several Country Villages, *viz.* Dublin,[5] Harford,[6] Merioneth,[7] and Radnor in Cambry;[8] all which Towns, Villages and Rivers, took their Names from the several Countries whence the present Inhabitants came.

The Air here is very delicate, pleasant, and wholesom; the Heavens serene, rarely overcast, bearing mighty resemblance to the better part of France; after Rain they have commonly a very clear Sky, the Climate is something Colder in the depth of Winter and Hotter in the height of Summer; (the cause of which is its being a Main Land or Continent; the Days also are two Hours longer in the shortest Day in Winter, and shorter by two Hours in the longest Day of Summer) than here in England, which makes the Fruit so good, and the Earth so fertil.

[1] Now Market.

[2] So named by one of the Virginia adventurers, Captain Samuel Argall, who visited the Bay in 1610, in honor of the then Governor of Virginia, Thomas West, Lord de la Warr, of whose alleged visit there no evidence is known.

[3] Lewes, in Sussex County, Delaware.

[4] Light boats used on rivers.

[5] Now Ogontz, Montgomery County, Pennsylvania.

[6] Haverford.   [7] Merion.

[8] Cambria, *i. e.*, the Welsh Tract, that area extending northwesterly from Schuylkill River and embracing at that time the townships of Merion, Haverford, and Radnor, occupied by Welsh people, many of them from the northern counties of Wales—principally Merioneth, Denbigh, Montgomery, and Flint.

The Corn-Harvest is ended before the middle of July, and most Years they have commonly between Twenty and Thirty Bushels of Wheat for every one they Sow. Their Ground is harrowed with Wooden Tyned Harrows, twice over in a place is sufficient; twice mending of their Plow-Irons in a Years time will serve. Their Horses commonly go without being shod; two Men may clear between Twenty and Thirty Acres of Land in one Year, fit for the Plough, in which Oxen are chiefly us'd, though Horses are not wanting, and of them Good and well shap'd. A Cart or a Wain may go through the middle of the Woods, between the Trees without getting any damage, and of such Land in a convenient place, the Purchase will cost between Ten and Fifteen Pounds for a Hundred Acres. Here is much Meadow Ground. Poor People both Men and Women, will get near three times more Wages for their Labour in this Country, than they can earn either in England or Wales.

What is Inhabited of this Country, is divided into Six Counties, though there is not the Twentieth Part of it yet Peopled by the Christians: It hath in it several Navigable Rivers for Shipping to come in, besides the Capital Delaware, wherein a Ship of Two Hundred Tuns may Sail Two Hundred Miles up. There are also several other small Rivers, in number hardly Credible; these, as the Brooks, have for the most part gravelly and hard Bottoms; and it is suppos'd that there are many other further up in the Country, which are not yet discover'd; the Names of the aforesaid Rivers, are, Hoorkill-River, alias Lewis River, which runs up to Lewis Town, the chiefest in Sussex County; Cedar-River, Muskmellon-River,[1] all taking their Names from the great plenty of these things growing thereabouts; Mother-kill alias Dover-River, St. Jones's alias Cranbrook-River, where one John Curtice[2] lives, who hath Three Hundred Head of Neat Beasts, besides great Numbers of Hogs, Horses, and Sheep; Great Duck-River, Little Duck-River, Black-Bird-River, these also took their Original Names from the great Numbers of those Fowls which are found there

---

[1] Mispillion.

[2] John Curtis (d. 1698), who was of the Whorekill, now Lewes, in 1679, soon after located on a plantation on St. Jones Creek in Kent County, Delaware. He represented Kent County in the Pennsylvania assembly and in the provincial council.

in vast quantities: Apequinemy-River,[1] where their Goods
come to be Carted over to Mary-Land,[2]   St. George's-River,
Christen-River,[3] Brandy-Wine-River, Upland alias Chester-
River, which runs by Chester-Town, being the Shire or County-
Town; Schoolkill-River, Frankford-River,[4] near which, Arthur
Cook hath a most Stately Brick-House; and Nishamany-River,
where Judge Growden[5] hath a very Noble and Fine House, very
pleasantly Situated, and likewise a Famous Orchard adjoyning
to it, wherein are contain'd above a Thousand Apple Trees of
various sorts; likewise there is the famous Derby-River,[6] which
comes down from the Cumbry by Derby-Town, wherein are
several Mills, viz. Fulling-Mills, Corn-Mills, etc.

There is curious Building-Stone and Paving-Stone, also
Tile-Stone,[7] with which latter, Governor Penn covered his
Great and Stately Pile, which he call'd Pennsbury-House,[8]
the Name it still retains. There is likewise Iron-Stone or Oar,
(lately found) which far exceeds that in England, being Richer
and less Drossy; some Preparations have been made to carry
on an Iron-Work: There is also very good Lime-Stone in great
plenty, and cheap, of great use in Buildings, and also in Manu-
ring Land, (if there were occasion) but Nature has made that
of it self sufficiently Fruitful; besides here are Load-Stones,
Ising-Glass, and (that Wonder of Stones) the Salamander-
Stone, found near Brandy-Wine-River, having Cotton in Veins
within it, which will not consume in the Fire; though held there
a long time.[9]

[1] Appoquinimink.

[2] To Bohemia River, a northeastern affluent of Chesapeake Bay. This was
the shortest and usual portage between the Delaware and Chesapeake.

[3] Christiana.   [4] Now Tacony Creek.

[5] Joseph Growden (d. 1730), gentleman, justice of the provincial supreme
court, speaker of assembly, and provincial councillor, was a son of Lawrence
Growden, of Trevose, parish of St. Merryn, Cornwall, England. As one of the
First Purchasers of Pennsylvania he brought over a ship loaded with his own
cargo in 1683 and located on his purchase of 5,000 acres of land on the Neshaminy
Creek in Bensalem Township, Bucks County. "Trevose," his "Noble and Fine
House," although altered is still standing. His daughter Grace became the
second wife of David Lloyd.

[6] Darby.   [7] Slate.

[8] Pennsbury House, Penn's country-seat, was in Pennsbury Manor, a tract of
over 6,500 acres of land, in Bucks County, about twenty-seven miles up the Delaware River from Philadelphia.   [9] Asbestos.

As to Minerals, or Metals, there is very good Copper, far exceeding ours in England, being much Finer, and of a more glorious Colour. Not two Mile from the Metropolis, are also Purging Mineral-Waters, that pass both by Siege and Urine, all out as good as Epsom; And I have reason to believe, there are good Coals also, for I observ'd, the Runs of Water have the same Colour as that which proceeds from the Coal-Mines in Wales.

Here is curious Diversion in Hunting, Fishing, and Fowling, especially upon that Great and Famous River Suskahanah,[1] which runs down quite through the heart of the Country to Mary-Land, where it makes the Head of Chesepeck-Bay, in which place there are an Infinite Number of Sea and Land Fowl, of most sorts, *viz.* Swans, Ducks, Teal, (which two are the most Grateful and most Delicious in the World), Geese, Divers, Brands, Snipe, Curlew; as also Eagles, Turkies (of Forty or Fifty Pound Weight) Pheasants, Partridges, Pidgeons, Heath-Birds, Black-Birds; and that Strange and Remarkable Fowl, call'd (in these Parts) the Mocking-Bird, that Imitates all sorts of Birds in their various Notes. And for Fish, there are pro-digious quantities of most sorts, *viz.* Shadds, Cats Heads, Sheeps-Heads, Herrings, Smelts, Roach, Eels, Perch. As also the large sort of Fish, as Whales (of which a great deal of Oyl is made), Salmon, Trout, Sturgeon, Rock, Oysters (some six Inches long), Crabs, Cockles (some as big as Stewing Oysters of which are made a Choice Soupe or Broth), Canok and Mussels, with many other sorts of Fish, which would be too tedious to insert.

There are several sorts of wild Beasts of great Profit, and good Food; *viz.* Panthers, Woolves, Fither, Deer, Beaver, Otter, Hares, Musk-Rats, Minks, Wild Cats, Foxes, Rackoons, Rabits, and that strange Creature, the Possam, she having a false Belly to swallow her Yonng ones, by which means she preserveth them from danger, when any thing comes to dis-turb them. There are also Bears some; Wolves are pretty well destroy'd by the Indians, for the sake of the Reward given them by the Christian for that Service. Here is also that Remark-able Creature the Flying-Squirrel, having a kind of Skinny Wings, almost like those of the Batt, though it hath the like

[1] Susquehanna.

Hair and Colour of the Common Squirrel, but is much less in
Bodily Substance; I have (myself) seen it fly from one Tree
to another in the Woods, but how long it can maintain its
Flight is not yet exactly known.

There are in the Woods abundance of Red Deer (vulgarly
called Stags) for I have bought of the Indians a whole Buck
(both Skin and Carcass), for two Gills of Gunpowder. Excellent
Food, most delicious, far exceeding that in Europe, in the
Opinion of most that are Nice and Curious People.   There are
vast Numbers of other Wild Creatures, as Elks, Bufalos, etc.,
all which as well Beasts, Fowl, and Fish, are free and common
to any Person who can shoot or take them, without any lett,
hinderance or Opposition whatsoever.

There are among other various sorts of Frogs, the Bull-
Frog, which makes a roaring noise, hardly to be distinguished
from that well known of the Beast, from whom it takes its
Name: There is another sort of Frog that crawls up to the tops
of Trees, there seeming to imitate the Notes of several Birds,
with many other strange and various Creatures, which would
take up too much room here to mention.

Next, I shall proceed to instance in the several sorts of
Wild Fruits, as excellent Grapes, Red, Black, White, Muscadel,
and Fox, which upon frequent Experience have produc'd
Choice Wine, being daily Cultivated by skilful Vinerons; they
will in a short space of time, have very good Liquor of their
own, and some to supply their Neighbours, to their great advantage; as these Wines are more pure, so much more wholsom; the Brewing Trade of Sophisticating and Adulterating
of Wines, as in England, Holland (especially) and in some other
places not being known there yet, nor in all probability will
it in many Years, through a natural Probity so fixed and im-
planted in the Inhabitants, and (I hope) like to continue.
Wallnuts, Chesnuts, Filberts, Heckery-Nuts, Hartleberries,
Mulberries, (white and black) Rasberries, Strawberries, Cram-
berries, Plumbs of several sorts, and many other Wild Fruits,
in great plenty, which are common and free for any to gather;
to particularize the Names of them all, would take up too much
time; tire, not gratifie the Reader, and be inconsistent with the
intended Brevity of this little Volume.

The common Planting Fruit-Trees, are Apples, which from

a Kernel (without Inoculating) will shoot up to be a large Tree, and produce very delicious, large, and pleasant Fruit, of which much excellent Cyder is made, in taste resembling that in England press'd from Pippins and Pearmains, sold commonly for between Ten and Fifteen Shillings per Barrel. Pears, Peaches, etc. of which they distil a Liquor much like the taste of Rumm, or Brandy, which they Yearly make in great quantities: There are Quinces, Cherries, Goosberries, Currants, Squashes, Pumpkins, Water-Mellons, Muskmellons, and other Fruits in great Numbers, which seldom fail of yielding great plenty. There are also many curious and excellent Physical Wild Herbs, Roots, and Drugs of great Vertue, and very sanative, as the Sassafras, and Sarsaparilla, so much us'd in Diet-Drinks for the Cure of the Veneral Disease, which makes the Indians by a right application of them, as able Doctors and Surgeons as any in Europe, performing celebrated Cures therewith, and by the use of some particular Plants only, find Remedy in all Swellings, Burnings, Cuts, etc. There grows also in great plenty the Black Snake-Root, (fam'd for its sometimes preserving, but often curing the Plague, being infused only in Wine, Brandy or Rumm) Rattle-Snake-Root, Poke-Root, called in England Jallop, with several other beneficial Herbs, Plants and Roots, which Physicians have approved of, far exceeding in Nature and Vertue, those of other Countries.

The Names of the Counties are as followeth; First, Philadelphia County; Second, Bucks County; Third, Chester County; Fourth, New-Castle County; Fifth, Kent County; Sixth, Sussex County.

The chiefest and most commodious places for raising Tobacco, as also for Breeding and Improving all sorts of Cattle, are the Counties of Kent and New-Castle; the other chiefly depend upon Raising and Improving English Grain, of which they have a prodigious Encrease, which I have particularly instanced in the beginning of this Book, both as to their Quality and Quantity: All those Counties also very much abound in all sorts of Cattle, both small and great, for the Use and Service of Man.

Their sorts of Grain are, Wheat, Rye, Pease, Oates, Barley, Buck-Wheat, Rice, Indian-Corn, Indian-Pease, and Beans, with great quantities of Hemp and Flax; as also several sorts of

eating Roots, as Turnips, Potatoes, Carrats, Parsnips, etc.,
all which are produc'd Yearly in greater quantities than in
England, those Roots being much larger, and altogether as
sweet, if not more delicious; Cucumbers, Coshaws, Artichokes,
with many others; most sorts of Saladings, besides what grows
naturally Wild in the Country, and that in great plenty also,
as Mustard, Rue, Sage, Mint, Tanzy, Wormwood, Penny-
Royal and Purslain, and most of the Herbs and Roots found
in the Gardens in England.   There are several Husband Men,
who sow Yearly between Seventy and Eighty Acres of Wheat
each, besides Barley, Oates, Rye, Pease, Beans, and other
Grain.

They have commonly Two Harvests in the Year; First, of
English Wheat, and next of Buck, (or French) Wheat.   They
have great Stocks both of Hogs and Horses, kept in the Woods,
out of which, I saw a Hog kill'd, of about a Year old, which
weigh'd Two Hundred weight; whose Flesh is much sweeter,
and even more luscious than that in England, because they
feed and fatten on the rich (though wild) Fruits, besides those
fatned at home by Peaches, Cherries and Apples.   Their Horses
are very hardy, insomuch that being very hot with riding or
otherwise, they are turn'd out into the Woods at the same
Instant, and yet receive no harm; some Farmers have Forty,
some Sixty, and from that Number to Two or Three Hundred
Head of Cattle: Their Oxen usually weigh Two Hundred Pound
a Quarter.   They are commonly fatter of Flesh, and yield more
Tallow (by feeding only on Grass) than the Cattle in England.
And for Sheep, they have considerable Numbers which are
generally free from those infectious Diseases which are incident to those Creatures in England, as the Rot, Scab, or Maggots; They commonly bring forth two Lambs at once, some
twise in one Year, and the Wooll is very fine, and thick, and
also very white.

Bees thrive and multiply exceedingly in those Parts, the
Sweeds often get great store of them in the Woods, where they
are free for any Body.   Honey (and choice too) is sold in the
Capital City for Five Pence per Pound.   Wax is also plentiful,
cheap, and a considerable Commerce.   Tame Fowls, as Chickens, Hens, Geese, Ducks, Turkeys, etc., are large, and very
plentiful all over this Countrey.

And now for their Lots and Lands in City and Countrey, in their great Advancement since they were first laid out, which was within the compass of about Twelve Years, that which might have been bought for Fifteen or Eighteen Shillings, is now sold for Fourscore Pounds in ready Silver; and some other Lots, that might have been then Purchased for Three Pounds, within the space of Two Years, were sold for a Hundred Pounds a piece, and likewise some Land that lies near the City, that Sixteen Years ago might have been Purchas'd for Six or Eight Pounds the Hundred Acres, cannot now be bought under One Hundred and Fifty, or Two Hundred Pounds.

Now the true Reason why this Fruitful Countrey and Florishing City advance so considerably in the Purchase of Lands both in the one and the other, is their great and extended Traffique and Commerce both by Sea and Land, *viz.* to New-York, New-England, Virginia, Mary-Land, Carolina, Jamaica, Barbadoes, Nevis, Monscrat, Antego,[1] St. Cristophers, Barmudoes, New-Found-Land, Maderas, Saltetudeous, and Old-England; besides several other places. Their Merchandize chiefly consists in Horses, Pipe-Staves, Pork and Beef Salted and Barrelled up, Bread, and Flower, all sorts of Grain, Pease, Beans, Skins, Furs, Tobacco, or Pot-Ashes, Wax, etc., which are Barter'd for Rumm, Sugar, Molasses, Silver, Negroes, Salt, Wine, Linen, Houshold-Goods, etc.

However there still remain Lots of Land both in the aforesaid City and Country, that any may Purchase almost as cheap as they could at the first Laying out or Parcelling of either City or Country; which is, (in the Judgment of most People) the likeliest to turn to account to those that lay their Money out upon it, and in a shorter time than the aforementioned Lots and Lands that are already improved, and for several Reasons. In the first place, the Countrey is now well inhabited by the Christians, who have great Stocks of all sorts of Cattle, that encrease extraordinarily, and upon that account they are oblig'd to go farther up into the Countrey, because there is the chiefest and best place for their Stocks, and for them that go back into the Countrey, they get the richest Land, for the best lies thereabouts.

[1] Antigua.

Secondly, Farther into the Countrey is the Principal Place to Trade with the Indians for all sorts of Pelt, as Skins and Furs, and also Fat Venison, of whom People may Purchase cheaper by three Parts in four than they can at the City of Philadelphia.

Thirdly, Backwards in the Countrey lies the Mines where is Copper and Iron, besides other Metals, and Minerals, of which there is some Improvement made already in order to bring them, to greater Perfection; and that will be a means to erect more Inland Market-Towns, which exceedingly promote Traffick.

Fourthly, and lastly, Because the Countrey at the first laying out, was void of Inhabitants (except the Heathens, or very few Christians not worth naming) and not many People caring to abandon a quiet and easie (at least tolerable) Life in their Native Countrey (usually the most agreeable to all Mankind) to seek out a new hazardous, and careful one in a Foreign Wilderness or Desart Countrey, wholly destitute of Christian Inhabitants, and even to arrive at which, they must pass over a vast Ocean, expos'd to some Dangers, and not a few Inconveniencies: But now all those Cares, Fears and Hazards are vanished, for the Countrey is pretty well Peopled, and very much Improv'd, and will be more every Day, now the Dove is return'd with the Olive-branch of Peace in her Mouth.

I must needs say, even the present Encouragements are very great and inviting, for Poor People (both Men and Women) of all kinds, can here get three times the Wages for their Labour they can in England or Wales.

I shall instance in a few, which may serve; nay, and will hold in all the rest. The first was a Black-Smith (my next Neighbour), who himself and one Negro Man he had, got Fifty Shillings in one Day, by working up a Hundred Pound Weight of Iron, which at Six Pence per Pound (and that is the common Price in that Countrey) amounts to that Summ.

And for Carpenters, both House and Ship, Brick-layers, Masons, either of these Trades-Men, will get between Five and Six Shillings every Day constantly. As to Journey-Men Shooe-Makers, they have Two Shillings per Pair both for Men and Womens Shooes: And Journey-Men Taylors have Twelve Shillings per Week and their Diet. Sawyers get between

Six and Seven Shillings the Hundred for Cutting of Pine-Boards. And for Weavers, they have Ten or Twelve Pence the Yard for Weaving of that which is little more than half a Yard in breadth. Wooll-Combers, have for combing Twelve Pence per Pound. Potters have Sixteen Pence for an Earthen Pot which may be bought in England for Four Pence. Tanners may buy their Hides green for Three Half Pence per Pound, and sell their Leather for Twelve Pence per Pound. And Curriers have Three Shillings and Four Pence per Hide for Dressing it; they buy their Oyl at Twenty Pence per Gallon. Brick-Makers have Twenty Shillings per Thousand for their Bricks at the Kiln. Felt-Makers will have for their Hats Seven Shillings a piece, such as may be bought in England for Two Shillings a piece; yet they buy their Wooll commonly for Twelve or Fifteen Pence per Pound. And as to the Glaziers, they will have Five Pence a Quarry[1] for their Glass. The Rule for the Coopers I have almost forgot; but this I can affirm of some who went from Bristol (as their Neighbours report), that could hardly get their Livelihoods there, are now reckon'd in Pensilvania, by a modest Computation to be worth some Hundreds (if not Thousands) of Pounds. The Bakers make as White Bread as any in London, and as for their Rule, it is the same in all Parts of the World that I have been in. The Butchers for killing a Beast, have Five Shillings and their Diet; and they may buy a good fat large Cow for Three Pounds, or thereabouts. The Brewers sell such Beer as is equal in Strength to that in London, half Ale and half Stout for Fifteen Shillings per Barrel; and their Beer hath a better Name, that is, is in more esteem than English Beer in Barbadoes, and is sold for a higher Price there. And for Silver-Smiths, they have between Half a Crown and Three Shillings an Ounce for working their Silver, and for Gold equivalent. Plasterers have commonly Eighteen Pence per Yard for Plastering. Last-Makers have Sixteen Shillings per dozen for their Lasts. And Heel-Makers have Two Shillings a dozen for their Heels. Wheel and Mill-Wrights, Joyners, Brasiers, Pewterers, Dyers, Fullers, Comb-Makers, Wyer-Drawers, Cage-Makers, Card-Makers, Painters, Cutlers, Rope-Makers, Carvers, Block-Makers, Turners, Button-Makers, Hair and Wood Sieve-Makers, Bodies-

---

[1] A square or lozenge-shaped pane of glass.

Makers, Gun-Smiths, Lock-Smiths, Nailers, File-Cuters, Skinners, Furriers, Glovers, Patten-Makers, Watch-Makers, Clock-
Makers, Sadlers, Coller-Makers, Barbers, Printers, Book-
Binders, and all other Trades-Men, their Gains and Wages are
about the same proportion as the forementioned Trades in
their Advancements, as to what they have in England.

Of Lawyers and Physicians I shall say nothing, because
this Countrey is very Peaceable and Healty; long may it so
continue and never have occasion for the Tongue of the one,
nor the Pen of the other, both equally destructive to Mens
Estates and Lives; besides forsooth, they, Hang-Man like,
have a License to Murder and make Mischief. Labouring-
Men have commonly here, between 14 and 15 Pounds a Year,
and their Meat, Drink, Washing and Lodging; and by the
Day their Wages is generally between Eighteen Pence and
Half a Crown, and Diet also; But in Harvest they have usually
between Three and Four Shillings each Day, and Diet. The
Maid Servants Wages is commonly betwixt Six and Ten Pounds
per Annum, with very good Accommodation. And for the
Women who get their Livelihood by their own Industry, their
Labour is very dear, for I can buy in London a Cheese-Cake for
Two Pence, bigger than theirs at that price when at the same
time their Milk is as cheap as we can buy it in London, and
their Flour cheaper by one half.

Corn and Flesh, and what else serves Man for Drink, Food
and Rayment, is much cheaper here than in England, or elsewhere; but the chief reason why Wages of Servants of all
sorts is much higher here than there, arises from the great
Fertility and Produce of the Place; besides, if these large
Stipends were refused them, they would quickly set up for
themselves, for they can have Provision very cheap, and Land
for a very small matter, or next to nothing in comparison of
the Purchace of Lands in England; and the Farmers there,
can better afford to give that great Wages than the Farmers in
England can, for several Reasons very obvious.

As First, their Land costs them (as I said but just now)
little or nothing in comparison, of which the Farmers commonly will get twice the encrease of Corn for every Bushel they
sow, that the Farmers in England can from the richest Land
they have.

In the Second place, they have constantly good price for their Corn, by reason of the great and quick vent [1] into Barbadoes and other Islands; through which means Silver is become more plentiful than here in England, considering the Number of People, and that causes a quick Trade for both Corn and Cattle; and that is the reason that Corn[2] differs now from the Price formerly, else it would be at half the Price it was at then; for a Brother of mine (to my own particular knowledge) sold within the compass of one Week, about One Hundred and Twenty fat Beasts, most of them good handsom large Oxen.

Thirdly, They pay no Tithes, and their Taxes are inconsiderable; the Place is free for all Persuasions, in a Sober and Civil way; for the Church of England and the Quakers bear equal Share in the Government. They live Friendly and Well together; there is no Persecution for Religion, nor ever like to be; 'tis this that knocks all Commerce on the Head, together with high Imposts, strict Laws, and cramping Orders. Before I end this Paragraph, I shall add another Reason why Womens Wages are so exorbitant; they are not yet very numerous, which makes them stand upon high Terms for their several Services, in Sempstering, Washing, Spinning, Knitting, Sewing, and in all the other parts of their Imployments; for they have for Spinning either Worsted or Linen, Two Shillings a Pound, and commonly for Knitting a very Course pair of Yarn Stockings, they have half a Crown a pair; moreover they are usually Marry'd before they are Twenty Years of Age, and when once in that Noose, are for the most part a little uneasie, and make their Husbands so too, till they procure them a Maid Servant to bear the burden of the Work, as also in some measure to wait on them too.

It is now time to return to the City of Brotherly-Love (for so much the Greek Word or Name Philadelphia imports) which though at present so obscure, that neither the Map-Makers, nor Geographers have taken the least notice of her, tho she far exceeds her Namesake of Lydia,[3] (having above

---

[1] Sale.   [2] Grain.
[3] Philadelphia in Lydia, Asia Minor. A marginal note in the original reads: "Three German Miles from Smyrna."

Two Thousand [1] Noble Houses for her Five Hundred Ordinary) or Celisia, or Cælesyria; yet in a very short space of time she will, in all probability, make a fine Figure in the World, and be a most Celebrated Emporeum. Here is lately built a Noble Town-House or Guild-Hall, also a Handsom Market-House, and a convenient Prison.[2] The Number of Christians both Old and Young Inhabiting in that Countrey, are by a Modest Computation, adjudged to amount to above Twenty Thousand.[3]

The Laws of this Countrey, are the same with those in England; our Constitution being on the same Foot: Many Disputes and Differences are determined and composed by Arbitration; and all Causes are decided with great Care and Expedition, being concluded (generally) at furthest at the Second Court, unless they happen to be very Nice and Difficult Cases; under Forty Shillings any one Justice of the Peace has Power to Try the Cause. Thieves of all sorts, are oblig'd to restore four fold after they have been Whipt and Imprison'd, according to the Nature of their Crime; and if they be not of Ability to restore four fold, they must be in Servitude till 'tis satisfied. They have Curious Wharfs as also several large and fine Timber-Yards, both at Philadelphia, and New-Castle, especially at the Metropolis, before Robert Turner's Great and Famous House, where are built Ships of considerable Burthen; they Cart their Goods from that Wharf into the City of Philadelphia, under an Arch, over which part of the Street is built, which is called Chesnut-Street-Wharf,[4] besides other Wharfs, as High-Street Wharf, Mulberry Street Wharf, and Vine-Sreet Wharf, and all those are Common Wharfs; and likewise there are very pleasant Stairs, as Trus[5] and Carpenter-Stairs,[6] besides

---

[1] This number doubtless is an exaggeration.

[2] The prison was in the centre of High (now Market) Street, a short distance east of Second Street. "The Cage," a small jail, built in 1683, was still standing at the intersection of High and Second streets.

[3] Probably an excessive estimate for that period.

[4] An error; Robert Turner's wharf was at Mulberry (now Arch) Street.

[5] Tresse's Stairs, built by Thomas Tresse from the bank or bluff of Front Street down to King Street, between High (now Market) and Mulberry (now Arch) streets.

[6] Carpenter's Stairs, built by Samuel Carpenter from Front to King Street, between Chestnut and Walnut streets.

several others. There are above Thirty Carts belonging to
that City, Four or Five Horses to each. There is likewise a
very convenient Wharf called Carpenter's Wharf,[1] which hath
a fine necessary Crain belonging to it, with suitable Granaries,
and Store-Houses. A Ship of Two Hundred Tun may load
and unload by the side of it, and there are other Wharfs (with
Magazines and Ware-Houses) which front the City all along
the River, as also a Curious and Commodious Dock[2] with a
Draw-Bridge to it, for the convenient Reception of Vessels;
where have been built some Ships of Two or Three Hundred
Tuns each: They have very Stately Oaks to build Ships with,
some of which are between Fifty and Sixty Foot long, and
clear from Knots, being very straight and well Grain'd. In
this famous City of Philadelphia there are several Rope-Makers,
who have large and curious Rope-Walks especially one Joseph
Wilcox.[3] Also Three or Four Spacious Malt-Houses, as many
large Brew-Houses, and many handsom Bake-Houses for Publick Use.

In the said City are several good Schools of Learning for
Youth, in order to the Attainment of Arts and Sciences, as
also Reading, Writing, etc. Here is to be had on any Day in
the Week, Tarts, Pies, Cakes, etc. We have also several
Cooks-Shops, both Roasting and Boyling, as in the City of
London; Bread, Beer, Beef, and Pork, are sold at any time
much cheaper than in England (which arises from their Plenty)
our Wheat is very white and clear from Tares, making as good
and white Bread as any in Europe. Happy Blessings, for
which we owe the highest Gratitude to our Plentiful Provider,
the great Creator of Heaven and Earth. The Water-Mills far
exceed those in England, both for quickness and grinding good
Meal, their being great choice of good Timber, and earlier
Corn than in the aforesaid Place, they are made by one Peter
Deal,[4] a Famous and Ingenious Workman, especially for in-
venting such like Machines.

All sorts of very good Paper are made in the German-Town;
as also very fine German Linen, such as no Person of Quality

---

[1] See p. 261, notes 1 and 2, *supra*.   [2] *I. e.*, Dock Creek.

[3] Joseph Wilcox, previously mentioned as having succeeded to his father's
rope-walk at the north end of the town. He was mayor in 1706.

[4] Peter Daile (d. 1703) of Pennypack Mills in 1703.

need be asham'd to wear; and in several places they make
very good Druggets, Crapes, Camblets, and Serges, besides
other Woollen Cloathes, the Manufacture of all which daily
improves: And in most parts of the Countrey there are many
Curious and Spacious Buildings, which several of the Gentry
have erected for their Country-Houses. As for the Fruit-
Trees they Plant, they arrive at such Perfection, that they
bear in a little more than half the time that they commonly
do in England.

The Christian Children born here are generally well-fa-
voured, and Beautiful to behold; I never knew any come into
the World with the least blemish on any part of its Body, being
in the general, observ'd to be better Natur'd, Milder, and more
tender Hearted than those born in England.

There are very fine and delightful Gardens and Orchards,
in most parts of this Countrey; but Edward Shippey[1] (who
lives near the Capital City) has an Orchard and Gardens adjoyning to his Great House that equalizes (if not exceeds) any
I have ever seen, having a very famous and pleasant Summer-
House erected in the middle of his extraordinary fine and large
Garden abounding with Tulips, Pinks, Carnations, Roses, (of
several sorts) Lilies, not to mention those that grow wild in
the Fields.

Reader, what I have here written, is not a Fiction, Flam,
Whim, or any sinister Design, either to impose upon the Ignorant, or Credulous, or to curry Favour with the Rich and
Mighty, but in meer Pity and pure Compassion to the Numbers of Poor Labouring Men, Women, and Children in England,
half starv'd, visible in their meagre looks, that are continually
wandering up and down looking for Employment without
finding any, who here need not lie idle a moment, nor want due
Encouragement or Reward for their Work, much less Vaga-

---

[1] Edward Shippen (1639–1712), a wealthy Quaker merchant, mayor, speaker
of assembly, chief justice, and president of the provincial council when it was
vested with the deputy governorship. Born in Methley, Yorkshire, England, he
removed to Boston, Massachusetts, in 1668 and thence to Philadelphia in 1693–
1694. His "Great House," which was on Second Street, north of Spruce, and
overlooked Dock Creek and the river beyond, was occupied for a time in 1699 by
William Penn and his family at their first arrival on the occasion of the Proprietor's
second visit to his province.

bond or Drone it about.   Here are no Beggars to be seen (it is a Shame and Disgrace to the State that there are so many in England) nor indeed have any here the least Occasion or Temptation to take up that Scandalous Lazy Life.

Jealousie among Men is here very rare, and Barrenness among Women hardly to be heard of, nor are old Maids to be met with; for all commonly Marry before they are Twenty Years of Age, and seldom any young Married Woman but hath a Child in her Belly, or one upon her Lap.

What I have deliver'd concerning this Province, is indisputably true, I was an Eye-Witness to it all, for I went in the first Ship that was bound from England for that Countrey, since it received the Name of Pensilvania, which was in the Year 1681.   The Ship's Name was the *John and Sarah* of London, Henry Smith Commander.[1]   I have declin'd giving any Account of several things which I have only heard others speak of, because I did not see them my self, for I never held that way infallible, to make Reports from Hear-say.   I saw the first Cellar when it was digging for the use of our Governour Will. Penn.[2]

I shall now haste to a Conclusion, and only hint a little concerning the Natives or Aborigines, their Persons, Language, Manners, Religion and Government; Of Person they are ordinarily Tall, Straight, well-turn'd, and true Proportion'd; their Tread strong and clever, generally walking with a lofty Chin. Of Complexion Black, but by design, Gypsie-like, greasing themselves with Bears-Fat Clarified, and using no defence against the Injuries of the Sun and Weather, their Skins fail not to be Swarthy.   Their Eyes are small and black.   Thick Lips and flat Noses so frequent with Negroes and East Indians,

[1] Of 100 tons burden. She departed from London in October, 1681, and arrived in Pennsylvania before December 15.

[2] Governor William Penn's house, built in 1682 in the centre of a large lot between Front, High (Market), and Second streets, patented in 1701 to his daughter Laetitia.   After his first visit (1682–1684) the house was occupied by some of the provincial offices for several years, the council meeting there.   Robert Turner's letter of 1685 (see p. 269, *ante*), stating that his house, built the year previously, was the first brick house erected in Philadelphia, would seem to discredit the generally accepted view that the so-called Laetitia House, the brick structure in Fairmount Park, removed thither from the above lot some years ago, is the house built for Penn in 1682.

are rare with them.   They have Comely Faces and Tolerable Complexions, some of their Noses having a rise like the Roman.

Their Language is Lofty and Elegant, but not Copious; One Word serveth in the stead of Three, imperfect and ungrammatical, which defects are supply'd by the Understanding of the Hearers.   Sweet, of Noble Sound and Accent.   Take here a Specimen.

Hodi hita nee huska a peechi, nee, machi
Pensilvania huska dogwachi, keshow a peechi
Nowa, huska hayly, Chetena koon peo.

Thus in English.

Farewel Friend, I will very quickly go to
Pensilvania, very cold Moon will come presently,
And very great hard frosts will come quickly.

I might Treat largely of their Customs and Manners, but that will not agree with my proposed Brevity.

As soon as their Children are born, they wash them in cold Water, especially in cold Weather.   To harden and embolden them, they plunge them in the River, they find their Feet early, usually at Nine Months they can go.   The Boys Fish till Fifteen, then Hunt, and having given proof of their Manhood, by a large return of Skins, they may Marry (else 'tis a shame to think of a Wife) which is usually at the Age of Seventeen or Eighteen; the Girls stay with their Mothers, and help to hoe the Ground, Plant Corn, bear Burdens, and Marry about Thirteen or Fourteen.

Their Houses are Matts, or Barks of Trees set on Poles, Barn-like, not higher than a Man, so not expos'd to Winds. They lie upon Reeds or Grass.   In Travel they lodge in the Woods about a great Fire, with the Mantle of Duffils they wear wrapt about them, and a few Boughs stuck round them.

They live chiefly on Maze, or Indian Corn rosted in the Ashes, sometimes beaten and boyl'd with Water, called Homine. They have Cakes, not unpleasant; also Beans and Pease, which Nourish much, but the Woods and Rivers afford them their Provision; they eat Morning and Evening; their Seats and

Tables are the Ground; they are reserv'd, apt to resent and retain long: Their Women are Chaste (at least after Marriage) and when with Child, will not admit of their Husbands Embraces any more till Deliver'd. Exceeding Liberal and Generous; Kind and Affable; uneasie in Sickness, to remedy which, they drink a Decoction of Roots in Spring-Water, forbearing Flesh, which if they happen to eat, it must be the Female; they commonly bury their Kettles and part of their Goods with their Friends when they die, suspecting (poor Souls) they shall make use of them again at the Resurrection. They Mourn a whole Year, but it is no other than blacking their Faces.

Their Government is Monarchical, and Successive, and ever of the Mothers (the surest) side, to prevent a Spurious Issue. The Distaff (as in France) is excluded the Regal Inheritance. Their Princes are Powerful, yet do nothing without the Concurrence of their Senate, or Councils, consisting chiefly of Old, but mixt with Young Men: slow and deliberate (Spaniard-like) in resolving, naturally wise, and hardly to be out-witted. Their Punishments are Pecuniary. Murder may be aton'd for by Feasts and Presents, in Proportion to the Quality of the Offence, Person, or Sex injur'd; for if a Woman be kill'd, the Mulct is double, because she brings forth Children. They seldom quarel, when Sober, and if Boozy, (which of late they are more apt to be, having learn'd to drink, a little too much Rum of the Christians, to their shame) they readily pardon it, alledging the Liquor is Criminal not the Man.

The way of Worship the Sweeds use in this Countrey, is the Lutheran; the English have four sorts of Assemblies or Religious Meetings here: as first, The Church of England, who built a very fine Church in the City of Philadelphia in the Year 1695.[1] Secondly, the Anabaptists:[2] Thirdly, the Presbyterians, and two sorts of Quakers (of all the most numerous by much) one Party held with George Keith;[3] but whether both Parties

---

[1] The site now occupied by Old Christ Church.　　[2] Baptists.

[3] George Keith (1639?–1714), a Scotchman, probably native of Aberdeenshire, holding the degree of M. A. from the University of Aberdeen, originally a rigid Presbyterian but by 1664 a persecuted Quaker minister, one of the ablest and most active of the age of Penn and Barclay, a companion of Penn and Fox in the tour of Germany in 1677, had removed to New Jersey in 1684–1685, serving

will joyn together again in one I cannot tell, for that Gentleman hath alter'd his Judgment since he came to England, concerning his Church-Orders in Pensilvania, by telling and shew-
ing them Precepts that were lawful in the time of the Law, but
forbidden under the Gospel to pay Tithes, or Ministers to
Preach for Hire, etc. As also to sprinkle Infants; and he
tells the Presbyterian Minister, That he must go to the Pope
of Rome for his Call, for he had no Scripture for it, and that
Water-Baptism and the Outward Supper are not of the Nature
of the Everlasting Gospel; nor essential Parts of it, see his
Truth Advanced page 173. He gives likewise a strict Charge
concerning plain Language and plain Habit, and that they
should not be concern'd in the compelling part of the Worldly
Government, and that they should set their Negroes at Liberty
after some reasonable time of Service; likewise, they should
not take the Advantage of the Law against one another, as to
procure them any Corporeal Punishment: These Orders he tells
his Followers, would make Distinction between them and Jews
and Moral Heathens, this was in the Year 1693. in Pensilvania:
But now the Year 1697. since he came to England, his Judgment is chang'd, for he tells his Disciples, that Water-Baptism
is come in the room of Circumcision; and by so doing, they
would distinguish themselves from either Jews, Pagans or

---

as surveyor-general of East Jersey and in 1687 locating the boundary line between
the east and west divisions of that province. Coming to Philadelphia in 1689
he had served but a year as teacher of the Friends' School when his restless and
aggressive spirit began to stir up trouble among the Friends. Feeling himself
leader of the denomination in America he was offended by the disregard by the
Philadelphia Friends of his proposed amendments to the code of "discipline" of
the Society. He questioned the orthodoxy of leading ministers and importuned
for a confession of faith. A ready writer and a keen polemic he raised a bitter
doctrinal controversy with stormy disputations and a pamphlet war which dis-
rupted the Society for a time, and was largely responsible for Penn's loss of his
province, 1693–1694. Keith was expelled from the Society, but not before he
had drawn to his side a considerable body of followers, including a few men of
prominence. He formed a separate body of "Keithites," which in breaking up
resulted in the growth of the Baptist denomination and the establishment of the
oldest Episcopal churches. He returned to England in 1693 and in 1700 received ordination in the Church of England. He revisited this country in 1702
upon a special mission of reclaiming the Quakers to the mother church. After
two years he went back to England and was given the small living of Edburton
in Sussex, where he ended his days as an Episcopal clergyman.

Moral Heathens: He keeps his Meeting once a Week at **Turners-Hall** in Fill-Pot-Lane, London, on Sundays in the Afternoon; he begins between Two and Three of the Clock and commonly ends between Four and Five.

Friendly Reader, by this thou mayst see how wavering and mutable Men of great Outward Learning are, if the Truth of this be by any Body question'd, let them look in the Creed, and the Paper against Christians being concern'd in Worldly Government, and the Paper concerning Negroes, that was given forth by the Appointment of the Meeting held by George Keith at Philip James's House in the City of Philadelphia, in Pensilvania; and his Letter also in Mary-Land against the Presbyterian Catechism, Printed at Boston in New-England in 1695. with the Answer to it bound up together in one Book and in *Truth Advanced*, page 173. And for what relates to him since in England, let them look into the *Quakers Argument Refuted, Concerning Water-Baptism and the Lord's Supper*, page 70. And now Reader, I shall take my leave of thee, recommending thee with my own self to the Directions of the Spirit of God in our Conscience, and that will agree with all the Holy Scriptures in its right place; and when we find our selves so, we have no need to take any Thought or Care what any Body shall say of us.

The End of the History of Pensilvania.

An Historical Description of the Province and Country of West-New-Jersey in America. A short View of their Laws, Customs and Religion: As also the Temperament of the Air and Climate; The fatness of the Soil, with the vast Produce of Rice, etc. The Improvement of their Lands (as in England) to Pasture. Meadows. etc. Their making great quantities of Pitch and Tar, as also Turpentine, which proceeds from the Pine Trees, with Rozen as clear as Gum-Arabick, with particular Remarks upon their Towns, Fairs and Markets; with the great Plenty of Oyl and Whale-Bone made from the great number of Whales they yearly take: As also many other Profitable and New Improvements. Never made Publick till now.

By Gabriel Thomas. London: Printed in the year 1698.

To the Right Honourable Sir John Moor, Sir Thomas Lane, Knights and Aldermen of the City of London, and to the rest of the Worthy Members of the West-Jersey Proprietors.

Worthy Friends,

To whom can the History of West. Jersey with more Justice pertain, than to you the Noble and Generous Proprietors.

That was the chief Motive that inclin'd me to this Dedication, which I hope will be the more acceptable to you, because the Account of that Country is so Sincere and Candid.

I have endeavour'd (by setting forth) the great Encouragements there are) to persuade the Poor, the Idle, the Lazy, and the Vagabonds of these Kingdoms and of Wales to hasten thither, that they may live plentifully and happily, and I doubt not but they will hearken to it, because it is their true Interest. I have done my best endeavours to possess them and others of the great Fertility and Plenty in those Parts, which I need not repeat to you, who must needs be well acquainted with the State of that Place. That it may Flourish and mightily tend to your Advantage, as also to the Benefit of England, the hearty desire of your Friend,

GABRIEL THOMAS.

The Preface to the Reader.

Courteous Reader,

My Chief Design in writing this short Account of West-New-Jersey, is to inform all (but especially the Poor) what Ample and Happy Livelihoods People may gain in those Parts, whereby they may subsist very well without either Begging or Stealing, for if they Steal, they are Whipt, and oblig'd to pay Four Fold; and if they are not of Ability to do that, they must abide in Servitude till they have made Satisfaction to the injur'd Person: And if they should be Lazy and turn to Beg, they will get nothing by that Base and Scandalous Imployment; But if they be so Poor that they have not of their own to supply their Wants and Necessities, nor are able to Work, they will have no need to Beg, for People out of their own free Compassion and pure Charity will relieve them in their Necessities. Now if this were all, (though it is not) it wou'd be a sufficient Encouragement to the Idle, the Sloathful, and the Vagabonds of England, Scotland, and Ireland to hasten thither, where besides this, they have a fair prospect of getting considerable Estates, at least of living very Plentifully and Happily, which Medium of Life is far better than lingering out their Days so miserably Poor and half Starved; or Whipping, Burning, and Hanging for Villanies, they will have little Temptation, nay or Inclination to perpetrate here. The French Refugees or Protestant People, wou'd soon find it their Interest to remove thither, where they wou'd live far better than in Germany, Holland, Ireland or England. Written by one who earnestly wisheth thy Wellfare and Prosperity in the ways of the Lord, and then thou canst not do amiss in this World.

GAB. THOMAS.

The History of West-New-Jersey.

WEST-NEW-JERSEY lies between the Latitude of Forty, and Forty two Degrees;[1] having the Main Sea on the South, East-Jersey on the North, Hudson's[2] Bay on the East, and Pensilvania on the West.

The first Inhabitants of this Countrey were the Indians, being supposed to be part of the Ten dispersed Tribes of Israel; for indeed they are very like the Jews in their Persons, and something in their Practices and Worship, for they (as the Pensilvanian Indians) observe the New Moons with great Devotion, and Reverence: And their first Fruits they offer, with their Corn and Hunting-Game they get in the whole Year, to a False Deity or Sham-God, whom they must please, else (as they fancy) many Misfortunes will befal them, and great Injuries will be done them. When they bury their Dead, they put into the Ground with them some House-Utensils, and some Money, (as Tokens of their Love and Affection) with other Things, expecting they shall have Occasion for them again in the other World. And if a Person of Note dies very far from the Place of his own Residence they will carry his Bones home some considerable time after, to be buried there. They are also very curious, nay, even nice in preserving and repairing the Graves of their Dead. They do not love to be asked twice their Judgment about one Thing. They are a People who generally delight much in Mirth, and are very studious in observing the Vertues of Roots and Herbs, by which they cure themselves of many Distempers in their Bodies, both internal or external. They will not suffer their Beards to grow; for they will pluck the Hair off with their own Fingers as soon as they can get hold of it, holding it great Deformity to have a Beard. They are very loving to one another; for if three or four of them come into a Christian's House, and the Master of it

---

[1] West New Jersey extended from Cape May on the south in about 39° N. to what was called, by the deed of agreement of 1676, the northernmost branch of the Delaware River. The line of division between West and East New Jersey —although a subject of dispute—ran from the latter point on the Delaware southeasterly to Little Egg Harbor.

[2] On the east of East Jersey but not of West Jersey.

happen to give one of them Victuals, and none to the rest, he will divide it into equal Shares among them: And they are also very kind and civil to any of the Christians; for I my self have had Victuals cut by them in their Cabbins, before they took any for themselves. Their chief Imployment is in Hunting, Fishing, and Fowling, and making Canows, or Indian Boats, and Bowls, in all which Arts they are very dexterous and ingenious: Their Womens Business chiefly consists in planting of Indian Corn, and pounding it to Meal, in Mortars, with Pestils, (as we beat our Spice) and make Bread, and dress their Victuals, which they perform very neatly and cleanlily. They also make Indian Mats, Ropes, Hats, and Baskets (some of curious Workmanship) of their Hemp, which there grows wild, and Natural, in the Woods, in great Plenty. In short, the Women are very ingenious in their several Imployments as well as the Men. Their Young Maids are naturally very modest and shamefac'd: And their young Women when newly married, are very nice and shy, and will not suffer the Men to talk of any immodest or lascivious Matters. Their Houses are, for the most part, cover'd with Chesnutt Bark, but very close, and warm, insomuch that no Rain can go through. Their Age in Computation may be compared with the Christians. Their wearing Habit is commonly Deer-Skins, or Duffles. They don't allow of mentioning the Name of a Friend after his Death; for at his Decease, they make their Face black all over with black Lead; and when their Affairs go well with them, they paint their Faces with red Lead, it being a Token of their Joy, as the other is of their Grief. They are great Observers of the Weather by the Moon. They take great Delight in Cloaths of various Colours. And are so punctual that if any go from their first Offer or Bargain with them, it will be very difficult for that Party to get any Dealings with them any more, or to have any farther Converse with them; And moreover it is worthy of Remark, that when a Company of them are got together, they never interrupt or contradict one another, 'till two of them have made an end of their Discourse; for if never so many be in Company only two must discourse at a time, and the rest must keep Silence. The English and they live very peaceably, by reason the English satisfies them for their Land.

As to the manner of their Language, it is high and lofty, with a Short Sentence. Their way of counting is by Tens, as to say Two Tens, Three Tens, Four Tens, Five Tens, etc.

I shall now proceed to show something of the manner and way of Discourse that happens between them and the Neighbouring Christians that use to deal and traffick with them, or when they meet one another in the Woods accidentally, one a looking for his Cattel, and the other a Hunting the Wild Deer, or other Game, by way of Questions and Answers. I shall put the Indian Tongue on one side of the Leaf, and the English just opposite. Their Discourse is as followeth.

The Indian Tongue.	*The English of it.*
Quest. Hitah takoman?	*Quest.* Friend, from whence com'st?
Answ. Andogowa nee week-in.	*Answ.* Yonder.
	Quest. Where yonder?
	Answ. My House.
Quest. Tony andogowa kee weekin?	*Quest.* Where is thy House?
Answ. Arwaymouse.	*Answ.* A r w a y m o u s e, which is the Name of an Indian Town.
Quest. Keco kee hatah kee weekin?	*Quest.* What hast got in thy House?
Answ. Nee hatah huska wees youse og huska chetena chase og huska orit chekenip.	*Answ.* I have very fat Venison, and good strong Skins, with very good Turkeys.
Quest. Chingo kee beto nee chase og youse etka chekenip.	*Quest.* When wilt thou bring me Skins and Venison, with Turkeys?
Answ. Hadopa etka nisha kishquicka.	*Answ.* To morrow, or two days hence.
Quest. Keco kee hata kee weekin?	*Quest.* What hast thou got in thy House?
Answ. Nee hata orit poonk og huska horit haloons etka nesket og marchkec ochqueon.	*Answ.* I have good Powder, and very good Shot, with red and blue Machcots.[1]

[1] Match-coats, made of match-cloth, a coarse kind of woollen cloth.

(O huskia orit.)

Quest. Kee namen neskec kabay og marchkec moos etka opeg megis?

Answ. Mata namen megis nee namen neskec kabay undogwa tekany.

Quest. Kee namen marchkec moos undogwa tekeny?

Answ. Mogy.

Quest. Kee squa og enychan hatah?

Answ. Mogy.

Quest. Kacha hatah?

Answ. Neo.

Quest. Benoingtid etka squatid?

Answ. Nisha benointid og nisha squatid.

Quest. Tongtid enychan hatah?

Answ. Mogy.

Quest. Etka aroosise?

Answ. Neo kishow.

Quest. Etka aroosise kee?

Answ. Pelenacheenckan katingan aroosis.

(Very well.)

Quest. Did'st thou see black Horses and red Cows, with white Sheep?

Answ. I saw no Sheep: I did see black Horses yonder in the Woods?

Quest. Did'st see red Cows yonder in the Woods?

Answ. Yes.

Quest. Hast thou a Wife and Children?

Answ. Yes.

Quest. How many hast?

Answ. Four.

Quest. Boys or Girls?

Answ. Two Boys and two Girls.

Quest. Hast got a young Child?

Answ. Yes.

Quest. How old?

Answ. Four months.

Quest. How old art thou?

Answ. Fifty years old.

In the next Place I shall give an account of their way in counting or numbering; which is as followeth.

The Indian Counting.	*The English of it.*
Kooty, nisha, nacha, neo, pelenach, Kootash, nishash, choesh, peskonk, telen.	One, Two, Three, Four, Five, Six, Seven, Eight, Nine, Ten.
Nishinchkan, nachinchkan, neochinchkan, pelenchinchkan.	Twenty, Thirty, Forty, Fifty, etc.

The Names of some of the Indians.

Anachkooting, Bussabenating, Okonycan, Potasko, Quindamen, Lames, Alpoongan, Kohonk, Hiton, Temeny.

The Dutch and Sweeds inform us that they are greatly decreased in number to what they were when they came first into this Country: And the Indians themselves say, that two of them die to every one Christian that comes in here.   Reader, I shall not insist any farther upon this Subject, because what is deficient or short here, is inserted already in the preceding History of Pensilvania; for the Natives both of that, as well as of this Country, speak the same Language, and live after the same manner; for my chief aim, in the next place, is to acquaint thee how, and after what manner the Christians live there.   And I hope I have pleased thee so far, as it may prove a means to encourage me to give a larger Description hereafter.

The next who came there were the Dutch; which was between Forty and Fifty Years agoe,[1] though they made but very little Improvement, only built Two or Three Houses, upon an Island (called since by the English) Stacies-Island;[2] and it remained so, till about the Year 1675, in which King Charles the Second (or the Duke of York, his Brother) gave the Countrey to Edward Billing,[3] in whose time, one Major Fenwick[4]

---

[1] At least seventy-five years before.

[2] Matinneconk, Stacys, or Burlington Island of about 400 acres in the Delaware River, just opposite Burlington, New Jersey.   It is mentioned in the records of the Swedes and Dutch on the Delaware.   Peter Jegou, a Frenchman, seems to have acquired it about 1668.   In 1678 Robert Stacy, one of the Yorkshire commissioners, leased it from Governor Andros for seven years.   In 1682 it was vested in the town of Burlington for the support of education.

[3] Edward Byllynge, who did not acquire West New Jersey directly from Charles II. or James, the Duke of York, about 1675, nor yet so simply as Thomas states, but by the more involved chain of title, with consequent disputes: (1) Charles II., the whole of New Jersey to the Duke, at the English conquest of New Netherland, in 1664; (2) the Duke, the same to his favorites Berkeley and Carteret, in 1664; (3) Berkeley, his moiety, West New Jersey, to John Fenwick, in 1674, in trust, as later alleged, for Byllynge.   Cf. pp. 179, 180, ante.

[4] Major John Fenwick (1618–1684), the Quaker founder of Salem and Fenwick's colony, the first permanent English settlement in West Jersey, in 1675, was the second son of William Fenwick (1581–1647), of Stanton Hall, lord of a

went thither, with some others, and built a pretty Town, and call'd it Salam;[1] and in a few Years[2] after a Ship[3] from London, and another[4] from Hull, sail'd thither with more People, who went higher up into the Countrey, and built there a Town, and called it Burlington, which is now the chiefest Town in that Countrey, though Salam is the ancientest; and a fine Market-Town it is, having several Fairs kept yearly in it; likewise well furnished with good store of most Necessaries for humane Support, as Bread, Beer, Beef, and Pork; as also Butter and Cheese, of which they freight several Vessels, and send them to Barbadoes, and other Islands.

There are very many fine stately Brick-Houses built, and a commodious Dock for Vessels to come in at, and they claim equal Privilege with Burlington for the sake of Antiquity; tho' that is the principal Place, by reason that the late Governor

manor in Northumberland. He studied law at Gray's Inn, London, 1639–1640, and perhaps longer; was described in 1649 as a member for several years of John Goodwin's Independent congregation in London, established in 1645; as early as 1648 he had married Elizabeth (d. about 1655), daughter of Sir Walter Covert, knight of Slaugham, Sussex, and was located as a farmer dealing extensively in sheep on an estate at Brockham, in Surrey. About this time he was commissioned as major in the army of Parliament, but it is not clear that he saw much military service. In 1652 he entered upon an additional estate at Worminghurst, in the adjacent county of Sussex—to which he changed his residence—possibly as the tenant of Gulielma Maria Springett, then aged eight, who had inherited from her father, Sir William Springett, Worminghurst Place, the most important house with large park and considerable lands in that parish, later (1677) the home of her and her husband, William Penn. In 1662 Fenwick had taken a second wife, Mary Burdett, and had become a Quaker. In 1674 (March 18, 1673/4) he made the purchase of West New Jersey from Sir John Berkeley for £1,000. In the subsequent settlement of the dispute with Edward Byllynge over the sale, effected through the mediation of William Penn, Fenwick in 1675 (February 10, 1674/5) relinquished to Byllynge's assignees nine-tenths of his purchase. The other tenth he retained and during the succeeding five months was busily engaged in exploiting its sale and in arranging to emigrate. Having disposed of over 150,000 acres, in tracts of from 500 to 20,000 acres, to about fifty purchasers, chiefly in London, he set sail from London late in July, 1675, in the ship *Griffin*, with a colony of about 150 persons, including his three daughters and ten servants. He arrived at the site of Salem in September of the same year, laid out the town and for the remainder of his life was concerned with the development of his colony.

[1] Salem.
[2] In 1677.
[3] The *Kent*, Gregory Marlow, master.
[4] The *Martha*.

Cox,[1] who bought that Countrey of Edward Billing, encouraged and promoted that Town chiefly, in settling his Agents and Deputy-Governors there, (the same Favours are continued by the New-West-Jersey[2] Society, who now manage Matters there) which brings their Assemblies and chief Courts to be kept there; and, by that means it is become a very famous Town, having a great many stately Brick-Houses in it, (as I said before) with a delicate great Market-House, where they keep their Market: It hath a noble and spacious Hall over-head, where their Sessions is kept, having the Prison adjoining to it.

Likewise in the said Town there are very many fine Wharfs and large Timber-Yards, Malt-Houses, Brew-Houses, Bake-Houses; and most sorts of Trades-Men (whose Wages are upon the same Foot with the Pensilvanians), *viz.* Cloath-Workers, who make very good Serges, Druggets, Crapes, Camblets (part Silk or Worsted, and part Camels Hair), and good Plushes, with several other Woollen Cloathes, besides Linnen.

There are many Fair and Great Brick Houses on the outside of the Town which the Gentry have built there for their Countrey Houses, besides the Great and Stately Palace of John Tateham Esq;[3] which is pleasantly Situated on the North side of the Town, having a very fine and delightful Garden and Orchard adjoyning to it, wherein is variety of Fruits, Herbs,

---

[1] Daniel Coxe (1641–1730), M.D., Cambridge, 1669, of London, physician to the queen of Charles II., and to Queen Anne, member of the Royal Society, before which he read papers, was a large landed proprietor in the colonies and, although he never came over, was one of the foremost promoters of undertakings there. In 1687, after the death of Byllynge (d. 1685) he acquired the latter's interest in West New Jersey and became the governor. He moved the seat of government to Burlington, started whale and cod fisheries, and initiated other helpful enterprises in the province. In 1692 he sold his West New Jersey property to the West New Jersey Society.

[2] The West New Jersey Society, to whose officers and members Thomas inscribes this *History of West-New-Jersey*, consisted of about forty-eight members, largely non-Quaker London merchants with head-quarters in London. The Society purchased West Jersey from Dr. Coxe in 1692, and governed it until 1702, when the whole of New Jersey became a royal province.

[3] John Tatham (d. 1700), gentleman, of Burlington, a rich man for that time and place, evidently a Roman Catholic, having at his death seven slaves, a silver crucifix, a silver plate of Saint Dominic, and other silver, a wooden cross with the image of Christ, and a collection of books, many of them being of a Catholic character. He was the New Jersey agent for Governor Daniel Coxe.

and Flowers; as Roses, Tulips, July-Flowers, Sun-Flowers (that open and shut as the Sun Rises and Sets, thence taking their Name), Carnations, and many more; besides abundance of Medicinal Roots Herbs, Plants, and Flowers, found wild in the Fields.

There are kept also in this Famous Town several Fairs every Year; and as for Provisions, *viz.* Bread, Beer, Beef, Pork, Cheese, Butter, and most sorts of Fruit, here is great Plenty and very Cheap; all those Commodities are to be bought every Market-Day.

A Ship of Four Hundred Tuns may Sail up to this Town in the River Delaware; for I my self have been on Board a Ship of that Burthen there: And several fine Ships and Vessels (besides Governour Cox's own great Ship) have been built there.

There are also two handsom Bridges to come in and out of the Town, called London and York-Bridges. The Town stands in an Island, the Tide flowing quite round about it. There are Water-Men who constantly Ply their Wherry Boats from that Town to the City of Philadelphia in Pensilvania, and to other places. Besides there is Glocester-Town, which is a very Fine and Pleasant Place, being well stor'd with Summer Fruits, as Cherries, Mulberries, and Strawberries, whither Young People come from Philadelphia in the Wherries to eat Straberries and Cream, within sight of which City it is sweetly Situated, being but about three Miles distance from thence.

There are several Meetings of Worship in this Country, *viz.* the Presbyterians, Quakers, and Anabaptists: Their Privilege as to Matter of Law, is the same both for Plaintiff and Defendant, as in England.

The Air is very Clear, Sweet and Wholesom; in the depth of Winter it is something colder, and as much hotter in the heighth of Summer than in England. Commonly (with them) the Days differ two Hours in length from ours here. The longest Day in Summer is shorter by two Hours than the longest Day in England, and the shortest Day longer by two Hours than with us here.

As for Corn, they have Wheat, Rye, Pease, Oates, Barley, Rice, etc., in vast quantities: Also Indian-Corn, Pease and Beans, likewise English Hemp and Flax, which prospers there exceedingly. Eating Roots, Pumpkins, Cashews, Water-Melons, Muskmellons, Cucumbers, Squashes, Carrots, Artichokes, Potatoes, Turnips, Garlick, Onions, and Leeks grow there in greater Plenty than in England. And for Herbs, they have Cabbages, Coleworts,[1] Savoys,[1] Lettice, Purslane, and other Sallads in abundance; beside Wild Herbs which are there very common, as Penny-Royal, Mint, Mustard, Sage, Rue, Tansey, etc., and likewise there are choice Phisical Roots, as Sassafras, Sarsaparilla, Black-Snake-Root, Rattle-Snake Root, and Poake Root, with divers others, which there is great store of.

Of Fish, they have Whales, Sturgeon, Cod, Scale-Fish, Cole and Hake-Fish, large Mackeril, Flat-fish, Rock, Shadds, Cattes, Eels, Perch, and many other sorts in prodigious Shoals: And Wild-Water-Fowl, as Geese, Ducks, Swans, Divers, etc., are very numerous, even beyond all expectation. As to Land-Fowl, Turkeys, Geese, Pheasants, Partridges, Pigeons, Wood-cocks, Blackbirds, etc., they are there in extraordinary great abundance, and very large. There is also that uncommon and valuable Bird (being near the bigness of a Cuckoo) called the Mocking-bird (known, but not very well in England, being so very Nice and Tender, that they usually die by the way) with several other Charming and Curious Birds, too tedious here to specifie.

As to the Wild Vermin, There are Otters, Beavers, Foxes, Mush-Rats Minx's, Wild-Cats, Rackoons, Pollcats, and also that cunning Creature the Possom, particularly mention'd and distinguish'd in the annex'd Account of Pensilvania for its remarkable Qualities, whither I refer the Reader, not in the least being fond of Tautology. This Creature is about the bigness of an English Cat, being of a light gray colour. Like-wise there were some Wolves and Bears, but now they are very rare to be seen, by reason the Indians destroy them (as before). Also that strange Creature the Flying Squirril, men-tion'd in the foregoing Book. There are great numbers of Wild Deer, and Red Deer also; and these wild Creatures are free and common for any to kill and take. And for Wild Fruits, there are Chesnuts, Filberts, Hickery-Nuts, Grapes, Mulberries, Strawberries, Rasberries, Huckleberries, and Craneberries, with several sorts of Plumbs, and all those Fruits in great plenty be-ing free for any Body to gather.

[1] Of the cabbage family.

Now I am a coming to the Planted Fruit-Trees, as Apples, Pears, Apricocks, Quinces, Plumbs, Cherries, Gooseberries, Currants, and Peaches, from which last they distil a liquor as in Pensilvania, much like Rumm or Brandy, in the taste; and all those Trees will come to bear in a little more than half the time, they do in England, the Soil is so rich; they have great plenty of the aforementioned Fruits, which are exceeding delicious. These, as also many other Fruits that come not to any pitch of Perfection in England, are the Natural Product of this Country, which lies warmer, being more befriended by the Sun's hot and glorious Beams, which without doubt is the chief Cause and true Reason, why the Fruit there so far excells the English. They have likewise great Stocks of Horses and Hogs, raised in the Woods; of the latter of which I have seen some of a Prodigious Weight that only fed there, their Horses are very hardy, strong, and of good Spirit for Labour or Travelling; they commonly go unshod (which in many Years saves much Money). Their Plow-shears require but small Reparation, wearing out but little. They Harrow their Ground with a Wooden-tyned-Harrow, and twice over does the business.

Of Bees also they are well provided, and abound in Sheep naturally very sound, and that stand well, the Rot, Scab, Maggots, etc., rarely invading them; they usually bring forth two Lambs at once, and their Wooll is very fine, white, and thick; they have great Stocks of Cattle, as Cows, Oxen, etc. Their Oxen commonly weigh well.

Tame Fowl there are (almost) incredible in numbers, *viz.* Geese, Turkeys, Hens, etc.

In this Country also is great Plenty of working Timber, as Oaks, Ash, Chesnuts, Pine, Cedar, Walnut, Poplar, Firr, and Masts for Ships, with Pitch and Rosin, of great Use and much Benefit to the Countrey. Here are several good Navigable Rivers, besides that famous River Delaware (which I have mentioned elsewhere, and where the Tobacco is excellent) being deep enough for Vessels to come in: First, Prince Morise's River,[1] where the Sweeds used to kill the Geese in great numbers, for their Feathers (only) leaving their Carcasses behind them; Cohansey River, by which they send great store

---

[1] Maurice or Prince Maurice River, in the southern part of New Jersey, flowing into Delaware Bay.

of Cedar to Philadelphia-City; Allaway-River; Salam[1]-River, which runs by Salam-Town (of greatest Antiquity;) Naman-River, Rackcoon-River,[2] which had its Name from the great numbers of those Creatures that always abound thereabouts; Old Man's River; Manto-River;[3] Woodberry-River; Great Eggharbor River (up which a Ship of two or three hundred Tuns may sail) which runs by the back part of the Country into the Main Sea; I call it back, because the first Improvement made by the Christians, was Delawar River-side: This Place is noted for good store of Corn, Horses, Cows, Sheep, Hogs, etc., the Lands thereabouts being much improv'd, and built upon: Little Egg-Harbor-Creek, which take their Names from the great abundance of Eggs, which the Swans, Geese, Ducks, and other wild Fowls off those Rivers lay thereabouts: Timber-River,[4] alias Glocester-River, which hath its Name (also) from the great quantity of curious Timber, which they send in great Floats to Philadelphia, a City in Pensilvania, as Oaks, Pines, Chesnut, Ash, and Cedars.   This River runs down by Glocester-Town, which is the Shire-Town; And Newton-River,[5] that runs by Newton; Cooper-River;[6] Pensokin-River;[7] Northampton-River,[8] with several others, at a convenient distance upon the Sea, the Shores whereof are generally deep and bold) of less Note, as Wissahiskonk-River,[9] that runs down into the great River Delaware, by Burlington.   The Countrey inhabited by the Christians is divided into four Parts or Counties, tho' the Tenth part of it is not yet peopled; 'Tis far cheaper living there for Eatables than here in England; and either Men or Women that have a Trade, or are Labourers, can, if industrious, get near three times the Wages they commonly earn in England.

Courteous Reader, As yet I have given thee no Account of East-Jersey, because I never was there, so in reality cannot properly or pertinently speak to that Matter.   I will not pretend to impose any thing on the World, but have all along, and shall still declare nothing but Verity; therefore one Word of that by and by.   I might have given thee a much larger Ac-

---

[1] Salem.   [2] Raccoon Creek.   [3] Mantua Creek.
[4] Big Timber Creek.   [5] Between Gloucester and present Camden.
[6] At present Camden, New Jersey.   [7] Pensauken Creek.
[8] Rancocas Creek.   [9] Assiscunk Creek.

ount of this Countrey, and have stretch'd this (now) Pocket
Volume to an extraordinary Bulk and Size; and yet without
straining or deviating in the least from the Principles of my
Profession, which are Truth it self. I have no Plot in my Pate,
or deep Design, no, not the least expectation of gaining any
thing by them that go thither, or losing by those who stay
here. My End chiefly in Writing, nay, indeed my great Aim,
is to inform the People of Britain and Ireland in general, but
particularly the Poor, who are begging, or near it, or starving,
or hard by it (as I before took notice in my Preface) to encourage them (for their own Good, and for the Honour and Benefit of their Native Countrey, to whom they are now a Scandal
and Disgrace; and whose Milk and Honey these Drones eat
up, and are besides a heavy Burden to the Commonwealth, in
the Taxes paid by every Parish in England, etc., to support
them.

Law-Causes are here (as in Pensilvania) speedily determined, in the second Court at least, unless in some difficult
Business. One Justice of the Peace hath Power to try a Cause,
and give Judgment therein, if the Original Debt be under
forty Shillings. And for Thieves and Robbers (as I hinted
before in the Preface) they must restore fourfold; which, if
they are not able to do, they must work hard till the injured
Person is satisfied.

I shall conclude with a Word or two on New-East-Jersey.
This Countrey is exceeding fruitful in Cattel, of which I have
seen great numbers brought from thence, viz. Oxen, Cows,
Sheep, Hogs, and Horses, to Philadelphia, the Capital of Pensilvania. The chiefest Manufactory (besides English and Indian Grain) fit for Traffick that this Countrey affords.

Now I shall give thee an Account of the English Manufactory, that each County in West-New-Jersey affords. In the
first Place I shall begin with Burlington-County, as for Peltage,
or Beavers Skins, Otter-Skins, Minks Skins, Musk-rats Skins,
Rackcoon, Wild Cats, Martin, and Deer-Skins, etc. The Trade
in Glocester-County consists chiefly in Pitch, Tar, and Rosin;
the latter of which is made by Robert Styles,[1] an excellent

---

[1] Robert Stiles (d. 1713), was living in 1711 on his farm of over 200 acres on
Pensauken Creek, in Chester Township, Burlington County, just over the line
from Gloucester (now Camden) County, New Jersey.

Artist in that sort of Work, for he delivers it as clear as any Gum-Arabick. The Commerce carried on in Salam-County, is chiefly Rice, of which they have wonderful Produce every Year; as also of Cranberries which grow there in great plenty, and which in Picle might be brought to Europe. The Commodities of Capmay-County, are Oyl and Whale-Bone, of which they make prodigious, nay vast quantities every Year, having mightily advanc'd that great Fishery, taking great numbers of Whales yearly.[1] This Country for the general part of it, is extraordinary good, and proper for the raising of all sorts of Cattel, very plentiful here, as Cows, Horses, Sheep, and Hogs, etc., likewise it is well Stor'd with several sorts of Fruits which make very good and pleasant Liquors, such as their Neighbouring Country before mention'd affords. Now Reader, having no more to add of any moment or importance, I salute thee in Christ; and whether thou stayest in England, Scotland, Ireland, or Wales, or goest to Pensilvania, West or East-Jersey, I wish thee all Health and Happiness in this, and Everlasting Comfort (in God) in the World to come. Fare thee well.

[1] About 1690 Dr. Daniel Coxe established a town and an extensive whale fishery on the bay side of Cape May.

CIRCUMSTANTIAL GEOGRAPHICAL DESCRIPTION OF PENNSYLVANIA, BY FRANCIS DANIEL PASTORIUS, 1700

INTRODUCTION

Upon the most trustworthy estimate, one-fifth of the blood of the United States is German. In Pennsylvania the proportion runs even higher. The German contribution to American civilization defies numerical estimate. Plainly, therefore, a book which aims at presenting typical narratives of Pennsylvania's foundation should include the chief writing relative to the beginnings of German colonization in that province, and especially if that principal writing should by chance have emanated from the chief figure in that earliest movement of German settlement. That classical position belongs so precisely to Pastorius's *Umständige Geographische Beschreibung Pensylvaniæ*, that it is surprising that it has never before been presented, save in fragments, in an English translation.

Francis Daniel Pastorius was born September 26, 1651, at Sommerhausen in Franconia, the son of Melchior Adam Pastorius, legal counsellor to the Count of Limpurg,[1] and of Magdalena Dietz, his first wife. His father's removal to the city of Windsheim, where the elder Pastorius became burgomaster and judge, brought it about that Francis was educated first at the gymnasium in that city, under a Hungarian schoolmaster named Tobias Schumberg.[2] In 1668 he proceeded to the university of Altdorf, and for the next eight years was engaged in studies, chiefly of law, there and at the universities of Strassburg, Basel, and Jena. Taking his degree of doctor of laws at Altdorf in 1676, he practised law at Windsheim and at Frankfort-on-the-Main till 1680, when as the companion of a young

[1] For a fuller account of Melchior Adam Pastorius, see below, p. 361, note 1.
[2] A poem of Pastorius addressed to his former schoolmaster is printed below, pp. 422–424.

nobleman he entered on a period of travel, lasting two and a half years, and extending through Germany, the Netherlands, England, France, and Switzerland.

Frankfort in 1682 was the very centre of the Pietists, who were endeavoring by revival of devout and practical Christianity, tinged often with mysticism, to melt and vivify the creed-bound theological and sacramentarian system of the Lutheran Church. That Pastorius would by natural sympathy be drawn into their circle is plain from the account of his spiritual development which he gives in the preface below. So when a kindred spirit, the Quaker William Penn, who in 1677 had paid a memorable religious visit to the Frankfort Pietists, became four years later a great landed proprietor in America, and through German translations of some of the documents already presented in this volume appealed to the Pietists and Mennonites of Germany to take part in his "holy experiment," it was natural that Pastorius should be strongly attracted. A Frankfort group bought 15,000 acres of land in the new province. He was made their agent, sailed for America in June, 1683, and arrived at Philadelphia in August. The main section of the first body of German immigrants to Pennsylvania, a Crefeld group, came in October. Uniting the interests of the German (Frankfort) Company and of the Crefelders, Pastorius by skilful management obtained favorable terms from Penn for the Germans, and before the end of October founded Germantown.

The development of this first of German townships in America can be followed during its first sixteen years in the pages which follow. Pastorius continued as agent for the German Company till 1700 only, but throughout his lifetime remained the chief citizen of Germantown, bailiff or clerk of the corporation in many years, justice of the peace, occasionally member of the General Assembly of the province. He shared in, perhaps wrote, the famous protest (1688) of the German Friends or Mennonites of Germantown against slavery. From 1698 to 1700 he served as schoolmaster of the Friends' School in Philadelphia, from 1702 till after 1716 he was master of the school in Germantown. Add to these occupations that of scrivener, in which capacity he was in much request, and it will easily be seen that no one was better qualified to testify as to the early days of the German village. In Germantown he lived until his death, which occurred between December 26, 1719, and January 13, 1720. The chief account of his life and writings, and an excellent one, based on most painstaking researches, is *The Life of Francis Daniel Pastorius, the Founder of Germantown*, by Professor Marion D. Learned (Philadelphia, 1908).

Pastorius was a man of wide learning, not only in legal and administrative matters, but in science, medicine, agriculture, history, theology, and business. His learning, his large library, his skill with the pen, his eagerness to do good, and, we must add, some willingness to display his talents, impelled him to most copious writing, now in vivacious if not too orderly prose, now in verses plainly meant to be, and thought of as being, poetry. Half a dozen printed books and a great mass of manuscripts remain to attest his literary zeal. The chief of the latter is the *Beehive*, a combination of commonplace-book and encyclopædia which he wrote for his children. The chief of the printed books is that which is here translated. From its pages, though the great waves of German immigration into America began several years after its publication, we can at least obtain priceless and abundant data regarding the first small beginning of that process.

The first printed account of Pennsylvania by Pastorius was an eight-page tract, headed *Sichere Nachricht auss America, wegen der Landschafft Pennsylvania, von einem dorthin gereissten Teutschen, de dato Philadelphia, den 7. Martii 1684* (Positive Information from America, concerning the Country of

Pennsylvania, from a German who has migrated thither, dated Philadelphia, March 7, 1684).[1] Of this excessively rare tract there is a copy in the city library of Zürich. A longer statement, entitled *Francisci Danielis Pastorii Sommerhusano-Franci Kurtze Geographische Beschreibung der letztmahls erfundenen Americanischen Landschafft Pensylvania* (Short Geographical Description of the recently discovered American Country Pennsylvania), was printed in Nuremberg in 1692 as an appendix to Melchior Adam Pastorius's *Kurtze Beschreibung Der H. R. Reichs Stadt Windsheim.* This also is rare, but there is a copy of it in the library of the Historical Society of Pennsylvania. The appendix fills only thirty-two pages. By expansion of these to forty-five and by many additions Pastorius composed his final treatise, *Umständige Geographische Beschreibung Der zu allerletzt erfundenen Provintz Pensylvaniæ, In denen End-Gräntzen Americæ In der West-Welt gelegen, Durch Franciscum Danielem Pastorium, J. U. Lic. und Friedens-Richtern daselbsten. Worbey angehencket sind einige notable Begebenheiten, und Bericht-Schreiben an dessen Herrn Vattern Melchiorem Adamum Pastorium, Und andere gute Freunde. Franckfurt und Leipzig, Zufinden bey Andreas Otto. 1700.* (Circumstantial Geographical Description of the Lately Discovered Province of Pennsylvania, Situated in the Farthest Limits of America, in the Western World, by Francis Daniel Pastorius, J. U. Lic., and Justice of the Peace in the Same, to which are Appended certain Notable Events, and Written Reports to his Honored Father, Melchior Adam Pastorius, and to Other Good Friends.) A second edition, without change of

---

[1] A translation of this interesting document, by the general editor of the series, has been substituted below, pp. 392–411, for those pages of the book of 1700 which present merely a brief summary of the *Sichere Nachricht.* Other versions may be seen in J. F. Sachse, *Letters relating to the Settlement of Germantown* (Philadelphia, 1903), and in S. W. Pennypacker, *The Settlement of Germantown* (Philadelphia, 1889), pp. 81–99. A photographic facsimile of the original may be found in Learned's *Pastorius*, between pp. 128 and 129.

substance, was issued under the same imprint in 1704. This usually has, bound up with it, a German translation of Gabriel Thomas's *Historical and Geographical Account,* and Daniel Falkner's *Curieuse Nachricht.* Friedrich Kapp republished Pastorius's part (Crefeld, 1884) with an introduction.

The *Umständige Geographische Beschreibung* is a small book, printed on paper 6⅜ x 3¾ inches in size, and contains xii+140 pages. It was edited for publication by the writer's father, Melchior Adam Pastorius, and the last twenty pages are occupied with his autobiography, supplied at the request of his grandsons. It is a very interesting document, but as its interest is wholly European, it has not been thought needful to include it in the present translation, which accordingly stops at page 120 of the original. As will be seen, the book opens with seventeen chapters of a more or less systematic treatise, but is continued by the printing, in nearly chronological order from 1683 to 1699, of various letters of Pastorius, together with a few written by his sons, his father, or William Penn. No one should look to it for a methodical history of Pennsylvania or of Germantown, but surely no one can look into it without catching vivid glimpses of early Germantown and Pennsylvania, without seeing, to some degree, "the very form and pressure of the time."

About a fifth of the book, in an imperfect English translation by Lewis H. Weiss, was printed in 1850 in the *Memoirs of the Historical Society of Pennsylvania,* volume IV., part 2, and reprinted in 1898 in no. 95 of the *Old South Leaflets.* The present version was made by the late Miss Gertrude Selwyn Kimball of Providence; Professor M. D. Learned has kindly revised it. The foot-notes are by the editor of the volume, Mr. A. C. Myers.

J. F. J.

CIRCUMSTANTIAL GEOGRAPHICAL DESCRIPTION OF PENNSYLVANIA, BY FRANCIS DANIEL PASTORIUS, 1700

Circumstantial Geographical Description of the Lately Discovered Province of Pennsylvania, Situated in the Farthest Limits of America, in the Western World, by Francis Daniel Pastorius, J. U. Lic., and Justice of the Peace in the Same, to which are Appended certain Notable Events, and Written Reports to his Honored Father, Melchior Adam Pastorius, and to Other Good Friends.
Frankfort and Leipzig: To be found at the Shop of Andreas Otto, 1700.

TO THE GENTLE READER

I herewith present to you the province of Pennsylvania, lately discovered by means of the expeditions sent out under Charles Stuart the First of England, and likewise its inhabitants, the Christians as well as the native savages, together with the laws, form of government, customs and habits of both of these, and also the towns which have already been settled, and the commerce which has been established, all most faithfully described, not only by the governor of the province, William Penn himself, but also by the local authorized representatives of the English and High-German Companies.

And it is worthy of remark that this province, as early as the year 1684, contained four thousand Christian souls; therefore, at the present time, at the end of sixteen years, it must, necessarily, have a much greater population, both because of the yearly arrival of settlers, and because of the natural increase of the Christian colonists, and must also have attained to a state of greater prosperity in agriculture, in dwellings, and in trade. This is especially the result of the inestimable vigilance, admirable bearing, and prudent conduct of the above-

mentioned governor, William Penn, to whom the English
King, Charles Stuart the Second, gave this country in perpetuity, as an English fief, upon the yearly payment of two
beaver-skins.   All of which will be learned more in detail in
the proper place.

Good health to the reader, whom I am ready to serve further, on receipt of further information.

N. B. The publisher received this from the hand of Melchior Adam Pastorius,[1] J. U. D., Councillor to the Prince of
Brandenburg and Historian, whose son now resides in Pennsylvania.

PREFACE

The method by which I have regulated the course of my
life, from the cradle, after laying-aside childish things, along
the path of this temporal state, toward a joyous eternity, is
well known to all my intimates; and also that in all my deeds
I have striven to learn the will of God, to fear His omnipotent
power, and truly to love, honor, and praise His unfathomable

---

[1] Melchior Adam Pastorius (1624–1702), doctor of civil and canon law,
father of Francis Daniel Pastorius, was a native of Erfurt, in Thuringia, springing from a prominent Catholic family, whose name was originally Scepers or
Schäffer (shepherd or pastor), then Pastor, and finally under humanistic influences fully Latinized to Pastorius.   The family was long resident in Warburg in
Westphalia, whence his father, Martinus Pastorius, a native of the latter town,
educated in the liberal arts and in the law, son of Fredericus Pastorius, town
councillor, had removed to Erfurt and become tribunal assessor.   Receiving an
early training in the humanities M. A. Pastorius, in 1644, joined the train of
Cardinal Rosetti, then on his way to the election of a new pope, went to Rome,
studied in the German College, pursued a course in law at the University Alla
Sapienza, practised in the Roman trials with his brother and for a few months
in 1648 held his brother's place as resident at Rome for the Elector of Trier.
Having made a grand tour of observation—interestingly recorded by him—
through Italy, Germany, Austria, and France, under the patronage of the Elector
of Mainz, in 1649, he became counsellor to the Count of Limpurg at Sommerhausen, in Franconia.   Here he changed to the Lutheran religion, married, and
had his son Francis Daniel born to him.   In 1659 he removed to the imperial
city of Windsheim, serving as counsellor, elder burgomaster, superior judge, and
councillor to the Prince of Brandenburg.   He was a man of much learning, knowing Latin, Italian, and French.   He wrote a history of Windsheim and many
other works in prose and verse, some of which have never been published.   His
later years were spent at Nuremberg, where he died.

goodness and mercy. And although I have, besides the ordinary courses in the liberal arts, happily undertaken and finished the study of law, and at the same time became sufficiently skilled in the Italian and French languages, and in good company made the so-called grande tour, through those countries, nevertheless, in all countries and places, my greatest industry and effort has been to endeavor to discover where and amongst what people and nations a true devotion, love, knowledge, and fear of God might be met with and acquired. I found, in universities and academies, learned men almost without number, but as many religions and sects as there were individuals; [I found] sharp wits and keen questionings, but, in fine, there was that great babbling and ostentation of frivolous worldly wisdom of which the apostle says: *Scientia inflat.*[1]

But that I saw anywhere, in the Netherlands or in France, a professor who, with the heart of a child and the soul of a disciple, earnestly pointed out the pure love of Jesus and a knowledge of the Holy Trinity—that [is something] which I cannot write with a clear conscience.

It is true that there is no lack of those Christians in name and in speech, who go about conceited in their worldly wisdom, and are really devoted to the lust of the flesh, the lust of the eye, and the pride of life (the *Trifolium* of the devil). But they who with fear and trembling thought to work out their own salvation, who lived without guile, and who penetrated to the centre to God, that highest good, with all the power of their being—such were *rara avis in terris.*[2]

I found, indeed, at last, in the University of Cambridge and in the city of Ghent, some in secret retirement who were devoted men, resigned to the Heavenly Father with their whole soul; these having perceived my earnest quest, taught me many good doctrines and strengthened me greatly in my purpose, and so aided me that the birth-chamber of the most glorious Emperor Charles the Fifth, in the royal palace at Ghent, was shown to me (it is four ells long and four ells wide), with the reminder that to this newborn prince was given by one of his god-fathers as a christening-present a richly-bound Bible with the inscription in gold: *Scrutamini scripturas,*[3] the

[1] Knowledge puffeth up.
[2] A rare bird in the lands.
[3] Search the Scriptures.

which he had read diligently, and therein learnt that he must die in the merits of Jesus Christ, which alone suffice.

I further saw, in my travels at Orleans, Paris, Avignon, Marseilles, Lyons, and Geneva, many thousands of youths from Germany, the greater part of them of noble rank, who habitually imitate only the frivolities of dress, speech, foreign customs, and ceremonies, and spend incredible amounts in learning to leap horses, to ride, to dance, fence, swing a pike, and wave banners; so that a large portion of their German patrimony is spent on the useless frivolities of this world, while no thought is given to the love of God, and to the wisdom of an imitation of Christ, well-pleasing in the sight of the Lord. Indeed, he who will discourse somewhat of the writings and communings with God of the holy Augustine, Taulerus, Arndius, and other men of godly wisdom, will be proclaimed a pietist, sectarian, and heretic; nor will the man who has drunk deep of the worldly wisdom of the school of Aristotle let himself be persuaded, or be admonished by the Spirit of God.

For these reasons, when my tour was ended, I withdrew into my study for a short retreat, and recalled to mind all that this world-spectacle had brought to my view, and could find no enduring pleasure in anything therein, and also I gave up all hope that, in the future, any place could be found in my native country, or in all Germany, where a man could abandon the old habit of mere *operis operati*,[1] and enter into the pure love of God with his whole heart and spirit, and with his entire strength, and love his neighbor as himself.

So the thought came to me that it might be better that I should expound for the good of the newly-discovered American peoples in Pennsylvania that knowledge given me by the grace of the highest Giver and Father of Light, and should thus make them participators in the true knowledge of the Holy Trinity, and the true Christianity.

But since the province and country of Pennsylvania is situated at the further limits of America, it is necessary that some few words should first be premised and set forth concerning the divisions of the globe, and in particular concerning America (the fourth part of the world). I divide the globe into four parts: the first is Europe, wherein are Spain, France,

[1] Dead works.

Italy, Greece, Germany, Hungary, Dalmatia, Croatia, Slavonia, Bulgaria, Muscovy, Poland, Denmark, Sweden, England, Ireland, Scotland, Holland, etc. This division is the smallest of them all, but because of its art and of the Christian religion, it is the most famous.

The second division is Asia, which lies toward the rising sun, or to the east, of Europe, and is almost as large as Europe and Africa together. In this part of the world Paradise was situated, and here Adam was created, and here too was the promised land of Canaan, wherein dwelt the patriarchs, Abraham, Isaac, and Jacob. It also contains Arabia, wherein is Mount Sinai, where God gave the law to Moses. In Asia are likewise found Syria, Judæa, Galilee, Babylon, and Niniveh. It also includes the East Indies, Tartary, and China, that land which lies the furthest to the east, and which is separated from its neighboring lands in part by lofty mountains, and in part by a wall twelve hundred miles in length.

The third division is Africa, divided from the south of Europe by the Mediterranean Sea, and from Asia by the Red Sea. It is a very hot, unfruitful, and partly uninhabited land, and full of venomous animals. It contains Egypt, Barbary, and the country of Prester John.

The fourth division of the world is America, or the so-called New World, which was discovered in part, A. D. 1492, by Christopher Columbus, and in part by Americus Vespucius, and by this last it was called America. It lies toward the setting-sun, or to the west, of Europe, and comprises the largest part of the globe, being almost as large as the entire Old World, Europe, Asia, and Africa, together. This is the country wherein are found in superabundance gold, silver, gems, sugar, spice, and many other rarities, as the silver fleets, coming from there every year, bear ample witness.

Besides these four principal divisions of the earth above mentioned, there are also the cold countries lying toward the North and midnight; such as Greenland, Nova Zembla, Iceland, etc. There is also that great unknown southern land, otherwise called Magellanica, which lies far to the south, near the south pole, and into which no man has dared to venture, up to this time, where it seems at night as if the whole region were on fire.

Since, however, my design at the present time is to write only of Pennsylvania, the newest portion of America, I forthwith proceed to the matter in hand.

THE FOURTH DIVISION OF THE WORLD, AMERICA,

is Divided by me into Two Principal Parts.

The first of these, to the south, includes:

1. Castilia del Oro,[1] comprising the provinces of Popayan,[2] New Granada,[3] Cartagena,[4] Venezuela,[5] New Andalusia,[6] Paria.[7]

2. The country of Guiana, belonging to the Dutch, from which they chose to make a grant of a fief, in 1669, to the Count of Hanau, of that part lying between the rivers Paria and Amazon.

3. The country of Brazil, belonging to Portugal, wherein are the cities of San Salvador, Olinda, and Pernambuco.

4. The country of Chile.

5. The country of Peru, in whose capital, Lima, the Spanish viceroy resides. This province is bounded by the Andes, in which the largest supply of gold is to be found, and where the aged men among the natives are gigantic in size, being ten feet tall.

There are, in this southern division, two principal rivers, the River Amazon and the River de la Plata. On the borders of this southern division flows the River Panama, or the Isthmus, by which the wealth of America is carried to the sea and thence to Spain.

---

[1] The name applied at that and earlier times to northwestern South America, including the present United States of Colombia and Venezuela.

[2] In the southern part of the present United States of Colombia.

[3] East of Popayan, and south of the then province of Venezuela.

[4] North of Popayan, bordering on the Caribbean Sea, in the present United States of Colombia.

[5] In the northern part of the present country of that name.

[6] East of the then province of Venezuela, on the Caribbean Sea, within present Venezuela. It is also called Paria by some geographers of the seventeenth century.

[7] South of New Andalusia, although by some geographers of the period made synonymous with the former. It is within present Venezuela.

The second Principal Division of America, to the North, includes:

1. The country of Nicaragua, Guatemala, Chersonesus or New Spain,[1] extends to the Gulf of Mexico.
2. The country of Florida.
3. The country of Virginia, belonging to the English.
4. New Netherland,[2] whose capital is New Amsterdam.[3]
5. New England, where, in the city of Cambridge, the Bible has been printed in the American language.[4]
6. Canada, New France, the land of Cortereal,[5] Labrador, and New Britain.[6] Until the year 1441 there was very scant information had in Europe concerning this entire division of the world, America, because none of the inhabitants had ever sailed over to us Europeans.

The first discoverer of this western world of waters was Christopher Columbus, an Italian, born in the little town of Cucurco,[7] in the territory of Genoa, of the noble house of Pilustroli,[8] a man of education and experienced in navigation.

After he had visited the island of Gades,[9] and ascertained that, at a certain season of the year, the winds blew steadily from the west for many days, and from that had concluded that they must come from some far-distant land, he resolved to explore this foreign land, and to sail beyond the Pillars of Hercules,[10] provided that the Republic of Genoa would equip some ships for him. Since the Republic was not willing to do

---

[1] The name given at first to Yucatan and afterwards in general to the whole of Mexico.

[2] "Novum Belgium" in the original.

[3] Called New York after 1664.

[4] *I. e.*, in the dialect of the Massachusetts Indians; the translation by John Eliot, the New Testament being published in 1661 and the whole Bible in 1663.

[5] Or Corterealis, marked on maps of the sixteenth century as in eastern Canada on the north shore of the Gulf of St. Lawrence.

[6] The country lying around Hudson's Bay.

[7] Cuccaro, in Montferrat, near Genoa, Italy, one of many towns claiming to be the birthplace of Columbus.

[8] The Pallastrelli or Perestrello family, originally of Italy, but later of Portugal, were ancestors not of Columbus but of his wife.

[9] Cadiz, Spain.

[10] Anciently applied to the two rocks on the respective African and European shores forming the entrance to the Mediterranean at the Strait of Gibraltar.

this, he went to King Henry VII.[1] of England, and to King Alphonso,[2] and as in both these countries his quest proved useless, he came to King Ferdinand,[3] and Queen Isabella of Castile. They furnished him with three ships and the necessary equipment, with which he, together with his brother Bartholomew,[4] set sail, in the August of 1492, and after some months they came to the island of Comera,[5] where he refreshed himself, and thirty days later he landed at the island of Guaraglysne.[6]

He also visited the island of Cumana[7] and the island of Hayti, which he called Hispaniola; and there he built a fort. When he saw the wealth of this land he decided to carry the good news to King Ferdinand, and returned in safety, without even the loss of a man, and the King gave him the surname of Admirandus.[8] After that he made other voyages, to the Fortunate Islands,[9] and to the Canary Islands, where there are two miraculous springs, of which one has this property, that whosoever drinks thereof begins at once to laugh, and never ceases until he has laughed himself to death, but if he be given to drink of the other spring, he is straightway set to rights again.

Columbus visited also the island of Teniriffa,[10] where there is a mountain that spouts fire. Finally he reached the Island of the Cannibals, or Man-eaters, and as it was on a Sunday, he called the place Dominica, and journeyed thence, by way of the Islands of Cuma[11] and Jamaica, back to Spain.

In the year of our Lord 1495, the above mentioned King Ferdinand sent the noble Florentine, Vesputius Americus,[12]

---

[1] There is no evidence of such a visit, although his brother Bartholomew did go to England to enlist the interest and assistance of King Henry VII. in the scheme.

[2] Affonso V. of Portugal. It was more probably João II.   [3] Of Aragon.

[4] Bartholomew Columbus did not accompany his brother on the first voyage to America in 1492, but brought out supplies to Santo Domingo on Christopher's second voyage.

[5] Gomera in the Canaries.   [6] Guanahani.   [7] Cuba.

[8] Columbus received the office of high-admiral.

[9] Of the ancients, i. e., the Canary Islands.

[10] Teneriffe.   [11] Cuba.

[12] Amerigo Vespucci, according to the most competent scholars of this day, did not visit the New World until 1499, then going over simply in a subordinate position, under Ojeda, to the previously discovered northern coast of South America.

with four great freight-ships, into this region, to search for still other lands, and he sailed far beyond the Canary Islands, and observed on the mainland men entirely naked, but turned back again to other islands, and on October 15, 1498, came happily back to Spain.

This new portion of the world was named America by this Vesputius Americus, and as time went on various fine colonies, cities, and trading-posts were built up by the Spanish, French, English, and Dutch, and prosperous commerce was established, as may be read more in detail in the *Natura Novi Orbis*, by Joseph à Costâ.[1]

After having set forth these matters, we come now to the last discovered province of America, Pennsylvania. This shall be taken up, chapter by chapter, in the briefest manner possible.

CHAPTER I.

Concerning the Discovery of the Country of Pennsylvania.

Although from the time of Christopher Columbus and Vesputius Americus many colonies and plantations have been successively built up, such as for example, New Spain, New France, Brazil, Peru, Castilia del Oro, Spaniola,[2] Cuba, Jamaica, New England, Florida, Virginia, etc., it has also further come to pass that, in the year 1665, through the expeditions under Charles Stuart I.,[3] King of England, an extensive new land, lying far beyond those already enumerated, was discovered. The aforesaid king found, during his life-time, no especial name to give this country, since the native inhabitants of the land wandered about, naked, in the woods, and had no civil assemblies, nor any established towns from which a name could have been taken, but they lived (as now) in little

---

[1] José de Acosta (*c.* 1540–1600), a learned Spanish Jesuit, after having resided many years in South America, returned to Spain, and in 1588–1589 published at Salamanca his *De Natura Novi Orbis*, descriptive of the New World.

[2] Northwestern part of South America.

[3] Pastorius makes sad confusion of English and early American colonial history, of which obviously he had very erroneous notions. Here apparently he has in mind Charles II., not Charles I., and the acquisition of New Netherland in 1664, not in 1665, not by discovery, but by conquest from the Dutch.

huts made of turf or of trees, here and there, throughout the wildernesses.

But since, at the time of this discovery of the country, under the first Stuart,[1] the Prince of York had in his dominions many useless persons, the greater part being Swedes,[2] he ordered that a settlement be built on the Della Varra[3] River, and that it be strengthened as time went on, and to this he gave the name of Neu-Castle, and gave the Swedes full authority to dwell there and to cultivate the land round about until more people should be brought over from England. These Swedes began to establish a little community and to employ themselves with agriculture and cattle-raising, until there occurred the most dreadful and unheard-of tragedy of the aforesaid King Charles I.,[4] namely, that he was persecuted, cast into prison, and finally beheaded, by his own subjects. His son, Charles II., hastily collected an army in order to avenge his father's death and to assert his own rights as king, and engaged in battle, but he was defeated on the field and sought for, that they might put him to death, and such would inevitably have been his fate had not his general, Lord Penn,[5] disguised him and taken him by ship to France. Because of this deed all of Lord Penn's manors, castles, and villages were

---

[1] Charles II., who is really meant, was of course the third Stuart.

[2] James, Duke of York, brother of Charles II., did not bring over the Swedes; they had long been settled on the Delaware before he came into possession of that region in 1664. The unfavorable allusion to the Swedes may be attributed to the death of Pastorius's grandfather and the loss of the family property at the hands of the Swedish soldiers at Erfurt during the Thirty Years' War.

[3] Delaware.

[4] In 1649, fifteen years before the English conquest of New Netherland with its Swedish settlements.

[5] Sir William Penn (1621–1670), knight, a native of Bristol, England, son of Giles Penn, a draper, springing from a yeoman family of Minety, Wiltshire, as a boy served in various mercantile voyages to the northern seas and to the Mediterranean, and became a lieutenant in the royal navy, thenceforth passing the whole of his life in that service. He attained the rank of admiral under the Parliament and the Protectorate, and was a general in the Dutch War, 1652–1654, receiving estates in Ireland from Cromwell in the latter year. Having secretly offered to bring Charles II. back to England during the Dutch War, he returned with the king at the Restoration in 1660, and was knighted at that time. He then became commissioner of the admiralty and the navy, governor of Kinsale, Ireland, and "great captain commander" under James, Duke of York, in the Dutch War of 1665. He died "in much peace," at Wanstead, in Essex.

laid in ashes, and he himself was driven into exile, where he died before Charles II. was restored to the royal throne.[1]

After[2] he had again obtained his sceptre and throne, William Penn (the only son of Lord Penn) came to him, and was very kindly received, and as a recompense for the loyal service rendered by his father,[3] this newly-discovered province, together with the fortress of Neu-Castle,[4] was given him in perpetuity, and by a public royal decree of the date of April 21, 1681, all the inhabitants, present and future, were directed to show him due obedience.

This William Penn caused it to be publicly proclaimed in London that he purposed to found some colonies and cities in this province, and that he was willing to sell land at no higher price than an English crown [*kopstück*, shilling (?)][5] an acre to such as had the desire to journey thither with him. Accordingly many persons entered their names in his book for a certain amount of land, and many families travelled with him to that country, where he accordingly founded the city of Philadelphia there for himself and them. Especially, however, a German Company,[6] which purchased several thousand acres

---

[1] To correct Pastorius's errors, Admiral Penn, it will be observed, (1) was not a general under Charles at the latter's defeat at the battle of Worcester, in 1651, but was then a naval commander under the Parliament; (2) he was not a "Lord," never receiving a higher title than knight; (3) he did not disguise Charles and assist him to flee to France; (4) his property was not laid in ashes, as he had no extensive estates at that time, but later received lands in Ireland from Cromwell; (5) he did not die in exile before the Restoration, but passed ten years of honored service under Charles II.

[2] In 1681, twenty-one years after the Restoration.

[3] And more especially for the debt of £16,000 due from the King to Penn's father, the admiral.

[4] Neither "the fortress of New-Castle" nor, in fact, any part of Delaware was included in the grant of Charles II. to William Penn. That territory was conveyed to Penn in 1682 by James, Duke of York, who had it from his royal brother Charles at the English conquest of New Netherland, in 1664. Nor, of course, was this region a "newly-discovered" land.

[5] Penn offered his land for sale (1) to First Purchasers, 5,000 acres at £100 and one shilling quit-rent per each 100 acres (*i. e.*, 50s.); (2) to renters at one penny per acre on tracts not to exceed 200 acres; (3) to servants and their masters at the end of the given time of service 50 acres each at a yearly rent of a half-penny per acre.

[6] Of Frankfort-on-the-Main, for which Pastorius came over to Pennsylvania as the agent.

of land, combined to establish a German colony there. But the entire province was named Pennsylvania (the wilderness of Penn), because it was entirely overgrown with forest and wilderness.

The Charter of King Charles Stuart II. to William Penn, etc., March 4, 1671.[1]

I. We give and grant, for various reasons, to William Penn and his heirs forever, the entire tract of the land in America, with all the islands thereto appertaining, That is to say, from the beginning of the fortieth degree of north latitude, twelve English miles above Neu-Castle, with its eastern boundaries running along the bank of the De la Ware River.

II. Free and undisturbed use and passage into and out of all harbors, bays, waters, streams, islands and mainlands belonging thereto, together with the soil, fields, woods, underwoods, mountains, hills, fens, swamps, islands, lakes, rivers, brooks, gulfs, bays, and inlets, that lie therein, or that belong to the aforesaid limits and boundaries. And all these the said William Penn shall hold and enjoy for his use and profit, forever, and it shall be held of Us as of Our castle of Windsor, for the delivery and payment every year of two beaver-skins only, as a free and public acknowledgement of his fief.

III. And of Our further favor We have thought fit to erect the aforesaid land and its islands into a province and a seigniory, wherefore We hereby erect and establish the same, and We do call it Pennsylvania, and it is Our wish that from henceforth for all time, it should be so called.

IV. By reason of the especial trust (and implicit confidence) which we repose in the wisdom and justice of the said William Penn, We grant to him and to his heirs, and to such persons as they shall appoint, [the power] to make and enact laws for the better and more prosperous ruling of the Province in general, and to publish the same under his seal, by and with the advice and approbation of the freemen, or freeholders so far as they do not run contrary to the laws of Our kingdom.

V. Also full authority to the said William Penn, etc., to appoint judges, magistrates, and other similar officials, by such means and in such form as may seem convenient to him.

Likewise, he shall also have authority to pardon and to punish misdemeanors and crimes, as is customary in well-regulated tri-

---

[1] Erroneous date, the correct year being 1681.

bunals. And We herewith also will, enjoin, and require that such laws and acts shall be fully observed and kept inviolable, and that all liege subjects of Us, Our heirs and successors, shall keep them inviolable, reserving only the final right of appeal to Ourselves.

VI. That the laws concerning individual property, whether in the case of the decease of a landed proprietor, or in the case of the inheritance of movable or immovable goods and chattels, shall be the same there as in England, and shall remain in force until the said William Penn, or his heirs, together with the freemen of the said province, shall otherwise ordain.

VII. In order that this new colony may happily increase by the multitude of people, We herewith grant to all Our liege subjects, both present and future, in behalf of Ourselves, Our heirs and successors, liberty to transport themselves thereunto.

VIII. Liberty to transport thither all sorts of goods and merchandise, upon payment of the impositions due Us in this country.

IX. The authority to divide this country into small districts or counties, of one hundred boroughs or smaller towns,[1] and to constitute markets and fairs with convenient privileges. All this [to be done] as may seem meet and serviceable to William Penn and to his heirs.

X. Permission to import the fruits of the soil, and the commodities made there, into England.

XI. Authority to establish ports, havens, bays, harbors, ports of entry, and other places for trade, with such rights, jurisdictions, and privileges, as the said William Penn may find expedient.

XII. The navigation laws shall not be broken, either by the governor, or by the inhabitants.

XIII. No alliance shall be made with any prince or state that wages war against Us and Our heirs.

XIV. Power for the security and defense [of the country] by such ways and means as may seem good to the said William Penn.

XV. Full power to assign, to grant, to lease, or to enfeoff, as many portions of the land and to such persons as William Penn shall consider fit to have and to hold the same, each person to rent it for himself and the heirs of his body, either for life, or for a term of years.

XVI. We give and grant to each of these persons to whom William Penn has granted an estate, the privilege to hold his own courts there, and [to make] regulations for better security.

---

[1] Pastorius mistakes the noun "hundreds" in the charter, meaning a subdivision of a county, for an adjective modifying boroughs.

XVII. Authority to these persons, that they may grant their lands and privileges in turn to another person, either in fee simple, or under certain conditions.

XVIII. We also covenant and affirm to the said William Penn, his heirs and assigns, that We will declare or impose no tax or imposition upon the inhabitants of the said province, nor upon the land, property, and goods of the inhabitants, nor upon the merchandise without the consent of the governor and inhabitants.

XIX. It is ordered that no one of Us or of Our heirs and successors, or officers of high or low degree, shall presume at any time to act contrary in the smallest thing to that herewith set forth, or in any sort to withstand the same, but that they shall aid and assist to the aforesaid William Penn, his heirs, and these inhabitants and tradespeople, their factors and attorneys, in the full use and fruition of this Our Charter.

XX. And, in case there should arise in the future any doubt or question concerning the true sense or meaning of a word or expression, contained in this Charter, We hereby ordain and command that at all times and in all things, such interpretation shall be made thereof and allowed by Our superior courts as that the said William Penn, his heirs and assigns, shall be judged in the most favorable and advantageous manner possible, providing that it be not contrary to a due allegiance to Ourselves and to Our heirs.

In witness whereof, We have caused these letters patent to be drawn up, and We Ourselves bear testimony thereto at West-Münster,[1] 4 March, 1681.

CAROLUS II.

After obtaining this princely gift William Penn caused the following proclamation to be posted up and circulated:

All persons who desire to negotiate with me in regard to this province may make their bargain here and obtain further satisfactory information from: Philipp Ford,[2] Thomas Rudyard,[3] Benjamin Klarc,[4] Jan Roelofs van der Werf, etc.

On April 2, 1681, all the inhabitants and planters already settled in this country were directed by the aforesaid King Charles II., in a written order, to show due obedience to William Penn, as the full lord and ruler of the property.

---

[1] Westminster.   [2] In Bow Lane, Cheapside, London.
[3] In George Yard, Lombard Street, London.
[4] Benjamin Clark, in George Yard, Lombard Street, London.

Chapter II.

The Manner and Method in which William Penn sought to pro-
cure Settlers for the uninhabited Province which he received
as a Gift.   The Offer for Sale.

1. He sent out a notice to the purchasers that they should
send in their names to certain places in London and enter into
agreements, [and] there he sold 3000[1] acres of land (Dutch
measure) for 100 pounds sterling, with the reservation of a
perpetual yearly payment therefor of an English shilling for
each 100 acres.   The money should be paid down for the receipt in London, and upon its presentation the amount of
land would be measured out for the purchaser.

2. To each person who has the necessary money for the
voyage, but has no means to establish himself upon his arrival,
and to buy land, William Penn gives fifty acres, with a perpetual yearly fee of a penny for each acre.   And this fee shall
give them as valid a claim as if they had purchased the land
for themselves and their heirs forever.

3. To the servants and children (to encourage them to
greater industry and obedience) he gives full permission to
take perpetual possession of a field of fifty acres, so soon as
they shall have worked out their stipulated time, and to pay
for each [acre] a yearly fee of only half a penny, and thus become their own masters.   Hereupon the book and register of
the purchasers was begun at the appointed bargain-place, and
the German Company, or Society, was the first to enter into
an agreement, and in the beginning paid down the money
in London for twenty thousand acres, upon the receipt of an
order of acquittance.

4. It is to be remarked that William Penn did not drive
forth the naked native inhabitants of the land with military
authority, but brought with him upon his arrival especial
clothing and hats for the principal Indians, and thereby secured their goodwill, and purchased their land (and territory)
to the extent of twenty leagues,[2] and they, thereupon, withdrew that much farther back into the wild forests.

---

[1] Five thousand acres (English).   [2] Sixty English miles.

CHAPTER III.

How the Survey of Lands for the German Company was Effected.

The entire German Company, or Association, had appointed Francis Daniel Pastorius, Licentiate of both Laws,[1] a man desirous to travel, as their fully authorized attorney. He went from Franckfurth-on-the-Mayn to London, where he concluded a purchase, took the order for the assignment of the land, and sailed, under the guidance of God, safely across the ocean,[2] and on March 7, 1684, sent back this report from Philadelphia:

The land which has been purchased is distributed in three different ways. First, fifteen thousand acres in one tract, and bordering on navigable water. Second, three hundred acres in the liberties of the city, which is the land between the rivers de la Ware and Scollkill. Third, three lots in the city, for building houses thereon.

When I now, upon my arrival, applied to William Penn for the warrants, to measure off the three portions, and take possession [of them], his first answer was: That as for the three lots in the city, and the three hundred acres in the liberties, the Company had no legal claim thereto because they were purchased after he, William, had left England, and the books in London had been closed. However, after I represented to him that the Germans were entitled to consideration because they were the first to conclude a compact with him he immediately caused three lots to be measured off for me from the portion of his younger son,[3] on the border of the city, one behind the other.

If now one counts in their order the houses situated on the Delu Waro River, the dwelling and trading-house of the German Company is the ninth.[4]

---

[1] Canon and civil law.

[2] Sailed from Deal, England, early in June and arrived at Philadelphia in August, 1683.

[3] William Penn, jr.

[4] At the southern end of the Philadelphia of that day, on the west side of Front Street, the lot being cut off from the lot of William Penn, whose remaining portion lay next south at the northwest corner of Front and Cedar (now South) streets.

The first of our lots in the city is one hundred feet wide and four hundred feet deep. At the end thereof is a street;[1] the second lot, lying behind this, is of the same length and breadth, and behind this is again a street.[2] The third lot is of the same size, and on the front of each lot two houses can be built side by side, and two on the rear, so that altogether twelve houses with their yards can be built, and all can front upon the streets.

At the end of November, 1684, Pastorius sent word to his Company:

That for the first few years they could make but little profit because of the notorious scarcity of money in the province, and because there was not yet any return cargo produced for England. And since the Governor, William Penn, holds it of the first importance to establish weaving and the cultivation of the Vine, it would be well for the Company to send out here a quantity of vine-stocks, together with all sorts of field and garden-seeds; also some large iron pots and nests of kettles; also an iron stove, some bed-clothes and mattresses, and likewise a few pieces of fustian, and white linen cloth, which may be sold to advantage in the trading-house.

On November 16th there was a fair held at Philadelphia, but at the Company's trading-house little more than ten thalers[3] worth was sold, because of the aforesaid scarcity of money, and because the new-comers from Germany and England for the most part bring so many clothes with them that for several years they need nothing more.

So far as concerns our newly-founded city, Germanopolis,[4] it is situated upon a rich black soil, surrounded by numerous pleasant springs. The main street is sixty feet wide, and the cross-street is forty, and each family has a farmyard of three acres in size.

[1] Front Street. [2] Second Street.
[3] About thirty shillings or $7.30, multiplied several times to equal present-day values.
[4] Germantown.

CHAPTER IV.

Concerning the Laws of the Province.

William Penn established the first [of these] with the concurrence of the public assembly:

1. The members of the council, and then the whole community come together each year upon a certain appointed day and choose their presiding officers and other functionaries by lot,[1] so that none may know who has voted for, or against, him. Thereby is prevented all improper use of money, and likewise the secret enmity of the defeated candidate. And if anyone has conducted himself improperly this year, a better man may be chosen next time.

2. No tax, excise, or other impost may be laid upon the public without the consent of two-thirds of the council.

3. In order to prevent litigation, law-suits, and quarrelling, a record will be kept, wherein will be registered all estates, mortgages, obligations, and rents. Thus all advocates and attorneys who demand money for their services are discarded.

4 and 5. That no one sect may raise itself above the others, each shall enjoy freedom of conscience, and no one shall be forced to be present at any public services for the worship of God, and no one shall be disturbed in his belief or religion.

6. In order to guard against whatever could tempt the people to frivolity, wantonness, insolence, audacity, ungodliness, and scandalous living, all worldly plays, comedies, games of cards, maskings, all cursing, swearing, lying, bearing of false witness (since an oath is not allowed), scandal-mongering, adultery, lewdness, duelling, and stealing, are forbidden under pain of the severest punishment.

7. If it should be discovered that one of the trades-people has cheated his employer he shall be sentenced not only to make full restitution, but also to pay a third more, as a punishment for his deceitful dealings. Because of this, the Deputies of the Provincial Council shall take care that upon the death of every factor whatever amount he may have had from his employer, which belonged to the employer, shall be assiduously delivered up to him again.

[1] Ballot.

Chapter V.

Concerning the Situation and the Rivers of the Province.

The situation of Pennsylvania is like that of Naples in Italy. This province begins at the fortieth degree of north latitude;[1] its boundaries run to the east along the de la Ware River. It is seventy-five German miles[2] long and forty-five[3] wide.

The adjacent islands are, Neu-Jersey, Marie-land, and Virginia.

In this province some new beautiful stars, whole and half, are seen which constantly maintain the same pole, and have not before been known to the European astrologers.

The dela Ware River is so grand that it has no equal in all Europe. Thirty miles[4] above Philadelphia ships of one hundred tons burden can conveniently sail thereon. It separates Neu-Gersey and Pennsylvania from one another. At Philadelphia it is two,[5] and at Castle three,[6] miles wide, it receives the ebb and flow of the tide, and abounds with fish, as does the Scolkil.

The fresh streams and springs are almost without number.

The shady underbrush and thickets are everywhere filled with birds, whose rare colors and varied notes magnificently set forth the praise of their Creator. And above all, there is a superabundance of wild geese, ducks, turkeys, partridges, wild pigeons, water-snipe, and similar game.

[1] So erroneously believed at the time.

[2] Two hundred and twenty-five English miles.

[3] If German miles are meant, this would equal 135 English miles.

[4] Evidently English miles, as the head of navigation is about thirty miles above Philadelphia at the Falls of Delaware, at Trenton.

[5] Less than an English mile wide.

[6] Slightly more than two English miles wide.

Chapter VI.

Concerning the Coming of William Penn.

On November 1, 1682,[1] William Penn arrived in this province with twenty ships,[2] having spent six weeks upon the voyage.   Even while they were yet far from the land there was wafted to them as delightful a fragrance as if it came from a freshly blossoming garden.   He found, upon his arrival, no other Christian people save those alone who upon the discovery of the province had been put there.[3]   Part of them dwelt in Neu-Castle, and part upon separate plantations.   Penn was received as their ruler by these people with especial tokens of affection, and they most willingly discharged their obligation of submission to him.   All that he required of them in return was: A temperate life and neighborly love.   On the other hand, he promised to protect them in both spiritual and temporal matters.

Chapter VII.

Concerning the Laws given by William Penn.

Firstly, no one shall be disturbed on account of his belief, but freedom of conscience shall be granted to all inhabitants of the province, so that every nation may build and conduct churches and schools according to their desires.

2. Sunday shall be consecrated to the public worship of God.   The teaching of God shall be so zealously carried on

---

[1] Penn arrived within the capes of Delaware Bay, October 24 (N. S., November 3); at New Castle, Delaware, October 27 (N. S., November 6); at Upland (now Chester), Pennsylvania, October 29 (N. S., November 8), 1682.

[2] Not as a convoy or fleet in company with Penn's ship the *Welcome*, but as the number of vessels arriving during the summer of 1682, or the shipping season of Penn's coming. "Here have come letters from Wm. Penn [in Pennsylvania] above a month since . . . and there had been that summer 21 sayl Ships arrived there with Passingers." (Letter of James Claypoole, London, January 16, 1682/3).

[3] Not true; Penn found a heterogeneous population of Indians, Swedes, Dutch, French, and English; the whites had been coming there since the first permanent settlement by the Swedes in 1638.

that its purity can be recognized in each listener from the fruits which arise from it.

3. For the more convenient bringing up of the youth, the solitary farmers living in the province shall all remove to the market-towns, so that the neighbors may help one another in a Christlike manner and praise God together, and that they may accustom their children also to do the same.

4. The sessions of the court shall be held publicly, at appointed times, so that everyone may attend them.

5. Justices of the peace shall be appointed in the rising cities and market-towns, to insure the observance of the laws.

6. Cursing, blasphemy, misuse of the name of God, quarrelling, cheating, drunkenness, shall be punished with the pillory.

7. All workmen shall be content with their definite stipulated wages.

8. Each child, that is twelve years of age, shall be put to some handicraft or other honorable trade.

CHAPTER VIII.

Concerning the Rising Towns of the Province.

The Governor William Penn laid out the city of Philadelphia between the two streams de la Ware and Scolkis, and gave it this name, as if its inhabitants should lead their lives therein in pure and simple brotherly love.

The river at the city is deep enough so that large ships can, without danger, sail up to the bank within a stone's throw of the city.

Another English Company[1] has built the new city of Franckfurt,[2] at a distance of an hour and a half, wherein, in addition to trading, they have set on foot some mills, glass-works, and brick-kilns.

Neu-Castle lies forty English miles[3] from the sea, on the de la Ware River, and has a good harbor. The city of Upland lies twenty English miles[4] from Castle, up the river, and is chiefly inhabited by Swedes.

---

[1] The Free Society of Traders.
[2] Frankford.
[3] Nearer fifty miles.
[4] Only about fifteen miles.

On October 24, 1685,[1] I, Francis Daniel Pastorius, with the good will of the governor, laid out another new city, of the name of Germanton, or Germanopolis, at a distance of two hours' walk from Philadelphia, where there are a good black fertile soil, and many fresh wholesome springs of water, many oak, walnut, and chestnut trees, and also good pasturage for cattle.   The first settlement consisted of only twelve families of forty-one persons, the greater part High German mechanics and weavers, because I had ascertained that linen cloth would be indispensable.

I made the main street of this city sixty feet wide, and the side streets forty; the space, or ground-plot, for each house and garden was as much as three acres of land, but for my own dwelling twice as much.   Before this, I had also built a little house in Philadelphia, thirty feet long and fifteen wide.   Because of the scarcity of glass the windows were of oiled paper. Over the house-door I had written:

Parva Domus, sed amica Bonis, procul este profani,[2]

Whereat our Governor, when he visited me, burst into laughter, and encouraged me to keep on building.

I have also acquired for my High-German Company fifteen thousand acres of land in one piece, upon the condition that, within a year, they shall actually place thirty households thereon; and for this reason, that we High-Germans may maintain a separate little province, and thus feel more secure from all oppression.

It would, therefore, be a very good thing if the European associates should at once send more persons over here, for the common advantage of the Company; for only the day before yesterday,[3] the Governor said to me that the zeal of the High-Germans in building pleased him very much, and that he preferred them to the English, and would grant them special privileges.

---

[1] Misprint for 1683.

[2] A little house, but a friend to the good; remain at a distance, ye profane.

[3] In this chapter Pastorius is drawing his account of Germantown and of his activities from his report of March 7, 1684.

CHAPTER IX.

Concerning the Fruitfulness of this Province.

As this province is situated like Mompellier[1] and Naples in respect to latitude, but is furnished with many more rivers and springs than either of the two, so it is not difficult to comprehend that such a country is well-adapted for many fine crops. The air is clear and pleasant, the summer longer and warmer than in Germany, and we have already in these parts satisfactory supply of all sorts of crops, and our work of cultivation is well rewarded.

We have also a large number of cattle, although, just now, all run free in the pasture together, until we shall have made better needful arrangements for them.

We get sugar and syrup from Barbados, and he who has no money exchanges goods for goods, as he comes to an agreement.

The trade between the savages and the Christians is in fish, birds, deer-skins, and all sorts of peltry, such as beaver, otter, fox, etc. Sometimes they barter for drink, sometimes they sell for their native money, which is only oblong corals, ground out of sea-mussels, sometimes white and sometimes light brown, and fastened on strings.

They know how to string this coral-money in a very artistic way, and they wear it in the place of gold chains. Their king wears a crown or hood of it.

Twelve of the brown are worth as much as twenty-four of the white pieces, which are equal to a silver penny of Franckfurt. They take their own money far more readily than silver coin, because they have often been cheated with the latter.

Besides this, the silver money, which we use here, consists of Spanish pieces of eight and English shillings. We have no precious stones found in these parts, nor do we desire them, and we cannot ascribe great praise to that man who first brought forth gold and precious stones out of the dark and hidden places of the earth, for these noble creations of God,

[1] Montpellier, France, which is in about the latitude of Lake Ontario, is too far north for Pennsylvania.

although good in themselves, are nevertheless terribly abused by their misuse, and, against their will, are made to subserve the uses of vanity.

Chapter X.

Concerning the Vegetation of this Province.

Although this far-distant portion of the world consisted of nothing but wildernesses, and it only within a short time has begun to be made ready for the use of Christian men, it is truly matter for amazement how quickly, by the blessing of God, it advances, and from day to day grows perceptibly. For although in the beginning we were obliged to have our victuals brought from Jersey, and to pay somewhat dearly for them with money, yet we are now able, praise be to God! to serve other neighboring communities.

We are supplied with the principal and most necessary handicraftsmen; the daily wage is regulated on a tolerable basis, and we have what is necessary in the way of mills and brick-kilns.

We sell our superabundance of grain and cattle in Barbados for brandy, syrup, sugar, and salt, but we send the fine peltries over to England.

We are especially desirous to advance the cultivation of the vine and the weaving of cloth in these parts, in order to keep the money in the province, and on this account we have already established yearly fairs, not for the sake of mere profit and gain, but that any thing which one man or another has, over and above his needs, may be made purchasable for the others, so that they need not, on this account, journey to the neighboring islands, and carry their money thither.

Chapter XI.

Concerning the Inhabitants of this Province.

Of these, three sorts may be found: 1. The natives, the so-called savages. 2. The Christians who have come here from Europe, the so-called Old Settlers. 3. The newly-arrived Associations and Companies.

So far as concerns the first, the savages, they are, in general, strong, agile, and supple people, with blackish bodies; they went about naked at first and wore only a cloth about the loins. Now they are beginning to wear shirts. They have, usually, coal-black hair, shave the head, smear the same with grease, and allow a long lock to grow on the right side. They also besmear the children with grease, and let them creep about in the heat of the sun, so that they become the color of a nut, although they were at first white enough by Nature.

They strive after a sincere honesty, hold strictly to their promises, cheat and injure no one. They willingly give shelter to others, and are both useful and loyal to their guests.

Their huts are made of young trees, twined, or bent, together, which they know how to roof over with bark. They use neither table nor bench, nor any other household stuff, unless perchance a single pot in which they boil their food.

I once saw four of them take a meal together in hearty contentment, and eat a pumpkin cooked in clear water, without butter and spice. Their table and bench was the bare earth, their spoons were mussel-shells, with which they dipped up the warm water, their plates were the leaves of the nearest tree, which they do not need to wash with painstaking after the meal, nor to keep with care for future use. I thought to myself, these savages have never in their lives heard the teaching of Jesus concerning temperance and contentment, yet they far excel the Christians in carrying it out.

They are, furthermore, serious and of few words, and are amazed when they perceive so much unnecessary chatter, as well as other foolish behavior, on the part of the Christians.

Each man has his own wife, and they detest harlotry, kissing, and lying. They know of no idols, but they worship a single all-powerful and merciful God, who limits the power of the Devil. They also believe in the immortality of the soul, which, after the course of life is finished, has a suitable recompense from the all-powerful hand of God awaiting it.

They accompany their own worship of God with songs, during which they make strange gestures and motions with the hands and feet, and when they recall the death of their parents and friends, they begin to wail and weep most pitifully.

They listen very willingly, and not without perceptible emotion, to discourse concerning the Creator of Heaven and earth, and His divine Light, which enlightens all men who have come into the world, and who are yet to be born, and concerning the wisdom and love of God, because of which he gave his only-begotten and most dearly-beloved Son to die for us. It is only to be regretted that we can not yet speak their language readily, and therefore cannot set forth to them the thoughts and intent of our own hearts, namely, how great a power and salvation lies concealed in Christ Jesus. They are very quiet and thoughtful in our gatherings, so that I fully believe that in the future, at the great day of judgment, they will come forth with those of Tyre and Sidon, and put to shame many thousands of false nominal and canting Christians.

As for their economy and housekeeping, the men attend to their hunting and fishing. The women bring up their children honestly, under careful oversight and dissuade them from sin. They plant Indian corn and beans round about their huts, but they take no thought for any more extensive farming and cattle-raising; they are rather astonished that we Christians take so much trouble and thought concerning eating and drinking and also for comfortable clothing and dwellings, as if we doubted that God were able to care for and nourish us.

Their native language is very dignified, and in its pronunciation much resembles the Italian, although the words are entirely different and strange. They are accustomed to paint their faces with colors; both men and women use tobacco with pleasure; they divert themselves with fifes, or trumpets, in unbroken idleness.

The second sort of inhabitants in the province are the old Christians, who came here from Europe.

These have never had the upright intention to give these needy native creatures instruction in the true living Christianity, but instead they have sought only their own worldly interests, and have cheated the simple inhabitants in trade and intercourse, so that at length those savages who dealt with these Christians, proved themselves to be also for the most part, crafty, lying, and deceitful, so that I can not say much that is creditable of either. These misguided people are wont to exchange the skins and peltry which they obtain for strong drink, and to drink so much that they can neither walk nor stand; also they are wont to commit all sorts of thievery, as the occasion may arise.

Owing to this, their kings and rulers have frequently complained of the sins of falsehood, deceit, thieving, and drunkenness, introduced here by the Christians, and which were formerly entirely unknown in these parts.

If one of these savages allows himself to be persuaded by a Christian to work, he does it with complaining, shame, and fear, as an unaccustomed act; he looks about him all the while on all sides, lest any of his people may find him working, just as if work were a disgrace, and idleness were an especial inborn privilege of the nobility, which should not be soiled by the sweat of toil.

The third sort of inhabitants of this province are the Christian Societies.

We, the latest arrivals, being Christians included in honorable associations and companies, after obtaining royal permission from England, in the year 1681, bought certain portions of the country for ourselves from the governor, William Penn, with the intention to erect new cities and colonies, and not only to gain thereby our own temporal advantage and support, but also to make the savages gentle and docile, and to instruct them in the true knowledge of God, insomuch that I live in the hope of being able to announce more good news of their conversion to Christianity within a short time.

CHAPTER XII.

Concerning the Magistrates of this Province.

The native savages have their own little kings. We Christians acknowledge William Penn as our ruler of the country, to whom this land was granted and ceded for his own by King Charles II., and the Christian inhabitants were instructed to give him personal allegiance. But this wise and God-fearing ruler did not, upon his arrival, wish to accept this inheritance of the heathen thus, for nothing, but he gave presents to the native inhabitants and their appointed kings, and compensated them, and thus bought from them one piece of land after another, so that they withdrew ever further into the wilderness. Penn, however, had bought all the land which he occupied by just right of purchase, and from him I bought at the start, in London, thirty thousand acres for my German Company.

And notwithstanding the aforesaid William Penn belongs to the sect of the Tremblers, or Quakers, yet he constrains no one to any religion, but leaves to each nation freedom of belief.

CHAPTER XIII.

Concerning the Religions in this Province.

The native naked inhabitants have no written articles of belief, since no traces can be found that any Christian teachers have ever come among them. They only know their native language by means of which the parents instruct their children through tradition, and teach them that which they have heard of and learned from their parents.

2. The English and Dutch are for the most part adherents of the Calvinist religion.

3. The Quakers are known in Philadelphia, through William Penn.

4. The Swedes and High-Germans are Evangelical. They have their own church, whose minister is named Fabricius, of whom I must declare with sorrow, that he is much addicted to drink, and is well-nigh blind in the inner man.

Here in Germanton, in the year 1686, we built a little church for the community, but did not have as our aim an outwardly great stone edifice, but rather that the temple of God which we believers constitute, should be built up, and that we ourselves should be, all together, holy and unspotted.

The Evangelical ministers could have had a fine opportunity here to carry out the command of Christ: Go forth throughout the world, and preach the Gospel, if they had pre-

ferred to be followers of Christ rather than servants of their
bodies, and if they had been devoted to the inner theology
rather than to verbal discourse.

CHAPTER XIV.

How the High-German Company is Managed in Pennsylvania.

The principal members of this Company were in the beginning:

> Jacob von de Walle, D. Johann Jacob Schütz, and Daniel
> Behagel, merchant, all three in Franckfurt am Mayn.
> In Duisburg there was D. Gerhard of Maastricht.
> In Wesel, D. Thomas von Wylich, and Johann Lebrunn.
> In Roterdamm, Benjamin Furly.
> In London, Philipp Fort.[1]

These send on from hand to hand the letters and goods
forwarded to them, until they reach the out-going ship; they
also lend a helping hand by means of advice and assistance,
to those who, with honest intent, wish to journey over to
Pennsylvania.

At the present time the management of the affairs of the
Company, in Pennsylvania, is confided to my unworthy self.

CHAPTER XV.

Concerning the Time for a Voyage to this Province.

From the month of April until autumn ships are sailing
from England to Pennsylvania, especially from the port of
Deal, yet there is no definite time appointed, either for the departure, or for the return, but one must wait for an opportunity.
As soon as from thirty-five to forty persons (not including the
ship's-crew) are at hand, a ship sails, and each grown person
must give six pounds sterling, or thirty-six thalers, for his
freight, the cost of his food, and one sailor's chest. For each
servant or domestic twenty-two reichsthaler. One pound sterling is equal to six thalers.

[1] Ford.

Chapter XVI.

Concerning my (Pastorius's) own Journey and Crossing-over.

After I had arrived at Deal from London I hired four men-servants, and two maid-servants for myself, and set forth, in the company of eighty persons.[1] The ship drew thirteen feet of water. Our treatment, as regards food and drink, was rather bad, for ten people received three pounds of butter a week, four jugs of beer and one jug of water a day, two dishes of pease every noontime, and four times in the week meat at noon, and three times, salt fish, which they must prepare for themselves with the butter that they had received, and there must always be enough saved from the noon meal to have something to eat at night. Now because this food is very tough, and is wont to taste about as much like flesh as fish, each one must provide himself with the means of nourishment when he comes to the ship, or he must carefully stipulate with the ship's master concerning the quality as well as the quantity of the food which he shall daily receive. In order however to bind him more precisely thereto, one must hold back some of the passage-money, and promise to pay it here; also, when it is possible, one should take passage in a ship that sails as far as the city of Philadelphia, because in the other ships, that stop at Upland, one is subjected to all kinds of inconvenience.

On the sixteenth of August, 1683, we came in sight of America, but reached the de la Ware River on the eighteenth of the same. On the twentieth of the same, we passed by Neu-Castle and Upland, and arrived toward evening safely at Philadelphia, where I was received by the Governor, William Penn, with affectionate friendliness, whose Secretary, Johann

---

[1] After attending to certain matters of business in London "I with Jacob Shoemaker (who came with me from Mentz), George Wertmuller, Isaac Dilbeck, his wife Marieke and his two boys Abraham and Jacob, Thomas Gasper, Cunrad Backer (alias Rutter,) and an English Maid, called Frances Simson, went a board of a Ship, which had the name of *America*, (the Captain whereof was Joseph Wasey,) and being gone the 6th of June [1683] from Gravesend, we arrived the 7th ditto. at Deal, and left England the 10th of the sd month of June" (Pastorius, *Beehive*, in Learned's *Pastorius*, p. 111). In his manuscript "Res Propriae," he states that he arrived in Gravesend June 3.

Lehennmann,[1] treated me with brotherly affection; also the governor frequently had me invited to his table, and allowed me to enjoy his edifying discourse.   When I was absent lately for eight days, he came himself to visit me, and bade me come twice in the week to his table, and testified in the presence of his council that he was very fond of me and of the High-Germans, and wished that they [the council] should feel the same.

Chapter XVII.

Concerning the Vocation of our Germans in this Place.

Besides the fact that the High-German Company has established a commerce in this place, in woollen and linen cloth and all conceivable wares, and has entrusted to me the superintendence thereof, it is still further to be remarked, that we have also purchased thirty thousand acres of land in order to establish a High German colony.   Meanwhile, in my newly laid-out city of Germanton, sixty-four households are already in a flourishing condition.   In order to support these present inhabitants, as well as others who are arriving, the fields must be cultivated, and the lands cleared.   Let one turn, however, in whichever direction he will, it is always true that: *Itur in antiquam sylvam,*[2] and all is overgrown with forest, so that I often wished for a few dozen stout Tyrolese who would have felled the thick ash-trees, which we have been obliged to do, little by little, for ourselves; whereat I pictured to myself that the very penance with which God punished the disobedience of Adam, namely that he should eat his bread in the sweat of his brow, was also, in this land, meted out and given to us his descendants, for here it may be said: *Hic opus, hic labor*

---

[1] Not Johann, but Philipp Theodor Lehnmann (d. 1687), son of Johann Georg Lehnmann, farmer-general of Saxony.   In 1680 he and his wife Theophila were living in St. Philip's parish, Bristol, England.   He was Penn's private secretary on the first visit of the Proprietor to Pennsylvania, 1682–1684, probably coming over on the *Welcome* in 1682.   He remained in Pennsylvania, being mentioned in 1685 as a Philadelphia merchant.   The next year, however he took up his residence on his plantation on Broad Creek, not far from Lewes, Delaware, where he died.

[2] One finds himself in the primitive forest.

est,[1] and it is not enough to bring money, but we must also
bring an inclination to work, and take into consideration the
motto of the Emperor Septimius Severus, which is: *Laboremus.
Absque labor nihil. Quo major, hoc laboriosior.*[2] For that man
is best off whom the devil does not find idle.

In the meantime we use the savages for work, hiring them
by the day; we are gradually learning their language, and little
by little instruct them in the teaching of Christ, invite them to
attend our worship of God, and hope soon to be able to announce with joy that the compassion of the Most High God
has permitted the light of His Holy Gospel to rise also over
these lands, and to shine forth, to the honor of His great
name, to Whom alone be praise, honor, thanks, and glory
without end.

Further News from Pennsylvania, of the 7th of January, 1684.

I had made known in my last how I was received upon my
arrival by the ruler of this province, William Penn, with most
affectionate friendliness. I must not now conceal how he permitted his kindness to me to be perceived daily more and more
by his actions. Also this province pleases me better the longer
I stay, so that I often wish to have my most estimable parents
and dear brothers and sisters with me, knowing well that such
a change would not be regretted by them, whom I love constantly and wish to serve. For although I am in the body deprived of their presence, I am nevertheless at times with them
in childlike love, and have them always in my mind and
thoughts. I live here in the labors of my calling, in singleness
of heart toward God and toward my fellow-Christians. I have
bought for myself six hundred acres of land, and brought a
good part thereof under cultivation, so that I am able to serve
others by giving of the superabundance granted me. I am
therefore heartily content with my condition, and have my
rest in God, the light of Whose grace I perceive more and more
in my heart from day to day, consequently I possess a gracious

---

[1] Properly, "Hoc opus, hic labor est"—"This is the work, this the labor."
Virgil, *Aeneid*, VI. 129.
[2] Let us labor. Without labor there is nothing. The greater one is, the
more laborious he is.

God and an unscathed conscience, two things which I greatly prefer to all the treasures of Egypt.

Whereby I can further truly assert that my soul is filled with love, reverence, and a desire to serve you and my dear brothers and sisters, whom I herewith greet and embrace from the bottom of my heart, with the assurance that for their sakes I would willingly make the journey once more to bring them hither, if I should only receive some lines bidding me to do so.   In the meantime I remain ever under the all-ruling protecting hand of our Emanuel, etc.

Positive Information from America, concerning the Country of Pennsylvania, from a German who has migrated thither; dated Philadelphia, March 7, 1684.[1]

To fulfill my duty as well as my promise made at my departure I will somewhat more circumstantially state what I have found and noted of these lands; and since I am not unaware that by imperfect relations many of you have been misinformed, I give my assurance beforehand that I with impartial pen and without deceptive additions will set forth faithfully both the inconveniences of the journey and the defects of this province, as well as that plentifulness of the same which has been praised by others almost to excess; for I desire nothing more in my little place than to walk in the footsteps of Him who is the way, and to follow His holy teachings, because He is the truth, in order that I may ceaselessly enjoy with Him eternal life.

I. Accordingly I will begin with the voyage, which is certainly on the one hand dangerous on account of the terror of shipwreck,[2] and on the other hand very burdensome on account of the bad and hard fare, so that I now from my own experience understand in a measure what David says in the 107th Psalm, that on the sea one may observe and perceive not only

---

[1] This, to p. 411, is a full version of the unique Zurich print, *Sichere Nachricht*, substituted for the abridgment printed in the *Umständliche Geographische Beschreibung*.   Translation by the general editor of the series.

[2] In a later account he mentions their escape "from the Cruel, Enslaving Turks, once supposed to be at our heels."

the wonderful works of God but also the spirit of the storm. As to my voyage hither,[1] I sailed from Deal the tenth of June with four men servants, two maid servants, two children and one young boy. We had the whole way over, for the most part, contrary winds, and never favorable for twelve hours together, many tempests and thunderstorms, also the foremast broke twice, so that it was ten weeks before we arrived here; yet *sat citò, si sat bene*,[2] considering that it seldom happens that any persons arrive here much more quickly. The Crefelders,[3] who arrived here on October 6, were also ten weeks upon the ocean, and the ship that set out with ours from Deal was fourteen days longer on the voyage, and several people died in it. The Crefelders lost a grown girl between Rotterdam and England, which loss however was made up between England and Pennsylvania by the birth of two children. On our ship, on the other hand, no one died and no one was born. Almost all the passengers were seasick for some days, I however for not more than four hours. On the other hand I underwent other accidents, namely, that the two carved lugs[4] over the ship's bell fell right upon my back, and on the 9th of July during a storm in the night I fell so severely upon my left side that for some days I had to keep to my bed. These two falls reminded me forcibly of the first fall of our original parents in

[1] *Cf.* Chap. XVI, *ante* p. 389.

[2] "Quickly enough, if well enough."

[3] A company of thirteen families, for the most part Mennonite or Quaker weavers, from Crefeld on the lower Rhine in Germany, not far from the Dutch frontier. A tract of 18,000 acres of land having been purchased from Penn by Jacob Telner, a Crefeld Mennonite doing business in Amsterdam, and five of his associates, these families came over to locate and to settle the land. Their passage having been engaged through the agency of Benjamin Furly of Rotterdam, they went by way of the latter city to England, and sailed about July 25, 1683, from Gravesend, on the ship *Concord*, of London, 500 tons burden, William Jeffries master. After a voyage of nearly eleven weeks they arrived at Philadelphia October 6. A large number of them found temporary shelter, as Pastorius states, in his newly-erected "dugout" house, at the south end of the town. Then, with the laying out of Germantown that same month, they took up their residence there, thus becoming, along with Pastorius, the founders of that town and the advance guard of the great German migration to America.

[4] "When the Lion fell upon my Back" is Pastorius's reference to the accident in a poem addressed in 1715 to his fellow voyagers, the daughters of Thomas Lloyd.

Paradise, which has come down upon all their posterity, and also of many of those falls which I have undergone in this vale of misery of my exile. *Per varios casus,*[1] etc. But praised be the fatherly hand of the divine mercy which lifts us up again so many times and holds us back that we fall not entirely into the abyss of the evil one. Georg Wertmüller[2] also fell down extremely hard, Thomas Gasper had an eruption of the body, the English maid [3] had the erysipelas, and Isaac Dilbreck,[4] who according to outward appearance was the strongest, succumbed for the greatest length of time. So I had a small ship-hospital, although I alone of the Germans had taken my berth among the English. That one of the boatmen became insane and that our ship was shaken by the repeated assaults of a whale, I set forth at length in my last letter. The rations upon the ship were very bad. We lived *medice ac modice.*[5] Every ten persons received three pounds of butter a week, four cans of beer and two cans of water a day, two platters full of peas every noon, meat four dinners in the week and fish three, and these we were obliged to prepare with our own butter. Also we must every noon save up enough so that we might get our supper from it. The worst of all was, that both the meat and the fish were salted to such an extent and had become so rancid that we could hardly eat half of them. And had I not by the advice of good friends in England provided myself with various kinds of refreshment, it might perhaps have gone very badly. Therefore all those who hereafter intend to make the voyage hither should take good heed that they either, if there

---

[1] The reference is to the *Aeneid*, I. 204. "Through various accidents, through so many hazards, we go on toward Latium."

[2] George Wertmüller, one of the four servants of the Frankfort Company brought over by Pastorius. He was an elderly Switzer, apparently from in or near Berne. A letter of his, dated March 16, 1684, descriptive of his new home, was one of the two letters printed in Dutch in Rotterdam the same year, as *Twee Missiven geschreven uyt Pensilvania.*

[3] Frances Simson, servant of the Frankfort Company.

[4] Isaac Dilbeck or Dilbeek, with his wife Marieke, servants of the Frankfort Company, bringing with them two children, Abraham and Jacob. He was a weaver. In 1700 he purchased 500 acres of land in Whitemarsh Township, now Montgomery County, Pennsylvania, and in 1710 was a deacon of the Reformed Church there.

[5] Medically and moderately.

are many of them, procure their own provisions, or else agree
distinctly with the captain as to both quantity and quality,
how much food and of what sort they are to receive each day;
and to hold him down the more completely to this agreement,
one should reserve some small part of the passage money, to
be paid on this side. Also when possible one should arrange
with a ship which sails up to this city of Philadelphia, since in
the case of the others which end their voyage at Upland, one
is subjected to many inconveniences.

My company consisted of many sorts of people. There was
a doctor of medicine[1] with his wife and eight children, a French
captain, a Low Dutch cake-baker,[2] an apothecary, a glass-
blower,[3] a mason, a smith, a wheelwright, a cabinet-maker, a
cooper, a hat-maker, a cobbler, a tailor, a gardener, farmers,
seamstresses, etc., in all about eighty persons besides the crew.
They were not only different in respect to age (for our oldest
woman was sixty years of age and the youngest child only
twelve weeks) and in respect to their occupations, as I have

---

[1] Thomas Lloyd, later governor.
   "Alone with him, I could in Latin then Commune:
   Which Tongue he did pronounce right in our German way."—Pastorius

[2] Cornelius Bom (d. 1688), Dutch cake-baker, who had lived in Rotterdam
(1675) and in Haarlem, came over to Pennsylvania in 1683 with Pastorius in the
America, and set up his bake-shop on the western outskirts of the little backwoods
town of Philadelphia, on a lot at the southeast corner of Third and Chestnut
streets. In 1684 he wrote a letter to Holland which was printed in Dutch at
Rotterdam the same year, along with another letter from George Wertmüller,
under the title *Twee Missiven geschreven uyt Pensilvania*. His letter was also
printed separately the following year at Rotterdam, with the title *Missive van
Cornelis Bom Geschreven uit de Stadt Philadelphia* (only known copy in America
in the collection of the Historical Society of Pennsylvania). "I have here a shop
of many kinds of goods and edibles," he states, "sometimes I ride out with merchandise and sometimes bring something back, mostly from the Indians, and deal
with them in many things. I have no servants except one negro whom I bought.
I have no rent or excise to pay. I have a cow which gives plenty of milk, a horse
to ride around, my pigs increase rapidly, so that in the summer I had seventeen
when at first I had only two. I have many chickens and geese, and a garden,
and shall next year have an orchard if I remain well; so that my wife [Agnes]
and I are in good spirits and are reaching a condition of ease and prosperity in
which we have great hopes."

[3] Joshua Tittery, from Newcastle-upon-Tyne, broad-glass blower, came over
on the *America* as a servant to the Free Society of Traders, to serve for four years
at £88 per annum.

mentioned, but were also of such different religions and be-
haviors that I might not unfittingly compare the ship that bore
them hither with Noah's Ark, but that there were more un-
clean than clean (rational) animals to be found therein.   In
my household I have those who hold to the Roman, to the
Lutheran, to the Calvinistic, to the Anabaptist, and to the An-
glican church, and only one Quaker.   On the 11th of August
we cast the lead for the first time and perceived that we were
close to the great sand bank, and so had to sail back and
around and consequently to run more than a hundred leagues[1]
out of our course.

On the 16th we came with joy in sight of America and on
the morning of the 18th arrived in Delaware Bay, which is
thirty English miles long and fifteen wide and is of such unequal depth that since our ship drew thirteen feet of water we
sometimes stuck upon the sand.

On the 20th we sailed past Neu Castle, Upland and Duni-
cum[2] and arrived at evening, praise God, safely at Philadelphia;
where I on the following day delivered to William Penn the
letters that I had, and was received by him with amiable
friendliness; of that very worthy man and famous ruler I
might properly

II. write many things; but my pen (though it is from an
eagle, which a so-called savage lately brought to my house) is
much too weak to express the high virtues of this Christian—
for such he is indeed.   He often invites me to his table and
has me walk and ride in his always edifying company; and
when I lately was absent from here a week, in order to fetch
provisions from Neu Castle, and he had not seen me for that
space of time, he came himself to my little house and besought
me that I should at least once or twice a week be his guest.
He heartily loves the [Germans], and once said openly in my
presence to his councillors and those who were about him,
I love the [Germans] and desire that you also should love them.
Yet in any other matter I have never heard such a command
from him.   This however pleased me so much the better
because it was entirely conformable with the command of
God (see John xiii. 23).   I can at present say no more than
that William Penn is a man who honors God and is honored by

---

[1] **Three hundred English miles.**   [2] Tinicum.

Him, who loves what is good and is rightly beloved by all good men. I doubt not that some of them will come here and by their own experience learn, that my pen has in this case not written enough.[1]

III. Of the nature of the land I can write with certainty only after one or more years of experience. The Swedes and Low Dutch who have occupied it for twenty years[2] and more are in this as in most other things of divided opinions; *laudatur ab his, culpatur ab illis.*[3] Certain it is that the soil does not lack fruitfulness and will reward the labor of our hands as well as in Europe if one will duly work and manure it, both which things are for the most part lacking. For the above mentioned old inhabitants are poor agriculturists. Some of them have neither barns nor stables, and leave their grain for years together unthreshed and lying in the open air, and allow their cattle, horses, cows, swine, etc., to run in the woods summer and winter, so that they derive little profit from them. Certainly the penance with which God punished the disobedience of Adam, that he should eat his bread in the sweat of his brow, extends also to his posterity in these lands, and those who think to spare their hands may remain where they are. *Hic opus, hic labor est,* and it is not enough to bring money hither, without the inclination to work, for it slips out of one's hands, and I may well say with Solomon: It has wings. Inasmuch as in the past year very many people came hither both out of England and Ireland and also from Barbadoes and other American islands, and this province does not yet produce sufficient provisions for such a multitude, therefore all victuals are somewhat dear, and almost all the money goes out of the land to pay for them. Yet we hope in time to have a greater abundance of both things, because William Penn will coin money and agriculture will be better managed. Working people and husbandmen are in the greatest demand here, and I certainly wish that I had a dozen strong Tyrolese to cut down the thick oak trees, for in whatever direction one turns,

[1] "How be 't nought in the World could mine Affection quench
  Towards Dear Penn, with whom I did converse in French."—Pastorius.

[2] Over forty years.

[3] "It is praised by these, it is reproached by those."—Horace, *Satires*, I. 2, 11.

one may say: *Itur in antiquam sylvam.*[1] It is nothing but forest, and very few cleared places are to be found, in which respect as also in some others the hope I had previously formed is deceived, namely, that in these wild orchards no apples or pears are to be found, and this winter (which indeed has been very cold) no deer, turkeys, etc., were to be had. The wild grapes are very small and better suited to make into vinegar than into wine. The walnuts have very thick shells, and few thick kernels within, so that they are scarcely worth the trouble of cracking. The chestnuts, however, and hazelnuts are somewhat more palatable; also the peaches, apples and pears are very good, no fault is to be found with them, except that there are not so many of them as some desire. On the other hand there are more rattlesnakes (whose bite is fatal) in the land than is agreeable to us. I must also add this, *tanquam testis oculatus*,[2] that on October 16 I found fine (March) violets in the bushes; also that, after I had on October 24 laid out the town of Germantown, and on the 25th had gone back there with seven others, we on the way found a wild grape-vine, running over a tree, on which were some four hundred clusters of grapes; wherefore we then hewed down the tree and satisfied all eight of us, and took home with us a hatfull apiece besides. Also as I on August 25 was dining with William Penn, a single root of barley was brought in which had grown in a garden here and had fifty grains upon it.[3] But all grains do not bear so much and it is as we say in the proverb, one swallow does not make a summer. Yet I doubt not that in the future more fruitful examples of this sort will present themselves, when we shall put the plow to the land in good earnest. I lament the vines which I brought with me, for when we were already in Delaware Bay they were drenched with seawater and all but two were spoiled. The abovementioned William Penn has a fine vineyard[4] of French vines planted; its growth is a pleasure to behold and brought into my reflections, as I looked upon it, the fifteenth chapter of John.[5]

---

[1] "We go into the primitive forest."   [2] "As an eye-witness."
[3] *Cf.* Penn's *Letter to the Free Society of Traders, ante*, p. 228.
[4] Penn's vineyard on the east bank of the Schuylkill, on the present Lemon Hill, in Fairmount Park, Philadelphia.
[5] "I am the true vine, and my Father is the husbandman," etc.

IV. Philadelphia daily increases in houses and inhabitants and presently a house of correction will be built in order that those who are not willing to live in a Philadelphian manner may be disciplined, for some such are to be found, to whom fittingly applies what our dear friend [Van de Walle] mentions in his letter, that we have here more distress from the spoiled Christians than from the Indians. Furthermore here and there other towns are laid out; for the Society[1] is beginning to build about an hour and a half from here[2] one bearing the name of Franckfurt, where they have erected a mill and a glass factory. Not far from there, namely two hours from here,[2] lies our Germantown, where already forty-two people are living in twelve dwellings. They are mostly linen weavers and not any too skilled in agriculture. These good people laid out all their substance upon the journey, so that if William Penn had not advanced provisions to them, they must have become servants to others. The way from here to Germantown they have now, by frequent going to and fro, trodden out into good shape. Of that town[3] I can say no more at present than that it lies on black fruitful soil and is half surrounded with pleasant streams like a natural defence. The chief street therein is sixty feet wide and the cross street forty. Every family has a house lot of three acres.

V. As to the inhabitants, I cannot better classify them than into the native and the engrafted. For if I were to call the former savages and the latter Christians, I should do great injustice to many of both varieties. Of the latter sort, I have already mentioned above, that the incoming ships are not altogether to be compared with Noah's Ark. The Lutheran preacher,[4] who ought as a *statua Mercurialis*[5] to show the Swedes the way to heaven, is, to say it in one word, a drunkard.

---

[1] The Free Society of Traders. *Cf. ante*, chap. VIII. of this *Description*, p. 380, and Penn's *Letter* to the Society, XXXIII., p. 241.

[2] From Philadelphia.   [3] *Cf.* this *Description*, chap. VIII., *ante*, p. 381.

[4] Rev. Jacob Fabritius (d. 1693), a Dutch or Polish Lutheran minister, who went from Holland to New York in 1669, and had charge for a time of a congregation in Albany. In 1671 he came to the Delaware, and in 1677 was made pastor of Gloria Dei, the new Swedish church at Wicaco, preaching the first sermon there on Trinity Sunday. In 1682 he became blind, and thenceforth had to be led to the pulpit.

[5] "Statue of Mercury," god and guide of travellers.

Also there are coiners of false money and other vicious persons here whom nevertheless, it may be hoped, the wind of God's vengeance will in his own time drive away like chaff. On the other hand there is no lack of pious, God-fearing people, and I can with truth affirm that I have nowhere in Europe seen the notice posted up, as here in our Philadelphia, that such an one has found this or that, and that the loser may call for it at his house; often however the converse, Lost this or that; he who returns it again shall receive a reward, etc.

Of these new engrafted strangers I will for the present say no more than that among them some High Germans are to be found who have lived already twenty years in this land and consequently are, so to speak, naturalized, namely, Silesians, Brandenburgers, Holsteiners, Swiss, etc.,[1] also a Nuremberg man named Jan Jaquet;[2] but will briefly give my account of those who are erroneously called savages.[3] The first who came before my eyes were those two who at Upland came in a canoe to our ship. I presented them with a dram of brandy. They attempted to pay me for it with a sixpence, and when I refused the money they gave me their hands, and said, Thank you, brother. They are strong of limb, swarthy of body, and paint their faces, red, blue, etc., in various ways. In the summer they go quite naked, except that they cover their private parts with a piece of cloth, and now in winter hang duffels upon themselves. They have coal-black hair, while the Swedish children born here have hair snow-white. I was once dining with William Penn where one of their kings sat at table with us. William Penn, who can speak their language fairly fluently, said to him that I was a German, etc. He came accordingly on the third of October, and on the twelfth of December another king and queen came to my house. Also many common persons over-run me very often, to whom how-

---

[1] Chiefly in and near New Castle.

[2] Jean Paul Jaquet (c. 1615-1620–1685), a native of Nuremberg, whose father came from Geneva in Switzerland, had served the Dutch West India Company for some years in Brazil. In 1654 he brought his family over to New Amsterdam, and in the following year was sent to Fort Casimir (now New Castle, Delaware) as vice-director on the Delaware. In 1676 he was made a justice of the court at New Castle, and continued his residence in or near the town until his death.

[3] Cf. this Description, chaps. IX., XI., XIII., XVII.

ever I almost always show my love with a piece of bread and
a drink of beer, whereby an answering affection is awakened
in them and they commonly call me "Teutschmann," also
"Carissimo" (that is, brother).   N. B. Their language is
manly and in my opinion is little inferior to the Italian in
gravity, etc.   As to their manners and nature, one must so
to speak sub-distinguish them into those who have associated
for some time with the so-called Christians and those who are
just beginning to come forth out of their burrows.   For the
former are crafty and deceitful, which they owe to the abovementioned nominal Christians.   *Semper enim aliquid hæret.*[1]
Such an one lately pledged me his strap[2] as security that he
would bring me a turkey, but in its place he brought an eagle
and wished to persuade me that it was a turkey.   When
however I showed him that I had seen many eagles he acknowledged to a Swede who stood by that he had done it out of de-
ception, in the belief that because we had lately come into the
land I should not know such birds so accurately.   Another at
my fireside tested the brandy thus: he stuck his finger into
it and then put the latter into the fire to see whether water
had been mingled with the liquor.   Those of the second class,
on the contrary, are of a reasonable spirit, injure nobody, and
we have nothing whatever to fear from them.   One thing lately
struck deeply into my heart when I pondered the sincere admonition of our Saviour, that we His disciples should take no
thought for the morrow, because thus do the Gentiles.   Ah,
thought I to myself, how entirely has all been now perverted!
When we Christians are not provided for a month and more
how displeased are we, while these heathen in so wonderful a
spirit of resignation refer their sustenance to God.   Just at that
time I saw four of them eating together.   The earth was at
once their table and their bench.   A pumpkin, cooked in
plain water, without butter or spice, was all their food.   Their
spoons were mussel-shells, with which they supped the warm
water.   Their plates were oak leaves, which they had no need
to clean after the meal, nor, when they needed others, to give
themselves much trouble about them.[3]   Now, dear friend, let
us not hesitate to learn contentment from these people, that

[1] "For always something adheres."   [2] By which things are carried.
[3] *Cf.* the same story in the *Description*, chap. XI., *ante*, p. 384.

they may not hereafter shame us before the judgment-seat of Jesus Christ.

Of those persons who came hither with me a half dozen are already dead. I and mine, however, have throughout the whole time found ourselves in good condition and good appetite, except that Isaac Dilbeck has for a week been somewhat indisposed, and Jacob Schumacher[1] on the first of October cut his foot severely with an axe and was for a week unable to labor. Of the Crefelders, no one has died thus far except Herman op de Graef's[2] decrepit mother, who, soon after her arrival, wearied of the vanities of the world, departed to enjoy the delights of heaven. The wife of Abraham Tunesen,[3] our farmtenant, has now lain for more than two months in my cottage very weak, and was for some time quite unconscious but now bids fair to get well.

Now as to the purchased land. It is divided into three kinds.[4] First, 15000 acres lying together in one piece, on a navigable stream. Secondly, 300 acres within the city liberties, which is the stretch of land between the Delaware and the Schuylkill. Thirdly, three lots in the town, on which to build houses. When after my arrival I applied to William Penn for warrants, to measure off these three parts, and to obtain possession of them, his first answer respecting this was:

---

[1] Jacob Shoemaker (died 1722), one of the servants of the Frankfort Company, brought by Pastorius from Mainz, in Germany, was a turner by trade. In 1693 he was sheriff of Germantown.

[2] Herman op den Graeff, linen weaver, from Crefeld, son of Isaac, with his mother and his two brothers, Dirck and Abraham and sister Margaret, as purchasers of 2000 acres of land from Telner, arrived with the first German company of Crefelders on the *Concord*, in 1683. "My mother died in Philadelphia on the nineteenth of November, [1683], and was buried in that very place. My brother's wife was delivered of a daughter here in Germantown, which was the first born here." Thus wrote one of the brothers, evidently Herman, in the earliest known description of conditions in that initial German settlement, in a letter, a copy of which is in the Könneken manuscript at Lübeck, published by J. F. Sachse in *Letters relating to the Settlement of Germantown*. Herman was one of the first four burgesses of Germantown. His brothers were signers to the first public protest against slavery in America, at Germantown in 1688. About 1701 he removed to Kent County, Delaware, and died there about 1704.

[3] Abraham Tunes, one of the first Crefeld company, was a burgess in Germantown in 1694.

[4] *Cf.* the *Description*, chap. III., *ante*, p. 375.

I. The three lots in the city, and the three hundred acres in its liberties, could not rightly go to the [Frankforters] [1] because they were bought after he, William Penn, had already left England and the books at London had been closed.   After I had represented to him, however, that you were the fore-runners of all Germans, and therefore to be regarded with more consideration, he caused three lots to be measured off for me at the beginning of the town, one after another, out of his younger son's [2] share.

etc.   12   11   10   9   8   7   6   5   4   3   2   1

The double lines represent the Delaware River, on which the town is situated.   The numbers, however, represent the following houses and farms: 1. Schwan, the Swede; [3]   2. the Lutheran Church; [4]   3. the pastor's house; [5]   4. an Englishman; 5. Andres, the Swede; [6]   6. William Penn's youngest son; [7]

---

[1] So given in the copy of the manuscript in the Könneken manuscripts at Lübeck.

[2] William Penn, jr. (1680–1720); the elder brother was Springett Penn (1675–1696).   William's lot, after the cutting off of the northernmost part for the German Company of Frankfort, was on the northwest corner of Front and Cedar (now South) streets.

[3] Sven Svensson, or Swanson (d. 1696), a native of Sweden, husbandman, living south of the town at Wicaco (now about Front Street and Washington Avenue, Philadelphia, centring at the old Swedes' Church built in 1700) evidently is meant.   He was a son of Sven Gunnarsson, or Gonderson, who was a culti-vator of tobacco at Fort Christina, in 1644, and who with his three sons, Sven, Olave, and Andrew, all of Wicaco, held title to a large part of the site of Phila-delphia under surveys from the Duke of York in 1664 and 1681.   Penn effected a surrender of their claims by an exchange for land on the west side of the Schuylkill.

[4] The Lutheran Church (Gloria Dei) of the Swedes at Wicaco, built as a block-house in 1669, was made a place of worship in 1675.   Its present site is occupied by the quaint Old Swedes' Church, built of brick in 1700, the oldest house of worship in the present city.   The Episcopal service is now held there.

[5] Of the Swedish Church at Wicaco.

[6] Andrew Svensson, or Swanson, of Wicaco, brother of Sven above.

[7] Simply the lot without buildings, apparently; William Penn, jr., was then (1684) only three years of age.

7. the [Frankforters]; 8. Philip Fort;[1] 9. the Society and its trading-house;[2] 10. the Blue Anchor Inn;[3] 11. James Claypoole; 12., etc. There are other houses, to name which is needless here. Thus in front lies the Delaware; then comes a broad street,[4] upon which falls our first allotment, a hundred feet broad and four hundred long. At the end of this[5] comes a lane;[6] then our second allotment, of the same breadth and length; then comes another lane,[7] and finally our third allotment. Upon each lot two houses in front and two behind can suitably be built side by side, consequently upon the three lots twelve houses with their appurtenant buildings; and yet all these give upon the streets. Necessarily, however, if we do not wish to lose these lots we must within two years build three houses, that is, one house upon each lot. Upon the front lot I have, with our man-servant, built already a small house, half under the ground and half above, which indeed is only thirty feet long and fifteen feet broad, yet, when the Crefelders were lodging here with me, could harbor twenty persons. On the oiled-paper window over the door I wrote: *Parva domus sed amica bonis, procul este prophani*.[8] This William Penn lately read, and was pleased.[9] Also I have a cellar[10] seven feet

---

[1] Philip Ford never came over.

[2] The Free Society of Traders, the trading-house being on the west side of Front Street, below Dock Creek.

[3] The Blue Anchor Inn, the first hostelry in Philadelphia, at this time (1684) was in the middle of Front Street, the main thoroughfare of the little town, on the high bank of the Delaware, and was about 146 feet north of Dock Creek, now Dock Street. The inn was opened as early as 1682, its owner being Captain William Dare. He sold the property on January 18, 1683, to Colonel Edward Hill, of Shirley, on James River, Virginia. Colonel Hill in the same year, 1683, sold to Griffith Owen, of Philadelphia, who was the owner at the time of Pastorius's writing. In 1686, Jones sold to George Bartholomew, who soon moved the inn off the street to his lot in the rear, to the westward.

[4] Front Street, the main street.

[5] *I. e.*, of the first lot, where Pastorius's house was built on the west side of Front Street, north of the lot of William Penn, jr., at the northwest corner of Front and Cedar streets.

[6] Second Street.   [7] Third Street.

[8] "A little house, but a friend to the good; remain at a distance, ye profane." *Cf.* Vergil's *Aeneid*, VI. 258.

[9] *Cf.* the *Description*, chap. VIII., *ante*, p. 381.

[10] Probably the cave in the bank of Front Street described in his reminiscences in after years, as follows:

deep and twelve broad and twenty long, dug on the banks of
the Delaware, and am now occupied with building a stable.
All three lots are cleared of the trees, and I shall immediately
fence them and plant them with Indian corn. N. B. It is
especially difficult and expensive to fence all the land, yet on
account of the horses, cattle, and swine running at large we
cannot dispense with doing it. Also one cannot, the first
year, plant either rye or wheat in such new land, but only Indian
(or as you call it, Turkish) corn, which however does not taste
nor satisfy so well.

II. As to the three hundred acres in the city liberties, I
have made various applications to William Penn in respect to
them, and have especially urged that B. Fürly[1] had promised
them in the sale, etc. He however for a long time would not
agree to this, the reason being that not more had been reserved
for city liberties than that for which buyers of five thousand
had been found while he was yet in England; and among
these the [Frankforters] were not comprised. Finally a few
days ago, when I again delivered to him a memorial, he gave
me the pleasing answer that he out of particular regard for
you would allow me the said three hundred acres additional,
but would give no more to any man who had bought after the

"The caves of that time were only holes digged in the Ground, Covered with
Earth, a matter of 5. or 6. feet deep, 10. or 12. wide and about 20. long; whereof
neither the Sides nor the Floors have been plank'd. Herein we lived more
Contentedly than many nowadays in their painted and wainscotted Palaces, as I
without the least hyperbole may call them in Comparison of the aforesaid Sub-
terraneous Catatumbs or Dens. Vide Hebr. 11: 38. I myself purchased one of
the old Tho. Miller for 5£ then Currt. Silver Money of Pennsylvania in the midst
of the Front-street at Philada., whereas the Servants, I had along with me, could
have made a far better in less than two days, had they but known how to handle
the spade."—Learned, *Pastorius*, p. 212.

[1] Benjamin Furly (1636–1714), a leading shipping merchant of Rotterdam,
an English Quaker and the chief agent of William Penn on the Continent for the
sale of lands, the issuing of descriptive pamphlets, and the general promotion of
the colonization of Pennsylvania. Beginning his career as a merchant in his
native town, Colchester, England, by 1660 he had removed to Amsterdam, thence
to Rotterdam. He was a prolific writer in English, German, Dutch, and French,
and gathered a remarkable collection of manuscripts and rare books. As a
patron of learning, his home became the rendezvous of Leclerc, Limborch, Al-
gernon Sidney, and Locke. Quaker meetings were held at his house, Fox, Penn,
Keith, and other leaders of the Society resorting there. Although a Quaker, he
was buried in the central aisle of the Groote Kerk, the chief church of Rotterdam.

closing of the books, no matter who he might be. It is
accordingly my intention, as soon as the Indian corn here
is in the ground, to make a beginning upon these three
hundred acres (which will not be more than a half-hour distant from this town), in order that I may better keep the cows
and swine, may raise more produce, and thereby help those
who come after me.

III. Concerning the fifteen thousand acres, two chief difficulties arose, namely, that William Penn did not wish to give
them all together in one piece in order that so very large a
space in the land might not lie uncultivated and empty, nor
on the Delaware River, where indeed everything had already
been taken up by others. But after I had repeatedly represented to him both orally and in writing that it would be very
prejudicial to us and our German successors to be so completely
wedged in among the English, and likewise that B. Fürly had
communicated to the [Frankforters] his, William Penn's, letter
in which he had promised otherwise to our nation, etc., he
finally gave me a warrant, to have our land in one tract, provided that we within a year would settle thirty families upon
the fifteen thousand acres, namely, three townships, each of
ten households, among which might be reckoned the three
which are already here (but in case thirty families do not come
he will not be bound to give the land in one piece). I for my
small part could indeed wish that we might have a small
separate province, and so might the better protect ourselves
against all oppression. Now if one of you could be free to
come hither and bring that number of families your own best
interests would be incomparably furthered thereby, for he,
William Penn, only the day before yesterday told me that in
that case he would give you the preference over all the English
who though they had bought earlier had not yet arrived here,
and would give you certain privileges in our new Francken-
land (for so he called the tract of land destined for us). If,
however, it is too difficult for you to transport so many families in so short a time, it would in my opinion, which of course
is not binding, be well that the friends of [Frankforters] should
take from you a few thousand acres and, out of the abundance
with which they have been blessed, send certain households
hither, in order that the fifteen thousand acres may come to us

undivided and without English neighbors intervening; especially as he will give these lands not too far away from this town, namely, on the Scollkill above the falls, where he himself intends to build a house and to lay out a small manse for himself. The land near the river is quite hilly, and not ill-suited to the cultivation of the vine. Farther in, however, it is level and fertile. The worst of it is, however, that one cannot go in a boat over the falls and the ledges, except when it has rained heavily and even then not without danger. Now since I could not know what you might conclude to do in these circumstances, and yet it was very important, and since moreover these often-mentioned fifteen thousand acres would cost 28 pounds sterling to survey, namely, 5 shillings of the local money for every hundred acres, which money however I did not have in hand, I was obliged to let the matter stand until I had received your decision, in order not to step over the limits of a faithful agent. In order, however, that I might settle the three families who had arrived upon their six hundred acres I have, in conjunction with the Crefelders (who have bought eighteen thousand acres, and though all here present cannot obtain the whole in one piece) taken up six thousand acres for a township, of which they have three thousand and we three thousand. This town I laid out on October 24, and called it Germantown. It lies only two hours' walk from here, on fertile soil, and near pleasant springs, which I have mentioned above. This I was obliged to do because William Penn will not give any man his portion separately but all must dwell together in townships or towns, and this not without weighty reasons. Among these the chief is that in that way the children can be kept at school and much more conveniently brought up well. Neighbors also can better offer each other loving and helpful hands and with united mouths can in public assemblies praise and extol the goodness of God. N. B. You might accordingly assign only a hundred acres to the families that you bring over here in the future and yet obtain almost as large an estate.

As for my domestic establishment, I very much wished to arrange it in the good High German manner and Jacob Schuemacher and the old Swiss[1] are very serviceable to me toward

[1] George Wertmüller.

this purpose. But the Hollanders whom I have with me adapt themselves but ill to this, especially the maid,[1] who cannot get on well with the English one,[2] so that I, to preserve the peace, must send the latter away because the former with her two children[3] cannot so easily remove or attach herself to another master. I greatly desire to obtain as soon as possible a High German maid whom I can trust better than, I am sorry to say, I now can do. If you wish not to be deceived in your hopes, send only Germans, for the Hollanders, as troublesome experience teaches me, are not so pleasant, which in this new land is a highly necessary quality. I have no carpenter among my servants, so a few ought to be sent over hither for the building of houses. In the making of the contract with them it may serve for your information that their daily wages are now much diminished, and beyond their board they receive not more than [two][4] shillings a day, though most of them for this reason do not work and are preferring to leave the country. N. B. A fixed price is set for all hand-workers, also not more than fifty per cent. gain must be made on merchant wares, though indeed perhaps three or four years from now there will be little profit to be made on these, as the Society is sufficiently aware. For (1) every newcomer brings so much clothing and provisions with him that he for some years needs nothing. (2) There is very little money here, although the desire for it is in the case of many persons so much the greater. On November 16 occurred the annual fair in our Philadelphia, where however I hardly took in a few pounds sterling. (3) One can not yet obtain from this land any return-goods to send to England. William Penn, to be sure, intends to establish weaving and wine-making and for this reason on several opportunities sends us good vines on whose prospering one can count. Also [send] all sorts of field and garden seeds, especially of lentils, millet, etc. Also, N. B., some great iron cooking-pots and nests of kettles.[5] Also an iron stove, because the winter

---

[1] Marieke, wife of Isaac Dilbeck.   [2] Frances Simson.

[3] Abraham and Jacob Dilbeck.

[4] "The wages are one-half rix-dollar per diem, including their keep." Op den Graeff's letter, dated Germantown, February 12, 1684.

[5] "Let him, now, who has an earnest resolve to come over, and is ready and fixed in this purpose, make use of this information: that he take with him butter,

here is usually as cold as with you and the rough north winds much harsher. Also some coverlets or mattresses, because I did not bring more with me than I immediately needed yet have already got an additional manservant. Finally, if you would also send me some pieces of fustian and Osnabrück,[1] linen cloth, it can be sold to good advantage.

A tanner can undertake his work with great profit, since here and in the neighboring lands we can obtain hides enough and indeed two raw for one dressed. Also the very best for a pair of shoes. But a certain capital must be employed for this, but since these sums of money thus expended would in a short time bring a rich revenue, I leave the matter to your riper reflection. The two most necessary things are: (1) upon the lots in this town to build suitable houses, which are expensive to rent and from which twelve per cent. per annum can be obtained; (2) to establish a brick-kiln, for which William Penn has promised to give us an excellent place, for so long as we make no bricks our house-building is only of wood. Other artisans may well wait at home a few years yet.

To the four questions I give this succinct reply: (1) William Penn has laid a good foundation for a righteous government and from time to time he publishes useful laws. (2) He maintains neighborly friendship with all the adjoining governors and hopes that the still-continuing contest with Baldimor[2] may soon be settled and removed by royal sentence. (3) William Penn is much loved and praised by all people, insomuch that even the old vicious inhabitants have to acknowledge that they have never before seen so wise a ruler. Ah, what impressive and penetrating sighs this dear man sent forth the first day of the new year to the heavenly heights and the throne of our Immanuel, because true "Philadelphia" and brotherly love is not yet so abundantly to be found in this our Philadelphia as he for his part desired and for whose advancement he has so earnestly busied himself as a true father of the land. (4) The Indians, of whose nature a little something has been said in a previous passage, grow less nu-

---

cheese, sugar, wine, brandy, spice, olive-oil, brain-sausage (*Cerbalár-Würst*), millet, rice, rolled barley, all kinds of field and garden seeds, iron pots, kettles, flint-guns, to shoot game, etc." (In the abstract in the book.)

[1] Osnaburg, a coarse linen.   [2] Lord Baltimore.

merous here daily, retiring some hundred miles[1] farther into the country.

Now you might perhaps ask whether I with a pure and undisturbed conscience could advise one and another of you to come over to this place. I answer with good deliberation that I would be heartily glad of your dear presence; yet unless you (1) find in yourselves freedom of conscience to go, (2) can submit to the difficulties and dangers of the long journey, and (3) can resolve to go without most of the comforts to which you have been accustomed in Germany, such as stone houses, luxurious food and drink, for a year or two, then follow my advice and stay where you are for some time yet. But if the things I have mentioned do not come too hard for you, depart the sooner the better from the European Sodom, and remember Lot's wife, who indeed went forth with her feet but left her heart and inclinations there. Ah, dear friends, I could well wish that with this eagle's quill I could express the love I bear you and could convince you indeed that it is not a mere lip-love but one that desires more good for you than for myself. My heart is bound to yours by the bonds of love. Then let us now grow up together as trees which the right hand of God has planted by streams of water, that we may bring forth not only leaves but fruit in good season: fruits of repentance, fruits of peace, fruits of righteousness. For what profits such a useless tree, though the gardener spares it yet for some years, digs about it with all diligence and cultivates it, yet finally, no improvement following, cuts it down and casts it into the oven? Forgive me this comparison, dear friend; we here encounter such unfruitful trees, hew them down and use them for firewood. It is at least a good-hearted warning, that can do no harm. I commend you all to the divine influence, without which our fruitfulness is incomplete. May the Lord who has given the desire give also the fulfillment! Amen.

Herewith I send a specimen of the Indian money used here, of which six of the white and three of the black make an English farthing; and these Indians will not sell anything more for silver money but will be paid with their own money,[2] since for the most part they wish to quit this land and to withdraw some hundred miles farther into the woods. For they have

---

[1] English miles probably.   [2] Cf. *Description*, chap. IX., *ante*, p. 382.

a superstition, that as many Indians must die each year, as
the number of Europeans that newly arrive.

Thus much I have to inform you, in order to comply with
my bounden duty, as one who has the greatest anxiety to be
found faithful, whereunto as well William Penn and other
reasonable people as my own conscience, which I value more
than thousands, can give an irreproachable witness.   That it
falls quite hard upon me in this expensive and unprotected
land to care for so many men-servants and married couples,
you can easily judge.   But trust in our heavenly Father over-
comes all.   Give all other acquaintances hearty greetings from
me.

I remain ever your true and devoted servant,

N. N.[1]

Francis Daniel Pastorius takes Leave of his Father and Friends.

From Deal, June 7, 1683.
After examining to my satisfaction the European provinces
and countries, and the impending *motus belli*,[2] and after taking
apprehensively to heart the vicissitudes and troubles of my
native country arising therefrom, I have suffered myself to be
moved by the special direction of the Most High to journey
over to Pennsylvania, living in the hope that this my design
will work out to my own good and that of my dear brothers
and sisters, but most of all to the advancement of the glory
of God (which is my aim above all else), especially as the audacity and sin of the European world are accumulating more
and more from day to day, and therefore the just judgment of
God cannot be long withheld.

I had in all my acts taken this frivolity and wickedness
greatly to heart, and pondered upon the final outcome thereof
with profound meditation, namely, how life, worldly possessions, honor, and lust will all once be subjected to death and
decay.   But let the soul be once lost, and it is lost forever.
Semel periisse aeternum est.[3]

In order therefore to escape evil both here and hereafter,
I have entered so much the more willingly upon this journey

---

[1] End of the *Sichere Nachricht.*   [2] Movements of warfare.
[3] "To have perished once is to have perished forever."

and passage across the mighty ocean, under the holy guidance of God; and, together with nine others of my people, sailed from Deal on June 7, 1683,[1] in the company of various respectable families, with the hope that the Lord, Who up to this hour had so richly blessed me, and commanded His angels to keep watch over me, would so govern my incomings and outgoings that His most holy Name would thereby be praised on the further side of the sea, in unknown places.

I therefore commit my honored father and all my dear ones to the protection of the Almighty, and as soon as the Lord helps me over to Pennsylvania, I shall give a more detailed account of everything. Should it however be His holy will to call me to Himself while on the way, I am ready with all my heart, and therefore I take leave of my honored father as becomes a child, with reiterated dutiful thanks for all the love and fidelity shown me in such abundance. May God reward him for it in time and in eternity!

I remember that while on my travels I read an epitaph which ran as follows:

> I, who the lines on many a foreign grave have read
> And in this book writ down those records of the dead,
> Now know not where, how, when, I go from mortal sight,
> And so, vain world, I say, a thousand times good-night.

If therefore we see one another no more on this side of the grave, we shall meet in Heaven. But if we fulfil the will of God here upon earth, which I desire from the depths of my soul, I remain until death

My honored father's
Truly obedient son,
F. D. P.

A Letter from the Same to D. Schütz of Franckfurth-on-the-Mayn, May 30, 1685.

It almost seems as if the greater number could not fully carry out their good intentions (namely, to serve God and righteousness in tranquillity of spirit, here in Pennsylvania), but that some of them, as it were against their will, were en-

---

[1] He did not sail from Deal until the 10th.

tangled in various affairs of this world, with neglect of the one thing needful.

I, for my part, can not now do otherwise than give my attention partly to Philadelphia and partly to Germanopolis, which I, nevertheless, would gladly turn ever toward the heavenly Jerusalem, the future city of God, which is to be sought for with every effort by me and by all who love the Lord. But the duties of a loyal superintendent, which have been confided to me, must also be administered with diligence and fidelity. My hearty greeting to all friends in Franckfurth, Wesel, and Duisburg. And let not my most worthy and dear friend doubt that I shall remain, under the commendation of the Most High, in unaltered affection until I die, etc.

Doctor Joh. Jacob Schütz made thereupon these sad comments: Alas, that this so-called New World should soil itself with unrighteousness and transgression, even as our Old World is entirely covered therewith, and instead of cleansing itself as is necessary, becomes each day more involved therein. Nevertheless, the Lord knows His own, and this is surely a valued seal for all who hold His coming dear.

Letters from Pennsylvania, October 10, 1691.

Dearly beloved and honored father:

I can not allow the present opportunity to go by without briefly informing you of the prosperous condition of myself and my associates, as well as conveying to you my cordial love and respects, wishing from the bottom of my soul that all may go well with my honored father and those belonging to him, and that the Almighty, according to His holy will, may preserve and deliver them all from His judgment of destruction which, in these our days, He is bringing upon the impenitence of Europe, by means of the Turks and the French.[1] Here, in this country, we have listened with compassion to the barbarous proceedings of the French, the laying waste and burning of so many beautiful cities, churches, and imperial sepulchres, and thereby have been strengthened in our belief that we should trust, not to our bodily strength and to fortified castles, but

[1] Under Louis XIV.

entirely and solely to the protecting hand of God, for Whom it is as easy to defend us against all assaults of the enemy as it is impossible for mere bulwarks of stone to do so.

We know nothing indeed of the condition of affairs in Upper Germany at the present time, for it is long since any ships have come in,[1] nevertheless we hold fast to the belief that these calamities will hardly cease until a reformation of life shall result therefrom.

In the meantime may the Most High grant to my honored father a constantly blessed prosperity, until such time as our correspondence can be again continued. May it only be vouchsafed us to grow, in Christlike tranquillity as respects the inner man, in upright love, and to embrace one another in heartfelt affection, as being one in Christ, which neither the remoteness of places, nor the dangers of pirates, nor any other circumstances are able to prevent.

I inform you further that our governor, William Penn, has sent us High-Germans certain concessions from England, and appointed me to be the first mayor and justice of the peace in this town,[2] so that now we have our own council and laws, provided that they are in accordance with the laws of England.

And as I drew up the proper regulations and laws for this, and on June 2, 1691, began the first Council Records of Germanton, I placed at the opening thereof the following holy admonitions:

There is no power but of God. Romans, xiii. 1.

For power is given you of the Lord, and sovereignty from the Highest, who shall try your works and search out your counsels. Wisdom, 6.

And thou shalt take no gift. Exodus, xxiii. 8.

Ye shall not afflict any widow, or fatherless child. Exodus, xxii. 22.

Do justice to the afflicted and needy. Deliver the poor and needy. Psalm lxxxii. 3, 4.

Ye shall not respect persons in judgment; but ye shall hear the small as well as the great. Deut. i. 17.

Ye shall do no unrighteousness in judgment. Lev. xix. 15.

Doing nothing by partiality. I Tim. v. 21.

[1] Shipping being interrupted by King William's War.
[2] Germantown.

Take you wise men, and understanding, and known among your tribes, and I will make them rulers over you.   Deut. i. 13.

A froward heart shall depart from me: I will not know a wicked person.   Psalm ci. 4.

And as ye would that men should do to you, do ye also to them likewise.   Luke vi. 31.

The said Council thus instituted has likewise its own seal, which is, as the impression bears evidence, a trefoil.   On one of the leaves a grape-vine is represented, on another a flax-blossom, and on the third a weaver's spool, with the inscription: *Vinum, Linum et Textrinum*,[1] to signify that one may in this place maintain himself by cultivating the vine, by growing flax, or by manufactures, to the satisfaction of God and his honor.

In the meantime we live peaceably and contentedly, with no desire for transitory riches; provided we have sufficient food and clothing for this our pilgrimage, for the rest we turn our eyes ever toward the heavenly Jerusalem, our true father-land.

I acknowledge it as an entirely unnecessary impulse of his fatherly affection that my honored father should affirm, in his letters to me, that he would gladly be able to do more for me in this world, and now, that God has bestowed a child upon me, I can judge of this far better than ever before, and comprehend far more deeply the axiom: *Amorem descendere potius quam ascendere*.[2]   My respected father has given me more than I have ever deserved, or than I shall ever be able to repay.   So that often when thinking of the past I say in my heart: Ah, if only my dear father had saved those sums which he sent me in cash at the universities to provide for himself in his old age, etc.   But that which is done cannot be altered by wishing. May God on High most richly reward him with His heavenly blessings, in time and in eternity, for all the love, fidelity, and kindness he has shown me.   With this petition, I remain until death, etc.

Oct. 10, 1691.

[1] "The vine, the flax, and weaving."
[2] "That love rather descends than ascends."

[1692.] On June 7, 1692, there was such a terrible earthquake in the island of Jamaica that it destroyed the greater part of the capital city, Port Royal, and annihilated about twenty-five hundred people, aside from the natives who have been buried by the mountains and hills. Among others my good friend and former fellow traveller, Mardochai Loyd,[1] was swallowed up in a hollow mountain, yet even in these circumstances he was saved through the miraculous providence of God; for he crept out again by means of a hole below, bringing forth his own life, as if it were a booty.

And at the time of this terrible earthquake, this marvel also came to pass, that some women dressed *à la mode*, who were going that way wearing high head-dresses and topknots, so that they appeared to have double heads, were buried in the earth up to the waist, and these it was not possible to dig out in any way, or to remove from the place before they became stiff in death, and were obliged to play the rôle as it were of the devil's pillory-posts.

Further News from Germanton, June 1, 1693.

After a most filial greeting and the wish for all the blessings of well-being, both for soul and body, I cannot refrain from saying what unparalleled joy comes over me when I receive letters bringing news of the good health and prosperity of my honored father and of the dear ones belonging to him, and since I suppose that similarly some in your country desire now and then to know somewhat of our condition, and how it fares with me in this new and somewhat desolate western world, on this account I have thought that in the following lines, in accordance with the request of my honored father, I would speak somewhat at length concerning the public affairs of this region, as well as of the private concerns of my own family. And first concerning the general condition of things:

The most holy God has so graciously sheltered this province under the wings of His mercy, during the ten years of my residence here, that no unfriendly clamor, whether of trumpet or musketry, has broken in upon our daily toil and nightly rest.

---

[1] Mordecai Lloyd (1669–1694), son of Governor Thomas Lloyd, came over with the other members of his family in 1683, as a fellow-voyager with Pastorius.

Indeed, in all these years, we have not been obliged to pay a farthing for war or other taxes, until, about five weeks past, the new governor, Benjamin Fletcher,[1] arrived in Philadelphia, with the royal decree and authority to govern this province in the name of King William III., until the vindication of William Penn should be fought out by way of the law, in Old England. To him, as compensation for the expenses of the journey, we have granted the 240th penny. This governor confirmed our Germanton charter anew, by virtue of which we are enabled to hold our own courts and council-meetings, and appointed me Irenarcha, or justice of the peace in the county of Philadelphia, after which he set forth from this place, with his retinue, for New York, in which place he is likewise governor, as also commander-in-chief over all the English islands and colonies in America.

I hope, and wish from my heart, that our former ruler, William Penn, may soon clear himself of all unreasonable suspicion of a treasonably-conducted correspondence with King James, and that he will shortly return to us again, seeing that his personal presence could prevent many contentions and disputes, in political as well as in religious matters, and could bring to naught the evil designs of many quarrelsome persons.

For the difference of belief [2] which arose here a year ago is not yet calmed or adjusted, for each believes that he knows the nearest and most direct way to Heaven, and can show it to others, although truly there has been One only Who could say of Himself with truth: I am the Way, the Truth, and the Life. *Via rectissima* (according to Thomas à Kempis) *Veritas suprema, Vita Beata, Via inviolabilis, Veritas infallibilis, Vita interminabilis, Via in Exemplo, Veritas in promisso, Vita in praemio, etc.*[3] This narrow path of sorrows brings us finally to so high a place that we shall have the stars under our feet.

---

[1] Colonel Benjamin Fletcher, a professional English soldier who had served under King William III. in the Low Countries and in Ireland, was Governor of New York, 1692–1698, and the first and only royal governor of Pennsylvania, 1693–1694, during the time when Penn was temporarily deprived of the province.

[2] The George Keith schism.

[3] "I am the invariable and perfect way; the supreme and infallible truth; the blessed, the uncreated, and endless life. I am the way thou must go, the truth thou must believe, and the life thou must desire." Chap. xxxix of Payne's ed. (London, 1842).

Although I have been requested by one party to suppress or drive out the other, I preferred to put off the matter for the arrival and decision of the proper governor, William Penn, and in the meantime I exhorted both parties to gentleness and harmony in the following verses—both in German and in English.[1]

I

The error of my brother
Fills me with holy horror,
   Yet may I not abide
That he by word of mine
Be forced to give some sign
   That shall his thought deride;
For such enforced submission
Redounds to his perdition
   And sets all truth aside.

II

Those who with pen or sword
Would prove their Master's word
   Durst not upon me call
For aught save deeds of peace—
For this I strive, nor cease,
   Whatever may befall.
Both friend and foe alike
I wish to serve aright,
   And to turn harm from all.

III

May no remorse nor sorrow
Darken for us the morrow,
   May naught arrive save joy.
Yes, joy that is of Heaven,
Where we from morn to even
   Shall dwell without annoy.
For so the Lord hath taught us,
And to His fold hath brought us,
   Where all is peace and joy.[2]

[1] Pastorius gives only his German; the English version here given, in the metre of the original, is by Miss Kimball.
[2] I Cor. xi. 16.   (Note in original.)

They who would serve the Lord
By empty deed and word
　Look not within the heart;
But they who seek His will
In quiet to fulfil—
　Such choose the better part.

N. B. The English verses are omitted here [*i. e.*, in the original] since I am unfamiliar with the language.

I now come to the so-called savages. I can say little of these native dwellers in these parts which will be satisfactory to those whose aim is rather to gain outward and worldly information than to put into practical exercise the precepts and prohibitions of Christ. In part they [the savages] are not unfitly to be compared with the son in the Gospel story, who went to work in the vineyard without promises and protestations, and nevertheless in real industry far surpassed his brother who promised much. They live more contentedly and with less thought for the morrow than we Christians. They overreach no man in business. They also know nothing of the pride of life, and of the fashions in clothes to which we cling so closely. They neither curse nor swear, are temperate in their food and drink, and if one occasionally drinks too much it is usually the nominal Christians who are to be blamed, who for their accursed self-interest sell strong drink to the savages.

In my ten years of residence here I have never heard that they have attempted to do violence to anyone, far less murdered anyone, although they have not only had frequent opportunity to do so, but also to conceal themselves in the thick and extensive forest. Therefore, in view of the horrible wickedness which is practised in Europe, among the nominal Christians, and, in mature comparison therewith, the candid simplicity of these my present West-Indian countrymen, I am always reminded of the sermon delivered before you by Herr Johann Augustin Litzheimers, upon Christianity brought to shame by a consideration of Heathendom, wherein the preacher asserts, on page 45: The nominal Christians crucify the Son of God, and scornfully spit upon their Holy Creator when they value the money and goods of this world more highly than the Word of God, or the well-being of this perishing life above

God and immortal bliss; on the other hand the heathen Seneca professes: *Semper magis nolo,*[1] *quod Deo [Deus] vult, quam quod ego, adjungar et adhaerebo illi velut Minister et assecla. Cum illo appeto, cum illo desidero. Nihil recuso omnium quæ ipsi videbuntur. Tu Deus quocunque me voles, ducito, quam vestem lubet, circumdato, si Magistratum me gerere vis, vel privatum in pauperie esse, ecce non tantum assentior, sed etiam apud alios te defendam et tuebor.*[2] Listen and ponder and blush over these things from the heathen.

But our nominal Christians are diametrically opposed to these heathen virtues, and seek their pleasure in eating, drinking, gambling, and debauchery, in usury, fraud, envy, cursing, and quarrelling. Oh, thou heathen Christendom! and yet thou dost nevertheless imagine to be even in such wise cleansed from thy sins. To assume this hypothetically, forsooth, is, unless improvement follow, a manifest error.

In conclusion, I must further add to the recommendation of my unsavage savages, that they are much averse to war and the shedding of human blood, and would far rather be at peace with all men; while, in contrast, nearly the whole of Christendom is under arms, and they rend and destroy one another in offensive and defensive warfare, with barbaric cruelty far exceeding that of the most horrid monsters. Concerning which the German poet makes complaint:

> Lion, wolf, and tiger still
> Are loth to work their comrades ill;
> How then can a Christian bear
> Fellowmen to rend and tear,—
> While their Lord enjoins these three,
> Love, and peace, and unity.[3]

---

[1] Evidently a misprint for *volo*.

[2] "I ever prefer that which God wishes to my own desires. I shall be joined to him and cling to him as a follower and a disciple. I shall be united with him in my strivings and longings. I refuse nothing, of what shall seem best to him. Thou, God, shalt lead me whithersoever thou desirest, thou shalt throw around me whatsoever garment thou wilt. If thou wishest that I should hold a magistracy, or that I should live in poverty as a private citizen, behold, not only do I assent thereto, but even in the presence of others I will defend thee, and maintain thy cause."

[3] John xiii. 34. (Note in original.)

I now inform you briefly of the particulars relating to myself. On November 26, 1688, I was married, here at Germanton, to the Jungfrau Anna Klostermannin, daughter of Henricus Klostermann, Doctor of Medicine, and a native of the Duchy of Cleves.[1] On March 30, 1690, my wife gave birth to a little son, whose name is Johann Samuel, and on April 1, 1692, to a second son, to whom the name Heinrich was given at the holy baptism.

May the Lord our God in mercy turn His holy countenance upon these my children, and all others, and bestow his Holy Spirit upon them, and may this lead them in the way of truth, and preserve them from error and false teaching; may He permit them to grow up in His service and obedience, may He comfort and strengthen them in trouble and temptation, that they together with us may fight a good fight, hold fast to the faith until the end, and thus win the crown of life and glory.

That furthermore God in His compassion has even up to this time preserved my honored father in His mighty protecting hand, from utter ruin in these dangerous events (especially now that the French Hannibal [2] has laid waste the Rothenburg frontier with fire and sword before your eyes), as also [for the fact] that my honored father has been selected by the regular election in the Council and by the gracious confirmation thereof on the part of His Majesty the Roman Emperor, to be chief justice of the city of Windsheim, for these things I congratulate him, since he has now obtained greater opportunity and power to render poor Windsheim beneficial service, according to the admonition of Saint Bernhard: *Vae tibi si praees, et non prodes.*[3] On this account, may we unceasingly bear in mind that the Most High Chief-Justice of the living and the

---

[1] Pastorius was married, November 6, 1688, to Ennecke Klostermanns (1658–1723), a native of Mülheim-on-the-Ruhr, daughter of Jan (not Henricus) Klostermanns. (Learned, *Pastorius*, p. 191.). She had a brother Heinrich Klostermanns.

[2] Evidently Louis XIV.'s commander, General Feuquières, the leader of the French forces in their terrible ravaging campaign in Southern Germany in 1689. Their operations extended to Rothenburg-on-the-Tauber, which, while surrounded by seventeen burning villages, made a valiant defense against the enemy. Rothenburg is only about twelve miles southwest of Windsheim, where Pastorious's father resided.

[3] "Alas for thee, if thou art high in place yet conferrest no benefits."

dead has not confided to us such judicial authority for our own
private advantage, but that it may be used for the good of all,
and that, in the great day of the last judgment He will demand
much from those to whom much was given. According to
the following words: *Potentes potenter tormenta patientur.*[1]
And this I write because of the compassionate desire which I
bear for the salvation of all our souls, considering that we as
followers of Christ are not obliged merely to pray for one
another, but also to encourage one another to holiness on all
occasions. Yes, even to true holiness! without which no one
can come to God. And I remain, under the true dispensation,
in the blessed hand of God, during my life's course, etc.

*Letter of Francis Daniel Pastorius from Pennsylvania to Tobias
Schumbergius,[2] his former Teacher.*

De Mundi Vanitate.

Vale, Mundi gemebundi colorata Gloria.
Tua bona, tua dona sperno transitoria.
Quae externe, hodierne splendent pulchra facie,
Cras vanescunt et liquescunt, velut Sal in Glacie.
Quid sunt Reges, quorum leges terror sunt mortali-
    bus?
Multi locis atque focis latent infernalibus.
Ubi vani, crine cani Maximi Pontifices?
Quos honorant et adorant Cardinales Supplices?
Quid periti, eruditi sunt Doctores Artium?
Quid sunt Harum vel illarum studiosi partium?
Ubi truces Belli Duces, Capita militiae,
Quos accendit et defendit rabies saevitiae?
Tot et tanti, quanti quanti, umbra sunt et vanitas,
Omne Horum nam Decorum brevis est inanitas:
Qui vixerunt, abierunt, restant sola Nomina,
Tanquam stata atque rata nostrae sortis Omina.
Fuit Cato, fuit Plato, Cyrus, Croesus, Socrates,
Periander, Alexander, Xerxes et Hippocrates,

---

[1] "The mighty ones will suffer terrible torments."

[2] Tobias Schumberg, a Hungarian, rector of the Latin school or gymnasium
at Windsheim. Pastorius came under his instruction as a small boy on the removal of the Pastorius family from Sommerhausen to Windsheim.

Maximinus, Constantinus, Gyges, Anaxagoras,
Epicurus, Palinurus, Demonax, Pythagoras,
Caesar fortis, causa mortis, tot altarum partium.
Ciceronem et Nasonem nil iuvabat Artium.
Sed Hos cunctos iam defunctos tempore praeterito
Non est e re recensere.   Hinc concludo merito:
Qui nunc degunt atque regunt Orbem huius seculi,
Mox sequentur et labentur velut Schema speculi.
Et dum mersi universi sunt in mortis gremium,
Vel Infernum, vel aeternum sunt capturi praemium
Hincce dei JESU mei invoco Clementiam,
Ut Is sursum cordis cursum ducat ad Essentiam
Trinitatis, quae Beatis summam dat Laetitiam.

[*Translation in the same metre, by the general editor of the series.*]

World of grieving, your deceiving glories bid I now adieu;
All your cheating joys, and fleeting, turn me with contempt
from you.
Though you render bright with splendor the appearance of to-
day,
Day revolves, your charm dissolves, and sinks, like salt in ice,
away.
Rulers regal, striking legal terrors into human hearts,
Now are lying low and sighing, smitten through with hellish
darts.
Old and hoary Popes, whose glory cardinals proclaim, and bow
Lowly bending without ending—lords of Rome, where are ye
now?
Where the learning of discerning Doctors full of scholars'
pride?
Where the hearty friend of party, blindly fighting for his side?
Where the famous chiefs, who shame us with the glory of their
deeds,
Whom the savage zeal to ravage ever on to warfare leads?
All the mighty are but flighty, spectral forms, and shadows
vain;
All the glory transitory, honors brief, and joys inane.
All are banished, all have vanished, naught but names remain
behind,
Illustrations, adumbrations, of the fate of human kind.
Gone is Cato, gone is Plato, Cyrus, Croesus, Socrates,

Periander, Alexander, Xerxes, and Hippocrates,
Maximinus, Constantinus, Gyges, Anaxagoras,
Epicurus, Palinurus, Demonax, Pythagoras,
Caesar glorious, the victorious, laying many chieftains low;
Nor could glowing speech or flowing Ovid save or Cicero.
Needless is it to revisit with our censure those who've gone
Through those portals. Hear, ye mortals, the conclusion I
    have drawn.
They that now are throned in power, they shall also pass away,
As there passes from our glasses imaged form or figure gay.
When Death's grievous hand shall leave us all beneath the
    churchyard stone,
Pains infernal, life eternal, we shall reap as we have sown.
Hence, adoring and imploring, Jesu's mercy loud I call,
That his leading and his pleading bring me to that heavenly hall
Of the trinal God, where final joy awaits the blessed all.

Letters from Pennsylvania, of March 30, 1694.

In my last, of June 1, 1693, I have given detailed information respecting the condition of public affairs in this country,
as well as the private concerns of my family. Since that time,
namely on February 8, 1694, I received your former letter as
well as that of my estimable brother, Augustine Adam,[1] so
that I am now briefly answering both of them. I especially
rejoice on account of the endurable circumstances of my honored father, and I rejoice in the Lord as the sole and eternal
source of tranquil contentment, the more because, at the present times of danger, many millions of our fellow-men are without, and in want of, such well-being, both of soul and body.
May God, the only good and powerful guardian of His Israel,
permit you to dwell yet longer, safe and tranquil, under the
shadow of his wings. May He give you that which is profitable for your eternal souls' good, both on this and the other
side of the grave.

I and my dear ones have, as yet, the same health and happiness, as I reported in my former letter, in a quiet and peaceful
mode of life, and although it is true that I am burdened with
the inspection of matters relating to the administration of
justice, in Germanton as well as in Philadelphia, nevertheless

---

[1] A half-brother, then aged twelve.

such external magistrate's business does not in the least hinder that inward consciousness of the mild and humble personal life in Jesus Christ, so that I can truly say, in the midst of each occupation: *revertere anima mea in requiem tuam.*[1]

An intimate friend wrote me from Franckfurt lately how the cold Lutheran preachers had been assailed and tossed about by the Pietists, and the Papist believers in good works by the Quietists, all which I regard as undoubted precursors of the speedy advent and appearance (God grant it!) of His dearly-beloved and only-begotten Son. Well then, and eternally well, for all those who have oil in their lamps, and are prepared to meet this blessed Bridegroom, and to go in with Him to the wedding-feast. I have, however, heard with astonishment, that both sides, Molinas[2] and his followers as well as the Pietists, who lay emphasis upon an effective faith, are almost violently persecuted as witnesses of the Heavenly truth, as if men desired to oppose the guidance of God and to rule over the consciences of men, which is the prerogative that God has reserved for Himself alone. These will one day see Whom they have assaulted. *Verbum Domini manet in aeternum.*[3] The Word of God and the Truth can not be suppressed.

Now to answer the questions of my dear brother Augustine Adam, what is the nature of the royal household among the savages here? It must be said that their royal residences are so ill-conditioned that I can not easily describe them. There is only one chamber, or room, in a hut made of trees and roofed over with bark, having neither chimney, stairs, nor place of retirement. These very kings go forth with the others to the hunt, shoot the wild animals, and support themselves by the work of their own hands. They have neither servants nor lacqueys, neither housemaids nor court-ladies, and what use has one for a master of horse who keeps no horse, but always goes on foot? In like manner, no court-steward is needed, where there is no one to be cared for besides one's self and one's

---

[1] "Return, my soul, to thy rest."

[2] Miguel de Molinos (1630?-1696), a Spanish mystic, author of an ascetical treatise, *The Spiritual Guide*, and a leader among Roman Catholics of the Quietistic movement. In 1685 he was cited before the Holy Office (Inquisition), and later his writings were condemned by it.

[3] "The Word of the Lord endureth forever."

wife and children.   They live in a poor way, and entirely in
harmony with nature, *quae paucis contenta est*.[1]   Their trade
with us Christians consists in this: they bring to market bear,
moose, deer, and other skins, likewise beaver, marten, otter,
and other furs, and also turkeys, game, and fish, and exchange
them for powder, lead, blankets, and brandy, the last of which,
and indeed all other strong drink, we are forbidden by our
laws to sell to them, because they misuse it, and it leads to
their hurt.

They use no ovens for baking, but cook their bread in the
ashes.   A great many of these savages have died, even since
I came here, so that there are hardly more than a fourth part
of the number now existing that were to be seen when I came
to the country, ten years ago.

On February 8 of this year, 1694, I also received a few lines
from my godchild Franz Jacob Mercklein[2] for whom I, in my
eighteenth year, stood as godfather, although I myself was then
unbaptized by the Holy Spirit, and had not yet put on Christ.
I beg you to greet him kindly for my sake, and earnestly to
admonish him that he shall keep with true zeal the bond into
which I entered with God on his behalf—renouncing in his name
the world, the flesh, and the devil—and that he shall not break
the same.   For such vows go far, far before all other duties,
and the true baptism is not the laying aside of the impurities
of the flesh, but it is the compact of a good conscience with
God, etc.

Is his honored father, Johann Caspar, and the brothers of
the same, Johann Jacob and Abraham, still living? and likewise my cousin Lucas Klein and Doctor Grimm, etc.?   I pray
you to give them my hearty love and most friendly greeting,
since I desire with Nazianzen that: *Ne quis illorum pereat*.[3]
And even though I do not count on seeing them in this mortal
dwelling or with the eyes of the body, on the other hand, it is
my sincere desire, and earnest supplication to God in Heaven,
that He may let His light shine upon all of us, give us new
birth through His Holy Spirit, and guide us toward all Truth,
and thus maintain us in His service and obedience, strengthen

---

[1] "Which is content with little."

[2] Born 1670, son of Johann Caspar Mercklein, probably of Windsheim.

[3] "That no one of them may perish."

us in trouble and temptation, and comfort us in those afflic-
tions which are our due, so that we may grow in true faith,
and in active ardent love, and in Christ-like good works, and
finally, when we shall have finished our appointed course, that
we may attain to that glorious kingdom of His dearly-beloved
Son Jesus Christ, and that there we may thank Him with
eternal Alleluias and evermore sing Holy, Holy, Holy.

With this, as well as a filial greeting from myself, my wife,
and two little sons, I remain, so long as I live, etc.

Germanton, March 30, 1694.

A Letter from Germanton of the last of April, 1695. P. P.[1]

Several months ago various Germans arrived here, and
again, a week since, an Hungarian named Saroschy[2] (who had
before that been staying for some time with Herr Schumberg),
but neither the one nor the other brought with him any letters
whatever from Windsheim, so that, in connection with meditation upon my own mortality, I also sometimes think, Has
perhaps my honored father finished his pilgrimage, and thus
reached the time of rest from all sorrow and misery? For to
those who die in the Lord, Death is no more than the portal
of paradise, *per quam itur ad Astra.*[3]

Our heaviest trouble and burden should pass lightly away
for this reason, that so long as the long-suffering God lengthens
our days in this earthly tabernacle, we are and live in Christ,
or rather Christ, by His holy and righteous Spirit, lives in us.
Therefore we should be well-assured that we should not die
without Him, nor be eternally destroyed.

Ah, may the Lord grant that we all, according to the measure of grace and understanding bestowed on us, may win the
imperishable crown of eternal glory by fulfilling the will of
God in patience and submission, and remaining steadfast unto
the end.

[1] "Praemissis praemittendis," *i. e.*, "titles to be supplied."

[2] Isaac Ferdinand Saroschi, a Hungarian, who had been a preceptor under
his compatriot, Tobias Schumberg, rector of the Latin School at Windsheim,
came to Germantown and after wandering about for two years returned to Europe
by way of Maryland.

[3] "Through which one reaches the stars."

As regards the conditions prevailing in this country, I can and must extol the benevolence and providence of God, for we live in peace and tranquillity, abundantly provided for, and supplied with all the necessaries of life.

King William III. of England has not only freely atoned to our governor, William Penn, for all accusations of a treasonable correspondence with King James, and once more re-instated him in the government of this province, but he has also elevated him to the rank of a prince,[1] so that he can now sign himself: William Penn, by the grace of God, and the favor of the King and Queen, Prince in Pennsylvania. We hope now for his speedy arrival. I and my two little sons are in as good health as could be wished. We greet our honored father and mother, our brothers and sisters, and all our acquaintances, most kindly, hoping with our whole hearts, that it is well with you all, in body and soul, wherewith, closing in haste, may we all be commended to the protecting hand of God, and I remain, etc.

A Missive from Germanton, of June 21, 1695.

May it please my honored father to receive the present lines as an echo of my former letter, in case that should not have been received in due course, concerning which the well-known uncertainty of the sea makes me doubtful; and also for that reason I dare not hope to receive many more letters from that worthy hand, to which I, however, cling in childlike fashion. Here, in this country, we are living in comfortable circumstances, in good health and in wished-for peace— two priceless gifts of the Supreme Being. We are on very good terms with our savage neighbors, whom I, in deed and in truth, find *melius moratos et hospitaliores in quoscunque advenas,*[2] than are the Christians with you, who know how to recount the acts of Christ historically, but by their ungodly lives disavow the power of the faith and the Imitation of Christ; and there is, accordingly, a noteworthy difference between sane Christians and vain Christians. The former are real, the latter

---

[1] By a royal order of August 20, 1694, Penn's government of Pennsylvania was restored to him, but he was, of course, not raised to the rank of prince as Pastorius states.

[2] "Better mannered and more hospitable towards all strangers."

nominal. The former are Christians in deeds, the latter are Christians in profession only. I often pray to God that He, in His infinite goodness and mercy, will pour out His Holy Spirit over these innocent savages, and bestow upon them the Light of the saving faith, in order to augment with them His eternal Heavenly kingdom.

And now may this true Shepherd of men, Who neither slumbers nor sleeps, henceforth graciously protect my honored father and all the dear friends and acquaintances belonging to your place from all destruction as well in regard to transitory and visible things, as also especially in regard to the eternal loss of the soul, and some time bring us together in the kingdom of His Son, there to praise and to glorify him with eternal songs of joy. Amen.

A Letter from Germanton, of March 1, 1697. P. P.

I inform you briefly that we, here in this province, live in wished-for peace, through the undeserved mercy of God, and find ourselves in good health, which we justly recognize and extol as a wonderful mercy and gift of God. I can also scarcely express with what joy I have learned from my honored father's last letter, your good condition (since the dear God has kept you unharmed in this ruinous flame of war); at the same time I had patiently resigned myself therein, neither to behold that honored person in this world, nor any letters by his hand, so often beneficently opened to me. May God fill the same again from time to time with His heavenly blessing, and reward most abundantly, in this life and in the life to come, all that has been done for me from my birth. May He protect my honored father together with all his family, in the present dangerous times from all harm and injury, according to the decree of His holy will.

I have previously, on December 1, 1688, written very much in detail to my good friend Herr Georg Leonhard Model,[1] rector of the schools in Windsheim, to which letter I refer for the sake of brevity. I had also suggested to him as respects the education of youth that each boy, according to his ability,

---

[1] Or Modelius, a native of Windsheim, with whom as a youth Pastorius was matriculated at the University of Altdorf, in 1668.

should learn an easy trade besides the knowledge of letters, in order to carry on the same in foreign provinces in case of necessity, and to assist himself therewith outside of the country, and to get his livelihood throughout the world, without dissipating his patrimony to the distress of his parents. For although in your country this is regarded as unimportant and contemptible, it is nevertheless far more conformable to the decree of God and the teaching of the apostles than all the scholastic vagaries. I myself would give forthwith some hundreds of reichsthalers if I had turned the precious time, which I employed in the acquisition of the sparrow-like physic, metaphysic and other unnecessary sophistic arguments and quibbles, to engineering, or the art of printing, which would be more useful to me now, and prove more profitable and more entertaining to me and to my fellow-Christians than such physic, metaphysic, and all the proofs and syllogisms of Aristotle, by means of which no savage or infidel can be brought to God, still less can a piece of bread be earned. Now it is over and done with, and I close. My two little sons greet their dearest grandfather in childlike simplicity, in their little letters which herewith are enclosed, and wish very much to see him.

The members of the German Company or Society in this country, still living, are: Abraham Behagel at Franckfurt-am-Mayn, Doctor Gerhard in Mastrich, the syndic of Bremen, Doctor Johann Petersen of near Magdeburg, Balthasar Jabert at Lübeck. My good friend in particular is, however, Pieter Hendricks living on the Keysers Graft [1] at Amsterdam, a man of sincere loyalty, who will not fail to care most assiduously for all my honored father's letters which come to him, and, further, to deliver them to me.

No more at this time, except that commending us all to God's almighty protection, shelter, and mercy, I remain, etc.

Germanopolis, March 1, 1697.

[1] Keisersgracht.

*Here follow two enclosures from the two young sons of Pastorius
to their honored grandfather, from the town of Germanopolis
in Pennsylvania.*

March 1, 1697.

Dearly-beloved Grandfather:

We, the two brothers undersigned, greet you most affectionately, and pray God that he will protect you from all misfortune, and that he will, on the other hand, bless you with all
the rich gifts of Heaven, and will preserve you to a long life,
according to His holy will. We also hope, that if not both, at
least one of us will have an opportunity to see our dear grandfather in this world; at last, however, in Heaven, to rejoice
with one another, and to remain near one another forever,
and always to praise and glorify God, with all the angels and
the elect, as Him to whose highest Majesty alone all praise,
all glory, all honor and love belongs, and is due.

Your dutiful grandchildren

JOHANN SAMUEL PASTORIUS. HENRICUS PASTORIUS.[1]

A Letter from Germanopolis of May 13, 1697.

I had already resigned myself (after I had received no
letters from my honored father for so long a time) to receive
nothing more from his dear hand, when by chance I received
his last in the street as I was going into our church-meeting,
and I could not read it through, without happy tears of affection. Above all, I was very glad to learn that my much loved
brother, Augustine Adam Pastorius, is inclined to come to
me, not doubting that we shall live together harmoniously in
brotherly love, and remain in unbroken, enduring, and un-
feigned heartfelt affection. But, however pleased I might be
to have him with me, nevertheless I herewith most kindly
entreat and beg of him, that he will not leave home without
the knowledge and consent of his honored parents, because in
such circumstances he would be extremely unwelcome to me.
It is almost repugnant to me to write long letters because the
French pirates plunder so many ships, and also those letters

---

[1] Aged seven and five respectively.

which I sent over during the past year by Richard Penn[1] (William Penn's cousin) got into their clutches as he informed me upon his return here.

The printer[2] who was here in Pennsylvania has removed to New York. If I had a little more skill in such work, I should myself establish a press here, for the use to the country. If, now, my dear brother Augustine Adam is much inclined to come here, with the consent of his honored father, he might learn this trade in a fourth part of a year, and it would not be difficult to teach the same later to others here.

This province still increases from day to day, in men and in human depravity, since religious quarrels are beginning with violence, and (in the absence of a Consistory) there is no end of the disputes.

That Hungarian of the name of Isaac Ferdinand Saroschi, who lived formerly with Herr Schumberg as tutor, and has wandered about in these regions for two years now, has betaken himself to Maryland with the intention to sail across to Europe once more. In case now he should speak slightingly of these colonies, his remarks thereupon should not be given entire credit, because he has not had a fixed abode in any place, nor lived with any Society, but has always been given to vagrancy which has become a fixed habit in him, and, after the manner of the Hungarians, he gathers only alms and gifts and has carried these away with him, but he did not wish to play the rôle of an apostolic preacher without a fixed recompense and salary, which is mistrust of the providence of God.

My two little sons thank their most dearly-loved and honored grandfather, with childish simplicity, for remembering them so affectionately. They much desire to see him and to be with him. They, together with myself, also commend him to the faithful protecting hand of God.

Germanton, May 13, 1697.

---

[1] Not identified; 10 Mo. (December) 24, 1696, Richard Penn witnessed a paper, Richard Lundy to Phineas Pemberton, two Bucks County men, of near Pennsbury (Pemberton MSS., in Etting Papers, I. 65, Hist. Soc. Pa.)

[2] William Bradford.

The Contents of a Letter of Francis Daniel Pastorius to Herr George Leonhard Model, Rector of the School of Windsheim.

Praemissis praemittendis.[1]

In order that my friend may be able to find this region on the maps, he must search thereon even to the 40° of latitude for New Amsterdam (now named New Eboracum).[2] One hundred English miles to the east [3] he will find the River de la Ware, thereon the capital of this province, Philadelphia, and two hours' distance from there Germanton which began in the year 1683 with thirteen families, and within five years saw some fifty houses erected, in the hope that from year to year more families and German workmen would come over here to us. We have, to be sure, at present, no other city-walls save such as Romulus made yonder with a plough, nevertheless there is no mischief-making Remus with us, and we do not need to apprehend any sudden hostile attack on the part of our neighbors, those native inhabitants, or savages, as they are quite humane and respectful to all strange guests coming to them. But how, and in what manner, and at what time these savages came across the Atlantic ocean hither? Of those things no well-grounded information can be given (because no single written document of this place is to be met with). They are people of the forest who instruct and teach one another by means of tradition, from the aged to the young. They are generally tall of stature, with powerful bodies, broad shoulders, and wide heads, hollow and austere foreheads, and black hair. They besmear the face with bear's grease and with various colors; they have no beards, are frank and ingenuous in disposition, and use few words, which, however, are emphatic. They can neither write nor read, but are nevertheless intelligent, cunning, serious, and fearless, hold fast to their preconceived opinion; they bargain closely, but pay for things with accuracy; they can long endure hunger, they love drunkenness, they do not work willingly, but all support themselves by hunting and fishing, and not one of them is accustomed to ride a horse. In summer they do not cover themselves at all, except what nature wishes covered, but in

[1] "The titles to be supplied."　　　[2] New York.　　　[3] Southwest.

winter they wrap themselves up in a coarse square cloth, and cover themselves in their huts with bear and deer skins; instead of shoes they use thin deer skin, and they have no hats.

The women are frivolous, backbiting, and arrogant. They fasten their hair together in a knot. They have full breasts and black necks, upon which, as also upon their ears and arms, they hang their coral money as decoration. While the men pursue the game, the women sow beans and plant Turkish [Indian] corn. They love their children passionately. They bind them on shingles as soon as they are born. When they cry the mothers move them rapidly to and fro, and so quiet them, and although they are still small they plunge them into the warm rivers that they may so much the sooner grow strong. In their infancy they are made to catch fish with hooks; afterwards, when they are grown stronger, they train themselves in the hunt. The young women that are of a marriageable age cover the face and thereby testify to their disposition to take a husband. They punish all their crimes by fines, even murder, and when one kills a woman he must give double the penalty, because the women bring forth children, which the men are not able to do. They believe that there is one God, and that the souls of men are immortal, and that God holds back the Devil from doing injury to human beings; they say that God dwells in the most glorious southern land, to which they also shall attain at some future time, after death. Their religion consists in two kinds of worship, namely in song and sacrifices. They slaughter the first fruits of their hunting as a sacrifice with such vigor that the whole body sweats.

When they sing, they dance around in a circle; while two, in the centre, lead the dance and raise a dirge, the entire chorus carries on a pitiful lamentation, weeps in addition, at one time gnashing the teeth, at another snapping with the fingers, at another stamping with the feet, and they execute this laughable spectacle quite ardently and seriously. When they become sick they eat of no animal that is not a female. When they bury their dead, they throw something costly into the grave with the dead by which they wish it to be understood that their affectionate good will toward the dead shall not fail.

They manifest their mourning (which continues for an entire year) by their blackened faces. They build their dwelling-huts of trees and bushes, and there is no one among them so inexperienced in the art of building that he cannot build such a hut for himself and his family, in three or four hours. Their language may be judged from the following dialogue: *Eitha-nithap*, Be greeted, good friend. *A eitha*, Be you greeted also. *Tankomi*, Whence come you hither? *Past ni unda qui*, Not far from here. *Gecho luensi*, What is his name? *Ans. Franciscus*. *O letto*, It is good. *Noha matappi*, Let him take a seat here by us. *Gecho ki Wengkinum*, What would he like? *Husko lallaculla*, I am very hungry. *Langund agboon*, Give me bread. *Lamess*, Fish. *Acothita*, Fruit. *Hittuck nipa*, There is a tree full. *Chingo metschi*, When do you journey again from this place? *Alappo*, to-morrow. *Nacha kuin*, day after to-morrow; and so on. Besides these, *ana* is mother; *squaa*, wife; *hexis*, an old woman; *Menitto*, the devil; *murs*, a cow; *kuschkusch*, a pig; *wicco*, the house; *hockihockon*, an estate; *pocksuckan*, the knife. Whatsoever professor digs out of this the origin and root of these Indian words, him will I praise. In the meantime the paper is becoming too small for me, the quills blunt, the ink will not longer flow, there is no more oil in the lamp, it is already late, my eyes are full of sleep. Fare you well. I close.

Sent from Philadelphia, on May 30, 1698.

I received in proper condition, on April 25, 1698, my honored father's latest, of August 15, and I was greatly rejoiced by the sight of his dear handwriting. But to answer his questions submitted, I would wish that my pen could reach down to the uttermost depth of my soul, for so should I do the same with more satisfaction than is the case now. Nevertheless I do not doubt that my honored father will supply by his keen apprehension that which is not perfectly expressed on this paper:

1.

Now as to the first question, concerning the ordering of the civil government.

William Penn is and remains lord of the proprietary and sanctioned prince over Pennsylvania, and although he has not been here with us for some years, nevertheless he has done us more service in England through his presence there, than probably might have been the case if he had remained here all the time.   The estimable man has very many enemies on account of his religion, who however rather overdo matters, since they, for their part, are not surely informed, much less can they see into another's heart.   We expect his arrival in this country without fail, this summer, or next autumn, if no ill-health or other hindrance occurs.

So far as relates to the form of the civil government here at Philadelphia, as the capital city, I state briefly that each year certain persons[1] are elected from the whole people, who make the necessary laws and ordinances for that year according to the condition of the time and the people, and thereby prevent encroaching vices and moreover, throughout the whole year, in all circumstances, they help to care for the common weal, by and with the governor of the province.   At the same time the aforesaid proprietary, William Penn, ordains a certain twelve, from among those thus elected, to be justices, who decide all disputes occurring according to the laws thus made, after the facts have been investigated by twelve neighbors.   And all this is done in open court, so that everyone, great and small, may enter and listen.

In my German city, Germanton, there is an entirely different condition of things.   For, by virtue of the franchise obtained from William Penn, this town has its own court, its own burgomaster and council, together with the necessary officials, and well-regulated town laws, council regulations, and a town seal.

The inhabitants of this city are for the most part tradespeople, such as cloth, fustian, and linen weavers, tailors, shoemakers, locksmiths, carpenters, who however at the same time

---

[1] The assembly.

are also occupied with the cultivation of the soil and the raising
of cattle.

This region would be sufficient to maintain twice as many
inhabitants as are now actually there.

This town lies two hours' distance from Philadelphia, and
includes not only six thousand acres (*morgen*) by the survey,
but twelve thousand *morgen* of land have also been assigned to
us by William Penn for the establishing of some villages.   As
to the taxation and tribute of the subjects, in this country, it
is treated as it is with the English nation, where neither the
king himself nor his envoys, bailiffs, nor governors may lay
any kind of burden or tax upon the subjects, unless those subjects themselves have first voluntarily resolved and consented
to give a specified amount, and, according to their fundamental
laws, no tax may remain in force for longer than a single year.

2. *To come to my honored father's second question.*

What form of government have the so-called savages and
half-naked people?   Whether they become citizens and inter-
marry with the Christians?   Again, whether their children also
associate with the Christian children and they play with one
another, etc.?

It may be stated in reply, that, so far as I have yet gone
about among them, I have found them reasonable people and
capable of understanding good teaching and manners, who
give evidence of an inward devotion to God, and in fact show
themselves much more desirous of a knowledge of God than
are many with you who teach Christianity by words from the
pulpit, but belie the same through their ungodly lives, and
therefore, in yonder great Day of Judgment, will be put to
shame by these heathen.

We Christians in Germanton and Philadelphia have no
longer the opportunity to associate with them, in view of the
fact that their savage kings have accepted a sum of money
from William Penn, and, together with their people, have
withdrawn very far away from us, into the wild forest, where,
after their hereditary custom, they support themselves by the
chase, shooting birds and game, and also by catching fish,

and dwell only in huts made of bushes and trees drawn together. They carry on no cattle-breeding whatever, and cultivate no field or garden; accordingly they bring very little else
to the Christians to market than the pelts, the skins of animals, and the birds which they have shot, and fishes, nor do
they associate much with the Christians; and certainly no
mutual marriage-contract between us and them has yet taken
place. They exchange their elk and deer-skins, beaver, marten, and turkeys, ordinarily, for powder, lead, blankets, and
brandy, together with other sweet drinks.

In the business of our German Company, however, we now
use in trade Spanish and English coins, as also the Dutch
thalers; with this difference only, that that which is worth
four shillings on the other side of the sea, passes for five here.

3. Concerning the third question: How our divine worship is regulated and constituted in this place?

The answer is that, as experience testifies that by the co-
ercion of conscience nothing else than hypocrites and word-
Christians are made, of whom almost the entire world is now
full, we have therefore found it desirable to grant freedom of
conscience, so that each serves God according to his best understanding, and may believe whatever he is able to believe.

It is certain, once for all, that there is only one single undoubted Truth. Sects however are very numerous, and each
sectarian presumes to know the nearest and most direct way
to Heaven, and to be able to point it out to others, though
nevertheless there is surely no more than a single One Who on
the basis of truth has said: I am the Way, the Truth and the
Life.

Although now each sect, with us, is accustomed to hold
undisturbed its assembly on the seventh day of the week, it
is nevertheless proved by experience and trial, that the most
part serve a God unknown to them out of mere habit, concerning Whom they have heard other people speak. But they
will neither feel nor listen to God Himself, nor taste His goodness; they are without spiritual apprehension, and their
fleshly senses do not comprehend what the Spirit of God is,

the verbal or historical narrative to which they listen does not reach the heart, and therefore does not edify them; so soon as the church-meeting is over, all is again forgotten; if the intention of their hearts is set upon usury, finance, deceit, and luxury before the service, it is still set thereon. Not once is amendment of life kept in mind, or how one shall put on Christ, or how Christ the Lord shall impress his image on them.

Such societies and sects one should reasonably avoid, and on the other hand seek his companions among those holy ones in the light of truth, who love the great goodness and truth of God with all their heart, trust His holy providence and highly extol His power, whose souls are in God and God is in them, of whose souls the Holy Ghost bears witness that they are the children of God.

We should follow yonder One our Master, Who has given us those words which His Heavenly Father gave to Him.

His true disciples abide by this His Word, and He gives His Spirit to these disciples, which the world neither perceives nor is able to receive, which also could not be purchased by Simon Magus for any money, but he who desires to have the same must turn from the old path of sin, renounce the world, cast himself into the father-heart of God, and resign himself entirely to the dear Lord, and beseech Him humbly, that He may draw him to Himself, for the Lord Christ says: No man can come to me except the Father which hath sent me draw him. John vi., and Eph. i.[1] It all depends on the mercy of God, and not at all on any man's wish or deed.

I must acknowledge that our age and the religious disputes are beyond my comprehension and understanding, and that with all the individual churches there is wanting the life of the inner man, and the life at one at Christ. Molinas and his sect of the Quietists have much alarmed the Papal See, in that he pointed out the way to Heaven through the inward faith of the heart and love to God and our neighbor, and not through works, pilgrimages, and penance. And because similar teachings will be also urged at the present time here and there among the Evangelical churches, by the Pietists, therefore, many of them, both clergy and laymen, men devoted to a luxurious life and to ease, are much alarmed, saying that man can not

[1] John vi. 44; Ephesians i. 5, 11.

be without sin, that there must be bad and good men together, that it may certainly be permitted to have a little Jesuitical drinking-bout in good fraternal spirit.

I for my part hold this as my entire secure hope, that I look up to God alone, and with my whole heart cling to and trust Him, under Whose protection alone is safety, and without Him there is neither safety nor Truth nor faith.   He alone can illumine the hearts of men, He can destroy the living, and bring the dead to life again, and knows how to protect His own in the midst of the fiery furnace.

But they that are joined unto the Lord are one Spirit with him.   I Cor. vi. 17.   They may become partakers of the divine nature.   II Pet. i.   And hereby know we that we dwell in him and he in us, because he hath given us of his Spirit. [I] John iv. 13.   We behold as in a mirror the glory of the Lord. II Cor. iii. 18.

And Luther, in vol. VI., Altenb., fol. 625, says clearly: "Thou shalt therefore so hold by the faith that thou shalt become by the same one with Christ, that out of thee and Him shall be, as it were, one person, Who will never permit them to separate or part from one another."   And in the *Kirchen-Postill,* fol. 243.   "We should become filled with the Spirit of God, so that, as respects the inner man, we may be entirely consecrated and sanctified."

The holy name of this great God should be at all times held in high esteem by us all, in the new as in the old world, and kept holy above all else.   And it is well with him, yes forever well with all those who desire the speedy coming of Jesus, and have oil in their lamps, and are ready to go in with the blessed Bridegroom to His eternal wedding-feast.

4. *Concerning the fourth question: How our German Company and Brotherhood is at present constituted.*

It should be stated that this same company was started by some pious and God-fearing persons, not so much for the sake of worldly gain, but rather to have a Pella or place of refuge for themselves and other upright people of their country, when the just God should pour out His cup of wrath over sinful Europe.

With this intention they arranged to purchase from the proprietor, through me, about thirty thousand acres of land in this country, of which the third part is now cultivated, but two-thirds still lie waste.

The principal members are, by name: Doctor Jacob Schütz, Jacobus von de Walle, Doctor Weilich, Daniel Behagel, Johann Lebrunn, Doctor Gerhard von Maastrich, the Syndic of Bremen, Doctor Johann Willhelm Peters of near Magdeburg, Balthasar Jabert of Lübeck, and Joannes Kembler, a preacher at the same place. Of these partners some were to have come over here to me and helped to bring the undertaking to the desired result, but up to this time that has not happened, because they fear the solitude and tediousness, to all of which I, thank God! am now well accustomed, and shall so remain accustomed until my happy end.

However, that the merciful God has so graciously preserved my honored father together with his dear ones in this recent devastation of the French war, gives me occasion to extol His everlasting goodness and fervently to beseech Him to protect you still further, with gentle fatherly care, from all chances of misfortune, but especially that He will bring us ever more and more into His holy fear and obedience, so that we may feel abhorrence to offend Him, and, on the contrary, may strive to fulfil His holy will with happy hearts.

In the meantime, my honored father's calm resolve to live his own life and to serve God, has much pleased and rejoiced me. A blessed foretaste of those things whereof we are to expect the fullness in eternity after laying aside this earthly tabernacle!

O blessed leading of the Holy Ghost! for what else should it be, or what could it be called, save the holy grace of God, that has also at last made my honored father (after he has become gray in the service of many offices at Windsheimb) so white in soul and temper that he has recognised the overwhelming wickedness of mankind, and on that account has gone out from Babel.[1] May the Heavenly Father of all Light preserve this gift of the Holy Spirit in my honored father's heart until his departure from this life and entering into eternity.

[1] Evidently refers to the father's retirement from Windsheim to Nuremberg.

5. *Concerning the fifth question: Whether William Penn, the proprietor of this country, is easy of access, and if one might address some lines of compliment to him.*

It may be stated, that this worthy man is a good Christian, and consequently entirely averse to the idle compliments of the world. But he who wishes to exchange sensible and truthful words with him, either by mouth or by letter, will find him not only easy of access, but also prompt in reply, since he is, from his heart, sweet-natured, humble, and eager to serve all men.

Furthermore, my two sons greet my honored father affectionately, and daily pray for his temporal and eternal well-being, wishing ardently either to see him once in person, or at least to obtain some information respecting the course of his life and the occupations conducted by him.

Finally, that my honored father has had troublesome dreams concerning me, and at the same time has regarded it as a bad omen that my little tree, planted in his garden before my departure, has withered, is truly not without [meaning], for I, my wife and youngest son have gone through severe illness, yet, praise be to God, are fully restored again. But such things are a reminder of our mortality. All must have an end, and therefore this letter also, in closing which I greet my honored father a thousand times, and kiss him (through the air) with the heart of a child, perhaps for the last time, and most trustingly commend you with us, and us with you, to the beneficent protecting and guiding hand of God; and I remain

My honored father's

Truly dutiful son,

Philadelphia   F. D. P.
30 May 1698.

Upon receiving all the above copious information I, Melchior Adam Pastorius, desired to have intelligence from a third person how it was faring with my son and his family in such a far away country. For this reason I caused the letter placed after this to be sent out from the city of Windsheim, to the proprietor, William Penn, on June 20, 1698.

Salutem ab ipso fonte Salutis Jesu
Christo quam plurimam.

Vir Praelustris Humanissime et in Jesu Dilecte.

Audaciam meam in scribendo facilè condonabis cum intellexeris ex paternâ id fieri solicitudine et affectione erga filium meum Franciscum Danielem Pastorium in Pensylvaniâ tuâ commorantem abs quo jam longo tempore nil literarum accepi, ideo naturalis et Paternus affectus me impulit, ut de statu ac vitæ genere ipsius pauca sciscitarer.

Speraveram ego quidem me in senectute mea in ipso baculum et solamen habiturum, sed spe mea frustratus sum, dum in Provinciam tam longè à me dissitam ipse se contulit.

Vive in Jesu felicissime et per ministrum quendam de tuo famulitio respondere desiderio et petitioni meæ dignare. Qui ipse toto corde exopto esse

Tuae Humanissimae Dominationis
servus ad omnia Mandata
paratissimus

Windshemii 20. Jun. 1698.   M. A. P.

In translation[1]:

Abundant salvation to you from the fountain of all salvation, Jesus Christ.

Most Illustrious and Beloved in Jesus:

You will readily pardon my boldness in writing when you know that it arises from my paternal anxiety and affection for my son, Francis Daniel Pastorius, who is living in Pennsylvania, from whom I have received no letter for a long time, and therefore my natural and fatherly affection has impelled me to make some inquiries in regard to his condition and method of life.

I had hoped, indeed, to find in him a staff and consolation in my old age, but I have been disappointed in my hope because he has betaken himself into a province situated so far from me.

[1] The original gives a free translation into German; we have instead rendered the Latin into English.

May you live most happily in Jesus, and deign to reply to my longing and petition through some servant of your household.

With my whole heart I desire to be
Your most humane Lordship's servant,
very ready to execute all your commands,

M. A. P.

Windsheim,
20 June, 1698.

Thereafter came by post to Neustatt-on-the-Aysch, on April 25, the following answer, in Latin:

Observande mi in Jesu Christo Amice.

Ex intimo amoris affectu te saluto praesentemque tibi et futuram exopto felicitatem, quæ constat in fidâ obedientiâ in Lucem et Cognitionem illam quam tibi per Christum Jesum impertiit Deus.

Nuper adhuc in vivis fuit filius tuus, et jam nunc Philadelphiæ agit. Irenarcha hoc anno est, aut nuperrimè fuit, aliàs Vir sobrius, probus, prudens et pius audit, spectatæ inter omnes, inculpatæque famæ, Familias pater est, quot vero filiorum, ignoro. Amoris tui pignus, cum literis valetudinis tuæ nunciis pergratum illi accideret.

Brevi Provinciam istam juvante Deo visurus sum, interea temporis quid velis et quid de eo expetas vel ad ipsum scribas vel in Literis ad me dandis exprimas.

Cum Votis itaque ut Deus unâ cum salutis suæ demonstratione dignetur seniles tuos annos sicuti olim Simeoni prolongare, valere te jubeo

sincerus tibi ex animo amicus,
Bristolii die 20. Mensis 2.
vulgo Februarii 1699.   WILLIAM PENN.

Inscriptio.
A Monsieur Monsieur Melchior Adam
Pastorius.
President, à Windsheim in Franconia.

In translation:

Respected friend in Jesus Christ:

With a deep feeling of love I salute you and I desire for your present and future that happiness which consists in faithful obedience to that light and knowledge which God has imparted to you through Jesus Christ.

Your son was recently among the living and is even now in Philadelphia. This year he is justice of the peace, or was so very lately. Furthermore, he is called a man sober, upright, wise, and pious, of a reputation approved on all hands and unimpeached. He is the father of a family, but how many children he has I do not know. An assurance of your love and a letter announcing your good health would be very pleasing to him.

With the help of God I shall, in a short time, visit that province. In the meantime, either you may write to him whatever you wish or what questions you desire to ask of him, or you may state these in letters to be entrusted to me.

And so, with prayers that God together with the proof of his grace, may deem it fit to prolong your aged years, as of old in the case of Simeon, I bid you farewell.

Your very sincere friend

WILLIAM PENN.

At Bristol, on the 20th day of the 2d month, commonly called February, 1699.

Addressed:

To Monsieur Monsieur Melchior Adam Pastorius, President. At Windsheim in Franconia.

Still further Information from Pennsylvania. March 4, 1699.
P. P.

I live here with my two little sons in the country, still in good health. I am bringing them up in the fear and love of God. They are always pleased when they hear anything concerning their honored grandfather, and when his letters arrive here they long to see him, and compel me to tell them frequently something of the journeys he has made, and of the

course of the life he has led, which is however not especially
known to me as yet in all respects.   So they are writing herewith to their honored grandfather himself, and would like
very much to know the origin of his family.

For the rest, this country still increases daily in men and in
human wickedness, nevertheless I hope things here will never
be conducted in a way so unbecoming men, as in those universities of Europe, in which a man must learn for the most
part things which are to be utterly forgotten.[1]   Many professors
waste their time on useless questions and clever trifling tricks,
and while they detain the minds of the learners on empty
questions they prevent them from aspiring to more solid matters.   They strive to investigate what Jupiter and Vulcan
may be, but not what Christ is.   They also attempt to throw
light upon the most sacred Word of God by means of the syllogisms of Aristotle, as if indeed that Holy Spirit (Who is the
only true Author and Dictator of the Scripture) could be
amended or explained by the accursed heathen mind of Aristotle wailing in the lower world.

Others pass the precious time with utterly useless questions and trickeries, as, Whether that sepulchral inscription at
Monte Fiascone is true: *Propter Verbum est est Dominus meus
mortuus est.*[2]   Others seek among the Greek declensions for
the ablative case, but wherefore they desire the same they
themselves know not.

Yea, the students now even begin to drink one another
(in actual fact one out of ten) to death, and to hand over the
miserable one to Satan in his kingdom of hell, which indeed is
much to be deplored, and it were to be wished from God that
the eyes of the understanding of those gentlemen, professors
as well as students, should be opened, that they might recognize how vain it is to boast of the Light of the Gospel, and yet
remain amidst such abominable works of darkness.

On these grounds also I grieve for my dear brother John
Samuel,[3] that when he has learned piety and the fear of God at
home from his dear parents and his house-tutor, he should lose
them again at the universities; and that he should learn, with

[1] From here to the end of the paragraph the original is in Latin.
[2] "On account of the word 'est est' my master is dead."
[3] A half-brother, born in 1675.

the utmost danger to his soul, so many things that are to be forgotten, and I would far rather counsel him with brotherly kindness that he should learn an agreeable and easy trade by which he might serve God and his fellow-Christian; the which, although it is considered contemptible and insignificant among you, is nevertheless much more in accordance with the divine command and the teaching of the Apostles than all the scholastic trickeries; since for the most part the most highly versed are the most highly perverted, and *scientia mundana inflat.*[1] Such high and haughty spirits are desirous to cut a great figure afterwards and for this they require large amounts of money, which they endeavor to obtain *per fas et nefas*[2] to the detriment of their neighbors, that their wives and children may be always able to loiter about, *à la mode.*

In contrast to this, humble people wise in divine things say with Antonius: *Non data non cupio,*[3] and agree with Palingenius, *contentum vivere parvo,*[4] with whom St. Paul agrees in his Epistle to the Hebrews, xiii. 5.

I now close for this time. I have written this letter in the confident hope that it will find you all together in prosperous circumstances, but should the French take it on the way from here to you, I am likewise contented with that if they only suffer themselves to be satisfied with such small plunder, and do not otherwise injure you. But should they, by the divine fore-ordering, do this also, then pray for them, that God may convert them, and give you a tranquil heart under all circumstances. To Whose all-powerful protecting hand I commend you all together, and I remain, etc.

Letters from the two younger Pastorii, from Germanton,
March 4. 1699.

Dearly-loved Grandfather:
Our father tells us that to repay thine outpouring love and affection for us is as impossible as to swim against the stream, which neither one of us can do. For this reason we thank thee heartily, and so far as relates to thy pictures sent over here, none of which we had ever seen before, there appeared among

---

[1] "Worldly knowledge puffeth up."   [2] "By right or wrong."
[3] "I do not desire that which is not given."   [4] "To live content with little."

them an unknown bird whose tail is larger than he is himself; he represents, so we are taught, proud people, from which sin may God defend us.

Further on, a boy in a red coat is falling down from the globe. Whether this was slippery, or whether the poor child did not know what to hold on by, subsequent experience shall teach us when we have become somewhat older. Thy rhymes written on the reverse side greatly please our parents, and they wish that we shall never forget them, especially the end of the poem:

> May we love Jesus Christ aright
> And be His service our delight.

We very often desire to be with thee. Oh, that thou wert here and didst dwell in our house in Germanton, which has a beautiful orchard, and at present stands empty because we are living in Philadelphia, and must go to school for eight hours every day, excepting the last day of the week, when we may stay at home in the afternoon. Because we do not dare to cherish the hope that we shall see thee, our dear and honored grand-father, here with us, we earnestly request thee to give us some information regarding thine origin and dear parents so that if any one of us should one day go from here to Germany, we could ask after our relatives. Wilt thou also greet our dear cousins most kindly on our behalf, and suggest to them to write letters to us frequently, which will also be very welcome to us, after our father's death, and we will not fail, with the help of other pious people, to continue the correspondence.

In the meantime we greet you all once more most affectionately, wishing from the bottom of our hearts that it may be well with you all, in time and in eternity, and we remain to the end of our lives, under the faithful guardianship of God, dearly-loved grandfather, thy dutiful grandsons,

JOHANN SAMUEL and
HENRICUS PASTORIUS.[1]

---

[1] Then aged respectively nine and seven. The remainder of the book, an autobiography of Melchior Adam Pastorius, written in response to this request of his grandsons, is omitted from the present translation as having no direct relation to American history.

LETTER OF JOHN JONES, 1725

INTRODUCTION

THE number of persons of Welsh descent in the province of Pennsylvania was much less than the number of the Germans. Yet they were a large body; the early Welsh settlers were of a high grade; they furnished many leaders to the province, in politics and in all three of the learned professions; and they for the most part settled as a compact body in one large area, commonly known as the Welsh Tract. Therefore, they made upon the life of the province so large a mark that they deserve to be represented in such a volume as the present.

The narrative which follows, great as its interest is, was not written by or concerning a member of the chief contingent of Welsh settlers. Thomas John Evan seems to have been the first Welsh colonist in Penn's province, arriving in April, 1682. But the mass of the first Welsh settlers arrived in August of that year. They were Quakers from Merionethshire who had felt the hand of persecution. They had bought from Penn in England five thousand acres of unsurveyed land, and had been promised by him the reservation of a larger tract, which they meant to keep exclusively for Welsh settlers. As the royal charter permitted Penn to erect manors, they perhaps expected to have a manorial jurisdiction. At all events, they had for a time some special privileges of local self-government, and the tract of forty thousand acres which they ultimately secured was often called the Welsh Barony. After their arrival in the province they found some difficulty in obtaining a survey laying out their promised amount of land in one tract, but finally received grants substantially covering six townships. Their tract lay on the west side of the Schuylkill

River, north of Philadelphia.   It is represented by the present
Welsh names of Merion, Radnor, Haverford, Bryn Mawr, and
Uwchlan, and the vigor and industry of the Cymry began early
to give it the garden quality it has to-day.

The writer of the following letter alludes, at the middle of
his text, to this main body of Welsh colonists, but the story
he has to tell is that of an earlier and isolated Welsh settler,
his father, Thomas Sion (John) Evan.   The son, after the
Welsh manner of giving patronymic names, was called John
Jones (*i. e.*, John son of John, or, in Welsh, John ap John).
The letter, which internal evidence shows to have been written
in 1725, was first printed in Welsh in July, 1806, in a Welsh
magazine published in London called *Y Greal* (The Historical
Magazine), no. V., pp. 210–214.   In this print nothing is said
of the source of the text, but a footnote says, "The editors
would be glad to receive information about the family of the
writer of the above letter, from any of his descendants, for
publication in the following number."

The letter was printed again at Bala, Wales, in January,
1831, in the Welsh magazine *Y Gwyliedydd* (The Sentinel),
VIII. 15–17.   This text differs somewhat from the earlier
print, not in anything essential, chiefly in certain orthographic
peculiarities which are more likely those of the original letter
than are the forms used in *Y Greal*.   The correspondent who
sent it to *Y Gwyliedydd* (his signature is simply "Gower," and
he writes from "Bryn yr Hydd"), had apparently not seen
the earlier print.   He writes, in Welsh, "I got the following
letter in a manuscript of the works of the late reverend bard,
Rowland Hugh of Graienyn, near Bala.   I have heard that it
was printed in the year 1806, in the publication called *Y Greal*,
. . . but since that excellent and entertaining book is so very
unfamiliar in the land that not one in a thousand knows anything about it I have not hesitated to send the letter for repub-
lication in *Y Gwyliedydd*."

In April, 1831, an English translation of the letter was printed in London in the *Cambrian Quarterly Magazine*, III. 141–144. From this source it was reprinted, but with omissions, in the *Pennsylvania Magazine of History*, XIII. 227–231, and in Mr. Thomas Allen Glenn's *Merion in the Welsh Tract* (Norristown, 1896, pp. 41–44). In the following translation, the passages omitted in these versions have been restored, and incorrect dates not found in the original but supplied by inference have been eliminated. In the process of revision of the English translation, the general editor of the series has been greatly aided by Dr. F. N. Robinson, professor of Celtic at Harvard University, and by Mr. Jasper M. Lawford of Baltimore. The foot-notes are by the editor of the volume, Mr. A. C. Myers, to whom the determination of the correct date of the letter is also due.

J. F. J.

LETTER OF JOHN JONES, 1725

My Kinsman, Hugh Jones:

I received a letter from you, dated May 8 last [1725];[1] and I was glad to find that one of my relatives, in the old land of which I have heard so much, was pleased to recollect me. I have heard my father speak much about old Wales; but I was born in this woody region, this new world.

I remember him frequently mentioning such places as Llanycil, Llanuwchllyn, Llanfor, Llangwm, Bala, Llangower, Llyn Tegid, Arenig Fawr, Fron Dderw, Brynllysg, Phenbryn, Cyffdy, Glanllafar, Fron Goch, Llaethgwm, Hafodfadog, Cwm Tir y Mynach, Cwm Glan Lleidiog, Trawsfynydd, Tai Hirion yn Mignaint, and many others.[2] It is probably uninteresting to you to hear these names of places; but it affords me great delight even to think of them, although I do not know what kind of places they are; and indeed I long much to see them, having heard my father and mother so often speak in the most affectionate manner of the kind-hearted and innocent old people who lived in them, most of whom are now gone to their long home. Frequently, during long winter evenings, would they in merry mood prolong their conversation about their native land till midnight; and even after they had retired to rest, they would sometimes fondly recall to each other's recollection some man, or hill, house, or rock. Really I can scarcely express in words how delighted this harmless old couple were to talk of their old habitations, their fathers and mothers, brothers and sisters, having been now twenty-four years[3] in

[1] This date determined by reckoning from the internal evidence. 1705 as supplied in the Welsh text in the magazine *Y Gwyliedydd* is erroneous.

[2] All these places are in North Wales; most of them are in Merionethshire, near the town of Bala, or in adjacent Denbighshire. Nearly all are easily identified. "Llanfor" is Llanvawr. Arenig Fawr is a mountain west of Bala. "Brynllysg" is Bryneglwys.

[3] The son apparently was recalling the reminiscences of his parents of about the year 1706, near the close of the father's life, or twenty-four years after 1682, the year of the father's arrival in Pennsylvania.

a distant and foreign land, without even the hope of seeing them more. I fear this narrative will be irksome to you; but I cannot forbear when I think of these innocent artless old people.

And now, my kinsman, I will give you an account of the life and fortunes of my dear father, from the time when he left Wales to the day of his death. Three weeks to the time when he first heard tell of Pennsylvania, at St. Peter's Fair in Bala he took leave of his neighbors and relatives, who were taking account of his departure for London.[1] He was waiting three months[2] for a ship; after boarding the first ship he set out [3] from England by [or upon] the name of William Penn.[4] He had a very tempestuous passage for several weeks; and when in sight of the river [Delaware], owing to adverse winds and a boisterous sea, the sails were torn, and the rudder injured. By this disaster they were greatly disheartened, and were obliged to go back to Barbadoes, where they continued three weeks, expending much money in refitting their ship. Being now ready for a second attempt, they easily accomplished their voyage, and arrived safely in the river [Delaware] on the 16th of April, being thirty weeks from the time they left London. During this long voyage he learned to speak and read English tolerably well.

[1] This sentence, which is translated literally, may be taken in either of two ways, but counting backward from the date of arrival in America—assuming that date as well as the length of the voyage to be correctly stated—the following would seem to be the acceptable interpretation: June 8, 1681, he first heard of Pennsylvania. Three weeks later in Bala at St. Peter's Fair, which occurred June 29, he took leave of his neighbors and relatives, who had gathered there to take account of his departure for London.

[2] Nearly three months, or possibly a week less than three months, to agree with the other dates given, and to allow several days, after June 29, for the journey from Bala, in Wales, to London.

[3] September 18, 1681, the day he left London, counting thirty weeks to April 16, 1682, the time of his arrival in Delaware River.

[4] That *William Penn* was the name of this ship is open to question. The meaning is obscure in the Welsh text, which is here literally translated. No vessel of that name, it may be stated, after some years' diligent search of printed and manuscript sources, in the compiling a list of merchant ships sailing to the Delaware in that period, has been found. The intention may be to state, as Professor Robinson suggests, that a company sailed under Penn's orders or patronage.

They now came up the river a hundred and twenty miles,[1] to the place where Philadelphia is at present situated. At that time there was, as the Welsh say, *na thŷ nac ymogor* (neither house nor shelter), but the wild woods; nor any one to welcome them to land. A poor outlook, this, for persons who had been so long at sea, many of whom had spent their little all. This was not the place for remaining stationary. My father therefore went alone where chance led him, to endeavor to obtain the means of subsistence. He longed very much at this time for milk. During his wanderings he met with a drunken old man, who understood neither Welsh nor English, and who, noticing the stranger, invited him to his dwelling, where he was received by the old man's wife and several sons in the most hospitable manner. They were Swedes. Here he made his home, till he had a habitation of his own.

As you shall hear, during this summer (1682) our governor, William Penn, Esquire, arrived here, together with several from England, having bought lands here. They now began to divide the country into allotments, and to plan the city of Philadelphia, (which was to be more than two miles in length), laying it out in streets and squares, etc., with portions of land assigned to several of the houses. He also bought the freehold of the soil from the Indians, a savage race of men, who have lived here from time immemorial, as far as I am able to understand. They can give no account of themselves, not knowing when or whence they came here; an irrational set, I should imagine; but they have some kind of reason, too, and extraordinary natural endowments in their peculiar way; they are very observant of their customs, and more unblamable, in many respects, than we are. They had neither towns nor villages, but lived in booths or tents.

In the autumn of this year several from Wales arrived here: Edward ab Rhys, Edward Jones of Bala, William ab Edward, and many others.[2] By this time there was a kind of neigh-

---

[1] It is only about ninety miles from the mouth of Delaware Bay to Philadelphia.

[2] This was the company of Dr. Edward Jones, of Bala, Edward ap Rhys, or Rees, of Bryn Lloyd, William ap Edward, of Ucheldri, and others—in all forty— who came over from Wales in this same year, 1682, sailing from Liverpool in the ship *Lyon*, John Compton, master, and arriving in the Schuylkill River, August

borhood here, although as neighbors they could little benefit
each other.   They were sometimes employed in making huts
beneath some cliff, or under the hollow banks of rivulets, thus
sheltering themselves where their fancy dictated.[1]   There were
neither cows nor horses to be had at any price.   "If we have
bread, we will drink water, and be content," they said; yet
no one was in want, and all were much attached to each other;
indeed much more so, perhaps, than many who have every
outward comfort this world can afford.

During this eventful period, our governor began to build
mansion-houses at different intervals, to the distance of fifty
miles[2] from the city, although the country appeared a complete wilderness.

The governor was a clever intelligent man, possessing great
penetration, affable in discourse, and a pleasant orator; a
man of rank, no doubt, but he did not succeed according to
his merit; the words of the bard Edward Morys[3] might be
applied to him:

> The old person did not keep a fragment of his sense;
> He fell away to the pursuit of wealth.

At this time my father, Thomas Sion Evan, was living with
the Swedes, as I mentioned before, and intending daily to return to Wales; but as time advanced, the country improved.
In the course of three years several were beginning to obtain
a pretty good livelihood, and my father determined to remain
with them.   There was by this time no land to be bought
within twelve miles of the city; and my father, having pur-

13. They settled on the west side of the Schuylkill River, in Lower Merion.   Dr.
Edward Jones's interesting contemporary narrative of the voyage and settlement
of the party is printed in the *Pennsylvania Magazine*, IV. 314–317 (1880).

[1] Many of Penn's first settlers made their temporary homes in caves or dug-
outs in the bank or bluff of the Delaware, in the town of Philadelphia, and in
other places on the Schuylkill and without the town.

[2] Penn's country-seat, Pennsbury, up the Delaware River in Bucks County,
was only about twenty-seven miles from Philadelphia.

[3] Edward Morris, Welsh poet, of Perthi Llwydion, near Cerryg y Drudion,
Denbighshire, Wales, was one of the best known writers of carols and ballads
during the second half of the seventeenth century in Wales.   He died in Essex,
England, in 1689, while travelling, no doubt in the pursuit of his occupation as
drover.

chased a small tract of land,[1] married the widow of Thomas Llwyd [2] of Penmaen.

> You have heard tell in Dyffryn Clwyd
> Of Thomas Lloyd of Penmaen.

He now went to live near the woods. It was a very rare but pleasing thing to hear a neighbor's cock crow. My father had now only one small horse; and his wife was much afflicted with the tertian ague. We might suppose that many things would be revolved in the mind of a man in such a situation as this; but I never heard him complain of the difficulties under which he labored. Everything was agreeable to these innocent people; although in want of some present necessaries, yet they were peaceable and friendly to each other. In process of time, however, the little which he had prospered, so that he became possessed of horses, cows, and everything else that was necessary for him, or even that he wished; indeed he never coveted much. During the latter years of his life, he kept twelve good milch cows. He had eight children, but I was the eldest. Having lived in this manner twenty-four years, he now became helpless and infirm, and very subject to difficulty of breathing at the close of his day's labor. He was a muscular man, very careful and attentive to his worldly occupations. About the end of July [1707], eighteen years to last July, he became sick, and much enfeebled by a severe fever; but asthma was his chief complaint. Having been thus five weeks indisposed, he departed this life,[3] leaving a small farm each for my brother and myself, a corresponding portion for my sister, and a fair dower for my mother. My sister married

---

[1] His farm of 300 acres was in the southern part of Radnor Township, in Chester, now Delaware County, about midway between present Bryn Mawr and Newtown Square. Ithan Creek flows through the eastern part, and Darby Creek through the western part. The Radnor Hunt Club is located on the tract.

[2] Thomas John Evan was married in 1686 to Lowery Jones, of Merion, widow of Thomas Lloyd. Thomas Lloyd, of "Penmaen," a township in the parish of Llanvawr, Merionethshire, Wales, was a bard of note before he became a Quaker. Some of his verses on the subject of his convincement were printed in the Welsh magazine Y Gwyliedydd, for March, 1824.

[3] Thomas John Evan died in 1707, and was buried in the Friends' burial ground near Radnor Meeting House.

Rhisiart ab Tomas ab Rhys, a man whom I much respected prior to his marriage, and still regard. My brother and I continue to live with my mother, as before, endeavoring to imitate our father in the management of his affairs; but we are in many respects unequal to him. Our mother is seventy-three years old, somewhat infirm, but enjoying pretty good health, considering her age.

And now, my kind kinsman, I have given you the history of my father and myself, and I hope you will be pleased with it. Do send me some news; if you should have anything remarkable to mention I should be glad to hear it.—I must conclude my letter.

Your kinsman,
HUGH JONES.[1]

[1] By error in the Welsh magazines for John Jones.

INDEX

INDEX